New Mexico Women

New
Mexico
Women

Intercultural
Perspectives

Joan M. Jensen
Darlis A. Miller

University of New Mexico Press
Albuquerque

Library of Congress Cataloging in Publication Data

Jensen, Joan M.
    New Mexico Women.
    Includes bibliographies and index.
    1. Women—New Mexico—Social conditions—Addresses,
essays, lectures. 2. Rural women—New Mexico—History—
Addresses, essays, lectures. 3. Women—New Mexico—
Economic conditions—Addresses, essays, lectures.
I. Miller, Darlis A., 1939–   .   II. Title.
HQ1438.N55J46   1986   305.4'2'09789   85–16526
ISBN 0–8263–0826–0
ISBN 0–8263–0827–9 (pbk.)

For the Women of New Mexico

Contents

Illustrations.

Introduction

N*ew Mexico Women: Intercultural Perspectives* brings the resources and techniques of women's history to the study of an area so rich in history and anthropology that over 10,000 years of women's work can be described through a careful analysis of their history. Here, on the land now marked off and defined politically as New Mexico, women began work as hiders, became millers, potters and builders, then weavers, farmers, ranchers, midwives and healers, teachers, politicians, writers and artists. It is a unique history and yet the continuous occupation of New Mexico for thousands of years allows the history of the working lives of these women to explain changes in women's lives elsewhere and at different times in human history.

Our approach has been to draw broadly on the methods of anthropology, history, cultural geography, sociology, literature, art, and political science but also to focus on how the work of women in different cultures changed in one relatively small geographical area over a long chronological span. Sources range from archaeological and ethnological reports and census returns to written memoirs and, for the twentieth century, a collection of taped interviews that we have conducted under an oral history project at New Mexico State University. Methods include quantitative anal-

1

ysis but the structure of this analysis is confined to separate tables
and the body of the work is written in a non-technical style meant
primarily for the lay reader. The work is carefully footnoted, however, so that students and other scholars can use this volume as a
guide for their own further research and study.

The first 8,000 years of Native American women's history can
be retraced through archaeology and ethnology. During this long
span of history, women moved from a gathering culture to an agricultural society. In these early southwestern cultures—called by
anthropologists Paleo-Indian, Desert, Mogollon, Mimbres, and
Pueblo—women took a major role in producing both subsistence
and material culture. While the food and clothing women produced
left only a few remains, the baskets and pots have left a particularly rich history of women's activities. (See Appendix A for a more
detailed history.)

On the pottery bowls left by the Mimbres about 1000 years
ago, historians have their first glimpse of these women. In designs
painted on pottery women appear in a great variety of activities.
With their string belts, these women are shown helping other
women giving birth, playing with children, fashioning pottery and
baskets, carrying pottery jars and burden baskets, and participating in rituals. These designs add greatly to our understanding of
the lives and work of early women.

Over the next five hundred years, women of the Pueblo culture developed an even more elaborate material culture. By the time
the Spanish arrived, the point at which Cheryl J. Foote and Sandra
Kay Schackel take up the story of New Mexico women, Indian
people were living in dispersed settlements along a few life-giving
waterways in the south and eighty to ninety compact pueblos along
the Rio Grande and elsewhere in the north. The people farmed large
plots of corn, sometimes at considerable distance from their villages, raised cotton and flocks of turkeys, and made lengthy hunting trips into the plains. The women of the Pueblos aided in farming,
gathered wild vegetable products, manufactured large quantities
of pottery, carried water, ground corn, plastered walls, and took
an active part in the ceremonial life of the community. Still farther
north and to the east were groups who still lived primarily as hunt-
ers and gatherers.

As Foote and Schackel point out, however, the lives of Indian
women were disrupted in many ways by the arrival of the Span-

ish. New diseases killed a frightful number of these women and their families. Some women who survived were sexually exploited, and many were forced by Spanish settlers to work as servants and as general laborers, building churches, collecting piñon nuts, processing dried corn, and weaving cotton blankets. Still, Indian women readily accepted some Spanish material culture and food items, such as metal tools, woolens, and mutton.

Indian women had contact with Hispanic women as early as 1540, since at least three Hispanic women accompanied Francisco Vasquez de Coronado on his famed exploration trip into modern day Arizona and New Mexico.[1] Hispanic women thereafter made important contributions to Spain's efforts to control and settle the frontier of northern New Spain. Indeed, at least one hundred thirty women signed on with Juan de Oñate, along with about four hundred armed men, to make the first permanent settlement in New Mexico in 1598.[2] These women cultivated and harvested fields of corn and other crops while the men were away on Oñate's long forays of exploration. They were also left to defend themselves against hostile Indians, and some women like Luisa Robledo received recognition in published documents for their courage and endurance.[3] On one occasion while the men were away exploring, Robledo organized the women of the small colony to ward off an impending attack by eastern plains Indians by positioning the women on flat rooftops of adobe houses and arming them with heavy stones to pelt the invaders. Confronted by these war-like women, the small band of Indians left the village unharmed.

The colony that Oñate established became the northern outpost of Spanish civilization, but its growth was exceedingly slow. Between 1598 and 1680, the Spanish-speaking population probably never exceeded 2,500. There was little in New Mexico to attract settlers, as agricultural resources were limited and Indian hostility prevented exploitation of minerals. Social distinctions were simpler on this frontier than found elsewhere in New Spain, though a clearly defined local aristocracy eventually arose based on family, service to the crown, and wealth. But for women and men of all classes, life on the frontier was rough, lacking the luxury and refinement found in more settled portions of New Spain.

The routine of everyday life in the colony was broken approximately every three years with the arrival of a new governor. In 1659, one of New Mexico's most notorious governors, Bernardo

López de Mendizábal, took up residence in Santa Fe along with his wife Teresa de Aguilera y Roche. Teresa and her husband soon clashed with the local agent of the Holy Office (Inquisition). In the lengthy document Teresa prepared to defend herself against charges of heresy, she laid bare the details of life and society in seventeenth-century New Mexico.[4] Historians have used part of her testimony to describe life in early Santa Fe, but future researchers need to re-examine Teresa's deposition for what it can tell us about roles women played on the northern frontier of New Spain.

The active participation of Hispanic women in the Pueblo Indian Revolt of 1680 is ably documented by Salomé Hernández in her essay on New Mexico women as refugees and reconquest settlers. By carefully sifting through Spanish colonial documents, Hernández is able to describe in detail the suffering that Hispanic women endured during the revolt as well as their important contributions to resettling New Spain's northern frontier. Her study is a prime example of how much information on women is available when a scholar reexamines documents relating to well-known historic events in order to illuminate women's central roles in them. Her article also reinforces the conclusions of historians about the importance and variability of women's work on other frontiers. Under the pressure of colonization, women performed both their own traditional work and, when necessary, traditional male work. The success of any frontier venture depended a great deal on the availability and willingness of women to perform these dual work roles.

Following the reconquest in 1692, Hispanic women and men gradually rebuilt farms and villages in north central New Mexico. In the eighteenth century the province experienced steady growth in population and expansion of settlements, as women and their families took up land along the Chama River and its tributaries and in the Albuquerque region. During these years, many *genízaros* (detribalized Indians) were incorporated into Hispanic society, Indians and Hispanos alternated making war and peace with one another, and Hispanic villagers quarreled among themselves over property boundaries. Women participated in all these events, chiefly as members of small farming and stock raising families. Occasionally some eighteenth-century women are identified in published accounts, as in the case of Josepha Baca, described as "a well-to-do widow and mistress of an hacienda at Pajarito just below Albuquerque," who in 1746 owned six hundred head of sheep and goats.[5] Most certainly other women's activities in the eighteenth century will emerge as significant when researchers focus their attention systematically upon women's activities in this century, as Hernández has done for the Pueblo revolt and its aftermath.

Turbulance and change characterized the history of New Mexico in the nineteenth century, beginning with Mexico's independence in 1821. Although local residents peacefully accepted transition from Spanish to Mexican rule, the new regime lifted old trade restrictions with foreigners, thus opening new commercial opportunities for energetic Hispanic and Anglo entrepreneurs. As a result of the quickened economic life, New Mexico's upper class increased in size, and distinctions between the classes sharpened. Debt peonage also was strengthened as more and more *ricos* leased sheep on shares to poor Hispanic families.[6]

Whether rich or poor, Janet Lecompte argues in her essay on the independent Hispanic women of New Mexico that Hispanic women shared certain legal and social advantages that American women justifiably might have envied. Lecompte also notes that Hispanic women practiced many occupations besides caring for children and home; they worked as bakers, weavers, laundresses, midwives, and a variety of other jobs that took them away from the home. Lecompte believes that unlike the women of a later era described by Darlis Miller in her essay on Lincoln County women, Hispanic women in the early nineteenth century did not perform heavy outdoor farm work. And she attributes a greater degree of sexual freedom and personal independence to Hispanic women than Miller does in her essay on cross-cultural marriages. Recent research indicates that some eastern women also had far more independence than Lecompte noted.[7] These differences underscore the need for further research on nineteenth-century New Mexican women, especially on Hispanic women of different classes living in different regions of New Mexico.

American conquest of the Southwest in 1846 brought further changes to New Mexican women as a consequence of having a new territorial government: military posts garrisoned by American soldiers, federal funds to subsidize public works, and an influx of Anglo men looking for investment opportunities. Although some Hispanos violently resisted American take-over, most quietly accepted the new regime, adapting their traditional Hispanic culture to changing social and economic conditions. Many Hispanic families welcomed young, unmarried Anglo males into their households, and as Miller describes in her essay on cross-cultural marriages, Hispanic women frequently chose to wed the Anglo newcomers. She suggests that the common practice of cross-cultural marriages muted ethnic hostility, a theory that needs further testing. Certainly by focusing research upon women and their families a more accurate picture of Anglo-Hispanic relations in the nineteenth century will emerge.

Very few Anglo women settled in New Mexico prior to the advent of railroads in the late 1870s. Among the few who came to the territory, however, were women attached to the United States army, as servants and wives of officers and enlisted men. Several black women also entered New Mexico as officers' servants. The special relationship of these women to military communities is discussed in Miller's essay on army women. Catholic nuns and protestant missionaries added their numbers to the small community of Anglo women. The Sisters of Loretto, for example, came to New Mexico in the 1850s and thereafter established girls' boarding schools in Santa Fe, Mora, Taos, Las Cruces, and Las Vegas. Alzina J. Reed and Emily J. Harwood, wives of missionaries, also fostered education, opening public schools in Santa Fe and La Junta. A few women, like Flora Spiegelberg, established homes in Santa Fe as young brides of prosperous Jewish merchants. Other Anglo women, however, like Ellen Casey of Lincoln County, arrived in ox-drawn wagons to begin farming and raising families in isolated but fertile regions of New Mexico.[8]

Following the Civil War, the number of women reported in the census as living in New Mexico nearly equalled the number of men, despite the few Anglo women present. The vast majority of these women, then, were Hispanic, living in long-established kin-related northern communities such as Tierra Amarilla or in new villages such as Lincoln and San Patricio in southeastern New Mexico. For the most part, these were farm women, who cared for their children and worked with husbands on small plots of land to produce subsistence crops. Some Hispanic families, particularly in Rio Abajo (the area south of Santa Fe to Socorro) labored on the estates of large landowners, primarily caring for large flocks of sheep. Fabiola Cabeza de Baca describes in her book *We Fed Them Cactus* life on such an estate in eastern New Mexico where her grandparents, people of wealth, employed many poor Hispanos as herders to care for thousands of sheep.[9] Her grandmother, Doña Estefana Delgado de Baca, aided ranch employees in difficult times, handing out food and clothing to those in need. The lives of farm and ranch women in southeast New Mexico are described in Miller's article on Lincoln County women.

Susan McSween Barber's career as a rancher, also described by Miller, epitomizes the independence that some nineteenth-century women found in the American Southwest. Surviving the death of one husband, Barber built her ranching enterprise while a second husband pursued a law career. She outwardly subscribed to nineteenth-century prescriptions regulating women's conduct, dressing and behaving as a proper Victorian lady. Yet she engaged in a male-dominated enterprise, and from all accounts her neighbors and friends recognized and respected her commercial success.

Other Anglo women who came to New Mexico late in the nineteenth century entered homestead and desert land claims as widows and single women, but we have no accurate count of how many proved up their claims or how successful they were as land owners. Jessie Farrington, an Englishwoman, homesteaded alone in 1901 in the Sacramento Mountains near Weed, New Mexico.[10] Her published memoirs reflect the challenge and satisfaction that she felt at having successfully managed her claim, surely sentiments shared by other New Mexican women who homesteaded.

As immigration increased after railroads made travel speedier and less expensive, more and more nineteenth-century New Mexico women became urbanites and spearheaded civic improvement projects in their local communities. Like eastern women, they joined a variety of special interest organizations, such as the Women's Relief Corps, Women's New Mexico Press and Literary Association, and the Woman's Christian Temperance Union. Still other women became officers and members of local populist political parties.

In the early twentieth century the majority of New Mexico women were still rural women whether Native American, Hispanic, Anglo, or black. Some were descendants of the Native American women who had survived the imported diseases of the early centuries and still lived in their pueblos or on reservations. Some were descendants of the early sixteenth-century immigrants who had come north from New Spain to colonize. Others were Anglo and black women who came west from Kansas and Oklahoma and east from California in the nineteenth century. Still others were

newer immigrants from Mexico, like the Duran women who came
north in the late nineteenth century to find land and establish small
homesteads in southern New Mexico. The Duran women remembered settling in the small community of San Miguel, living in a
jacal, and working on *el sembrado,* their plot of land. Women from
Mexico brought their culture north, making pottery, processing
food, and also working the land. Immigration kept alive the Mexican culture in the southern part of the state, adapting it to the new
environment, preserving what seemed most valued, adopting the
most desirable. Migration kept on through the twentieth century
with an increasing number of women migrating after the Mexican
revolution of 1910.[11]

In the North, the Hispanic villagers arrived at a compromise
with the newer Anglo immigrants. Keeping much of their older
culture, they too incorporated what they needed of the Anglo material culture into their own. In turn, Anglo immigrants also adopted part of the local culture. Meanwhile, Anglo homesteaders, eager
for land, streamed into the eastern part of the state. Living very
similarly to the Hispanic villagers, though in more isolated areas,
they hoped their bare two-room houses would be the beginning of
a family farm that they could pass on to their children. These
migrants were looking for better times. The Hispanic people, meanwhile, were finding it harder to survive on their earlier small plots
of land as Anglos brought in more and more consumer goods and
encouraged them to join in consuming what they could not produce. The story of Hispanic and Anglo farm people is described in
greater detail in the chapter by Joan Jensen on rural women. "I've
worked, I'm not afraid of work," one farm woman reminded her
interviewer. That phrase summed up the history of the rural majority of New Mexico women.[12]

During the twentieth century, while rural women worked hard
for the survival of their families, family patterns changed. New
Mexico proved to be only slightly behind other states in changes
like lower fertility rates, rising rural mobility, urban migration,
increase in divorce, female headed households, and the poverty of
these households. Early twentieth-century economic conditions sent
rural men out of their homes to obtain what work they could and
the family was never the same. Recent studies show extreme mobility patterns and fragmentation of families in the late nineteenth century as well as the twentieth century. Sandra Stephens' study of the

Amador family clearly illustrates this pattern of fragmentation and trial, even in a wealthy Hispanic family. The family was the basic unit of society, where shocks and hurts could be absorbed. At this level one could see security and protection but also the pain and suffering—in death, disease, accident, separation, and dreams deferred.[13] All the pressures of change bore in on the family, and it is through individual family histories like that of the Amadors that the fissures in society are revealed.

New Mexico was in many ways a healthy environment. Thousands came from the East in the late nineteenth and early twentieth centuries to be cured of tuberculosis, arthritis, and other seemingly incurable diseases. Many lived long lives, though many others died just as surely in the land of enchantment as they would have elsewhere. Still many women found employment taking in invalids and nursing, helping run ranch resorts, and sanatoriums. For native New Mexicans, the influx of ailing Anglos, increased mobility, and poverty combined to make the first years of life the most unhealthy. Before the state public health programs of the 1920s, the nutrition programs of agricultural extension, and improved water supply, infant mortality was higher for New Mexico than for most states. By the 1930s, with the expansion of health programs, the rates dropped. New Mexico began to be a good place to begin life as well as to end it.[14]

While poorer women struggled to provide for families, middle-class women established social institutions—hospitals, public schools, libraries, parks. Middle-class women became reformers because they individually lacked the resources of wealthier families to provide a healthy, stimulating, and aesthetically pleasing environment. They organized, lobbied, pressured, cajoled, and wheedled their way to what they wanted—a range of social structures that would provide social services for themselves and others. At the local level, clubs were the most visible institutions. The Woman's Improvement Association of Las Cruces, for example, established a park, built and staffed a library, obtained water fountains, arranged for dusty streets to be watered down, and improved their community. Other women's clubs functioned similarly in small towns, especially from 1890 to 1930, as they took the lead in developing urban services as well as campaigning for women's legal rights.[15]

If rural women seemed to retain what was most uniquely traditional in pioneer Hispanic and Anglo cultures, urban women retained it least. Socially, they shared the most superficial similarities with eastern women. They participated in the political movements of the day as pointed out in the article on the suffrage movement. Women also moved into political participation in the 1920s and 1930s. The Depression of the 1930s hit city women hard. Without the support structure created by rural women, with jobs difficult to locate, and family members scattering to fend for themselves, urban women found times difficult. While no careful study has yet traced the hardships of these women, they likely responded as did urban women elsewhere—doubling up with relatives, stretching and making do, taking jobs for low wages when they could, and hanging on.

Village women could still rely on kin but their separate sources of income shriveled. Hispanic village women continued to trade and sell produce. Native American women survived the depression in separate ways, by taking wage labor in cities, and as Terry Reynolds shows in her study of Acoma, by continuing to supplement meagre family income with pottery sales. Both Hispanic and Indian women also passed on cultural and linguistic traditions during these years, dramatic illustration of how central their place was in the survival of their communities both physically and spiritually.[16]

World War II brought boom times, jobs, and a certain prosperity to New Mexico women. The government mailed one-half of soldiers' paychecks to wives, giving women control over more cash than they had ever known. Single, divorced, and widowed women found work at army bases, driving taxis, and in service occupations. Thousands of others headed west to work in defense plants. Still the social costs of war were high. High military death rates because of New Mexico's prominent role in the Philippines and the Bataan death march left many struggling widows on small pensions. For those women who received physically and psychically disabled veterans back into their homes, the costs were also high. Conditions in housing and schools were crowded both during and after the war. Albuquerque particularly suffered but even the isolated women in families at Los Alamos suffered from crowding, tensions, and relaxation of social mores that seemed to make it difficult to keep track of husbands and of teenage children.[17]

The 1950s were not much different in urban areas of New Mexico than in other southwestern towns, again at least superficially. Carol Lee Sanchez seemed to catch the mood of nights along the

Rio Grande just right in "The Way I Was." Cherry cokes, juke-boxes, bobby socks—it was a fluid teenage society in which young people groped for security and solidarity, sometimes elusively in sex, drugs, and teenage gangs.[18]

For young black women in towns like Las Cruces there were the experiences of segregated and then integrated schools. In Las Cruces and elsewhere Chicanas also experienced increased contact with Anglo dominated institutions and subsequent discrimination and prejudice. Patricia Luna, for example, remembered the blatant racism she encountered. "My friends who were darker than I really were discriminated against," she said later. More than one Chicana remembered harassment for speaking Spanish in school, and difficulty in getting jobs or renting apartments. These were the days when both blacks and Hispanics built up outrage against discrimination. The era marked the beginning not only of intensified awareness of racial and ethnic discrimination but also assertations of cultural identity.[19]

Soon after the war middle-class Anglo women also renewed their battle for equal rights. Increasing numbers of national women's clubs had endorsed the Equal Rights Amendment in the late 1930s and early 1940s. By 1944 both parties had endorsed the ERA. In southern New Mexico, a state women's rights movement gathered strength. There, as the chapter on legal reform shows, women began to organize to change the community property laws to allow women to inherit their property when husbands died without a will and for wives to be able to write their own wills and dispose of their community property. Later, reformers organized and campaigned for a state ERA that changed 60 laws and made men and women equal before the law.[20]

A few groups of women, mostly in the north, remained isolated from these poor or middle-class women. There had always been a wealthy few who set the social standards, women who by their activities cemented the status and power of their husbands. To this group belonged some of the wealthiest farm and ranch women, generally living isolated lives until fast automobiles and private planes brought them into the mainstream of upper class culture. More common were wealthy business and professional families where the women's activities were important in securing social alliances. This was a full time job. Wives of officials, even if sometimes not wealthy by birth, had to learn these tasks. Some, such as

Katherine Burn Mabry clearly were uneasy or made their own image in these tasks. Others, such as Carrie Wooster Tingley, brought with them social standards learned in a more stratified society. Like other upper class women, these in some ways were the least powerful of women—powerless among the powerful—as their husbands often managed and controlled the community property imperiously. It would be good to know more about these women. They are, despite their high social visibility, the least personally visible of all New Mexico women.[21]

A second group of wealthy women, always separate, were the literary and artistic elite. These new immigrants mainly settled near Santa Fe. Beginning with Mabel Dodge Luhan, these women used their money and influence to impose a shadow society on Taos and Santa Fe. They provided support for the arts among individual artists and in the community, tried to revive colonial crafts, helped keep Santa Fe from drifting permanently into midwestern architecture, and generally stood guard against the collapse of traditional society in the face of the invasion of other eastern Americans. Sometimes they risked petrifying the local community to achieve this defense but together they left a rich cultural legacy. Mabel Dodge Luhan, Georgia O'Keeffe, Mary Austin, and Laura Gilpin remain responsible for leaving a female tradition in the formal arts that took its place next to a rich female folk art tradition.[22]

Just how much these early artists had to do with the later renaissance of women's art and literature is still impossible to say. Like women in other parts of the country, a new generation of New Mexico women were able to discover their cultural and female traditions because of access to education and to financial support. Native Americans like Leslie Silko, Joy Harjo, Paula Gunn Allen, and Luci Tapahonso achieved national recognition for their writings. Hispanic and Anglo women were touched by the same movement and created poetry, short stories, novels, drama, and visual art that signified a woman's renaissance in the arts. Vera Norwood analyzes this reaching back into their cultural past by women in "Thank You for My Bones."[23]

Other women used their energy to continue political battles. New reformers, sometimes more militant and radical than the old, became visible. Indian women organized within their own communities. Black and Hispanic women helped develop community programs and political action campaigns. Anglo women made common cause or struck out on their own.[24]

Despite these activities, New Mexico women remained the poorest residents of one of the poorest states. Artists, professional, and middle-class women floated above the vibrant mass of women struggling with the daily chores of their existence. Women above derived strength from this struggle below. Some supported it with their work. In the 1980s, intercultural perspectives were only beginning to emerge. Whether or not women could forge coalitions to address their political needs, create visual, performing, and literary traditions necessary to nourish women's spiritual needs, and create a culture for New Mexico remained a question as yet unanswered.

Notes

1. Herbert E. Bolton, *Coronado, Knight of Pueblos and Plains* (reprint; Albuquerque: University of New Mexico Press, 1974), 62.
2. Fray Angelico Chavez, *My Penitente Land* (Albuquerque: University of New Mexico Press, 1974), 33.
3. Chavez, *My Penitente Land*, 46.
4. See France V. Scholes, "Troublous Times in New Mexico, 1659–1670," *New Mexico Historical Review* 12 (April, October 1937): 134–74, 380–452 and 15 (July, October 1940): 249–68, 269–417.
5. Marc Simmons, *Albuquerque, A Narrative History* (Albuquerque: University of New Mexico Press, 1982), 114.
6. David J. Weber, *The Mexican Frontier, 1821–1846, The American Southwest Under Mexico* (Albuquerque: University of New Mexico Press, 1982), 122–46, 207–37.
7. See particularly Nancy A. Hewitt, *Women's Activism and Social Change: Rochester, New York, 1822–1872* (Ithaca: Cornell University Press, 1984) and Joan M. Jensen, *Loosening the Bonds: Mid-Atlantic Farm Women, 1750–1850* (New Haven, Ct.: Yale University Press, in press). A more detailed account of New Mexico women in this period will soon be available in Deena J. González, "The Spanish-Mexican Women of Santa Fe: Patterns of Their Resistance and Accommodation, 1820–1880," (Ph.D. diss., University of California, Berkeley, 1985). A portion of this dissertation, "The Unmarried Women of Santa Fe: Assessments on the Lives

of a Widowed Population, 1820–1880," and Martha O. Loustaunau, "Hispanic Widows and their Support Systems in the Mesilla Valley of Southern New Mexico, 1910–1940," are part of the final report on *Widowhood and Aging: The American Southwest, 1848–1939,* Project for the Department of Health and Human Services, National Institute on Aging, Grant #1R01–AG03042–02, BES, an interdisciplinary project sponsored by the Southwest Institute for Research on Women, 1984. A view of the ideological constraints on earlier Hispanic women is in Ramón Gutírrez, "Marriage, Sex and the Family: Colonial New Mexico, 1690–1846," (Ph.D. diss., University of Wisconsin, 1980), "From Honor to Love: Transformation of the Meaning of Sexuality in Colonial New Mexico," in Raymond T. Smith, ed., *Love, Honor, and Economic Fate: Interpreting Kinship, Ideology, and Practice in Latin America* (Chapel Hill: University of North Carolina Press, 1984,; and "Honor, Ideology, Marriage Negotiation, and Class-Gender Domination in New Mexico, 1690–1846," Center for Advanced Study in the Behavioral Sciences, Stanford, California, 1983.

8. Nancy C. Benson, "Pioneering Women of New Mexico," *El Palacio* 85 (Summer 1979): 34; Michael L. Lawson, "Flora Langermann Speigelberg: Grand Lady of Santa Fe," *Western States Jewish Historical Quarterly* 8 (July 1976): 291–308.

9. Fabiola Cabeza de Baca, *We Fed Them Cactus* (Albuquerque: University of New Mexico Press, 1954).

10. Jessie de Prado Farrington, "Rocking Horse to Cow Pony," *New Mexico Historical Review* 30 (April, July, October 1955): 115–35, 221–51, 313–39 and 31 (January 1956): 38–67.

11. Maria Duran Apodaca's account is in Joan M. Jensen, *With These Hands: Women Working on the Land* (Old Westbury: Feminist Press, 1980), 120.

12. For women's village life one of the best descriptions is in the film *Luisa Torres.* See also Gioia Brandi, ed., "The Words of an Old One, Luisa Torres Writes of Her Life in Guadalupita, New Mexico," *El Palacio,* 84 (Fall 1978).

13. The unpublished work of Lillian Schlissel and Byrd Gibbens document this dislocation among Anglo families. Byrd Gibbens, "Dislocation: A Family in Crisis on the New Mexican Frontier," paper delivered at the New Mexico Family and Community Conference, July 1983, in Albuquerque gives a particularly descriptive case study for southern New Mexico. See also Gibbens' "Impact of the Western Frontier on Family Configuration: The Charles Albert Brown Collection of Letters (1874–1930), A Study in Literary Analysis of Correspondence," (Ph.D. diss., University of New Mexico, 1983), 2 volumes.

14. For health see Myrtle Greenfield, *A History of Public Health in New Mexico* (Albuquerque: University of New Mexico Press, 1962); J.

Rosslyn Earp, "The Public Health Program in New Mexico," *New Mexico Business Review* 5 (Jan. 1936), 117–23; and Rose Ethel Hubbard, "Infant Mortality in New Mexico: A Study of Certain Factors Related to Its Incidence," (Master's thesis: Tulane University, 1942). Several dissertations, some still underway, will be helpful in describing conditions of nineteenth and twentieth century women further. Sarah Deutch, "Culture, Class, and Gender: Chicanas in Colorado and New Mexico, 1900–1935," is being completed at Yale University. Sandra Schackel, University of New Mexico, is studying women in the 1930s in New Mexico. Cheryl J. Foote, University of New Mexico, is focusing upon New Mexico women during the territorial period. Twila Turpen is completing "Conflict and Intermarriage in Territorial New Mexico, 1850–1912: Simmel's Bipolar Concepts" at the University of New Mexico. See also Kate H. Parker's " 'I Brought With Me Many Eastern Ways': Euro-American Income-Earning Women in New Mexico, 1850–1880," (Ph.D. diss., University of New Mexico, 1984).

15. The story of reform is only partially documented in the chapters by Jensen.

16. See oral histories in Nan Elsasser, Kyle MacKenzie, and Yvonne Tixier Y Vigil, *Las Mujeres: Conversations from a Hispanic Community* (Old Westbury: Feminist Press, 1980), and Marta Weigle, ed., *Hispanic Villages of Northern New Mexico* (Santa Fe: Lightening Tree, 1975). The activities of New Mexican women mirrored those described by Karen Blair, *The Clubwoman as Feminist: True Womanhood Refined, 1868–1914* (New York: Holmes and Meier, 1980).

17. The history of wartime New Mexico is poorly documented but see Peggy Pond Church, *The House at Otowi Bridge* (Albuquerque: University of New Mexico Press, 1960).

18. Carol Lee Sanchez, "The Way I Was," in *Message Bringer Woman,* (Taurean Horn Press, 1977), 26–28.

19. Elsasser, MacKenzie, and Tixier Y Vigil, *Las Mujeres,* 88, 93; Charlotte K. Mock, *Bridges: New Mexican Black Women, 1900–1950* (Albuquerque: New Mexico Commission on the Status of Women, 1985); and Joan M. Jensen, "Women Teachers, Class, and Ethnicity: New Mexico, 1900–1950," *Southwest Economy and Society* 4 (Winter 1978/79).

20. The history of the ERA has yet to be written.

21. Eunice Kalloch and Ruth K. Hall, *The First Ladies of New Mexico* (Santa Fe: Lightening Tree, 1982), 85–9 and 103–09 for Mabry and Tingley.

22. Vera Norwood, "The Photographer and the Naturalist: Laura Gilpin and Mary Austin in the Southwest," *Journal of American Culture* 5 (Summer 1982): 1–27; Augusta Fink, *I–Mary: A Biography of Mary Aus-*

tin (Tucson: University of Arizona Press, 1983); and Lois Rudnick, *Mabel Dodge Luhan: New Woman, New Worlds* (Albuquerque: University of New Mexico Press, 1984).

23. Below are only the most recent publications of the Native American women: Paula Gunn Allen, *Shadow Country* (Los Angeles: UCLA American Indian Studies Center, 1981); Joy Harjo, *She Had Some Horses* (New York: Thunder's Mouth Press, 1983); Leslie Silko, *Storyteller* (New York: Seaver Books, 1981); Luci Tapahonso, *One More Shiprock Night* (San Antonio, Texas: Tejas Art Press, 1981). See also Paula Gunn Allen, "The Grace That Remains: American Indian Women's Literature," *Book Forum,* 5, No. 3 (1981): 376–82.

24. Beth Wood and Deb Preusch, *New Mexico Women Working for Change* (Albuquerque: New Mexico People and Energy, 1981) is a preliminary attempt to document these activities.

⋙ 1 ⋘

Indian Women of New Mexico 1535–1680

Cheryl J. Foote and Sandra K. Schackel

In 1535, when the first Spaniards arrived in the region now known as New Mexico, they inaugurated a new era for Indian women. With their arrival began a period of painful testing, adjustment, and accommodation for the women as well as for men of the major cultural groups in the area. Three forces—the entrance of European society, the rapid decline of the Indian population, and a shifting of old friendships between Indian groups—had a significant impact on the lives of Native American women. In the records left by those first European arrivals, historians can begin to glimpse what the lives of these women were like during the first century and a half of this new era.

The Spaniards who arrived in 1535 were searching for more of the fabulous wealth they had found in the Aztec and Inca empires of Mexico and Peru. In succeeding decades, several parties explored the area, and in 1598 a permanent colony was established in the northern part of the state. During the next eighty years, the newcomers attempted to assimilate and Christianize indigenous residents of the province, the Pueblo Indians, until these native peoples overthrew the Spanish and drove them south to the El Paso, Texas, area in the great Pueblo Revolt of 1680.[1]

The advent of Spanish political control of the area, as well as the arrival of European material culture precipitated a process of cultural exchange between Indian women and their Hispanic overlords and hastened cultural borrowing already under way between Pueblo women and two other Indian groups, the Apaches and the Navajos. Pueblo women, pressed into service by the conquerors, incorporated Hispanic foods, livestock, and tools into traditional tasks. Pueblos who fled to the Navajos and Apaches to escape Spanish domination carried with them expectations of women's work roles that influenced women in Apache and Navajo societies.

The Indian women with whom Spaniards had the greatest contact in New Mexico were these Pueblos, who were also the most numerous of the native peoples. At the beginning of the seventeenth century, about fifty thousand Pueblos lived in some ninety villages scattered along the Rio Grande and to the west beyond the present Arizona–New Mexico border. These village dwellers shared a number of cultural traits, although each pueblo was self-governing and a variety of languages existed. Women gathered, prepared, and preserved foodstuffs, cared for children, tended two domesticated animals, the dog and the turkey, built and plastered walls, and created pottery. Men hunted and grew crops of corn, beans, squash, and cotton in irrigated fields. Social structure and religion were complex and intertwined, and the nuclear family was less important than the extended family, the clan, or the village.[2]

Trade among the Pueblos took place to a limited degree, but a more significant exchange occurred between Pueblos and the Apaches and Navajos, nomadic Athapaskan peoples who traversed the region in search of buffalo. Pueblos traded agricultural produce for buffalo hides and meat that the Athapaskans brought to the villages. Because the Apaches and Navajos shared many cultural traits in addition to a common language, early Spanish accounts often failed to distinguish between the groups. During the period 1540 to 1680, the Navajo probably inhabited the northwestern quadrant of New Mexico, while Apaches migrated across the eastern plains as well as the southern regions of the state and west into eastern Arizona. Prior to the arrival of the Spaniards to the region, the only domesticated animal of these nomads was the dog, which women hitched to travois to carry possessions as they followed the buffalo herds. Before Europeans came, Apaches and Navajos enjoyed peaceful relations with their trading partners, the Pueblos. From the more sophisticated village dwellers the Athapaskans acquired a number of cultural traits, including a knowledge of agriculture, which they began to practice in a limited fashion about 1600. Because Hispanics and these Athapaskan people interacted far less than did Hispanics and Pueblos in the seventeenth century, the experience of Athapaskan women merits separate discussion.[3]

Although several Spanish expeditions entered New Mexico between 1540 and 1598, no settlement was attempted, and thus little cultural borrowing between newcomers and Pueblos took place.[4] But despite Spanish failure to find mineral wealth, the presence of settled Indians excited interest in the area as a mission field and a site for settlement. In 1598 Don Juan de Oñate established the first Hispanic colony at San Gabriel, near the pueblo of San Juan. For the next eight decades, a small Hispanic population (never numbering more than three thousand)[5] molded the native peoples into a labor force and attempted to convert them to Catholicism and to assimilate them to Hispanic values, a process that, if successful, would extinguish significant portions of native culture.

Destruction of the native peoples, however, was not Spain's formal policy or intent. Although one cannot say the Spanish appreciated native culture and sought to preserve it—for the most part, the Spanish were supremely ethnocentric, convinced that their religion and way of life were superior to any other—an important qualification must be made. These Europeans did not view Indians as obstacles to progress who must be annihilated or removed; they considered indigenous peoples a labor force with souls to be saved. The Spaniards pressed Indian women as well as men into service, and integrated parts of native culture into their own, just as Native Americans adapted to Hispanic tools, livestock, and foods. During the seventeenth century, a blending of cultures and a mingling of blood (through the unions of Hispanic men and Indian women), rather than the extermination of the aboriginal population, took place. For example, Pueblo women, although forced to labor for the conquerors, did not abandon traditional roles, but modified them with the material culture Spaniards introduced. The Spanish reconquest of New Mexico following the Pueblo Revolt ended Pueblo control of the region, but the Pueblos successfully maintained many of their cultural traits throughout the first century of contact and subsequent ones as well.

The advent of the European colony in 1598 brought numerous changes to the lives of the Pueblos of New Mexico. The Spanish established a system of government that abolished Pueblo autonomy, and more importantly, placed an economic burden upon these Indians. Spanish overlords (*encomenderos*) were entitled to collect cotton blankets and corn from each village as tribute, which meant that the work load of the native peoples greatly increased. Women struggled to preserve enough food for their families in addition to satisfying Hispanic demands. In times of drought or crop failure, tribute was still demanded, and starvation haunted Pueblo villages.

Starvation, in fact, played a part in the most devastating change that occurred among the Pueblos during the first century after the Spanish settlement, the drastic reduction of Pueblo population. The primary cause, however, was disease, including smallpox and measles. Native Americans had no resistance to these scourges that the Europeans unwittingly introduced. A secondary cause of death—warfare—also was the result of European entrance in the region. The Apaches quickly acquired the horse from the newcomers, and increased mobility transformed Apache society. They turned to raiding Spanish and Pueblo villages, further depleting Pueblo ranks. By the end of the seventeenth century, Pueblo population had declined from perhaps fifty thousand to sixteen thousand, and the number of pueblos shrank from ninety to nineteen.[6] The psychological impact of such destruction—as women watched husbands, children, parents, and siblings perish—must have been as profound as it was unmeasurable.

Despite these cataclysmic events, Indian women of New Mexico continued to perform important economic and social roles in Native American societies and provided a work force for the Spanish as well. These newcomers quickly appreciated Native American women as workers. Chroniclers of the early expeditions found labor among Pueblo people equitably divided, and approvingly recorded descriptions of women's work roles. Pueblo women, observers reported, cared for children and tended the homes. Their most significant contribution to Pueblo society was gathering, preserving, and preparing foodstuffs. Although men tended the crops of corn, beans, and squash, women assisted in clearing out and repairing irrigation ditches. Moreover, they augmented the foods men grew with piñons, berries, and other wild plants they gathered.[7] Men assumed major responsibility for hunting, but Pueblo women may have fished and sometimes assisted in communal rabbit hunts.[8] Once food was acquired, women prepared or preserved it. They dried corn, beans, and other plants, and made meat into jerky. When mealtime approached, the women, often working together, used *manos* and *metates* (grinding stones) to reduce the dried beans and corn into meals, from which they made breads and tortillas.[9]

As an adjunct to cooking and storing food, Pueblo women adeptly produced pottery storage vessels, water jars, and cooking utensils. These items served an aesthetic as well as utilitarian purpose, and drew admiring comments from Spanish observers. Pedro de Castañeda, a chronicler of the Coronado expedition of 1540–42, reported that Pueblo women made "earthenware glazed with antimony and jars of extraordinary labor and workmanship, which were worth seeing." And a member of another expedition was even more enthusiastic in his description: "These vessels are so excellent and delicate that the process of manufacture is worth watching; for they equal, and even surpass, the pottery made in Portugal."[10]

Pueblo women also exhibited skill with textiles. Although in many pueblos men were the primary spinners and weavers (noted particularly for the blankets they wove for their brides as wedding gifts), in some villages women also wove cotton into cloth on upright looms. Women decorated the cloth with intricate embroidery or painted designs, and fashioned it into items of clothing. Skillful female hands also worked turkey feathers into blankets, capes, and ceremonial garments.[11]

Most of the chores of Pueblo women, such as child care, cooking, and preparing clothing, were consistent with Spanish concepts of "women's work," but other activities of Native American women seemed foreign and intriguing to Hispanics. For example, Pueblo women tended the flocks of turkeys, prized for their feathers in addition to their meat. More significantly, Spaniards were surprised to discover that among the Pueblos, women not only built and plastered the houses, but owned them as well.[12]

The comments of Spanish chroniclers indicate that Hispanics were interested in Pueblo women as a potential workforce, but they also serve to reveal the position women held in Pueblo society. In recent studies, anthropologists have suggested a number of factors that may influence women's status. These include women's contributions to subsistence, female control of dispersion of food, ownership of property, matrilocal residence (a husband moves in with the wife's family after marriage), and matrilineal descent (reckoning descent through the mother). Clearly, Pueblo women made significant contributions to subsistence, played a vital role in dispersing food supplies, and owned the houses. Although some Pueblos were bilocal (that is, after marriage a couple might live with either the husband's or wife's relatives), others favored a matrilocal system, and many of the Pueblos were matrilineal. Thus, Pueblo women likely held considerable status in Pueblo society, although such status was never revealed in the political spheres as was the case with Iroquois women.[13]

Soon after their arrival in the Southwest, Hispanics called upon the services of Native American women. One of the first work roles Indian women performed for Spanish explorers was that of interpreter. During the conquest of Mexico, Hernán Cortés established the custom when he took Doña Marina, an Indian woman, as his interpreter, and other Spaniards attempted to follow his example on the northern frontier. Members of the Antonio de Espejo expedition (1582) returned to Mexico with a Hopi woman, planning that she might "enlighten us regarding those provinces and the route to that region" on a return trip that never materialized.[14] A few years later, Gaspar Castaño de Sosa also returned to Mexico with an Indian woman whom the Spanish christened Inés. She accompanied Oñate back to her homeland in 1598, but was unable to carry out her role, as Oñate explained in his diary of the expedition:

> On the 22nd July 1598 we went to the pueblo of San Cristóbal, where Doña Ines was born. She is the Indian woman we brought from Mexico like a second Malinche [Doña Marina], but she does not know that language or any other spoken in New Mexico, nor is she learning them. Her parents and almost all of her relatives were already dead, and there was hardly anyone who remembered how Castaño had taken her away.[15]

After permanent Spanish settlement in New Mexico began, Native American women integrated Spanish material culture into traditional activities. They learned to prepare and preserve foods the conquerors brought from Spain (for example, peaches, apricots, apples, and melons), or from the valley of Mexico (chiles and tomatoes). Wool, made possible by the Spanish introduction of sheep, eventually replaced cotton as the principal fiber in Pueblo textiles. Also, Pueblo women no longer produced only for home or village consumption, or a little trade with nomadic tribes. As a result of the Hispanic presence, Indian women expanded the context of traditional tasks and may have added new work roles to those they had previously filled in Pueblo society. Spanish demand for tribute placed a severe burden on Pueblo economy, and it is likely that female involvement in spinning and weaving increased as the native peoples struggled to supply enough blankets to satisfy the Europeans.

Some Indian women tried to supplement Pueblo economy by wage work; the *residencia* (investigation of his performance in office) of Governor Bernardo López de Mendizábal, whose term of office occurred near mid-century, provides an illuminating glance at the types of tasks Hispanics hired Indian women to perform. To obtain supplies from Mexico, colonists needed items to exchange, and Indian women's labor helped to provide not only materials for local use, but for New Mexico's exports. Spaniards sought Indian seamstresses to produce blankets and various articles of clothing, for export as well as for domestic use. For example, Governor Mendizábal probably planned to export the black silk scalloped trim that he ordered an Apache woman named Madalena to make, in addition to the sixteen pairs of hose that he had ordered from Juana, a woman from San Felipe pueblo.[16] Another valuable export was piñon nuts, which Indian women, often working together, gathered. On one occasion, the women of Tesuque pueblo shared a goal as well as a task; they gathered fourteen *fanegas* of piñons to exchange for cattle for the village.[17]

Another significant contribution Pueblo women made to the emerging Spanish society was in construction. Although Europeans initially expressed surprise at seeing Indian women building and plastering the houses, they soon accepted the idea. Oñate's colonists turned to Indian women for assistance in repairing Hispanic homes, and missionaries employed Native American women as laborers on the mission churches. When Fray Alonso de Benavides visited the province in 1626, he admired the architectural accomplishments of these women, commenting "It will seem an enchantment to state that sumptuous and beautiful as . . . [these churches] are, they were built solely by the women and boys and girls. . . ." He went on to relate that when Hispanics tried to enlist the aid of the Pueblo men, the women laughed and the men ran off.[18] Indian women learned that a small piece of sheepskin made plastering easier than using twigs, again integrating Spanish material cultural into traditional tasks. In this case, however, cultural borrowing went in two directions. Hispanics in New Mexico integrated women as plasterers into Hispanic culture, and when Anglo-American traders entered the area in the nineteenth century, they commented upon Hispanic women plastering the houses, revealing as much amazement as the Spanish had demonstrated when they first witnessed Pueblo women performing this task. Into the twentieth century, plastering has remained a firmly entrenched role for women in Hispanic communities in New Mexico.[19]

Most Pueblo women remained in their villages while they worked for the Spaniards, but settlers pressed others into domestic service in Hispanic homes and missions. Such arrangements frequently led to sexual abuse, and in 1630 the ecclesiastical head of the province, Esteban de Perea, forbade the "allotment of Indian women as servants in the houses of Spaniards" unless these women went of their own volition and their husbands accompanied them.[20] It is doubtful, however, that the edict had much effect. (Sexual relations between Hispanics and Indian women will be discussed in greater detail below.) As Spanish demand for Indian servants to function as cooks, bakers, laundresses, and wet nurses increased, colonists traded for slaves that the Pueblos acquired from Plains Indians. Many of these captives were Apaches captured in childhood. Although Spanish law prohibited enslavement of Indians, masters were permitted to "ransom" captives in order to Christianize them. The Spaniard was then entitled to the servant's labor in return for instruction in the faith and for the food and clothing the master provided. Occasionally these female captives were included as a part of a tribute payment or as a gift to a prominent official, and these *criadas* (maids) were prized in Hispanic homes. Eventually, this increased demand for slaves provoked hostility between the Pueblos and their ancient trading friends, the Apaches, who turned to raiding the pueblos where the trade took place.[21]

In addition to valuing Indian women for the occupational skills, many Spaniards were also intrigued and attracted to the physical appearance of these women. On the whole, Hispanics commented favorably on the dress and physical characteristics of the Pueblo women they encountered. A member of an early expedition reported that he found Pueblo women "handsome and fairskinned," and noted that "like the men, [they] bathe frequently." Espejo, leader of another group, observed that Pueblo women are "fairer than the Mexican [Indian] women."[22] The fact that these women were clothed, for the most part, also generated Spanish approval, and most descriptions concur that Pueblo women wore colored cotton skirts, embroidered or painted, topped by a blanket woven in bright colors that was draped over one shoulder and pinned or tied.[23] In cold weather, women wore leather leggings and shoes or mocasins,[24] and they were often adorned with turquoise jewelry.[25] Hairstyles varied among the Pueblos, and included bangs, braids, and the whorls at the side of the head that are now called "squash blossoms."[26] Although woolen garments replaced cotton ones, the dress of Pueblo women was little changed by contact with the Spanish, and most of the garb described by sixteenth-century observers may today still be seen in New Mexico pueblos on ceremonial occasions.

Hispanics were more favorably impressed with the indigenous females they encountered than were other Europeans, and appreciated the kindness, generosity, and docility of these women. Not only were such traits consistent with Hispanic ideals for the female sex, but Pueblo women provided a pleasing contrast to the naked, primitive Chichimec tribes the Spanish encountered in northern Mexico. Moreover, Pueblo women did not serve as burden carriers, a practice among other groups that provoked European disgust.[27] Because Hispanic men found Native American women clean, attractive, and culturally sophisticated, it is understandable that the most pervasive context in which Indian women appear in the documentation of the period is a sexual one.

Like other Europeans who came in contact with aboriginal societies, Spaniards observed and described sexual customs among the native peoples, and often had sexual relations with Indian women.[28] Spanish commentary about Pueblo marital and sexual practices reveals variations among these village dwellers as well as the chroniclers' confusion. Hispanics made little mention of expectations regarding premarital chastity or postmarital fidelity for Pueblo men; perhaps, coming from a society that tacitly condoned a double standard, they saw little need to comment on these activities. However, they found Native American customs regarding female virginity, adultery, prostitution, divorce, and polygamy intriguing and perplexing.

Although Spaniards observed that most women of the Pueblos wore sophisticated costumes, they were fascinated to see that among some of these village-dwellers, young women went about naked even during cold weather. Castañeda, chronicler of the Coronado expedition, investigated the matter and reported that

> virgins . . . go nude until they take husbands, because they say that if they do anything wrong then it will be seen and so they do not do it. They do not need to be ashamed because they go around as they were born.[29]

Other chroniclers agreed with Castañeda regarding the importance of virginity in Pueblo culture; however, these Spaniards expressed surprise to learn that despite the importance of premarital virginity, fidelity after marriage was not expected for women. One Spanish chronicler commented that "the women are not faithful to these Indians, nor do the men punish them."[30] But other observers contradicted their colleagues, indicating that among the Pueblos, women were common property before marriage but were expected to be chaste afterwards.[31]

Hispanic evidence, because it is so contradictory, reveals the confusion chroniclers experienced when confronted with a society with a more relaxed and permissive attitude toward sex. Women may have experienced a higher degree of sexual freedom in Pueblo society as compared with Hispanic practices or with other Native American societies (Apache, for example). Such freedom surprised the Spanish, as a chronicler of the Espejo expedition revealed when he commented that Pueblo women "are not at all opposed to hiring themselves out to the men . . . and the men take whatever women they like and the . . . [women] the men they fancy."[32]

That marriage among the Pueblos was not necessarily intended to last for life also seemed curious to Hispanic observers. One witness made a lengthy observation about Pueblo marriages and the conditions whereby a union could be ended.

> The Indian talks to the girl he likes and gives her two, three, or four blankets, according to the esteem in which she is held. She takes him to her house, for the houses belong to the women, they being the

ones who build them. She keeps the man with her three or four months, which they call moons. If she becomes pregnant during this time, the man supports her, and she cares for him all of her life and remains his wife. If she does not become pregnant, the man abandons her and she is marked with two roses in her hair. This indicates that she is ready to marry [sic] any man, if she is paid.[33]

Other accounts reveal that divorce also occurred for reasons other than the wife's infertility, and women as well as men could initiate it. If a woman no longer wished to be married, she piled her husband's belongings outside the home and he returned to his parents' dwelling.[34]

Unaccustomed to such ease in shedding spouses, Spaniards may have confused serial monogamy (a succession of mates, but not more than one at a time) with polygamy on some occasions. However, many accounts contain commentary about polygamous marriages, and indicate that although men had multiple wives, women had only one husband. How widely polygamy was practiced among the Pueblos is difficult to determine, but it appears to have been firmly entrenched in Pueblo society. In any case, polygamous unions generated a determined opposition from the Catholic church. In an effort to abolish polygamy, friars meted out punishments, which included physical chastisement, to Indians who persisted in polygamous marriages.[35] Still, Indians were exempt from the Holy Office of the Inquisition, which investigated a number of bigamy cases during the seventeenth century, while Hispanics involved were castigated because their bigamous unions set a bad example for the Indians, who chafed under new rules seeking to eradicate ancient customs.[36] Although Pueblos continued to oppose forced monogamy before and after the Pueblo Revolt, the church persevered in its efforts to abolish multiple marriages. Ultimately the church was successful; in the late nineteenth and early twentieth centuries, ethnologists would confidently state that the Pueblos had always been a monogamous people.[37]

Hispanics could not have been too critical of the marriage practices of Indians when Hispanic society in New Mexico often violated the sexual standards the church espoused. Despite official condemnation by the church, many priests, as well as soldiers, settlers, civil officials, and governors, engaged in extramarital relations involving Indian women. A sexual encounter such as this, in fact, brought about the first hostility between Native Americans and Europeans in New Mexico. Estevanico, the Moorish guide of the Fray Marcos de Niza expedition (1538–39), demanded supplies and Indian women at the Zuni pueblo of Hawikuh, and the Zunis, incensed by his insolence, killed him.[38] Estevanico was only the first in a long line of those Spaniards who sought Indian women as sexual partners. Chroniclers of later expeditions usually recorded tales of the rape of Indian women,[39] as well as the fearful reactions of Pueblo women when Spaniards arrived in their villages. At Santa Clara, Castaño de Sosa reported that the natives "showed very great fear at seeing us, especially the women, who wept very much," and at another village he observed, "not an Indian woman was willing to come out of the houses."[40]

Although Hispanic communities including Hispanic women were established early in the seventeenth century, unions between Hispanic men and Indian women persisted. At least three factors encouraged these interracial relationships: Spaniards found Native American women attractive and desirable, Hispanics perceived that Pueblos condoned sexual relations outside of marriage, and, at least in the early years of the century, Hispanic women were in short supply. For example, the muster roll of Oñate's colonizing force lists 129 men, and only 29 women or girls, as well as a mention of a small number of children (sex unspecified) and Indian servants. Even if all these children and servants were female, which is doubtful, the sex ratio could hardly have been equalized. When replacements joined Oñate's colony in 1600, the muster roll contained the names of 72 men, 15 Hispanic women and girls, and 16 Indian women and girls who accompanied the expedition as servants.[41] Since the number of Hispanic males seeking sexual partners far exceeded the number of available Hispanic women, some Spanish men turned toward Pueblo communities for partners. Marriages between Hispanics and Indians were not uncommon, but many other liaisons were illicit. Mutual attraction and affection probably played a significant role in many of these relationships, as Indian women must have sought or consented to relations with Spanish men. But other unions rested upon physical and psychological coercion.

Sexual exploitation of Indian women continued throughout the seventeenth century, and the topic figured frequently in acrimonious charges that clergy and civil officials flung at each other in the ceaseless struggle for domination of the province.[42] While some accusations were inflated or false, many, no doubt, were based on fact. Documents clearly indicate that clerics violated ecclesiastical law as well as civil law in their unions with Indian women. For example, a charge of murder was brought against a priest at Taos for the "crime of forcing a woman, cutting her throat, and burying her in an office or cell." Another complaint against the clergy alleged that some "pueblos were full of the children of friars. . . ." And, on another occasion, an irate Indian complained that a priest had "taken his wife from him, and had obliged her every night to arise from her husband's side to go and sleep with him."[43]

Charges of clerics against civil authorities, even if only partially true, indicate that these officials were also not above reproach. Lengthy transcripts of the trial of Governor López de Mendizábal contain numerous complaints against the notorious governor. These include allegations that he raped Indian servants in his home as well as female prisoners awaiting trial.[44] Officially, of course, Spanish policy (however unsuccessfully) attempted to reduce sexual harassment of Indian women by friars as well as civil authorities. On a visit to the convent at Galisteo pueblo, a governor reviewed a parade of Indian women bakers and "said to them that their faces were too pretty for them to be bakers, and that . . . [the friars] should look for others who were old."[45]

Although Pueblos resented Hispanic exploitation of Pueblo women, Pueblo men also evinced a willingness to use women as sexual pawns. In 1680, leaders of the Pueblo Revolt urged their followers to throw off the overlay of hated Spanish domination and revert to the old ways, declaring that any Indian who killed a Spaniard would receive an Indian woman for a wife and "he who kills four will get four women, and he who kills ten or more will have a like number of women."[46] Later, Indian leaders hoped to use women as bait in a planned attack on Governor Antonio de Otermín's forces during a reconquest attempt in 1681. Alonso Catití, one of the leaders of the Indian resistance, planned a peaceful reception for the Spanish when they arrived at Cochiti. He instructed the most attractive of the young women of the pueblo to bathe and arrange their hair attractively to be ready to seduce the Spanish. Then, after the Europeans were asleep, Cochiti men would descend from the nearby mesa and kill the invaders. The plan failed, however, when the girls, arrayed in their best, saw the large Hispanic contingent approaching and fled.[47] Although Pueblo women no doubt shared the goals of their men in wishing to keep the Spaniards at bay, they refused to participate in the manner proposed.

The refusal of Pueblo women to carry out Catití's demands illustrates women's status in Pueblo political life. Although women did not serve as political leaders, they participated in the decision-making process of each village. An observer from Oñate's colony noted that Pueblo men consulted the women before arriving at a decision.[48] While Indian women did not participate in the Spanish governmental process, they apparently retained a voice in the internal affairs of each pueblo. In testimony given after the Pueblo Revolt, witnesses reported that many Christianized Indians (as well as those who had not been converted), and "particularly the women" had clamored to "be done with all the Spanish and put all our strength toward killing them."[49] Although records do not reveal whether women participated in the bloody slaughter of the Revolt, they were not unfamiliar with defensive warfare. For example, during a battle at Pecos when Castaño de Sosa's group arrived, women assisted in the defense of the pueblo, and Spaniards remarked that the "women showed immense fortitude."[50]

Women's roles in Pueblo religious life are even more difficult to define precisely than their political roles. Although Spaniards attempted to suppress Pueblo religion, these village dwellers did not abandon their old beliefs. Instead, they literally went underground and retreated to their *kivas* (underground ceremonial chambers) to conduct religious rites that remain shrouded in secrecy to the present day. Women, prohibited from entering kivas except to bring food to the men, thus were excluded from these religious ceremonies.[51] Also, their involvement in healing rituals, part of religious ceremonies, is unclear. To construe this to mean that Pueblo women were barred from most aspects of Pueblo religious life would be erroneous, however. For example, chroniclers indicated that women attended the dances, although they did not dance.[52] Women also belonged to scalp societies and performed the important tasks of caring for and ritually feeding the scalps.[53] In Pueblo mythology, Spider Woman and the Corn Maidens are significant benign figures whose roles reflect the important nurturing and feeding tasks Pueblo women perform.[54] In addition, since religion permeates Pueblo existence, women likely participated in many ways that escaped Spanish notice.

A precise definition of the legal status of Pueblo women in

seventeenth-century New Mexico is also elusive. Spanish law designated Indians wards of the Crown, and a special official known as the Protector of the Indians was appointed to safeguard their rights. Although large discrepancies no doubt existed between ideals expressed in statutes and administration of justice in the remote province, Indian women participated in legal proceedings. A sampling of Inquisition cases and other proceedings indicates that Indians of both sexes functioned as witnesses, and that their testimony carried equal weight with that of other deponents. Similarly, Indian women apparently enjoyed the same recourse to the Protector of the Indians that their male counterparts did, and their appeals to this official indicate that they were aware of their rights to his advocacy.[55] Further conclusions, however, will elude historians until they undertake a thorough examination of the functioning of the legal system in seventeenth-century New Mexico.

In the seventeenth century, unintentional depletion of Pueblo population and introduction of Spanish material culture had profound effects upon the native peoples. Women continued to make substantial contributions to Pueblo economy, however, and demands Hispanics made may have necessitated an expansion of women's work roles. Correspondingly, it appears that the status of Pueblo women did not suffer appreciably within Pueblo society in this crucial period of cultural exchange.

In fact, during this period, Pueblo culture exerted strong influence upon the nomadic Athapaskan peoples, and women in Apache and Navajo society adopted many of the work roles of Pueblo women. Since the Spanish had far less contact with either Apaches or Navajos than with Pueblos before the Pueblo Revolt, a much less complete picture of Apache and Navajo women emerges from the records. In general, however, Spaniards commented about work roles, marriage customs, and personal appearance of women in these cultures in much the same way they recorded their impressions of the Pueblos.

Athapaskan women had primary responsibility in their societies for child care and for food preparation. Presumably they helped to prepare the jerky that was a staple in their diet, and they gathered wild plants to supplement the meat.[56] Moreover, the nomadic lifestyle of Apaches intrigued Spanish observers, who noted with surprise that women and children accompanied the men when whole villages moved in search of the buffalo.[57] In this effort, women had charge of the travois and cared for the dogs who pulled it. Also, they made and maintained the tipis that served as family homes.[58]

The costumes of Apache women, mostly chamois, also favorably impressed Hispanic observers. Coronado's chronicler, Castañeda, called Apache women "well-made and modest," and Fray Alonso de Benavides echoed Castañeda's observations nearly a century later when he noted that Apache women "go clad in *gamuzas,* which are the skins of deer, very well tanned and adorned in their fashion, . . . the women gallantly and honestly clad."[59] In fashioning these garments, Apache women demonstrated great skill with needlework. So impressed were Hispanic women with the workmanship of the Apaches that soon after arriving they adopted the garb of these Native Americans, but the custom apparently died out, perhaps when production of woolen cloth in the province began.[60]

As with the Pueblos, Spaniards displayed interest in Athapaskan marriage customs. Hispanic testimony indicates that Apaches, like Pueblos, practiced polygamy, and all witnesses agreed that for women in Apache society a strict code prohibited dalliance after marriage. Indeed, the Apache woman who committed adultery faced a severe penalty. To mark her shameful behavior, her nose, and sometimes her ears as well, were cut off, and her people repudiated her. Noseless Apache women could still be seen in New Mexico and Arizona in the early twentieth century.[61]

As a result of increased demand for Apache slaves to function as domestic servants in Spanish homes, Apaches grew to regard Pueblos as Hispanic allies, and animosity developed between Apaches and their former trading friends. Despite increasing hostility, however, Apaches borrowed a number of traits from the Pueblos during this period. Some groups began to practice a limited amount of agriculture, and at some point Apaches acquired pottery skills from the Pueblos. Indeed, women among the Jicarilla Apache became so proficient at manufacturing small pots and baskets that their tribe derived its name from the containers they made.[62]

While relations between Apaches and Pueblos became increasingly hostile, Pueblos were developing closer ties with the Navajos. Pueblos who could not endure Spanish domination joined the Navajos, and during the reconquest of the province following the Pueblo Revolt, many Pueblos fled to these Athapaskans. Some scholars suggest that Navajos acquired Pueblo cultural traits during the post-reconquest period, but other evidence suggests that the process of cultural exchange probably began much earlier.[63] Like the Apaches, Navajos acquired knowledge of agriculture from the Pueblos. Also, they learned weaving from the village dwellers. Pueblo techniques, including the upright loom (as opposed to Hispanic horizontal looms) influenced the development of Navajo weaving, as Navajo women, borrowing a work role from women among the Western Pueblos, became skilled weavers.[64]

Another indication of possible Pueblo influence upon Navajo culture appears in the sheep tending role of Navajo women. In Pueblo society, women cared for domesticated turkeys, but Spanish settlers of the seventeenth and eighteenth centuries apparently did not adopt this female work role into Hispanic society. Herding and tending livestock was not, in Spanish eyes, part of women's work, even for Native American domestic servants.[65] Navajo women, however, became responsible for the sheep the tribe acquired in the seventeenth century, adopting Pueblo women's work role that Hispanic society spurned. These Athapaskan women also acquired the dress of Pueblo women by the beginning of the eighteenth century. In addition, Navajo women assumed responsibility for plastering the hogans, much as Hispanic women adopted this role from the Pueblos.[66]

Still another cultural trait these Athapaskan peoples may have borrowed from the Pueblos was matrilineal descent and matrilocal residence. Since among Navajos women own the house and the sheep, these expansions of power and work roles no doubt enhanced the status of women in Navajo and perhaps Apache society.[67] Unfortunately, records for the seventeenth century are so sparse that it is difficult to determine to what extent Athapaskan women participated in tribal politics or religion. It appears, however, that women could join war societies among both groups, and women emerge as important figures in mythology (Changing Woman and Spider Woman among the Navajos, for example, and White Painted Woman among the Apaches).[68] Recently, scholars have postulated that Plains Indian women suffered a diminution in status during the eighteenth and nineteenth centuries when their societies became dependent upon the horse.[69] But evidence suggests that Apache and Navajo women did not face a loss of status among their people during the seventeenth century, despite the introduction of the horse and other livestock; rather, they may have enjoyed increased status as a result of new work roles.

It is, of course, impossible to adequately measure the psychological effects of these events upon Indian women, but a few clues suggest that women suffered much stress. For example, pottery, a female contribution that generated so much admiring comment from early Hispanic visitors to the areas, declined in quality throughout the century, and by 1700 decorated pottery had disappeared.[70] Although the importation of Spanish manufactured goods undoubtedly reduced some of the market for Pueblo vessels, the abandonment of an aesthetic outlet for Pueblo women probably reveals more than an inability to compete in the marketplace.

Nonetheless, Pueblo women survived this stressful period with most of their roles intact or expanded rather than diminished. They continued to make important contributions to Pueblo society with food preparation and preservation, with weaving and other work with textiles. They learned to utilize Spanish material culture in traditional tasks, but they also became a work force for the conquerors. Some of the most enduring monuments of their labors are the impressive mission churches at Quarai and Abó state monuments. Similarly, Navajo and Apache women experienced an expansion of their roles during this century of cross-cultural contact, as they learned to tend livestock, make pottery and baskets, and to weave. These roles for women persist today in these Indian cultures, as do female ownership of property, matrilineal descent, and matrilocal residence among some of the Pueblos. In the competition for cultural dominance in seventeenth-century New Mexico, no group assumed complete cultural domination over the others. Although the mixing of races and the conflict of cultures created a good deal of turmoil during the 145 years between 1535 and 1680, Indian women of New Mexico adapted to the new circumstances and, for the most part, preserved their cultural identity.

Notes

1. For the purpose of this study, "Spanish," "Spaniard," "European," and "Hispanic" refer to cultural, not racial identity. Many settlers who came to New Mexico were not full-blooded Europeans, but mesti-

zos (Mexican-Indian/Spanish) or mulattos (black/Spanish). Unfortunately, Indian residents of the Southwest in the sixteenth century left no written records as did the Aztecs who inhabited the valley of Mexico. Aztec codices permit scholars to examine that culture from an Aztec perspective as well as from the viewpoint of the conquering Europeans. For a discussion of women in Aztec society see Alfredo Mirandé and Evangelina Enríquez, *La Chicana: The Mexican American Woman* (Chicago: University of Chicago Press, 1979). However, the Europeans who settled New Mexico compiled a body of documentary evidence that, in addition to ethnological and archaeological reports, provides the basis for study of Native American populations in the area. Although most of the official records of the province were destroyed during the Pueblo Revolt, copies or supplementary materials are extant in the archives of Spain and Mexico. Unfortunately, parish records of births, marriages, and deaths cannot be reconstructed. The documents that remain are the products of Hispanic males, and thus contain inherent cultural and sexual biases. Nonetheless, they provide eyewitness and contemporary observations. In addition, ethnological and archaeological records enhance and corroborate contemporary evidence.

2. The term "Pueblo" implies a homogeneity that did not exist. The Pueblos are divided into the Eastern Pueblos (those clustered around the Rio Grande) and the Western Pueblos (including the Zunis and Hopis). Edward Dozier made two major linguistic and cultural divisions among the Eastern Pueblos, the Tanoan and the Keresan. Keresans display a closer connection with the Western Pueblos than do the Tanoans. See Dozier, *The Pueblo Indians of North America* (New York: Holt, Rinehart, and Winston, 1970), and Dozier, "Rio Grande Pueblos," in *Perspectives in American Indian Culture Change,* ed. Edward H. Spicer (Chicago: University of Chicago Press, 1961), 94–186.

3. Spicer, *Cycles of Conquest: The Impact of Spain, Mexico, and the United States on the Indians of the Southwest, 1533–1960* (Tucson: University of Arizona Press, 1962), 210–29, 229–61; Evon Z. Vogt, "Navaho," in *Perspectives in American Indian Culture Change,* 278–336. Spelling of "Navajo" varies. We use the spelling with a *j* unless we are quoting.

4. Albert H. Schroeder, "Rio Grande Ethnohistory," in *New Perspectives on the Pueblos,* ed. Alfonso Ortiz (Albuquerque: University of New Mexico [UNM] Press, 1972), 41–70.

5. Oakah L. Jones, Jr., *Los Paisanos: Spanish Settlers on the Northern Frontiers of New Spain* (Norman: University of Oklahoma Press, 1979), 110.

6. Schroeder, "Ethnohistory," 48, and Dozier (who offers a more conservative estimate of population), "Rio Grande Pueblos," 136.

7. "Investigations of Conditions in New Mexico, 1601," in *Don Juan de Oñate, Colonizer of New Mexico, 1595–1628,* 2 vols., ed. George

P. Hammond and Agapito Rey, Coronado Cuarto Centennial Publications, 1540–1940, vols. 5 and 6 (Albuquerque: UNM Press, 1953), 2:660.

8. Gaspar Pérez de Villagrá, *A History of New Mexico,* trans. Gilberto Espinosa (Chicago: Rio Grande Press, 1962), 144; Dozier, "Rio Grande Pueblos," 102–3.

9. "[Hernán] Gallegos' Relation of the Chamuscado-Rodríguez Expedition," in *The Rediscovery of New Mexico, 1580–1594,* ed. Hammond and Rey, Coronado Cuarto Centennial Publications, 1540–1940, vol. 3, (Albuquerque: UNM Press, 1966), 84.

10. "Translation of the Narrative of [Pedro de] Castañeda" in George Parker Winship, *The Coronado Expedition 1540–1542* (Chicago: Rio Grande Press, 1964), 270; Hammond and Rey, "Gallegos' Relations," 85.

11. Hammond and Rey, "Gallegos' Relation," 86; Hammond and Rey, "Investigations of Conditions in New Mexico," in *Don Juan de Oñate,* 2:627.

12. "Diego Perez de Luxán's Account of the Antonio de Espejo Expedition into New Mexico, 1582," in *Rediscovery of New Mexico,* 187; "Narrative of Castañeda," 264; "Captain Velasco to the Viceroy," in *Don Juan de Oñate,* 2:610; *The Memorial of Fray Alonso de Benavides, 1630,* trans. Mrs. Edward E. Ayer, annot. Frederick Webb Hodge and Charles Fletcher Lummis (Albuquerque: Horn and Wallace Publishers, 1965), 33.

13. Judith K. Brown, "A Note on the Division of Labor by Sex," *American Anthropologist* 72 (October 1970): 1073–78; Peggy R. Sanady, "Toward a Theory of the Status of Women," *American Anthropologist* 75 (October 1973): 1682–1700; Louise Lamphere, "Strategies, Cooperation, and Conflict Among Women in Domestic Groups," in *Woman, Culture, and Society,* ed. Michelle Zimbalist Rosaldo and Louise Lamphere (Stanford: Stanford University Press, 1974), 97–112; Dozier, *Pueblo Indians,* 128–29, 137, 145.

14. "Report of Antonio de Espejo," in *Rediscovery of New Mexico,* 231.

15. "Itinerary of the Expedition," in *Don Juan de Oñate,* 1:321.

16. "Concurso a los bienes de . . . Mendizábal," Tierras 3268, AGN, typescript UNM–SC, 25.

17. A *fanega* was equal to 1.5 bushels. "Concurso a los bienes de Don Diego de Penalosa y Don Bernardo de Mendizábal," Tierras 3268, Archivo General de la Nación (AGN), Mexico City, typescript available in University of New Mexico Library, Special Collections Department (UNM–SC), 22–23, 33, 34.

18. Benavides, *Memorial,* 33.

19. Josiah Gregg, *Commerce of the Prairies,* ed. Max L. Moorhead (Norman: University of Oklahoma Press, 1954), 145; W. W. H. Davis, *El Gringo: New Mexico and Her People* (1857; reprint ed., Lincoln: Uni-

versity of Nebraska Press, 1982), 177; Nan Elsasser, Kyle MacKenzie, and Yvonne Tixier y Vigil, *Las Mujeres: Conversations from a Hispanic Community* (Old Westbury, N.Y.: The Feminist Press, 1980), 24, 107.

20. France V. Scholes, "Church and State in New Mexico, 1610–1650," *New Mexico Historical Review* 11 (April 1936): 155.

21. "Concurso a los bienes de . . . Mendizábal," Tierras 3268, AGN, typescript UNM–SC, 61, 93.

22. Hammond and Rey, "Gallegos' Relation," 85–86, and "Report of Antonio de Espejo," 230.

23. Hammond and Rey, "Gallegos' Relation," 85, and Albert H. Schroeder and Dan S. Matson, *A Colony on the Move: Gaspar Castaño de Sosa's Journal 1590–91* (Santa Fe, N. Mex.: School of American Research, 1965), 100.

24. "Investigations of Conditions in New Mexico, 1601," in *Don Juan de Oñate,* 2:645.

25. "Translation of the letter from Mendoza to the King, April 17, 1540," *Coronado Expedition,* 313.

26. For descriptions of Pueblo women's hairstyles, see "Investigations of Conditions in New Mexico," in *Don Juan de Oñate,* 2:645; "Luxán's Account," 180; and "Report of Antonio de Espejo," 220.

27. For a discussion of European perceptions of Indian women in Anglo America, see Valerie S. Mathes, "A New Look at the Role of Women in Indian Society," *American Indian Quarterly* 2 (Summer 1975): 131–39, Rayna Green, "The Pocahantas Perplex: The Image of Indian Women in American Culture," *Massachusetts Review* 16 (Autumn 1975): 698–714, and Glenda Riley, "Some European (Mis)Perceptions of American Indian Women," *New Mexico Historical Review* 59 (July 1984): 237–66.

28. The reactions of other Iberians to Indian women are treated in John Hemming, *Red Gold: The Conquest of the Brazilian Indians* (Cambridge, Mass.: Harvard University Press, 1978).

29. Winship, "Narrative of Castañeda," 272.

30. "Investigations of Conditions in New Mexico," in *Don Juan de Oñate,* 2: 636, and "Luxán's Account," 206.

31. Villagrá, *History of New Mexico,* 140, and "Investigations of Conditions in New Mexico," in *Don Juan de Oñate,* 2: 636.

32. "Luxán's Account," 206.

33. "Investigations of Conditions in New Mexico," in *Don Juan de Oñate,* 2: 636.

34. Hodge, *Handbook of American Indians North of Mexico,* 2 vols., Smithsonian Institution of American Ethnology Bulletin 30 (New York: Greenwood Press, 1969), 2: 323.

35. Scholes, "Troublous Times in New Mexico, 1659–1670," *New Mexico Historical Review* 12 (April 1937): 144; a number of articles by Scholes

remain the standard works on seventeenth-century New Mexico. See "Troublous Times," *New Mexico Historical Review* 12 (April, October 1937): 134–74, 380–451, and 13 (January 1938): 63–83, and 15 (July, October 1940): 249–68, 369–417, and 16 (January, April, July 1941): 15–40, 184–205, 313–27, "Church and State in New Mexico, 1610–1650," *New Mexico Historical Review* 11 (January, April, July, October 1936): 9–76, 145–78, 283–94, 297–349, and 12 (January 1937): 78–106, and "Civil Government and Society in New Mexico in the Seventeenth Century, *New Mexico Historical Review* 10 (April 1935): 98.

36. "Carta contra Juan Lopez y Juan Anton por casado dos veces, 1634," Inquisición 380, AGN, typescript UNM–SC; "Proceso y causa criminal contra Juan Baptista mulato por casado dos o tres veces, 1657," Inquisición 571, Exp. 8, AGN, typescript UNM–SC.

37. Hodge, *Handbook of American Indians,* 2: 323, and Adolph F. Bandelier, "Documentary History of the Rio Grande Pueblos, New Mexico," *New Mexico Historical Review* 4 (October 1929): 303–34.

38. Winship, "Narrative of Castañeda," 191.

39. Winship, "Narrative of Castañeda," 219; "Proceedings of the [Lieutenant] Governor of New Mexico with Regard to Breaking Camp" in *Don Juan de Oñate,* 2: 676; Charles Wilson Hackett, ed., *Historical Documents Relating to New Mexico, Nueva Vizcaya, and Approaches Thereto, to 1773,* 3 vols. (Washington, D.C.: Carnegie Institution, 1937), 3: 210, 214.

40. Schroeder and Matson, *A Colony on the Move,* 123, 102.

41. "Inspection Made by Juan de Frias Salazar of the Expedition," in *Don Juan de Oñate,* 1: 199–308, and "The Gordejuela Inspection" in *Don Juan de Oñate,* 1: 514.

42. Scholes, "Church and State," and "Troublous Times."

43. Hackett, *Historical Documents,* 3: 214–16, 202, 214.

44. Hackett, *Historical Documents,* 3: 210.

45. Hackett, *Historical Documents,* 3: 205.

46. "Declaration of Pedro García, an Indian of the Tagno nation, a native of Las Salinas," in *Revolt of the Pueblo Indians of New Mexico and Otermin's Attempted Reconquest 1680–1682,* 2 vols., ed. Hackett, trans. Charmion Clair Shelby, Coronado Cuarto Centennial Publications, vols. 8 and 9 (Albuquerque: UNM Press, 1942), 1: 24.

47. "Declaration of Juan Lorenzo and Francisco Lorenzo, brothers," in *Pueblo Revolt,* 2: 252.

48. "Investigations of Conditions in New Mexico," in *Don Juan de Oñate,* 2: 635.

49. "12 de noviembre, 1684," Provincias Internas, tomo 37, exp. 4, AGN, typescript p. 72, UNM–SC.

50. Schroeder and Matson, *A Colony on the Move,* 87.

51. Winship, "Narrative of Castañeda," 269.

52. Hammond and Rey, "Luxán's Account," 99–100.

53. Dozier, "Rio Grande Pueblos," 114.

54. Pat Carr, *Mimbres Mythology* (El Paso: Texas Western Press, 1979), 21–28; also see Dozier, *Pueblo Indians*.

55. "Concurso a los bienes de . . . Mendizábal," Tierras 3268, AGN, typescript UNM–SC; Charles Cutter, a doctoral student at the University of New Mexico, wrote a master's thesis entitled "The Protector of the Indians in Spanish New Mexico" (University of New Mexico, 1984). We are grateful to him for sharing some of his conclusions with us.

56. Vogt, "Navajo," 288.

57. Benavides, *Memorial,* 55.

58. Gertrude B. Van Roekel, *Jicarilla Apaches* (San Antonio, Tex.: The Naylor Company, 1971), vii.

59. Benavides, *Memorial,* 40.

60. "Testimony of Joan [sic] de Ortega," 31 July 1601, Mexico 26, Archivo General de Indias, Seville, Spain, cited in Jack Forbes, *Apache Navajo and Spaniard,* (Norman: University of Oklahoma Press, 1960), 120.

61. Benavides, *Memorial,* 40, and S. Lyman Tyler and H. Darrell Taylor, "The Report of Fray Alonso de Posada in Relation to Quivira and Teguayo," *New Mexico Historical Review* 33 (October 1958): 303.

62. Hubert Howe Bancroft, *Arizona and New Mexico 1530–1888,* vol. 12 in *History of the Pacific States of North America* (San Francisco: The History Company, 1888), 665; Van Roekel, *Jicarilla Apaches,* vii.

63. W. W. Hill, "Some Navaho Culture Changes During Two Centuries (With a Translation of the Early Eighteenth Century Rabal Manuscript)," *Smithsonian Miscellaneous Collections* 100 (1940): 395–415.

64. Joe Ben Wheat, "Rio Grande, Pueblo, and Navajo Weavers: Cross-Cultural Influences," in *Spanish Textile Tradition of New Mexico and Colorado* (Santa Fe: Museum of New Mexico Press, 1979), 29–36; and Wheat, "Spanish-American and Navajo Weaving, 1600 to Now," in *Collected Papers in Honor of Marjorie Ferguson Lambert,* ed. Albert H. Schroeder, Papers of the Archaeological Society of New Mexico no. 3 (Albuquerque: Albuquerque Archaeological Society Press, 1976).

65. "Querella de dos Yndias genízaras sirbientes contra sus amos, 12 octubre 1763," Spanish Archives of New Mexico, available on microfilm from the State Records Center and Archives, Santa Fe, roll 9, fr. 524–26. We are indebted to Charles Cutter, who called this document to our attention. In this case, two Indian women brought charges against their masters for requiring them to tend livestock. Governor Tomás Vélez Cachupin ruled in favor of the women, assigning them to other homes where they would devote themselves only to the "household services and duties appropriate for a woman."

66. Hill, "Some Navaho Culture Changes," 395–415; Laila Sayid

Shukry, "The Role of Women in a Changing Navaho Society" (Ph.D. diss., 1954; Ann Arbor Michigan, University Microfilms).

67. Important studies of these Athapaskan groups include Clyde Kluckhohn and Dorothea Leighton, *The Navaho* (revised ed., Cambridge, Mass.: Harvard University Press, 1979), and Morris Edward Opler, *An Apache Life-Way: The Economic, Social, and Religious Institutions of the Chiricahua Indians* (New York: Cooper Square Publications, Inc., 1965).

68. Spicer, *Cycles of Conquest,* 383; Opler, *An Apache Life-Way,* 281–82.

69. For example, see Margot Liberty, "Hell Came With Horses: Plains Indian Women in the Equestrian Era," *Montana, the Magazine of Western History* 32 (Summer 1982): 10–19.

70. Schroeder, "Rio Grande Ethnohistory," 53.

⇒ 2 ⇐

Nueva Mexicanas as Refugees and Reconquest Settlers

1680–1696

Salomé Hernández

On 9 August 1680 the Pueblo Indians of New Mexico rose up against the Spaniards who had levied tributes upon their towns and had tried to change their customs and religion. The explosive events of the rebellion, which affected more than two thousand Spanish citizens during the decades that followed, have understandably served as the subject of many historical studies. Yet none of these studies has pointed out that the majority of the affected Hispanos were women. The crucial role played by women as victims of the Indian vengeance, as besieged colonists, as immigrants escaping to safer territory, as active participants in the struggle to survive in El Paso, and as active settlers in the four main recruitment and settlement attempts organized by Captain Diego de Vargas Zapata Luján Ponce de León is the focus of the following study.[1]

An analysis of refugee and expedition lists, rolls, petitions, and testimonies makes it clear that female heads of households participated in the New Mexican reconquest process in a dramatic manner, though their role has not received sufficient recognition. Indeed, although women lived and worked alongside male settlers, their very presence on the frontier of Mexico has often been ignored by historians, perhaps because women did not make the military and

41

administrative decisions that scholars traditionally study. Male political and military leaders made scant mention of women in official
reports. Yet, even though women were mentioned only indirect-
ly, it is clear that they worked as productive and necessary members of the colony and in that manner helped make the reconquest
expeditions a success.

After the reconquest, women continued to perform essential
tasks as New Mexico colonists. All colonists suffered from the harsh
climate, the lack of tools and seed, and the need for more laborers.
Living conditions, as one colonist noted, were such that the colonists lived "huddled together each lamenting his fate." While colonists had expected Indians to provide a willing labor force, this
was often not the case. In fact, some Hispanic men complained that
their "wives and children were forced to work for the Indians, carrying water and wood in order to live." Thus Hispanic women
were not only present on the New Mexico frontier but the frontier
experience shaped and changed their lives. The women came as
settlers, not merely as wives subordinate to settler husbands. Living on the seventeenth-century frontier of Mexico forced women
to perform tasks that were seldom demanded of them in the more
settled regions of Mexico.[2]

Refugees of the Revolt

The frontier women who were caught up in the Pueblo Revolt
shared a social make-up similar to that of all Spain's colonies. There
were, of course, many native Indians, but there were also socially
and economically well-to-do settlers. One of the most well-known
señoras was European-born Doña Teresa de Mendizábal, the unfor-
tunate wife of a seventeenth century New Mexican governor. Most
upper-class women were referred to as Hispanas, that is colonists
of European background, even when they might have more Indian blood than they would admit. Reconquest documents refer to
most settlers as mestizas, a mixed blood of Indian and European
ancestors. Mention is also made of mulatas (a mix of European and
African), *lobas* (a mix of Indian and African), *coyotas* (a mix of mes-
tiza and Indian), as well as several other common racial types that
resulted from the marriage of these three key groups.

Both before and after the revolt these frontier women, from

all spheres, coped with the daily fear of being killed or kidnapped alive by hostile Indians especially when their husbands, fathers, or brothers left them alone with the responsibility of caring for households and administering ranches or farms. In 1680 the nightmares became a reality as entire families, men, women, and children, fell victim to the vengeance of the Pueblos during the first week of hostilities. The plans for revolt had been laid out for years by Popé, an Indian medicine man, who united the disgruntled Pueblo leaders against the Spaniards. In utmost secrecy, the Indians agreed to kill all white men on August 13, 1680 but moved the date up when the Spaniards learned of the plot four days earlier. The colonists were unable to prevent Indians from immediately rising up against those whom they considered intruders in their homeland. Some four hundred Hispanos died at the hands of the rebels; left were some two thousand survivors, mostly women and children. Among those who lost loved ones was Juan Leiva who had left his family in Galisteo while he went on escort duty. The Indians immediately killed all the family except for his three daughters, whom they kidnapped only to kill them later in retaliation for losses suffered during the siege of Santa Fe.[3]

After an attempt at fending off the Indians, most Hispanos realized that they could not withstand an extended siege and gathered for mutual protection at two collection points. Approximately one-half of the refugees went to Santa Fe, where they sought protection under Governor Antonio de Otermín. For convenience, these northern refugees will be called the Santa Fe group. The other one thousand survivors, those in the southern region, united at Isleta under the command of Captain Alonso García. This group will be referred to as the Isleta group.[4]

García wrote that only 120 persons, from among the many noncombatants who gathered under his protection, were capable of bearing arms. He decided that his primary responsibility was to see to the safety of the women and children who made up the majority of the group. After scouring the region for survivors, on advice of his officers, he broke camp and headed southward to El Paso with the refugees, their male and female servants, and some Indian allies. Thus he put their welfare before that of a governor whose fate was unknown.[5]

In the north some one thousand Hispanos faced a similar and perhaps more precarious situation as the Pueblo Indians laid siege to Santa Fe on August 15. The governor echoed García's complaint that "there are not one hundred men who could fight, all the rest being women and children who must necessarily march on foot through the countryside in the sight of the enemy."[6] Soon the Indians cut off the water supply to the Casas Reales for two and one half days and everyone within the gates began to suffer from thirst and hunger. Governor Otermín commented on being surrounded by the "wailing of women and children," who took comfort in praying "constantly and with much fervor" for themselves and for male loved ones, who left the compound to fight the Indians. Otermín saw no other alternative and decided to move south. He ordered the distribution of eight thousand pesos of his personal goods to the "Spanish soldiers, to all the families, and servants, the Mexican natives, and to all classes of people." Since there were only twenty carts, most of the Hispano women were obliged to march on foot, bringing only the clothes they wore, and carrying only a few possessions.[7]

Only some of the female refugees, in both the Santa Fe and Isleta group, who suffered the great distress and hardships of the war and its aftermath, can be identified individually. In the Isleta group is Doña Teresa Varela, who had the good fortune to have the protection of her husband, Captain García. Since his military duties kept him busy, she assumed the responsibility for two sons, two daughters, their spouses, an unwed son, a grandchild, and twenty-two servants. Other women such as the childless Doña Magdalena Varela de Losada took on the responsibility of feeding and clothing several brothers-in-law. Doña Juana Valencia supervised four servants, and later muster rolls indicate that she took in several orphans and women who had been abandoned. The widowed Ana de Tapia traveled as the head of household of a thirty-two member household.

Accompanying the Santa Fe group were Ana de Anaya and María González, who were left behind by husbands who were on escort duty with Father Francisco Ayeta, the commisary general. Others who accompanied the governor were Doña Luisa Hurtado, the wife of Captain Fernando Chávez, who traveled with her four adult offspring and two servants, and Blas Griego's mother who headed a thirty-four member family.[9]

In addition to the few women who are specifically mentioned in accounts, there were countless others. Some were young, others aged, some childless, some in their first pregnancy, and others with large families. Some traveled with a husband or a male protector; other widowed or single women traveled alone or with servants. While a few had material wealth, most did not. They journeyed barefooted, hungry, and penniless. Their poverty forced them to pool their resources for protection and comfort during the trip through the arid and rugged desert.

The Isleta group, according to reports, included "many children and women on foot, naked, and dying of hunger." When they met Father Ayeta, who was on his way northward to New Mexico with a wagon train of supplies ordered months before the revolt, he was moved to note that these survivors looked almost dead. Their appearance also touched the hearts of the hardened soldiers under Ayeta's command and increased their fears that loved ones might be lost. They hoped to speed northward to find their families among the survivors, "children and women marching through the country on foot" and to offer them food and transportation. The military junta, in a move that received Ayeta's approval, voted to leave the noncombatants from Isleta in a safe place and go in search of the Santa Fe group.[10] Meanwhile, the Santa Fe group left on August 21, moving cautiously because of the people on foot and for fear of Indian attack and gathering proof of the murders of priests, men, women, and children, the desecration of churches, and the destruction of property.

Upon arrival in Isleta, Otermín was disappointed to find that the pueblo had been attacked and that García had retreated. Otermín immediately sent an order to García commanding him to appear before him.[11] When Otermín finally met García weeks later, he ordered García arrested for desertion. García defended his position, saying "I was forced to seek the means of saving and receiving the many people that this jurisdiction contains, both women and children who are in manifest danger." His Council of War, agreed with his analysis and argued "your lordship can see with your own eyes the misfortunes of hunger and nakedness which afflict us and hear the clamor of the many women and children who would have inevitably perished either of hunger or at the hands of the enemy." Otermín was persuaded by their arguments to free García. Indeed, although the noncombatants were not consulted, and thus did not give their opinion, no decision could be made without taking them into consideration.[12]

Otermín himself had no choice left but to follow García south. He also hoped to meet Ayeta, whom everyone expected to be making his way northward with provisions to feed all the New Mexican residents. Ayeta met the second wave of refugees as they neared El Paso and was inspired to write:

> I remained with the governor for fifteen days camped on the banks of the river, well supplied with provisions, receiving the people who arrived in groups and in such misery that there was no heart that was not moved by compassion nor was it easy to find words for expressing it for such unhappiness and pitiful tragedy, with the need corresponding to the great number, and the poor women and children on foot and unshod, of such a hue that they looked like dead people, inspired one with horror.

Otermín ordered a general muster roll to ascertain the total number of refugees under his care. That roll listed 150 male heads of households capable of bearing arms and 1,795 "women, children, servants, widows, and orphans."[13]

The noncombatants were not all females or minors, indeed the list included 317 male and female Mexican Indians, twenty-three bachelors, fourteen widowers, and an unknown number of males among the four hundred servants listed with no mention made of age, sex, or status. There is no way to ascertain if they were slaves, free wage earners, or Apache Indian captives.[14]

The muster specifically identifies only 112 women who traveled with García or Otermín and does not include all the names of the married or single women who traveled with husbands or other relatives. Indeed, official documents indicate the number of arms and beasts of burden with more accuracy than they do the female citizens or their children, *agregados* [companions], or servants. The 1680 list does specifically mention nine widows traveling alone as heads of household. They included Doña Catalina Zamora, who presented herself before the governor with four grown nieces and five servants, the only survivors of a family of thirty. Doña Inez Luz passed muster on foot with the responsibility of two recently widowed daughters and four small grandchildren. The fifty-year-old Francisca Abrega, the Mexicana Angelina, Magdalena García, Catalina Bernal, María Hernández, and Isabel Archuleta, and Ana Tapia, who are listed as poor, penniless, naked, and on foot, passed muster with families of from four to nine children. The widows demonstrated their independence by journeying alone rather than joining an extended family. Four years later, in the 1684 muster, however, only the poor Francisca Abrego is listed as a head of household, with several children, an orphan, and an Indian servant.[15]

Refugees at El Paso

The presence of the large numbers of women and children continued to influence the decisions of the governor. After sending a delegation to Chihuahua to buy supplies for these refugees, Otermín turned to the task of finding a level place to set up a camp in which to "withstand the rigors of the impending winter," especially for the "very old persons and some who are ill, and women with newborn children, without any place to live or any shelter from the inclemencies of the weather." Governor Otermín decided to set up camp. On October 5 the surviving refugees moved to several sites surrounding the monestary of Guadalupe, near present day El Paso, where pasture, firewood, and water were more abundant. These selected sites were still within the New Mexico frontier since the soldiers and refugees believed that the reconquest was a foregone conclusion.[16]

There the refugees began immediately to construct suitable and durable *jacales* of four forked poles. Since all building materials "had to be carried on their shoulders," every able bodied person, men, women, and children, participated in the activity. According to one account, "wives made the mud and with their own hands overlaid the said huts." Eventually the refugees organized their camps "in an orderly manner, each one living in a house which he has made of sticks and branches with his own hands."[17]

The governor set up his headquarters in the new capital, El Paso, which was surrounded by various small settlements. San Lorenzo, the most important, was initially founded some thirty-three miles away, until 1684 when it was destroyed by Indian attacks and moved to a site three miles away. Corpus Cristi de Isleta and other smaller Hispano settlements including Nuestra Señora de Guadalupe, San Pedro de Alcántara, and Nuestra Señora de Alcántara and also several Indian settlements such as Sacramento of the Tiquas,

Socorro of the Piros, San Antonio de Senecu of the Piros and Tompiros surrounded El Paso.[18]

Although the economy of these towns was based on agriculture and livestock, the communities retained a military flavor. This is especially true because the refugees found it difficult to accept the fact that they would have to remain in the El Paso area for a long period of time. They could not forget that the reconquest itself had as one of its goals winning back the lost homes of the refugees. After completing the construction of shelters, Otermín turned to his military responsibilities. He began recruiting soldiers to reconquer the lost colony. Even in this decision, Otermín had to consider the refugee families who would accompany the troops and was forced to recruit fifty soldiers to guard them. He also recognized his responsibility toward the families which the soldiers left behind. The viceroy in Mexico City offered to equip the soldiers with arms, saddles, hats, "shoes for themselves and their wives, and 200 *varas* of fine brayant linen for shirts, and [promised] that he would see to it that the wives and families were supplied with everything necessary for their well-being."[19]

Despite the viceroy's promises, several persons excused themselves, such as Captain Pedro Marqués, stating that he could not abandon his twenty-one member family. Seventy year old Sergeant Major Pedro Duran y Chávez, who had similar family responsibilities, added that he was too old. Cristobal Enríquez offered to return to New Mexico if he could be assured of the safety of his wife and seven children. The family was an important element in the decisions of the soldiers as well as the officers.[20]

When the soldiers left on reconquest expeditions, the women assumed family responsibilities as heads of households. They wove blankets to ward off the cold with the wool supplied by Ayeta. They "cut open the land," sowed and took care of the crops and overcame difficulties occasioned by the lack of seed, the harsh winters, the scarcity of water, the rough terrain, and the fear of Indian attack. While waiting for the crops to mature, they sold all they owned to buy food. When their food supply dwindled, hunger often forced them to eat the immature ears of corn, to slaughter their milk cows and other livestock, and even to eat "roots and weeds."[21] To aid the poor families, the Santa Fe *cabildo* requested victuals, provisions, clothing, and arms from Mexican officials, especially for these impoverished "families and the poor and the orphaned

young girls." They also suggested that viceregal officials recruit
settlers from among Mexico City's idle and poor by offering them
land and titles.[22]

The families suffered greatly during the two months the soldiers were on the expedition. Upon their return, the great poverty
of so many poor women and children and so many orphans and
widows prompted many of the soldiers to ask for permission to
leave for another place where they could maintain their own persons and that of their wives because all were perishing from hunger. Despite the fact that the governor denied such licenses on the
grounds that it would depopulate the area and leave "only women
and children who would be in danger of dying of hunger," many
persons left.[23]

The situation did not improve for these families in the years
that followed. The 1684 roll with 161 families, ranging in size from
one to fifty-five persons, totaled fewer citizens than the 1680 roll.
More harvests were lost and the families complained to the viceroy and king in terms such as these:

> The food which we now have is of roots and *mescales* because not a
> kernel of corn can be found, and the need has come to such a point
> among the neighborhood that they [the thieves] no longer care to be
> discovered and are risking it all. They are destroying the tame milk
> cows belonging to certain citizens and it has come to the point that
> not even the he goats within the corrals are safe.[24]

The settlers continued to hope that the king would hear "the cries
and shouts of the *vecinos* [citizens], especially the poor women and
children." As more soldiers died on later expeditions, the number
of poor widows continued to increase and they began to take on
an increasingly important role in the history of the area. The soldiers who returned to their homes found "their families so thoroughly poor and naked that they cannot fulfill the requirements of
our Holy Mother Church, because they do not have anything to
cover their bodies so as not to feel public shame."[25]

In September of 1684 Governor Domingo Jironza Petriz de
Cruzate personally visited 109 families and miscellaneous persons
in Isleta, El Paso, and Guadalupe. Although the widows made up
only five percent of all the heads of households in 1680, four years
later they constituted twenty-five percent of the muster roll in Isleta,

five percent in San Lorenzo and twenty-one percent in El Paso, a
substantial increase. In Isleta he found the condition of the twenty-
one families, including the five widows among them, to be very
similar. The typical entry read:

> The family of the widow of Francisco Valencia is made up of twen-
> ty persons. [She] has no supplies nor a field because she lost what
> she sowed due to lack of water. Their clothing is not sufficient. The
> aforementioned widow is indecently dressed and the rest [of the fam-
> ily] is almost naked.[26]

The Mexicana Clara Susana was described as "infamously poor."
The widow of Juan Martín complained that, if she had been supplied with seed, she and her family of twelve would have harvested a crop, thus implying they would have been better-off.[27]

The thirty-six vecinos visited by the governor in the Real de
San Lorenzo seemed to be materially better off than their Isleta com-
patriots. Not only women, such as Doña Magdalena Varela de Losada, who were married to prominent citizens, but widows such as
Juana Leiva, who had the responsibility of a ten member family,
were able to dress with "some decency" as were the fifty-three vecinos in El Paso. Indeed, thirty-three families harvested from three
to twenty-five *fanegas* of corn. Ana de Tapia, who organized her
thirty-two members family into an effective work force, harvested the second largest 1684 crop. Doña Bernardina Trujillo, Doña
Catalina Lucero, Isabel de Vera, and the widow of Perea averaged
harvests of three fanegas, an amount below that of their male counterparts but indicative of their labor. Most vecinos indicated that
they looked forward to a brighter and more promising year in 1685.

While local documents include the names of many of these married, widowed, or single women as active participants in such mundane actions as writing wills, giving testimony, and selling land or
other merchandise, they offer few personal details. Most pre-1680
documents were destroyed by the Pueblos and most postrevolt documents and historical works give more attention to the members
of higher social, military, or economic spheres and ironically to
the horses and arms of the soldiers. Official documents seemed to
take the woman's presence for granted, yet recognized that these
female settlers contributed to Spain's success in holding on to her
colonies by fulfilling the domestic chores of grinding corn, mak-

ing tortillas, having babies, and caring for a family. To these household tasks can be added others held in greater esteem on the frontier such as feeding the troops, laundering their clothing, augmenting the population by their presence, giving logistical support on the home front, and managing home industries, all of which were crucial to the reconquest. Even as these women and their families struggled in the daily battle to survive, the military reconquest was never out of the minds of the political and military leaders.[28]

Recruitment

It is obvious that General Diego Vargas Zapata, who was appointed Governor and Captain General in 1692, recognized the need for both male and female recruits when he requested financial backing for recruitment of settlers as well as soldiers to augment the families in El Paso. The viceroy authorized twelve thousand pesos and later an additional 29,723 pesos to be drawn on the treasuries of Zacatecas and Durango for the recruitment of settlers, their maintenance for one year, and for the soldiers of the presidio of Santa Fe. Vargas Zapata gave his support to four recruitment efforts. He brought some recruits with his entourage; he commissioned Páez Hurtado to recruit settlers in Mexican states to the south; he backed recruitment in Mexico City; and, of course, he recruited old New Mexican families in El Paso.[29]

Before his departure for New Mexico, Vargas Zapata himself recruited nineteen racially mixed families, including eight women traveling alone or as a head of household. Five years later these recruits, each of whom had received the title of vecino testified about their experience in an inquiry against the governor.[30] Among the witnesses was the vecina of Santa Fe, the sixty-year old black, Mariá Rodríguez, who testified that she had enlisted with her daughter Pascuala Guerrero just three days before Vargas Zapata departed from Sombrerete on June 13, 1692. Páez Hurtado, Varga Zapata's second in command, had contacted her and given her one hundred pesos in cloth and fifteen pesos for a new wardrobe. She complained that the latter sum was not enough, since tailors charged up to three pesos for each skirt or petticoat. The vecinas, Juana de Enciso, a sixty-year old black from Fresnillo and Juana de la Ríos, a thirty-six year old mulata head of household from Sombrerete were among several recruits who received goods, money "to pay a debt," cash to buy supplies, and wages for the time they awaited departure.[31]

Generally, all settlers, whether male or female, were to receive a basic ration which consisted of a bowl of flour and one sixteenth of a steer a week. Nonetheless, almost every one of the recruits complained that the ration was not sufficient to live on and that they had to use their own money or that of a third party to survive. Documents specifically note the presence of many women dependent upon a male relative, but little mention is made of several exceptions which destroy the stereotype of the dependent female camp follower. One example is Diego Brito who received seventy pesos in goods, but received neither rations or wages because he attached himself to the General's family. Gregorio Vicente, a twenty year old Spaniard from Zacatecas, received thirty-five pesos but no rations because he "attached himself to the soldiers' female cook who gave him to eat while they remained in the city." Thus, some women were not only heads of households but had male dependents.

Either Juana Torres, the fourteen year old *coyota* from Zacatecas, who had enlisted "alone and single" or the fifty-seven year old Tarascan Indian, Juana de la Cruz, both of whom enlisted as independently employed women, could have been the female cook to whom Vicente referred. Although Juana received a petticoat worth seven pesos, an overcoat, a pair of shoes, a hat, three *varas* of baize cloth, a saddle, and two shirts for a total of twenty-eight pesos, as "a servant in the kitchen of the cited general," she received no rations in Sombrerete and Zacatecas. The young maiden aided the older cook, Juana de la Cruz, to whom Vargas Zapata gave fifty pesos in Sombrerete and hired her at eight pesos a month or five and one-half reales a day to cook for the muleteers. She complained he did not give her family any goods. It is important to note, however, that these two women, on the two ends of the age spectrum journeyed without husbands, earned their own wages, and hoped to contribute to the settlement process.

Reconquest

The dedication of Vargas Zapata and his nineteen recruits, did not allay the fear of the New Mexicans or fulfill the needs of the frontier. The old settlers continued to seek permission to leave the region. Some stated "We have been residing in this country without the means to keep ourselves decently on corn alone because the place is unsuitable, for the land is so sterile that except by constant watering no grain can be gathered." But the governor's plan to reconquer New Mexico necessitated the aid of every man, woman, and child. Thus he denied licenses to leave, ordered a muster roll, and began a recruitment process.[32]

From 21 August to 16 October 1692, Vargas Zapata recruited a sizable number of soldiers who left on yet another expedition leaving behind many families. Although the harvest had ended, the administrative responsibility assumed by the women was still great. It was not a novel experience for such women as Doña Luisa Hurtado who had demonstrated her capabilities during the trek to El Paso with four small children, had borne four other offspring, helped her husband Don Fernando de Chávez in the field, and generally proven her qualities as a productive and active frontier dweller. For some, the experience was new. Francisco Anaya, who had lost his family in 1680 while he was on escort duty, left a young wife, three children, and a widowed sister to work in the fields and garden plot.[33]

The soldiers were the most visible participants of this initial military expedition, yet several women also played a role in this reconquest expedition. Female participation began when several Indian women offered to serve as messengers. As the reconquest progressed, soldiers freed several captured Hispana women. On September 25, Vargas Zapata freed the first such prisoners: two elderly Indian women, a young Indian maiden, and the son of the deceased Cristobal Anaya. In the weeks that followed he freed Doña Petrona, with her husband's two sons and three daughters, as well as a son born of a Pueblo Indian; Juana de Arzata; Catalina a single woman with a small child; the daughter of a Janos soldier Joseph Nevares; Juana Domínguez with five children; Lucía the wife of Pedro Muzquís and a daughter; a mulata with four children; and Juana, a Tegua Indian.[34]

The latter's case reveals some of the psychological hazards these women faced on returning from captivity. Juana refused to return to her soldier husband, who had petitioned for her return as his legal spouse. Vargas Zapata stated "having assured her that she would not be harmed in any way, I turned her over to him." The husband showed great joy at being reunited with his wife despite the presence of two small children born during her captivity.[35]

These freed captives followed the expedition for a whole month suffering cold and hunger with the soldiers until Vargas Zapata ordered their return to El Paso via the Hacienda Mejía. Along with the Indian allies, Pueblo captives, and the tired horses, they traveled under the protection of their kinsmen "with whom they have come out from the reduced and conquered kingdoms." Vargas Zapata and the group reunited at El Ojito del Zuñi and entered El Paso on 20 December 1692.[36]

Recruiting Anew For Resettlement

When Vargas Zapata returned to El Paso, he immediately began recruiting colonists to join his resettlement effort. From among the seventy-nine families which he visited in San Lorenzo and El Paso fourteen heads of household responded affirmatively to his inquiry. Of those who immediately stated their readiness to go, four were headed by loyal female subjects. Catalina de Esparza, a single woman with a fifteen year old nephew, two young nieces, and six servants, stated her readiness "to enter with all her family to settle said kingdom." The widows María Luján and Doña Luisa Jaramillo both stated they "would go whereever his majesty would order." Doña Juana de Almaza, a recent widow, stated "when they give her the financial aid to be able to move her family, they will enter to settle the kingdom."[37]

Several males refused to take their family until they had built a house and sowed a crop in the new settlement. Twenty-one others stated individually that if equipped with "enough supplies he would take his wife and family . . . to which I [Vargas] responded that no one would lack supplies to make the trip at that time."

In Senecu, Vargas Zapata interviewed nineteen Mexican Indian families. Women headed six families, which encompassed forty percent of the population. None indicated they were not planning to go northward, and indeed the 1697 census indicated that three did make the journey; Agueda Morán with two of the four persons with whom she is initially listed in a previous census, Josefa de la Cruz, who enlisted alone in 1692 had two sons in 1697 although she was still listed as Laureano's widow; Magdalena de Ogaño with two children and two orphans in both musters. In Isleta and So-corro de los Piros, only five of the thirty-three families showed any enthusiasm for leaving immediately. Ana María Montoya, María de Tapia, and the widowed Inez Herrera with nine children, seven orphans, and a mother-in-law between them, stated they "would willingly go to said kingdom" and indeed made it north.

Most of the families were so poor that Vargas Zapata was prompted to make the following observation:

> With my own eyes [I] saw the great poverty of said *empadronados* and also the complete nakedness of women, children, and the domes-tics to whom they have to give the title of servants and yet must raise. Likewise their offspring and the orphans whom they feed with them, their nakedness is so equal that the offspring cannot be distin-guished from their servants.

Despite the poverty, the black drummer Sebastián Rodríguez pub-licly announced the upcoming departure of the citizens and in mid-October all the carts and the seventy poor New Mexican families moved northward following a route with good pasture, water, and firewood.[38]

The suffering of the colonists did not abate during the jour-ney. Years later a number of these recruits also testified against Var-gas Zapata. Their testimony is found in depositions taken during the governor's *residencia* in December of 1697. The first witness, Diego Montoya, lived in Bernalillo. His wife, Doña Josefa, cared for four nephews in addition to her own seven preteenage children. She complained that although they were to have received the basic ration of one bowl of flour and one sixteenth steer each week, had she not brought her own supplies, they might have died. Almost all the other settlers, bachelors, young couples, widows, and estab-lished families, echoed the complaint speaking of the hardships, espe-cially the lack of food that drove them to eat "the sweat soaked protectors of the horses . . . horse meat, and even worse, dogs and cats." The witnesses also noted the death of many travelers, espe-cially the young and newborn children.[39]

The settlers came from all social classes and had families which ranged in size from one to six members. Many were female heads of household whose ages spanned the gamut from the eighty-seven year old mulata, Francisca García to the twenty year old *coyota*,

Clara de Chávez, who brought her Apache mother and brother with her. There was a majority of middle-aged settlers. Four women, Phelipa Martín, Ana de Arriata, María Martín, and María López Ocanto, had lost their husbands after the journey and testified on their own behalf.

The number of female heads of households interviewed in El Paso was fifty-four of a total of ninety-nine area families. Vargas Zapata was moved to state that of the seventy families he recruited in El Paso "among them are many widows, bachelors, and single women." These settlers included Hispanas, Mexican Indians, New Mexican Indians, blacks, mulatas, *lobas, coytas,* and mestizas who were listed as vecinas and received rations, wages, and goods. The El Paso families complained later that the Zacatecas families were only black female vendors—*"negras* and *tamaleras"* or "old Black, *coyota* and *loba* widows which he had recruited as settlers . . . to whom he paid forty and fifty pesos each, while giving the more than one hundred families he brought from El Paso only ten, fifteen, twenty, and twenty-five pesos per each four to six member family."[40]

The 1697 census and court testimony indicate women's importance as settlers. While many women were mentioned because of their social or economic position, other women traveled as settlers in their own right. Although these women are rarely mentioned, many of these female *agregadas* attached themselves to most large families, widowed mothers, maiden sisters, aunts, orphans, and servants. They often later married or remarried and took on the role of active participants in resettlement. Many of these women voiced no plans to travel to Santa Fe on the reconquest yet are noted in future musters. They included women such as Leonor Martín, a widow with two grandchildren; María Romero with four children; and Juana Leiva who died and left seven orphans two years later. Proportionately, a greater percentage of women than men journeyed northward. Other women are known because they lodged official complaints in their capacity as persons with legal rights and did not hesitate to make their opinions known.[41] For example, four Bernalillo women, Doña María de Salazar, the Indian Sebastiana Fresqui, María Ortega, and Isabel García, testified for their absent husbands according to Spanish law. They complained that officials "took one half of a steer to give to their women and only gave the *vecinos* some pieces that did not last two days. . . ." The sixty-year old Doña Bernardina de Salas, who traveled with two nephews, also stated that she was deeply affected by the execution of four deserters whose death "left their wives and children perishing without the poor protection they had had from them [the husbands]."[42]

According to most of the witnesses, the settlers, including the women, also received a ration of dry goods. Juan Lucero and his wife, Isabel de Salazar, received a typical allotment consisting of eight *varas* of canvas, eight *varas* of baize, five *varas* of scarlet, one breath of rouen, two hats, one saddle, one cuirass, shoes for women, two blankets, four breadths of cloth for petticoats, and four cloaks. She also received the following goods:

> fourteen *varas* of glossy silk, five *varas* mitan, one and one-half ounce of satin, two pesos of white thread, twelve *varas* silk ribbon, eight *varas* of ribbon, one saddle, two and one half *varas* petticoat cloth, one *vara* brittany cloth, and one *vara* Chinese rouen.[43]

The settlers did not complain about these particular supplies as much as they did about other abuses.

Mexico City Settlers

Vargas Zapata was not the only official who actively sought to populate and colonize New Mexico anew. The junta in Mexico City began its endeavor by hiring someone to go to the four corners of the capital's *plaza mayor* to proclaim the recruitment process, "to the sound of the war drum," seeking "white, married [settlers] with sons and daughters of distinct ages." The recruits were to receive 300 pesos; an allotment of dry goods; a wage while they awaited departure; transportation for the families; and a promise of livestock, land, equipment, and a year's subsidy. In return the settlers lost their prerogative to end the contract. "If a family did not show up or fled in the city or on the road, it would be punished with exile to the Philippines without pay."[44]

These promises attracted sixty-six families for a total of 234 persons, all but one headed by males. Only the thirty-three year old Petronila de la Cueva, described as a woman of "medium height, aquiline face, large eyes, and a scar on the lower part of the left cheek," traveled alone when her husband Juan de Góngora died shortly before the departure. She made the difficult decision to continue the journey with three daughters and two sons. The only other single women were daughters of the settlers, whose very presence necessitated special care so that no bachelors would live or mix with the families.[45]

The lack of female heads of families does not diminish the importance of the wives who made the journey. Most of them courageously left their homes at a young age. For example Gertrudes de la Conde Jariaguerra, Josefa Sedano, Juana de Góngora, and Francisca Morales were twelve, thirteen, fourteen, and seventeen years old respectively and traveled with one or two children. Several other young wives, such as Gertrudes Trujillo, and María de la Encarnación, Gregoría Rúiz, Mariana Coronado, and María Rúiz all added a son or daughter to the volunteer ranks.[46] The unusual case of Doña María Mirabal, a fifteen year old bride, indicates that the official inspector questioned all members of the expedition, male and female, about their willingness to settle the frontier. She later ran away from her husband and eventually took him to court for abusing her. This action indicates that she and other women were not pawns in their husbands' hands but could seek the protection of the law.[47]

Administrative complaints of inadequate supplies, unpaid wages, and corruption plagued the families on the difficult journey from Mexico City. Their hopes for a brighter future as hidalgos in a new land were dashed when they arrived in El Paso only to hear that Vargas Zapata had already departed for Santa Fe. Undaunted by this information and a dearth of supplies, the expedition set off in thirteen carts, although most of the women and children were forced to walk when hundreds of the beasts of burden died. The settlers suffered from hunger and thirst. Their confessor and guide, Father Francisco Farfán was moved to write, "they have not even a tortilla with which to aid me, nor even some wild greens."[48]

This expedition arrived in Santa Fe too late to sow crops. Nonetheless, Vargas Zapata greeted them and gave orders that they be cared for at least a year. The settlers were destined to pay for this aid when soon after their arrival, the governor called upon them to join in a campaign against the Indians. They complied but they also reminded the governor that when the viceroy persuaded them to leave their homes to come and populate New Mexico, he promised them a land free of enemies.[49]

The Hurtado Settlers

These Mexican families, the El Paso refugees, and Vargas Zapata's recruits did not meet the needs of the province. In the years that followed these settlers complained that they did all but "sell their children and women" to survive and sustain themselves with their small herds. To fulfill the obvious need, in June 1694 Vargas Zapata commissioned Captain Páez Hurtado to recruit more settlers in his name.[50]

Páez Hurtado set out, with orders from the *fiscal,* Juan Escalante y Mendoza, and the junta general to recruit settler families, not bachelors. A family of four was to receive three hundred pesos and those with larger families, three hundred and fifty pesos. The families were also to receive a ration of goods which varied depending on the size of the family. Each member of the family was considered a valuable settler and as such also entitled to receive a wage of one and a half *reales* per day while awaiting the departure.

The volunteers signed up from December 7, 1694 to February 13, 1695 in Parral, Zacatecas, and Sombrerete. Although the captain seemed satisfied with the quality of the recruits, officials of Nueva Viscaya, complained that the people he selected were vagabonds and when they arrived in New Mexico, the El Paso families labled them black *tamaleras.* By February 11 Páez Hurtado wrote Viceroy Gálvez "I have forty-three families and will leave within three days." An official Páez Hurtado muster listed forty-six families. Among them were listed twelve female heads of families.[51]

Existing testimony taken from the recruits in 1697 reveals complaints which highlight discrepancies and irregularities not only in the number and composition of families on the official list but also in the recruitment process and Páez Hurtado's administration in general. Such charges were noted by both individuals traveling alone, several male heads of household, single males and females, and nine female heads of households, who complained that, as a policy, Vargas Zapata considered the clothing, arms, horses, and other goods given the recruits in Zacatecas and during the journey as a loan for which he "discounted the costs from their first year's wages." Speaking of the recruitment itself, vecinos complained that they did not receive a full ration, while others complained that Páez Hurtado took "them to the store several times [instead of once] and kept their money." Páez Hurtado apparently took the extra supplies and money and kept both for himself. He is also accused of making some families "buy their own supplies" and use their own money to make the journey.[52]

The testimony draws attention to Páez Hurtado's manipulation of families and single persons in order to form artificial families, thus allowing him to deprive them of their just pay and rations. The testimony also reveals that women contributed more to resettlement than was previously believed. Several witnesses stated that Páez Hurtado listed about twenty-five persons who never made the journey. Parents complained that Páez Hurtado took their children and put them "with different mulatas to make families of them." Single persons complained that, after enlisting alone, they were attached to other families "who were neither siblings, nor relatives." One *coyota* testified that, when Páez Hurtado enlisted her, he asked her to say "that she was a widow who had two daughters named María and Antonia de San Nicolás, although in truth she was eighteen years old, single, and had never had any daughters." She further stated that these two girls never left Zacatecas.[53]

Witness upon witness interviewed in different towns at different dates collaborated the statements of fellow settlers. Indeed, it was a common belief that Páez Hurtado "made relatives of strangers and married people of bachelors who later married other persons in this city and many have not married." In addition, the testimony provides evidence indicating that a larger number of women than previously thought truly settled New Mexico.

Despite the existence of the Páez Hurtado list, an analysis of the later census and the testimony of the recruits themselves indicate several things. There were in reality twenty-one families and twenty individuals, of different racial background, rather than the forty-six families listed by the Captain. The official list included twelve female heads of households composing fifty-four percent of the population, in families ranging from one to seven persons. Six more females can be added to this list of heads of households since they did not travel under the control of a male. Several of these unprotected females were teenagers who seemed to be more easily exploited by Páez Hurtado who took their money and gave them fewer goods. Indeed, regardless of age or marital status women played a more important role in this settlement process than has heretofore been believed.[54]

The families left during this unusually harsh winter and arrived in El Paso too late to sow crops. Nonetheless, Páez Hurtado set out again using the carts belonging to the *Custodio* of New Mexico. From the time of their arrival in Santa Fe the Zacatecas families were housed in dwellings vacated by the Mexican families who moved to Santa Cruz de la Cañada and were subsidized for a year.[55]

The *Nueva Mexicanas* were as responsible and competent as men in the day-to-day process of survival. They fulfilled the tasks reserved by Spanish society for women, but on the frontier, they also took on added responsibilities in times of peace as well as war. An analysis of the colonial documents indicates that the full extent of their active participation has been overlooked in the past. Hispanic and Indian women became involved as victims and refugees in the first hours of the revolt. As the Spaniards fled southward they made up a sizable percentage of the weary travelers. In the years that followed, women became even more important as heads of households as many of the men fled farther south with their families or died on military expeditions leaving behind widows and orphans. As the reconquest expeditions were organized and reversed the exodus, the women, as settlers, were again a prominent and numerically strong segment of the frontier element that again gave Spain her foothold in the region. It is obvious that women played an important role during the reconquest period that followed the 1680 Pueblo Revolt.

Notes

1. The most valuable publications are: Charles W. Hacket, ed., *The Revolt of the Pueblo Indians of New Mexico and Otermín's Attempted Reconquest, 1680–1682,* 2 vols. (Albuquerque: University of New Mexico Press, 1942) hereinafter cited as *Revolt* (a translation of an entire *legajo* from the Archivo General de Indias in Sevilla) and Ralph Twitchell, ed., *Spanish American Archives of New Mexico,* 2 vols. (Torch Press, 1914) hereinafter cited as *SANM*. Archives of importance include the New Mexico Archives

(both book form and microfilm) found in the Special Collections Room of Zimmerman Library of the University of New Mexico, hereinafter cited as NMA; Archivo General de Indias cited as AGI; Archivo General de la Nación, México cited as AGNM; and Archivo Franiscano, Biblioteca Nacional-Universidad Autonoma de México, to be cited as AF/BN.

2. Cabildo to Cubero, Santa Fe, [November 24, 1697], NMA, Doc. 60c.

3. Generally "the wives, children, and unmarried daughters of the settlers were forced to work in the corn fields" before the revolt and after, Auto Procurado en Santa Fe, October 21, 1661, AGNM/Tierras, 3268: 184–87. "The Viceroy of New Spain makes a report to your majesty on the general uprising of the Indians of the Province of New Mexico, and the measures and means which have been adopted for their restoration," Mexico, February 28, 1681, *Revolt,* 1:3; "None was spared, except that a few beautiful women and girls were kept as captives," Hubert Howe Bancroft, *Arizona and New Mexico, 1530–1888,* (San Francisco: The History Co., 1889) 17:178; the Indians killed every Spaniard, "not sparing even innocent babes in arms," [Opinion of Cabildo de Santa Fe, La Salineta, October 3, 1680], Francisco Xavier, et. al., *Revolt,* 1:178; and List of Dead, August 12, 1680, AF/BN, 20/434/3v; Auto and Declaration of the Maestre de Campo, Francisco Gómez, Santa Fe, August 12, 1680, 1:9; Declaration of Pedro García, [Near San Cristobal Anaya, August 25, 1680], *Revolt,* 1:23; Letter of the very Reverend Father, Procurador and Visitador of the Holy Custodia of the Province of New Mexico to [the Viceroy], El Paso, August 31, 1680, *Revolt,* 1:47–54.

4. There are many muster rolls and censuses, among them are: Auto for passing muster, reviewing arms, and horses, and other things, [the Place Opposite La Salineta, September 29, 1680], *Revolt,* 1:134–59; List of Families in this Town of Corpus Christi de Isleta . . ., September 11, 1680, Juan Severino Rodríguez, AF,BN-21/446.1/61–68v; Description and register and receipt book of the soldiers and male colonists under pay for the reconquest of New Mexico, September 22–October 16, 1681, Twitchell, *SANM,* 2:386–451; Muster of settlers, September 9–16, 1681, Otermín, AF/BN, 20/436.1/1–188; Muster of the settlers, September 12–October 22, 1681, *Revolt,* 2:34–68, 70–86; 2:35, 94–134; Muster of September 10–14, 1684, AGNM/Provincias Internas, 37/na/50–59; List of Families, AGNM/Provincias Internas, 37/2/94–108; List of Families, El Paso, Isleta, San Lorenzo, September 14, 1684, AGNM/PI, 37; List of Settlers, 1692, Doc. 54b, NMA; and Testimony of the *visita* and personal list of the *vecinos* for the settlement of the Newly Conquered Kingdom of New Mexico, Vargas Zapata, AGNM/Historia, 37/7/452–end and AF/BN, 22/455/n; and Muster, May 1697, AGI/AG, 141; General Muster Which I, Don Diego de Vargas Zapata Luján Ponce de León, Governor

and Captain General of this Kingdom and Provinces of New Mexico, do personally, December 22, 1692, AGNM/Historia, 37/7/448–75; Depositions for the Sentence against Vargas Zapata, October 26–December 16, 1697, Auto Against Don Diego de Vargas Zapata, First Book, Second Book, and Third Book, Documents 71–74c, NMA. This footnote will be referred to as Musters.

5. Opinion of Luis Granillo, August 26, 1680, *Revolt,* 1:82; [Auto of Alonso García], El Socorro, August 24, 1680, *Revolt,* 1:73; Auto of Alonso García, Place Opposite El Socorro, August 26, 1680, *Revolt,* 1:83; Letter of the Governor and Captain General, Don Antionio de Otermín, from New Mexico [to Francisco Ayeta] in which he gives him a full account of what has happened to him . . ., [September 8, 1680], *Revolt,* 1:94–105; Auto of the March and the halting places places, Antonio Otermín, August 24–26, 1680, AGNM/Historia, 26/n/20; Viceroy Conde de Paredes to [King], February 28, 1681, AGI/AG, 138/116.

6. Musters; [Auto of Antonio de Otermín], Fray Cristobal, September 13, 1680, *Revolt,* 1:114; Auto, Otermín, et. al., Santa Fe, August 21, 1680, *Revolt,* 1:18; Otermín to [Ayeta], September 8, 1680, *Revolt,* 1:94–105.

7. Musters; Otermín to [Ayeta], September 8, 1680, *Revolt,* 1:94–105; Auto, Otermín, *et. al.,* Santa Fe, August 21, 1680, *Revolt,* 1:18; and [Auto of Antonio de Otermín], Fray Cristobal, September 13, 1680, *Revolt,* 1:114; [Auto of the Place Opposite El Socorro, September 7, 1680], *Revolt,* 1:88.

8. Otermín to [Ayeta], September 8, 1680, *Revolt,* 1:94–105; Auto [Antonio de Otermín], San Cristobal, September 13, 1680, *Revolt,* 1:114. Certification and Notice of Departure, Francisco Xavier, Santa Fe, August 21, 1680, *Revolt,* 1:19; Opinion of the Cabildo, [Fray Cristobal, September 14, 1680], *Revolt,* 1:120; [Opinion of Luis Granilla, Place of El Socorro, August 26, 1680], *Revolt,* 1:80.

9. Musters; Declaration of Pedro García . . ., near Cristobal Anaya, August 25, 1680, *Revolt,* 1:23; Ayeta, *et. al.,* El Paso, August 25, 1680, *Revolt,* 1:33.

10. Musters; Letter of the Lt. Governor for our Father Visitador in which he advises him that the governor is alive and that he is retreating, Alonso García, [Fray Cristobal, September 4, 1680], *Revolt,* 1:58; Auto of Alonso García, *et. al.,* the Place Opposite El Socorro, August 26, 1680, *Revolt,* 1:82; "Auto in which it is decided by the people who were with Francisco Ayeta to go to the aid of the governor, Pedro Leiva, *et. al.,* [El Paso, August 29, 1680], *Revolt,* 1:44; "Letter of the Governor and Captain General, Don Antonio Otermín . . ., [September 8, 1680], *Revolt,* 1:94–104; García to Leyva, September 4, AF/BN, 24/433.1/1v; Opinion of Luis Granillo, August 26, 1680, Place Opposite El Socorro, *Revolt,*

1:82; and Ayeta to [Viceroy], n.d., AGI/AG-139/41; Letter of Pedro Leiva and other officials [to the Viceroy], El Paso, August 29, 1680, *Revolt*, 1: 44; Auto of the Junta, Ayeta, *et. al.*, El Paso, August 25, 1680, *Revolt*, 1:29–34; Letter of the Lt. Gov. for our Father Visitador . . ., [Fray Cristobal, September 4, 1680], AF/BN, 20/433.1/1.

11. [Auto of Antonio de Otermín, Fray Cristobal, September 13, 1680], *Revolt*, 1:112; Auto of the march and halting places, Otermín and Francisco Xavier, August 24–26, 1680, *Revolt*, 1:21.

12. Opinion of the Reverend Father, the Maestre de Campo, and all other persons, Fray Cristobal, [September 14, 1680], *Revolt*, 1:116–20; Notification and arrest [of Alonso García, El Alamillo, September 6, 1680], *Revolt*, 1:65–73; Auto of El Socorro, Alonso García, El Socorro, August 26, 1680, *Revolt*, 1:73; and Otermín to Ayeta, September 8, 1680, *Revolt*, 1:105.

13. Letter of Fray Francisco Ayeta written to the Father Commissary General, [Real Chico, September 20, 1680], *Revolt*, 1:212–14; Auto of El Socorro, Alonso García, August 24, 1680, *Revolt*, 1:73; The Viceroy of New Spain makes a report to your Majesty . . ., Mexico, February 28, 1681, *Revolt*, 2:3 & 12; Opinion of Luis Granillo, August 26, 1680, Place Opposite El Socorro, *Revolt*, 1:82; and Ayeta to [Viceroy], n.d.; AGI/AG, 139/41.

14. Musters.

15. Musters. *Agregados* were male or female relatives, orphans, or less well off persons who attached themselves to an extended family. Although some persons were listed with families or as individuals in 1680, many disappeared by the next muster as they fled further south, remarried, or joined another family. Families split up as youngsters grew up, married, and set up their own households.

16. Auto of Junta de Guerra, [La Salineta, October 2, 1680], *Revolt*, 1:160–64; AGI/AG, 139/41. Certification of Cabildo of Santa Fe, El Paso, October 12, 1680, *Revolt*, 1:198; "Testimonio de autos originales remitidos por el Señor Don. Antonio de Otermín Governador y Capitán General de las Provincias de Nuevo Mexico y Presidio de ellos al Excelentísimo Señor Conde de Paredes, Marквéz de la Laguna," January 17, 1681, AF/BN, 20/436.11/1–188; Opinion of the Cabildo of Santa Fe, Juan Lucero de Godoy, *et. al.*, La Salineta, October 3, 1680, *Revolt*, 1:177; [Opinions given in the Junta de Guerra, La Salineta, October 2, 1680], Tomé Domínguez de Madrid, *et. al.*, *Revolt*, 1:160–81; The winter was so harsh that "the men spread mud on their faces just like the women to protect their skin and save their sight," Letter of Juan Lucero of Godoy, *et. al.*, n.d., El Paso, AGI/AG, 139/100.

17. Musters; Letter of Fray Francisco Ayeta Written to the Commissary General, [Real Chico, December 20, 1680], *Revolt*, 1:214–15; Peti-

tion of the Cabildo of Santa Fe, n.d., AF/BN, 20/436.1/1/50–55v. The Santa Fe Cabildo kept its name despite the fact that it was headquartered in El Paso until the reconquest.

18. Van Hastings Garner, "The Dynamics of Changes: New Mexico, 1680–1690," *Journal of the West,* 18 (January 1979):4–13.

19. Conde Paredes to [King], Mexico, February 28, 1681, AGI/AG, 138/n.p.; Reply of Fiscal, Mexico, [January 7, 1680], AGN/ Hist., 25/ 14/170v; Ayeta to the Commisary General, [Real Chico, December 20, 1680], *Revolt,* 1:214; Auto of Otermín, *et. al.,* El Paso, October 13, 1680, AGI/AG, 138/n.p.; Memo of the list of things needed for the new conquest of New Mexico, Otermín, El Paso, [October 12, 1680], *Revolt,* 1: 200.

20. Musters; Testimony of Original Autos, January 17, 1681, AF/ BN, 20/436.1/1–188; Autos and judicial proceedings concerning certain persons excusing themselves from royal service, [El Paso, September 29, 1681], *Revolt,* 2:143–50.

21. Memo of the list of things needed for the new conquest of New Mexico, Otermín, El Paso, [October 12, 1680], *Revolt,* 1:200; Cabildo of Santa Fe, El Paso, March 17, 1682, AF/BN, 20/437.4/8v; Auto of Ayeta, El Paso, September 21, 1681, *Revolt,* 2:32; Auto of Juan Lucero de Godoy, *et. al.,* El Paso, March 7, 1682, AF/BN, 21/440/1; Auto de Guerra, Juan Domínguez, *et. al.,* Plaza de Armas, San Lorenzo de Tome, March 5, 1682, and Junta de Cabildo, Francisco Xavier, San Lorenzo de Tome, March 1, 1682, AF/BN, 20/437.4/8–11v; [Cabildo of Santa Fe to Governor Cubero, n.d.], NMA, Doc. 73.

22. *Ibid.,* Memo of the list . . ., *Revolt,* 1:200–2; Memo of García, April 30, 1682, *Revolt,* 2:214.

23. Reply of Sr. Fiscal, 1:225–26; [Memorial of Fray Francisco Ayeta to Viceroy, January 9, 1681], *Revolt,* 1:237; Auto, Juan Lucero de Godoy, *et. al.,* El Paso, February 6, 1682, AF/BN, 21/440/1; Junta de Cabildo, Francisco Xavier, San Lorenzo de Tome, March 1, 1682, AF/BN, 20/ 437.4/10–11v.

24. Musters; Auto, Juan Domínguez, *et. al.,* El Paso, March 4, 1682, AF/BN, 20/437.4/8–11v; Auto, Plaza de Armas, El Paso, March 17, 1682, AF/BN, 20/437.4/8–11v; Auto, Lázaro Mesquía, *et. al.,* September 27, 1685, AGNM/PI, 37/n/3.

25. Musters; Auto, Lázaro Mesquía, *et. al.,* September 27, 1685, AGNM/PI, 37/n/3; Report of Viceroy to the King, Mexico, February 28, 1681, *Revolt,* 2:7–12; Cabildo de Santa Fe, Francisco Anaya Almázar, *et. al.,* n.d., AGNM/PI, 37/3/145.

26. Musters; [Auto], Francisco Gomez Robledo, *et. al.,* El Paso, August 26, 1685, AF/BN, 21/446.28/146.

27. Musters. Just as Francisca Abrego is the only widow listed in both

1680 and 1684, only the Trujillo, Durán, and Leiva widows, and Clara Susana are listed in both 1684 and 1692.

28. Van Hastings Garner, "The Dynamics of Change: New Mexico, 1680–1690," *Journal of the West,* 18 (January 1979):4–13.

29. Musters; General Muster Which I . . . do personally, AGN/AG, 513; Depositions for the Sentence against Vargas Zapata, October 26–December 16, 1697; Auto Against Don Diego de Vargas Zapata, First Book, Second Book, and Third Book (May 22, 1698), NMA, Documents 71–74c; Vargas Zapata to [Viceroy], El Paso, September 12, 1692, Twitchell, *SANM,* 2:98–91. Vargas Zapata asked for five hundred settlers to aid the poor Nuevo Mexicanos and soldiers to protect them, Fiscal Report, n.d., NMA/Misc, 1692; The order to aid the recruitment effort was sent to the Zacatecas treasury, Vargas Zapata to Conde de Galve, Santa Fe, June 3, 1694, AGI/AG, 140/277–78v; Vargas asked for money for the fifty soldiers, Conde de Galve to Junta de Guerra, May 28, 1692, AGN/ History, 38/1/1–5.

30. Musters. These same persons were among the group that journeyed to Santa Fe along with the El Paso recruits. Interestingly enough the El Paso recruits later criticized the social and racial make up of these and later Zacatecas area recruits.

31. Musters. The cases of women being bound to the expeditions through loans made by Vargas Zapata, are not unique to the sex. In one case, the *mulato* Pedro Rojas and his father joined after being lent forty pesos.

32. Musters. Vargas Zapata asked the Viceroy and King for more families from Zacatecas and Mexico. He even suggested recruiting Jews from the Inquisition. He also asked for food and clothing for those "sons, wives, orphans, and widows" who remained in New Mexico. Letter to the Viceroy, Vargas to Conde Juan Ortega de Montañes, March 8, 1695, AGI/AG, 141/45; Reply of his Excellency Conde de Galve to Don Diego Vargas Zapata, Mexico, November 24, 1692, *Revolt,* 2:192–96; Vargas Zapata to Conde de Galve, October 16, 1692, *Revolt,* 2:160; Vargas Zapata to [Viceroy], El Paso, October 13, 1693, Twitchell, *SANM,* 2:89. There were many petitions to leave.

33. Musters.

34. Vargas stated that several of the Hispanas "came before my presence dressed like Indians with their hair cut." Auto, Vargas Zapata, September 22, 1696, AGI/AG, 141/50; Auto, Vargas Zapata, September 25, 1696, AGI/AG, 141/51; One list had a total of sixty-one captives, seventeen males and forty-four females. The other list had seventy-four names. List of Captives, Vargas Zapata and Roque Madrid, October 29, 1692; List of the Captives who arrived at this waterhole with their children, November 13, 1693, Vargas Zapata; and Auto de Remisión, El Paso, Jan-

uary 8, 1693, Vargas Zapata, in NMA/Misc., 1685–1693, Doc. 53b–53c.; List of the Persons Who were to be found in the Pueblos of New Mexico at its reconquest, 1692, AF/BN, 22/455.1/1–71; Vargas Zapata, *et. al.,* El Paso, September 30, 1692, AGI/AG, 139/428v.

35. *Ibid.;* Vargas Zapata, *et. al.,* Hacienda de México, October 29, 1692, AF/BN, 22/455.1/1–71.

36. The harsh winter trek was difficult and "every day many of the captives died and others suffered frostbite." Vargas Zapata, November 7, [1692], AGI/AG, 141/85; Many of the Indian captives were to be distributed among the soldiers and vecinos, Vargas Zapata, November 9, 1696, AGI/AG, 141; Auto de Remisión, El Paso, January 8, 1693, Vargas Zapata, NMA/Misc, 1685–1693; Vargas Zapata to Viceroy, El Paso, October 16, 1692, AF/BN, 22/455.1/1 or *Revolt,* 2:160.

37. Musters.

38. Vargas Zapata to [Viceroy], El Paso, January 3, 1693, AGNM/History, 37/7/474–75; Viceroy Galvez to [King], September 4, 1693, AGI/AG, 140/n; Vargas to [Viceroy], El Paso, [October 22, 1693,] NMA, 1693, Doc. 54a; Testimony of the auto of the last entry and conquest made by Don Diego de Vargas Zapata Luján Ponce de León, Governor and Captain General of the Kingdom of New Mexico, 1694, AGI/AG, 140.

39. Musters. Vargas Zapata indicates that he left El Paso with 800 persons. Vargas Zapata to Viceroy Gálvez, October 13, 1693, Twitchell, *SANM,* 2:89–91. The settlers also note the death of many travelers, especially thirty young children. Petition of Cabildo, Santa Fe, May 23, 1698, NMA, Doc. 74b; [Cabildo of Santa Fe to Governor Cubero, n.d.], NMA, Doc. 73; and Vargas Zapata to [Viceroy], November 18, 1693, AGI/AG, 40/55v; Memoria de los generos de la tierra de Castilla . . ., Vargas Zapata, El Paso, December 4, 1693, AGI/AG, 140/507; Testimony of the Auto of the last entry and conquest made by Don Diego De Vargas Zapata . . ., 1694, AGI/AG, 140.

40. Vargas Zapata Statement, June 23, 1694, NMA, Doc. 55c; [Cabildo of Santa Fe to Governor Rodríguez Cubero, Santa Fe, November 24, 1697], NMA, Doc. 60c; Auto Requistorio against Páez Hurtado, April 29, 1698, Santa Fe, NMA, Doc. 74d; Vargas Zapata Statement, June 23, 1694, NMA, Doc. 55c.

41. Musters; Of 101 men listed by Vargas Zapata, only 29 are in the 1697 census; however, thirty-eight percent of the women are listed.

42. Musters and Memorandum and list of things . . ., [El Paso, October 12, 1680], *Revolt,* 1:200–1.

43. Musters; Memorandum of the items from Castilla . . ., Vargas Zapata, El Paso, December 4, 1693, AGI/AG, 140/507.

44. Gaspar de Sandoval to Viceroy Conde de Galve, Mexico, February 25, 1693, AF/BN, 22/455.2/68–71; List of Settlers, AF/BN, 22/

455.25/129v–133; Conde de Galve to [King], Mexico City, March 13, 1693, AF/BN, 22/455.2/71–72; Sebastian Guzmán de Cordova to [Viceroy], March 17, 1693, AF/BN, 22/455.5; José María Aguilera to [Galve], March [11], 1693, AF/BN, 22/455.5/73v–74; Junta General to Galve, April 8, 1693, AF/BN, 22/455.5/76v; Sebastian Guzmán to [Viceroy], May 20, 1693, AF/BN, 22/455.11/90–94; Miguel González, *et. al.,* to [Viceroy], March 14, 1693, AF/BN, 22/455.2/172.

45. Father Francaisco Farfán to Viceroy, July 13, 1693, AF/BN, 22/455.15/111–111v; Licenciado Francisco de Serase to Viceroy, Mexico, May 28, 1693, AF/BN, 22/455.11/92v; List of Families, AGI/AG, 140/9–12.

46. List of the families that will travel to New Mexico, Mexico, March 20, 1693, AF/BN, 22/455.17/112–14; List of Families, September 4, 1693, AF/BN, 22/455.25/129–33; List of Families, AGI/AG, 140/9–12. The version of Doc. 54a found in Twitchell lacks the first ten names, Twitchell, *SANM,* 1:92–105. Special studies were made for women and children. Roque Madrid to [Vargas], Santa Cruz, July 19, 1696, AGI/AG, 141/300.

47. Doña Ana de Tordecillas to Galve, n.d., AF/BN, 22/455.19/113; Galve, Memo, Mexico, September 4, 1693, AF/BN, 22/455.19/166v; Testimony of various witnesses, AF/BN, 22/455.19/117–21; [Maria de Mirabal to Viceroy, Mexico], July 8 and September 5, 1693, AF/BN, 22/455.19/117v–120v; Judgement, September 7, 1693, AF/BN, 22/455.19/119v; also found in AGI/AG, 140.

48. Sebastian Guzmán y Cordova [to Vargas Zapata], March 17, 1693, AGI/AG, 139/356; Antonio Silva, *et. al.,* to [Viceroy], [September 1, 1693], AF/BN, 22/455.21/122–23; Testimony of Joseph Angulo, September 10, 1693, AF/BN, 22/455.21/122–23; Pedro Velasques de Cadera to [Viceroy], May 8, 1693, AGI/AG, 139/375; Vargas Zapata to Galve, El Paso, October 13, 1693, AF/BN, 22/455.24/127v; Vargas Zapata to [Viceroy], April 8, 1694, AGI/AG, 140/177; Francisco Farfán to Vargas, Paraje de Patos, April 13, 1694, AGI/AG, 140/180.

49. Vargas Zapata to [Viceroy], May 4, 1694, AGI/AG, 140/212; Cabildo of Santa Fe, Lorenzo Madrid, *et. al.,* June 3, 1694, AGI/AG, 140/282v.

50. Cabildo of Santa Fe, Lorenzo Madrid, *et. al.,* June 3, 1694, AGI/AG, 140/282v; Vargas to Viceroy, June 22, 1694, AGI/AG, 140/325; Vargas to Viceroy, June 23, 1694, AGI/AG, 140/328; Vargas Zapata to [Viceroy], June 3, 1694, AGI/AG, 140/292–300; Junta General, July 16, 1694, AGI/AG, 140/330v.

51. Clevy Lloyd Strout, "The Resettlement of Santa Fe, 1695, The Newly Found Muster Roll of Páez Hurtado," *New Mexico Historical Review,* 53 (July, 1978):261–63; "Santa Fe Redidiva: The Muster Role of the Juan Páez Hurtado Expedition of 1695," unpublished manuscript, Clevy Lloyd Strout, has the same information plus some additional details; Petition

from the Settlers of Zacatecas for a refund . . ., Santa Fe, 1697, NMA. Doc. 66a; Auto de Diego y Ulloa . . ., AGI/AG, 140/656. Vargas Zapata to [Viceroy], Santa Fe, January 11, 1695, AGI/AG, 140/690–91v; Vargas Zapata Statement, June 23, 1694, NMA, Doc. 55c; [Cabildo to Governor Rodríguez Cubero, Santa Fe, November 24, 1697], NMA, Doc. 60c; Auto Requistorio against Páez Hurtado, April 29, 1698, Santa Fe, NMA, Doc. 74d; Vargas Zapata Statement, June 23, 1694, NMA, Doc. 55c.

52. [Cabildo to Cubero, Santa Fe, November 24, 1697], NMA, Doc. 60c. Again the musters and testimony given as part of some legal proceedings give a fount of details, which indicate that many official documents were not correct.

53. Musters. It is possible to trace the witnesses through the later census and muster rolls. Those who are said not to have traveled are not included in any list.

54. Vargas Zapata to [Viceroy], Santa Fe, November 22, 1693, NMA, Doc. 54b. Vargas Zapata was not the first nor the last governor or citizen of New Mexico to ask for more settlers and recruits.

55. Páez Hurtado to Galve, February 11, 1694, AGI/AG, 140^{7}01; Nicolás de Medina and Joseph Viche to Páez Hurtado, Durango, August 3, 1694, AGI/AG, 140/505–506v; Vargas Zapata to Galve, September 2, 1694, Santa Fe, AGI/AG, 140/518; Vargas Zapata to Galve, Santa Fe, September 6, 1694, AGI/AG, 140514; Testament of the Autos made before the Real de Zacatecas on request of captain Juan Páez Hurtado acting on behalf of Governor Vargas Zapata, July 16, 1694, AGI/AG, 140/636–38; Junta General, December 22, 1694, AGI/AG, 140/667; Auto de Diego y Ulloa and José Urristi to Viceroy, Mexico, July 14, 1694, AGI/AG, 140/656.

⋙ 3 ⋘

The Independent Women of Hispanic New Mexico

1821–1846*

Janet Lecompte

The culture of New Mexicans, and especially of New Mexican women, was distinct in many aspects from that of central Mexico or other Mexican frontier territories. In costume, language, religion, government, and legal rights of women, the people of New Mexico kept strong ties to sixteenth-century Spain. Their ancestors had marched boldly through deserts inhabited by hostile Indians to found a Spanish colony in New Mexico in 1598. From that time until 1821 the deserts and Indians, as well as Spanish policy prohibiting foreign commerce, kept New Mexico more or less isolated. New Mexicans developed traditions in response to this isolation, to climate and terrain, and to their sedentary Pueblo Indian neighbors and the nomadic tribes with whom they alternately fought and traded. In 1821 Mexico declared independence of Spain, became a republic, and opened its borders to foreign commerce. Henceforth foreign trappers, traders, and travelers further altered the lives of New Mexicans with the introduction of new materials, new skills, and attitudes.[1]

The purpose of this essay is not to trace the origins of this unique

*Reprinted by permission of the *Western Historical Quarterly* 12 (January 1981):17–35.

culture but to describe the position occupied in it by New Mexican women in the Republican period from 1821 to 1846. Accounts of American (and a few European) visitors that provide the only general descriptions, marred though they are, by ignorance and cultural bias are the primary sources, supplemented by the New Mexico archives. These archives not only correct foreigners' misconceptions but also give a clear picture of women's social and legal rights as demonstrated in the alcalde courts.

The first American woman to see New Mexico was young Susan Magoffin, who accompanied her trader-husband to New Mexico in 1846. Susan's delightful diary portrayed New Mexican women in terms that told as much about her own culture as theirs. In Las Vegas the eighteen-year-old Susan was startled to see women dressed only in chemises and petticoats, which American women wore as undergarments. Around their heads and arms these women wore rebosos, or large shawls, under which some of them had their babies, "I shant say at what business," wrote Susan. As the traders' wagons passed villages, Susan saw children running about naked and women pulling their skirts up over their knees and paddling across creeks like ducks. "It is truly shocking," wrote Susan; "I am constrained to keep my veil drawn closely over my face all the time to protect my blushes." No sooner had Susan become accustomed to the bare legs and bosoms of New Mexican women than she was exposed to their repugnant views on marriage. One old lady was amazed that Susan had left her home and parents "just for a husband" and laughed heartily at Susan's assertions that a husband was the whole world to his wife. Another New Mexican woman suggested slyly that Susan's husband might at that moment be off with "his other senorita," which distressed Susan to the point of tears. Susan was appalled at women smoking cigarettes, gambling, shopping, and paying visits on the Sabbath. But as the New Mexican women came to her carriage to shake hands, bring her gifts of food, and call her "pretty little girl," Susan succumbed to their warmth and kindness and described them in her diary as "decidedly polite, easy in their manners, perfectly free."[2]

Several Americans called this freedom of demeanor "boldness" and contrasted it unfavorably with the modesty of American women.[3] In the emerging industrial United States of the early nineteenth century, the urban, middle-class American woman lost her economic importance. Her influence often became limited to moral and cultural spheres, and her position in society was usually subordinate to men. A married woman lost almost all legal rights, and her property and wages belonged to her husband. She was believed to have no sexual urges, from which arose a double standard of behavior that allowed a man to exercise his sexual needs, but not a woman. She was expected to be pious, chaste, and self-sacrificing, and her place was in the home.[4]

In contrast, a New Mexican woman retained her property, legal rights, wages, and maiden name after marriage, like her Spanish ancestors. As we shall see, she was measured by no such ideals of character or double standard of sexual behavior, nor was she assumed to be subordinate to men, except by Americans who carried to New Mexico their image of true American womanhood and judged New Mexican women by it.

The first thing Americans noticed were the dark skins of New Mexican women: "Instead of the black-eyed Spanish women, we found ourselves amongst a swarthy, copper-colored, half-Indian race."[5] New Mexican women valued light skins and protected their faces from the sun with a thick bone-meal paste or the juice of a red berry. Some claimed pure Spanish blood and hidalgo (noble) ancestors; many more were mestizos but thoroughly hispanicized and thus designated *españoles* in the caste system imposed by Spain. Mexico discarded the caste system after Mexican independence from Spain, and wealthy or important citizens, whether *español* or mestizo, were honored with the respectful title of don or doña. In New Mexico, where centuries of poverty had tended to erode social barriers, even affluent men with many peons to tend their fields and flocks called themselves "farmers" in the census and were in fact only a generation or two removed from peasantry. Master and servant were usually of the same ethnic mix, spoke the same dialect, wore the same style of clothing. Rich and poor worshiped together, danced together, attended each other's family baptisms, weddings, and funerals. In the 1830s and 1840s, traders' wagons brought luxuries that widened the material differences in class, but Republican New Mexico remained essentially an open society, offering its poor, its Pueblo Indians, its mestizos, and to some extent its women, opportunities to rise as high as their talent or good luck could take them.[6]

W. H. H. Davis described New Mexican women as healthy, graceful, and athletic. They wore loose, low-cut blouses and full

short skirts; in this easy costume they did their work, much of it
outdoors. Their diet was full of nutrients. They baked bread with
unbolted flour containing both husk and germ of the grain; they
dried fruits, vegetables, and strips of meat in the sun for later use;
and included in nearly every meal fresh or dried chili peppers—
high in vitamins—and fresh and dried beans—high in protein. Their
adobe houses, with thick walls and high ceilings, were cool in summer and warm in winter, and easy to clean. Their rooms had little
corner fireplaces for cooking and heating, but were almost barren
of furniture. Ordinary families slept on thin mattresses which they
rolled against the walls during the day to serve as sofas. Only the
rich had kitchens, beds and bedrooms, imported carpets, draper-
ies, silver table service, and servants to maintain these luxuries.[7]

"A woman's work is never done" was a popular phrase describing the housewifery of American women, but it did not apply
in New Mexico. Some Americans regarded New Mexican women
as idle, which in the Anglo-Saxon work ethic was a form of sin.
"They work but little," wrote one American; "the fandango and
siesta form the diversion of time." Another said that women were
taught only to "grind corn on a rock, make tortillas and dance."[8]
But American accounts show women at many other tasks, often
in cheerful groups: "maidens with merry faces" in the vineyard
with flat baskets of purple grape clusters on their heads, girls chat-
ting as they filled their Indian water jars at the spring or passed in
dignified procession balancing the huge jars on their heads, women
wading in the river as they laundered cloths, or watching intently
as they washed placer gold from sand in wooden platters or goat
horns. One woman was seen outdoors spinning yarn on an upright stick at the same time she suckled her child.[9]

New Mexican women were likely to have other occupations
besides caring for home and children. The censuses of New Mexico employ no single word for housewife, unless it was the frequent designation *costurera* or seamstress, perhaps referring not only
to women who made clothes or produced elegant embroidery but
also to those whose work was primarily in the home. Many paid
occupations for women were listed in the census—servants, bakers, weavers, gold-panners, shepherds, laundresses, stocking-
knitters, healers, midwives, ironers, and prostitutes. Women were
often in the town plaza selling products of their domestic animals
or gardens, or vending whiskey and traders' goods in stalls along

the main streets, or dealing cards in gambling games. Vending was not despised: Doña Barbara Baca kept a stall in Santa Fe and went to court about a fifteen-peso debt, which turned out to be an error in her own ledgers; a sister of Governor Manuel Armijo sold whiskey to American soldiers out of an old coffee pot on a street in Albuquerque; the widow of another governor owned the only billiard table in Santa Fe, which she rented to gamblers for five to six pesos a week.[10]

Nor were women and children barred from men's work. In 1807 Zebulon Pike passed along the Rio Grande near Albuquerque as irrigating ditches were being opened and saw men, women, and children "at the joyful labor . . . the cultivation of the fields was now commencing and everything appeared to give life and gaiety to the surrounding scenery." Forty years later Lieutenant William Emory described the high glee of men, women, and children as they see-sawed on the lever of a molasses press. Yet women apparently did not do the heavy work of farming, and crops were not sown when men were off on campaigns against hostile Indians.[11]

A woman without means was supported by her extended family, which often included half her acquaintances through intermarriage and compadrazgo—the intimate, lifelong relationship between a child and his baptismal sponsors. Even *criados,* who were Indian children redeemed from wild tribes and brought into families as servants, were baptized with the family name, and when they married they became full citizens of the Republic. New Mexico had no hordes of beggars such as blighted the cities of Mexico. Almost no one was without family, and those who were depended upon the mercy of the courts or the charity of the community.[12]

As Americans noticed, a New Mexican woman's life was not a weary round of endless chores. The simplicity of her costume, food and dwelling left her time to take siestas at mid-day and enough energy to enjoy frequent dance parties, called fandangos, where she appeared radiant, powdered, perfumed, and jingling with necklaces and earrings. Foreigners were amazed at the democratic aspect of these affairs. Everybody was welcome, from the priest to the criminal released from jail for the evening; everybody danced—the lady with the ragged peon, the old man with the little girl. On political or religious holidays fiestas involved people of all ages in races, cock-pulls, cock-fights, folk dramas, and fandangos, or in watching puppeteers, traveling players, tumblers, and fireworks.

They sang, danced, and gambled at *chusa,* or monte, far into the
night, the women gambling with as much abandon as the men.
Most fiestas were festivals of the Roman Catholic church, to which
all Hispanic New Mexicans belonged. American observers deplored
what they saw as a desecration of the Sabbath. In church, as the
priest recited his service at the altar, women would chat and gig-
gle; as the same musicians of last night's fandango struck up the
same tunes in church, women would toss their heads and count
their beads in time to the music. After church everybody mingled
in the plaza—shopping, dancing, gambling.[13]

Many Americans would have agreed with George V. Kendall
that New Mexican women were "joyous, sociable, kind-hearted
creatures, easy and graceful in their manners." Kendall enjoyed the
warmth of the close embrace with which both sexes greeted each
other, in contrast to the restraint imposed upon Anglo-Saxons by
"cold, conventional rules." The hospitality of New Mexican women
did not always stop at a warm embrace. Visitors from the land of
the double standard blamed New Mexicans' sexual freedom entirely on the women: "The standard of female chastity is deplorably low," wrote W. H. H. Davis; "the women deem chastity no
virtue," wrote Alfred Waugh. Jacob Fowler described an attempted
seduction of his negro servant by a Taos wife, and James O. Pattie
told of the friendliness of New Mexican ladies they had met at a
dance, who expected the Americans to escort them home and spend
the night.[14]

Marriage in New Mexico, according to Josiah Gregg was "a
convenient cloak for irregularities." W. H. H. Davis wrote that
three-quarters of the married population of New Mexico had lovers, "and the feelings of society are in no manner outraged by it."
This assertion was not quite true, as our examination of court records will show. Concubinage, a Spanish tradition, was more common than marriage and was generally accepted. Americans remarked
on the priests of New Mexico who had concubines and families,
and many American traders took concubines from respectable New
Mexican families. Foreigners usually blamed concubinage on high
marriage fees charged by priests, for there was no alternative civil
marriage in New Mexico. Bearing children out of wedlock was
common among all classes; birth records show that many babies
were given their mothers' name, their fathers being recorded as
"unknown."[15]

Josiah Gregg assumed that all marriages were "forced and ill assorted, and without the least deference to the wishes or inclinations of the young lady." In fact, betrothals arranged by parents were investigated by the priest to ensure that the bride was acquainted with the groom and wished to marry him. W. H. H. Davis assumed that "a young girl can hardly put her nose outside the door without an old duena [sic] tagging after her," but the term dueña scarcely appears in the records. In fact, New Mexican girls would hardly have needed a dueña, for they were married or living with men as early as twelve years old.[16]

In general, American accounts show an unawareness of Mexican customs, particularly the social and legal rights of women. What these rights were and how they were exercised is illustrated by cases from the records of the alcalde courts. An alcalde combined the civil duties of mayor with the judicial duties of judge. His court was meant to provide inexpensive and prompt legal remedy for most civil complaints, as well as initiatory stages of ecclesiastical and criminal proceedings. In most civil cases plaintiff and defendant appeared before the alcalde, called *juez* in his judicial capacity, for an attempt at conciliation. If the juez could not reconcile the parties, each named an arbitrator, or *hombre bueno,* whose opinion the juez considered before pronouncing his judgment of conciliation. If plaintiff and defendant did not agree with the judgment, the case was dropped, or the plaintiff made a formal charge whereupon witnesses were called, testimony taken, and the proceedings sent to the governor for a verdict. Appeal from the governor's verdict was made to the superior tribunal at Guadalajara (later Chihuahua), a slow and costly process.[17]

Alcalde courts were not ruled strictly by national law. Laws promised by the republican constitution of 1824 for the governance of New Mexico had never been promulgated, and national laws in force sometimes did not serve this remote territory because of differences in customs. Furthermore, New Mexico had no native lawyers. Serving occasionally as attorneys were a handful of former deputies sent to the national Congress, where they picked up a little legal lore and returned to annoy the alcaldes in their courts. With this questionable legal assistance and an occasional opinion of lawyers from "below," the *juez* (who was often nearly illiterate) attempted to provide judgments based on what law he knew, but more on common sense and compassion.[18]

A New Mexican woman could own, inherit, loan, convey, or pawn property, as records of the alcalde courts show. Suits involving women's property were many and diverse—over a woman's fat hog or half-interest in a burro inherited from her mother, over a pawned cloak or a pledged gun, over rooms in a house which one woman sold another with stipulation as to use, over a nugget of gold found by a woman in a borrowed placer basin, of which she was allowed half the value. Property suits often concerned the most seemingly trivial things, but New Mexicans were chronically short of clothing, hard money, metal objects, and trinkets commonplace elsewhere. A list of items stolen from Doña María Manuela Martínez of Taos indicates what was worth stealing: a *tunica* (European-style gown) of fine cotton, a multi-colored blanket, a linen mantle, two cigarette boxes decorated with mock pearls and spangles, a spangled suit, a yellow-metal rosary, a man's muslin shirt, a serape, a pair of white canvas stools, and a bordered kerchief. Money was so scarce that when Doña Peregrina Domínguez demanded that Felix García pay his hundred-peso debt to her in hard money, the court gave him a month to collect it.[19]

A few wealthy women of New Mexico used the courts frequently. Doña Ursula Chávez was the wife of Don Antonio Sandoval of Las Padillas, one of the richest men in New Mexico. She too was wealthy, and although illiterate, she managed her own property. In 1815 she brought suit against her neighbor, Don Pedro Bautista Pino, for two hundred pesos she had loaned him. In 1818 she sued José Sánchez, another neighbor, for the value of 351 sheep. In 1832 the same José Sánchez, now city councilman of Las Padillas, declared a conflict of interest in a suit Doña Ursula had brought against another neighbor, because Sánchez's livelihood depended on a partido contract with Doña Ursula (meaning that he managed her sheep for a percentage of the annual lamb crop). With her wealth came a measure of concern for the commonweal: in 1835 she complained to the governor that the alcalde of Valencia had appropriated funds belonging to the church. Her complaint was promptly investigated.[20]

Even more independent than Doña Ursula was Doña Gertrudis Barceló, the famous La Tules who earned a fortune as the leading monte dealer of New Mexico. She often used the alcalde courts to collect debts contracted in her gambling hall and to defend her rather free style of life by means of suits for slander against the gossips of Santa Fe. She signed these proceedings with her name and rubric, for she was one of the few literate women of New Mexico, where schools meant for both boys and girls were attended only by a few boys, and girls were taught at home, if at all. La Tules was public spirited, giving to charity and in 1846 lending the United States Army money to pay its troops after the American invasion. La Tules was a brilliant woman, and her counsel was sought on public matters by her friend, Governor Manuel Armijo. She contributed to the "forced loan," a sporadic and inequitable taxation, but there is no evidence that this brought her representation in the election of electors or the opportunity to hold public office.[21]

Women occasionally stated, according to Mexican custom, that their appearance in court was with permission of their husbands, but in New Mexico their deference was merely courtesy, as is indicated by the many cases in which the wife appeared not only without her husband's permission but with a complaint against him. Permission or lack of it was often on the other side, as in the suit brought by Doña Gregoria Quintana against her husband Jesús Martínez for selling her grain mill without her consent. The juez and *hombres buenos* proposed that the new owner of the mill grind twelve fanegas of grain for Doña Gregoria every year until her death and pay the fee for a certificate of cleanliness; the new owner agreed to do so. In another case, the wife of José Sandoval took her husband to court for gambling away her burro to another man. The court ordered the burro returned to the wife and fined the men two pesos each for gambling.[22]

An example not only of the independence of New Mexican women but also of the practice of law in New Mexican courts is the case of Manuel Sánchez, who went to court to nullify a conciliation between himself and his brother-in-law on grounds that Sánchez did not have his wife's power of attorney to act for her. Antonio Barreiro, a lawyer from "below" who served a few years as legal advisor to the Territory of New Mexico, gave the opinion that power of attorney was not needed. The learned lawyer's opinion was ignored, as the juez sided with Sanchez in ordering a rehearing of the case.[23]

If Mexican law was disregarded in New Mexican courts, the common law of the United States was entirely ignored. In the United States, widows were liable for their husband's debts; not so in New Mexico, as some Americans discovered in trying to collect a debt owned by the estate of Alexander Branch from Branch's widow, Paula Luna. The Americans seized the widow's house and evicted her and her ten dependents, including her own children and six Indian *criados,* aged five to fifteen. The widow appealed to the governor, who ordered her house restored to her since she was not a partner in her husband's business and therefore did not assume his debts. The Americans then managed to have the widow jailed for debt. Again the governor rescued her, ordering that she be freed immediately "because no one in New Mexico could be jailed for lack of property."[24]

A married woman of New Mexico was protected by the Spanish law providing that her property acquired before marriage was not part of the community property after marriage. A wife could not make donation of her noncommunity property to her husband, nor demand a share of his, unless he was squandering hers. This principle was lucidly explained to the local juez by Padre Antonio José Martínez, a former deputy, during a suit brought by the padre's niece against her husband, whose gambing debts had exhausted all the income and part of the principal of her inheritance. As her attorney, Padre Martínez wrote that the husband's attorney, former deputy Juan Bautista Vigil, had attempted to destroy the inventory of her inheritance and had threatened her life if she refused to donate the property to her husband. On Padre Martínez's petition, the governor ordered the husband jailed and the property put in the hands of a trustee. At this threat the husband ended the litigation by dismissing his attorney and agreeing to pay his wife all he owed her.[25]

Alcalde courts had jurisdiction over children whose rights or property were threatened. One juez had to choose between two women seeking guardianship of a four-year-old orphan who had inherited from his mother a third of the product of a piece of land. After choosing a guardian, the juez ordered the boy's property held in trust until he was old enough to manage it. Either father or mother could serve as guardian for minor children, and children could be legally adopted. Dolores Griego de Barceló went to court over Pedro Sandoval's daughter, whom he had given her with a "public document of adoption." Sandoval now declared that he wanted his daughter back, for the child had come to his house to live with him. The court ordered the girl returned to her adoptive parent, for she was not in need and there was no legitimate reason for giving her to her father. In another case, Alexander Tibeau had obtained possession of his two-year-old daughter by a prostitute of Real del Oro. When the mother of the child brought suit for custody, Tibeau, who was married to a New Mexican, said that the prostitute set the child a bad example and that he could provide an education for the child. One of the *hombres buenos* thought the child should go to Tibeau, who could give her a better environment. But since Tibeau could not prove he was the child's father, the juez delivered her to her mother.[26]

Promiscuity was less tolerated than the Americans believed. Alcaldes were charged with protection of public morals and issued edicts against women who walked the streets at night, men who violated the marriage bed of women of the house where fandangos were held, and habitual adulterers or fornicators of either sex. In 1832 the juez of Pecos was ordered by the juez of Santa Fe to identify the men and women living "the bad life," whether married or not and whether or not husbands were aware of the bad life their wives were leading with other men. "The bad life" described the relationship of the soldier Rosario Gabaldón with Gertrudis Valencia, who had been confined in a private home for her immorality. When Gabaldon asked the alcalde to release Gertrudis to him on bond, the official was outraged, fulminating in the record that the soldier had a nerve asking that the women be released, as though the alcalde were his pimp! In 1842 Ana María Rendón and another woman living in her house were evicted for their bad life as *amasias* (concubines), although this relationship was rarely cause for court action. This particular judgment may have had a hidden instigator, for La Rendón had accused the powerful La Tules of illegal cohabitation some years earlier.[27]

Because of early maturation of New Mexican girls and lack of shame surrounding sexual activity, girls were frequently living in concubinage or indulging in illicit relations at early puberty. Juan de Jesús Archuleta brought proceedings against a young man for cutting his daughter's face with a razor at ten in the morning because the youth had found the girl in "bad circumstances" with a soldier. The girl denied involvement with the soldier, stating instead she had had sexual relations with the defendant and afterwards told him she did not love him, which caused his anger. This girl was single, living with her parents, and fourteen years old.[28]

Alcaldes were not the only defenders of public morality. Rosalia Sandoval and her daughter, both servants of Governor Armijo, were outside the governor's palace when Manuel Leyva came by and cut off the daughter's braids with his sword because both mother and daughter had had illicit relations with men. The braid-snipper was banished to San Miguel del Bado for three months, and the Sandoval women were ordered to court to defend their virtue.[29]

In the absence of lawyers and marriage counselors, alcalde courts served as the first resort in marital difficulties. Many married couples appeared in the courts seeking reconciliation, looking to the juez and hombres buenos for advice and guidance as well as legal means of assuring better treatment from their spouses. One jealous wife persuaded the court to order her rival to stop following her husband around or be punished by law and the husband to cease scolding his wife or suffer three months in prison. Doña Rafaela Sánchez, wife of Don Juan Bautista-Vigil, withdrew her divorce suit when the court ordered her husband to give bond for her satisfaction with his behavior. The court was not always successful in achieving conciliation. Doña Simona Pineda, sixty-year-old wife of Don José Maria Alarid, complained of her husband's "maltreatment with words" and asked the court to order her husband out of the house. The husband refused to go, on grounds that her complaints were insufficient to disrupt his life. The court agreed with him, but Doña Simona did not agree to conciliation. Another husband whose "maltreatment with words" included a threat of death was banished to Galisteo until he could prove his good intentions toward his wife. Two persons, one in Galisteo and one in Santa Fe, were to watch over the conduct of this couple.[30]

Divorce, meaning legal separation, was obtainable only from an ecclesiastical court after all attempts at conciliation through the courts and through appeal to the governor had failed. One woman seeking divorce appeared before the juez alone, "for lack of words to assert her rights in company with her husband." The juez ordered her to return to her husband; she appealed to Governor Armijo to suspend the juez's order. The governor decreed that none who had contracted matrimony should be forced to live together if there was sufficient cause for divorce and that the wife need not return to her husband.[31]

The governor's view of "sufficient cause of divorce" was different from that of the ecclesiastical judge to whom Doña Seferina Sandoval appeared during a long court case. Seferina was young but educated. She characterized Martin Aragón her husband of four years, as uneducated, incompetent, unemployed, and inclined to violence, which she attributed to the fact that his father had been executed for murder. In a well-written petition to the ecclesiastical judge (the leading priest of New Mexico), Seferina begged for divorce. She recited some valid causes—that her husband did not provide necessities for her, that he once suggested that she sell her body to obtain food, and that he struck her, causing a miscarriage. Then she listed some annoyances that only weakened her case—that while she was dangerously ill after the miscarriage her mother-in-law would not allow her *comadre* (baptismal sponsor) to see her, that her husband refused to take her to a dance because she did not invite his mother to join them, that the husband sided with his sister instead of Seferina in a quarrel. Aragón responded that Seferina's charges were false or exaggerated, that she was young and naive—the source both of her charm and her silliness—and that he strongly desired reconciliation. Four times Seferina appeared in court refusing conciliation. She was put in deposit in her parents' and other houses for fifty-three days, at the end of which she was as determined as ever on divorce. The ecclesiastical judge gave the opinion that there was insufficient cause for divorce. The husband, he wrote, was well intentioned, but the wife was stubborn. Nevertheless, he would seek a decree from the ecclesiastical court in Durango, which could take a very long time, and in the meantime Doña Seferina would have to live with her husband.[32]

Governor Armijo participated in a divorce case that indicates the healthy state of women's rights in New Mexico or else the astonishing liberality of the governor. In 1827 a woman sought a divorce because her husband insisted on living in the tiny village of Isleta, while she preferred Albuquerque. The case was referred to the governor, who weighted the "multitude of inconveniences" suffered by his wife at Isleta against the needs of the husband to live where he worked. The governor's decision was that the man's needs were no more compelling than his wife's, and he ordered the couple to choose a new location satisfactory to both.[33]

Men and women were often punished equally for adultery. For example, Doña Francisca Romero brought Doña Rosaria Domínguez to court for adultery with her husband, and both lovers were put in prison. Later the husband was released upon petition of his wife, but Doña Rosaria remained in jail. Adultery did not necessarily lead to divorce, as in the case of Don José Francisco Baca y Pino, who had suspected for five years that his wife Doña Dolores Ortiz was having an affair with José Tenorio. Don José put up with the situation until his suffering became so acute that he feared he might kill his wife or Tenorio, and he appealed to the governor to have Tenorio banished. The governor ordered that the guilty couple should suffer fines and punishment the first and second times they were caught. The third time would mean banishment for Tenorio because he was a bachelor without occupation or fortune and would not be harmed by living elsewhere. The third time occurred one evening when Don José found them bedded down in a neighbor's kitchen. Tenorio was banished to Albuquerque for a year and five months; then he returned to Santa Fe and was jailed for a time and released. The lovers were warned that if they succumbed again to their passion they would both be put in jail until the supreme tribunal should determine their fate, which could take years.[34]

If Don José's pride allowed him to put up with an adulterous wife, John Scolly's Celtic temper did not. Scolly was a rich, middle-aged Irish merchant of Santa Fe who had married Don Vincente Lopez's young daughter, Juana. A year later Juana went to court with a complaint against Scolly, and they were reconciled, Scolly agreeing to pay his wife's father a hundred and twenty-five pesos for his wife's subsistence every time she returned to her father's house after a quarrel. A year later Juana returned to her father's house, where she spent the night with an American teamster. The next morning she was seen at the camp of American traders near Santa Fe, very drunk on whiskey, and crying as her lover left with the wagons. Scolly died two years later, probably before he received the divorce he sought.[35]

Although concubinage was generally accepted, except by the church, adultery was not. The law was invoked in many cases, and even those who failed to report the adultery of others were subject to arrest. Bautista Espinosa deserted his wife and family to live with Rafaela Rael. When the deserted wife made a complaint, Rafaela's relative Luis Rael was put in jail along with the lovers for tolerating their adultery. In similar cases a man was punished for not reporting the adultery of his wife, and a mother was accused of consenting to her daughter's "bad life."[36]

Court records seem to show that standards of behavior were essentially the same for both sexes, as was the behavior. Men were hauled into court for gossip and slander against women, and women for physical assault on men. During a quarrel, Doña Antonia Suárez called Don Rafael Pacheco "old and ruptured," to which he responded, in front of her children, that she was a "whore, thief, pimp and vagabond." The court ordered both to beg the other's pardon and to cease quarreling or be treated as criminals. Mariano Ortiz brought Franklin Brown to court for reviling the honor of his daughter in accusing her of living "the bad life" with Luis Anaya for two years. Brown brought in two American friends to support the truth of his accusation and to testify that Brown had been drinking whiskey at the time. Neither the truth nor Brown's drunkenness served to mitigate the insult. Brown apologized and retracted the offending words, but he was sent to jail for eight days anyway.[37]

As men were sued for slander, so women were sued for attacks on men. One woman beat a soldier so badly that he was seriously injured; another was accused with her lover of murdering her husband. The power of a woman in the courts is apparent in the case of María de la Cruz Barela, whose personal rights were respected above a man's property, even when the man was wealthy and even when her own actions were not above reproach. María de la Cruz did her laundry in the river and spread it to dry on the nearby adobe wall of Don Miguel Sena. Don Miguel was tired of having to repair his wall after laundresses put their wet clothes on it, so he told her to stop. Shouting improper words, she picked up a rock to attack him. He took her by the shoulder and pushed her to the ground. She took Don Miguel to court, where it was determined that he was at fault in throwing her to the ground and should choose a different course of action in the future.[38]

In communities with separate jails, women were incarcerated as well as men, and they worked out their subsistence by providing meals for inmates. According to national law, as recited by Juan Bautista Vigil, jails were meant only for detention of suspects while a case was being tried, but in New Mexico offenders were often sentenced to jail. Women were more often detained in private homes or freed on bond, even when accused of what Americans would regard as serious felonies. Doña Ignacia Sandoval was convicted with her husband of robbing a Santa Fe store. She was detained in a room of the alcalde's house for twenty-one days and then released on bond upon her petition that her twelve-year-old daughter was alone at home taking care of the younger children. Her husband remained in jail.[39]

Lest the reader conclude that New Mexican women were viragos, it might be well to cite a murder case that portrays the life of poor women in New Mexico more typically than many of the examples above. Rafael Montoya and his wife set out from Belén on a journey and stopped for the night at a house in Corrales. In the middle of the night the couple went outside to make water in the road, and there Montoya stabbed his wife. Before she died she told the owner of the house that her husband was jealous of everything, although she had never given him cause. The husband later testified that his wife had refused to return to bed with him that night and that he suspected her of adultery because she had some new shoes and stockings that he had not given her. The public prosecutor wrote in his charge that the woman had probably bought the clothes to make the journey, for even poor women had a little money of their own, earned at spinning or given to them by husbands or relatives. The prosecutor stated that murder of a wife was defensible only if the husband caught her in adultery and that public vengeance demanded execution of this man, which required a sentence from the supreme tribunal.[40]

Servants often exercised their rights in the alcalde courts. The servant of Madam María Brown, Mexican wife of an American storekeeper, sued her mistress for her salary of twelve pesos a month. Madam Brown was ordered to pay the salary, less two pesos for the value of a cup the servant had broken. Another servant was ordered by her master to clean the sala and fetch water; the servant refused, and the master refused to pay her. The servant followed the master's wife around the house remonstrating until it became intolerable and the master hit her. The court decided that the master had a habit of not getting along with his servants and not paying them, and it ordered him to pay the servant what he owed her.[41]

Employers had rights too. An employer could slap a servant but not cause injury, and he could hold her to a contract. A young kitchen maid was struck by the master and denied her three pesos a month because of her incompetence. Her mother brought the employer to court where he was told to pay the girl her salary, but he was not punished for striking her because he had not caused her injury. Another little maid was sent into service under contract be-

tween her mother and her employer. After seventeen days she became ill and was sent home. She did not improve; her mother could
not leave the sick girl to take her place in service, and the mistress
refused to pay her. The mother went to court; the judgment was
that the mistress should allow the child two more days to regain
her health, but if she died, the mother was to return the salary already paid her.[42]

A special court—the tribunal de vagos—had been set up in colonial days to deal with vagabonds or people without decent occupation, like two prostitutes being held in the Real del Oro jail. One
was a refugee from the interior of Mexico who had fled to New
Mexico to escape her husband. The court decided she should be
kept in detention in a reputable house until her mother could come
and take her home or else be sent back to her own province. Another was María Antonia Baca, a Mexican girl captured by Indians
and redeemed by Governor Bartolomé Baca, who raised her in his
own family. She was now without family; the court ordered her
to be put in household service to earn her keep and her natural son
to be employed in Robidoux's tannery.[43]

This brief look at New Mexican women should suggest a need
for more research—on New Mexican social classes in different regions at different dates, on women's Spanish and Indian legal heritage, on influences of their matrilineal Navajo and Pueblo Indian
neighbors, on the frontier conditions that shaped their lives for the
two hundred-odd years before the Republican period, and on New
Mexican men whose edicts and judgments allowed women such
unusual freedom.

The extraordinary independence of New Mexico women, in
full flower during the Republican period, came to an end in 1846
when New Mexico was invaded by United States soldiers, convinced of their own superiority and disdainful of the natives. Very
quickly New Mexicans submitted to their conquerors and to many
of their foreign ideas. Only fifteen years after the American conquest, the New Mexican woman had all but abandoned her easy,
graceful costume and was yielding to the fashionable tyranny of
corsets, hoop-skirts, and bonnets. Her fandangos were corrupted
beyond recognition by strong American whiskey and rough American frontiersmen. Her legal rights upheld in alcalde courts were
curtailed in American courts. Her Sunday merriment became a private thing, as foreign priests swept fandango music and gaiety out

of the churches, and American officials banned other Sabbath activities. As years went by, ethnic discrimination denied her husband political power and jobs, her children were forbidden to speak Spanish in school, and her folk festivals and folk art were scorned. Her way of life was gone. But the Hispanic woman of today has not lost the values that once gave her joy and confidence. She stubbornly fights to retain her culture, with the strength born of an independence that has not forsaken her.[44]

Notes

1. Max L. Moorhead, *New Mexico's Royal Road: Trade and Travel on the Chihuahua Trail* (Norman: University of Oklahoma Press, 1958), 28, 32.

2. Stella M. Drumm, ed., *Down the Santa Fe Trail and into Mexico: The Diary of Susan Shelby Magoffin, 1846–1847* (New Haven, Connecticut: Yale University Press, 1926), 93–95, 98, 160, 210–12.

3. Lewis H. Garrard, *Wah-to-yah and the Taos Trail,* ed. Ralph P. Bieber (Glendale, California: A. H. Clark, 1938), 238; George Rutledge Gibson, *Journal of a Soldier under Kearny and Doniphan, 1846–1847,* ed. Ralph P. Bieber (Glendale, California: A. H. Clark, 1935), 210.

4. Barbara Welter, "The Cult of True Womanhood, 1820–1860," Ronald W. Hogeland, ed., *Woman and Womanhood in America* (Lexington, Massachusetts: Heath, 1973), 103–13; Lorna Duffin, "Prisoners of Progress: Women and Evolution," Sara Delamont and Lorna Duffin, eds., *The Nineteenth Century Woman: Her Cultural and Physical World* (New York: Barnes & Noble, 1978), 57–91.

5. Gibson, *Journal of a Soldier,* 195.

6. For cosmetics, see Josiah Gregg, *Commerce of the Prairies,* ed. Max L. Moorhead (Norman: University of Oklahoma Press, 1954), 153; and "Journal of Marcellus Ball Edwards, 1846–1847," Abraham Robinson Johnston, Marcellus Ball Edwards, and Philip Gooch Ferguson, *Marching with the Army of the West, 1846–1848,* ed. Ralph P. Bieber (Glendale: A. H. Clark, California, 1936), 165. For hidalgos, see W. H. H. Davis, *El Gringo; or, New Mexico and Her People* (New York, 1857), 215–16, and Fray Angelico Chavez, *My Penitente Land: Reflections on Spanish New Mexico* (Albuquerque: University of New Mexico Press, 1974), 35, 231. For castes, see Ralph H. Vigil, "The Hispanic Heritage and the Borderlands," *Journal of San Diego History* XIX (Summer 1973), 32, 39. For luxuries, see Drumm, ed., *Down the Santa Fe Trail,* 133, 154. For the open society, see Robert

Archibald, "Acculturation and Assimilation in Colonial New Mexico," *New Mexico Historical Review* 53 (July 1978), 205–14.

7. Davis, *El Gringo,* 190, 216; Erna Fergusson, *Mexican Cookbook* (Albuquerque: University of New Mexico Press, 1934); E. Boyd, *Popular Arts of Spanish New Mexico* (Santa Fe: Museum of New Mexico Press1974), 2–30, 246–65, 286–87.

8. "Santa Fe and the Far West," letter dated Santa Fe, July 29, 1841, reprinted in *New Mexico Historical Review* V (July 1930), 299–304; testimony of Calvin Jones, April 9, 1885, Trinidad, Colorado, *Transcript of Record, Maxwell Land Grant and Railway Co., et al v. Guadelupe Thompson et al,* Supreme Court, Territory of New Mexico, July term 1894, no. 581.

9. "Report of the Secretary of War, communicating . . . a report and map of the examination of New Mexico, made by Lieutenant J. W. Abert . . .,, *Sen. Exec. Docs.,* 30th Cong., 1st sess., no. 23 (serial 506), 29, 35, 48; Garrard, *Wah-to-yah,* 247–48; "Journal of Marcellus Ball Edwards," 179.

10. Virginia Langham Olmsted, *New Mexico, Spanish & Mexican Colonial Censuses, 1790, 1823, 1845* (Albuquerque, n.d.); Santa Fe census, 1841, microfilm publication, State of New Mexico Records Center and Archives (Santa Fe, c. 1969), roll 30, fr. 339–89, Mexican Archives of New Mexico (hereafter MANM). For vending, see John Francis McDermott, ed., *Travels in Search of the Elephant: The Wanderings of Alfred S. Waugh, Artist in Louisiana, Missouri,* and *Santa Fe, in 1845–1846* (St. Louis: Missouri Historical Society, 1951), 120–21; Gibson, *Journal of a Soldier,* 227, 236; Doña Barbara Baca v. Doña Isabel Urioste, April 25, 1835, Jusgado 2°, Santa Fe, roll 20, fr. 388–89," MANM. For Armijo's sister, see "Diary of Philip Gooch Ferguson, 1847–1848," Beiber, ed., *Marching with the Army of the West,* 321, 328. For the billiard table, see Doña Peregrina Domínguez v. Doña Josefa Baca, Jusgado 2°, Santa Fe, December 16, 1837, roll 20, fr. 455–58 and roll 25, fr. 319–68, MANM.

11. Donald Jackson, ed., *The Journals of Zebulon Montgomery Pike, with Letters and Related Documents* (2 vols., Norman: University of Oklahoma Press, 1966), I, 401; W. H. Emory, "Notes of a Military Reconnaissance, from Fort Leavenworth, in Missouri, to San Diego, in California . . .," *Sen. Exec. Docs.,* 30th Cong., 1st sess., no. 7 (serial 505), 46; Proceedings, New Mexico Territorial Deputation, January 23, 1828, roll 8, fr. 169–71, MANM.

12. Marianne L. Stoller, "Spanish-Americans, Their Servants and Sheep: A Culture History of Weaving in Southern Colorado," *Spanish Textile Tradition of New Mexico and Colorado* (Santa Fe: Museum of New Mexico Press, 1979), 42–44; Lorin W. Brown, *Hispano Folklife of New Mexico: The Lorin W. Brown Federal Writers' Manuscripts* (Albuquerque: University of New Mexico Press, 1978), 50, 72, 102, 130; Gibson, *Journal of a Soldier,* 249.

13. For siesta, see Gregg, *Commerce of the Prairies,* 157. For fandangos, see George F. Ruxton, *Life in the Far West* (New York, 1849), 196–98.

For fiestas, see Waugh, *Travels in Search of the Elephant*, 126–27; Emory, "Notes of a Military Reconnaissance," 41–52. For the church, see ibid., 34; "Dr. Willard's Journal, 1827–1830," Reuben Gold Thwaites, ed., *Early Western Travels, 1748–1846* (32 vols, Cleveland, 1905), 28, 337; Gregg, *Commerce of the Prairies*, 179–80; Gibson, *Journal of a Soldier*, 236.

14. George Wilkins Kendall, *Narrative of the Texan Santa Fe Expedition . . .* 2 vols. (New York, 1844), 1: 321, 2: 335; "Santa Fe and the Far West," 299–304; Davis, *El Gringo*, 221; Waugh, *Travels in Search of The Elephant*, 121; Elliott Coues, ed., *The Journal of Jacob Fowler, Narrating an Adventure from Arkansas through the Indian Territory, Oklahoma, Kansas, Colorado, and New Mexico to the Sources of Rio Grande del Norte, 1821–22* (New York, 1898), 107–8; *The Personal Narrative of James O. Pattie*, 190.

15. Gregg, *Commerce of the Prairies*, 182–84; Davis, *El Gringo*, 221–22. For statistics on marital status, see Lansing B. Bloom, "New Mexico under Mexican Administration, 1821–46," *Santa Fe* 1 (July 1913), 29, 33 n. For concubines, see Janet Lecompte, *Pueblo Hardscrabble, Greenhorn: The Upper Arkansas, 1832–56* (Norman: University of Oklahoma Press, 1978), 72; baptismal records, Archives of the Archbishop of Santa Fe, Records Center and Archives, Santa Fe.

16. Gregg, *Commerce of the Prairies*, 182; Diligencias Matrimoníales, Archives of the Archbishop of Santa Fe; Davis, *El Gringo*, 227; Olmsted, *New Mexico, Spanish and Mexican Colonial Censuses*, 210–31, fr. 420, 422, 425.

17. Antonio Barreiro, "Ligera explicación," 1833, roll 16, fr. 1000, MANM.

18. Gregg, *Commerce of the Prairies*, 164–65; David J. Weber, ed., "El Gobierno Territorial de Nuevo México—La Exposición del Padre Martínez de 1831," *Historia Mexicana*, 25 (no. 2, 1975), 310–15; Manuel Armijo to the territorial deputation regarding administration of justice, January 26, 1828, roll 8, fr. 216–18, MANM; Antonio Barreiro, "Supplement," *Three New Mexico Chronicles: The Exposición of Don Pedro Bautista Pino, 1812; the Ojeada of Lic. Antonio Barreiro, 1832; and the additions by Don José Agustín de Escudero, 1849*, ed. H. Bailey Carroll and J. Villasana Haggard (Albuquerque, 1942), 60–61.

19. For the fat hog, see Bentura Romero v. Doña María Antonio Zúares, January 14, 1835, Jusgado 1° de Santa Fe, roll 20, fr. 12–14, MANM. For the burro, see Jesús Domínguez v. Tomás Gallegos, March 6, 1844, Jusgado 2° de Santa Fe, roll 36, fr. 227–29, MANM. For the cloak, see Doña Barbara Cordero v. Don Juan Furnie, April 4, 1839, Jusgado 1° de Santa Fe, roll 26, fr. 694–95, MANM. For the gun, see José Ortiz v. Juana Gonzales, January 27, 1842, Jusgado 1° de Santa Fe, roll 32, fr. 2–4, MANM. For rooms, see Doña Ana María Rendón v. Doña Juliana Gonzáles, June 19, 1845, Jusgado 2° de Santa Fe, roll 19, fr. 156–57, MANM. For the nugget, see Miguel Benavides v. Reyes Trujillo, Sep-

tember 9, 1845, Jusgado 1° de Santa Fe, March 8, 1842, roll 32, fr. 36–38, MANM; Doña Peregrina Domíngues v. Felix García, Jusgado 1° de Santa Fe, September 30, 1839, roll 26, fr. 624–25, MANM.

20. Doña María Ursula Chávez v. Don Pedro Bautista Pino, Santa Fe, August 1815 to March 1818, and Doña Ursula Chávez v. Don José Sanchez, Santa Fe, February 15, 1818, Spanish Archives of New Mexico, Records Center and Archives, Santa Fe, microfilm publication (Santa Fe, c. 1968), roll 18, fr. 139–235 and roll 19, fr. 603–4; petition of José Gavriel Sánchez to the governor, Plaza de los Padillas, September 18, 1832, roll 14, fr. 609–10, MANM; José Antonio Chávez, Jusgado de la Ysleta to alcalde Don Manuel Vijil, Valencia, July 12, 1835, roll 19, fr. 901–2, MANM.

21. Janet Lecompte, "La Tules and the Americans," *Arizona and the West* 20 (Autumn 1978), 215–30.

22. Doña Gertrudis Barceló v. Don Santiago Clerce [Kirker], August 13, 1839, Jusgado 1° de Santa Fe, roll 26, fr. 623, MANM; Doña Barbara Cordero v. Don Juan Furnie, April 4, 1839, Jusgado 1° de Santa Fe, roll 26, fr. 694–95, MANM; Doña Gregoria Quintana v. Jesús Martínez, January 10, 1844, Jusgado 1° de Santa Fe, roll 33, fr. 769–70, MANM; Francisca Romero v. José Sandoval, October 9, 1843, Jusgado 2° de Santa Fe, roll 33, fr. 827, MANM.

23. Manuel Sánchez v. Don José Francisco Ortiz, Jusgado 2° de Santa Fe, February 16–May 10, 1832, roll 15, fr. 24–82, MANM.

24. Doña María Paula Luna v. Patrick Ryder, March 30 and April 23, 1841, Santa Fe, roll 29, fr. 168–70, 173, MANM; Governor Manuel Armijo's Book of Decrees, February 12, April 23, April 26, 1841, roll 27, fr. 1168–1173, MANM.

25. Antonio José Martínez on the rights of matrimony, Taos, September 19, 1836, roll 22, fr. 335–38, MANM; Doña María Manuela Martínez v. Tomás Lucero, Jusgado 1° de Taos, August 8, 1836–April 1, 1837, roll 22, fr. 339–57, MANM.

26. Ermenegilda Sandoval v. Josefa García, September 26, 1843, Jusgado 2° de Santa Fe, roll 33, fr. 824, MANM; Doña Dolores Griego de Barceló v. Pedro Sandoval, May 24, 1839, Jusgado 1° de Santa Fe, roll 26, fr. 617–18, MANM; María Gertrudis Baca v. Alexo Tibu, July 9–10, 1840, Jusgado 1° de Santa Fe, roll 26, fr. 639–42, MANM.

27. Bando, Alcalde 1° de Santa Fe, February 12, 1832, roll 14, fr. 989, MANM; bando, Prefecto del 1° distrito, January 26, 1845, roll 38, fr. 1064, MANM; alcalde 1° de Santa Fe to Teniente de Pecos, March 3, 1835, roll 19, fr. 934, MANM; libro de borradores, Jusgado 1° de Santa Fe, June 1, 1842, roll 32, fr. 10, MANM; Jusgado 2° de Santa Fe to Sec.° de Gobierno, June 9, 1842, roll 29, fr. 158, MANM; Doña Gertrudis Barceló v. Doña Ana María Rendón, March 3, 1835, Jusgado 1° de Santa Fe, roll 20, fr. 131–32, MANM.

28. Juan de Jesús Archuleta v. Juan José Salaíses, March 19, 1844, Jusgado 1° de Santa Fe, roll 36, fr. 144–47, MANM.

29. Rosalia Sandoval v. Manuel Leyva, February 18, 1842, Jusgado 2° de Santa Fe, roll 32, fr. 88–97, and September 17, 1842, roll 32, fr. 88–89, MANM.

30. María Josefa Rodríguez v. María Soledad Ortiz, March 5, 1835, Jusgado 1° de Santa Fe, roll 20, fr. 93–95, MANM; Rafaela Sánchez v. Don Juan Bautista Vigil, April 9, 1836, Jusgado 1° de Santa Fe, roll 20, fr. 114, MANM; Doña Simona Pineda v. Don José María Alarid, September 4, 1840, Jusgado 2° de Santa Fe, roll 28, fr. 179–80, MANM; María de la Luz Pena v. José Silva, August 7, 1845, Jusgado 1° de Santa Fe, roll 39, fr. 29–30, MANM.

31. Petition of Tomasa Tenorio to the governor, June 4, 1840, roll 27, fr. 1035–36, MANM.

32. Doña Seferina Sandoval v. Don Martín Aragón, May 10 and September 1, 1836, Jusgado 2° de Santa Fe, roll 22, fr. 136–60, MANM.

33. Governor Manuel Armijo to the Vicar Foraneo and curate of Tomé, Don Francisco Ygnacio de Madariaga, August 10, 1827, roll 6, fr. 1226–27, MANM.

34. Doña Francisca Romero v. Doña del Rosaria Domíngues, April 23, 1835, Jusgado 2° de Santa Fe, April 23, 1835, roll 20, fr. 464–65, MANM; Don José Francisco Baca y Pino v. José Tenorio, January 15, 1828–November 14, 1829, Jusgado de Santa Fe, roll 8, fr. 311–46, and roll 9, fr. 378–79, MANM.

35. Don Juan Escolem v. Doña Juana López, April 8 and April 16, 1844, Jusgado 1° de Santa Fe, roll 35, fr. 82–88, MANM; Don Juan Escole v. Exsequios Arison, May 4–9, 1845, Jusgado 1° de Santa Fe, roll 39, fr. 117–31, MANM.

36. Francisca Gonzáles v. Bautista Espinosa, July 11, 1836, Jusgado 2° de Santa Fe, roll 20, fr. 413–14, MANM; Alcalde 2° de Santa Fe to Lic. D. José María Yrigoyen, Chihuahua, July 15, 1835, roll 19, fr. 1039, MANM; Josefa Sena v. Ana María Villapando y Gertrudis Espinosa, May 31, 1839, Jusgado 2° de Santa Fe, roll 26, fr. 716–17, MANM.

37. Doña María Antonio Suáres v. Don Rafael Pacheco, August 1, 1843, Jusgado 2° de Santa Fe, roll 33, fr. 833–34, MANM; Mariano Ortiz v. Franklin Brahon, January 19, 1836, Jusgado 2° de Santa Fe, roll 20, fr. 401–3, MANM.

38. Pablo Domínguez v. María Guadalupe Trugillo, January 4, 1844, Jusgado 1° de Santa Fe, roll 33, fr. 768–69, MANM; Antonio Sandoval, prefecto 2° distrito to Guadalupe Miranda, Sec.° de Gobierno, September 2, 1840, roll 27, fr. 1055–56, MANM; María de la Cruz Varela v. Don Miguel Sena, May 14, 1836, Jusgado 2° de Santa Fe, roll 22, fr. 117–19, MANM.

39. Juan Bautista Vigil y Alaríd to Francisco Ortiz y Delgado [Santa Fe], November 19, 1838, roll 25, fr. 259–60, MANM; Manuel Delgado, Santa Fe, March 27, 1844, roll 37, fr. 550, MANM; petition of Pedro Sandoval, April 28, 1838, Jusgado 1° de Santa Fe, roll 25, fr. 235–41, MANM; Cornelio Vigil to Miranda, April 2, 1842, Jusgado 1° de Taos, roll 30, fr. 897–99, MANM; Don Justo Pastor Pino v. Doña Ygnacia Sandobal, August 18–31, 1841, Jusgado 2° de Santa Fe, roll 29, fr. 328–414, MANM.

40. Proceedings against Rafael Montoya, Corrales, December 22, 1842–January 16, 1844, roll 32, fr. 131–62, MANM.

41. Chiquita Manuel de Anda v. Madama María Brown, July 8, 1836, Jusgado 2° de Santa Fe, roll 20, fr. 411–12, MANM; Estefana Sandobal v. Don Anastasio Sandobal, September 17, 1845, Jusgado 2° de Santa Fe, roll 29, fr. 159–60, MANM.

42. María Francisca Sena v. Don Benito Larragoita, February 25, 1845, Jusgado 2° de Santa Fe, roll 40, fr. 470–72, MANM; Peregrina Saens v. Señora Ortega, February 25, 1845, Jusgado 2° de Santa Fe, roll 39, fr. 144–45, MANM.

43. Tribunal de Bagos, July 22, 1835, roll 20, fr. 154–55, MANM.

44. James F. Meline, *Two Thousand Miles on Horseback, Santa Fe and Back: A Summer Tour through Kansas, Nebraska, Colorado, and New Mexico, in the Year 1866* (New York, 1868), 169, 184–86, 190–91; Clinton E. Brooks and Frank D. Reeves, eds., *Forts and Forays: James A. Bennett, A Dragoon in New Mexico, 1850–1856* (Albuquerque: University of New Mexico Press, 1948), 20; Aurora Hunt, *Kirby Benedict, Frontier Federal Judge, An Account of Legal and Judicial Development in the South-West, 1853–1874* (Glendale: A. H. Clark, California, 1961), 41–55; Frances Leon Swadesh, *Los Primeros Pobladores: Hispanic Americans of the Ute Frontier* (Notre Dame, Indiana: University of Notre Dame Press, 1974), 68–72.

⋙ 4 ⋘

Cross-Cultural Marriages in the Southwest

The New Mexico Experience 1846–1900*

Darlis A. Miller

Approximately 75,000 Spanish-speaking people were living in the Southwest at the time of the American conquest in 1846. Although sharing a common language, religion, and Iberian heritage, they were not culturally homogeneous but were separated into several population centers, each with its distinct culture. Different dates for migration and settlement as well as geographic isolation, environmental conditions, and Indian populations contributed to the diversity among Hispanic societies in Texas, California, Arizona, and New Mexico.[1]

Similarly, each center of population developed its own pattern of assimilation of Anglo-American culture. The adjustment made by Nuevo Mexicanos, for instance, was different from that made by Californios. But in each area, cross-cultural marriages between Hispanic women and Anglo men contributed to the assimilation process. Recent sociological studies have emphasized the important role that intermarriage plays in assimilation. It is used as an index of social distance and has been called the "crucial test of acceptance of one group by another."[2] In all sections of the South-

*Reprinted by permission of the regents of the University of New Mexico and the editor of the *New Mexico Historical Review*.

west, continuous and intimate contact between Hispanic and Anglo spouses helped to bridge cultural differences and eventually led
to partial assimilation of some wives and their offspring into Anglo society.

Despite claims of one writer, who attributes cross-cultural marriages to Anglo-American land hunger,[3] Hispanic women were valued by Anglo men for many reasons: as helpmates, links to powerful
Hispanic families, and as mothers, companions, and lovers. Still,
women who married Anglo men typically were forced to adjust to
changing environments, primarily because exogomous marriages
disrupted primary group relationships and thus undermined the co-
hesiveness of Hispanic society.

Although cross-cultural marriages occurred throughout the
Southwest, scant information is available concerning their frequency,
quality, or socioeconomic impact.[4] Jane Dysart, in her study of
Hispanic women in San Antonio, gives the most complete in-depth
analysis of mixed marriages in Texas. She found that interethnic
marriages between high-status Hispanic women and Anglo men
were relatively frequent in San Antonio, where at least one daughter in almost every mid-nineteenth-century upper-class Hispanic
family married an Anglo. This unleashed a process of assimilation
that resulted in the Americanization of Anglo-Hispanic families; in
the vast majority of cases, sons and daughters of high-status mixed
marriages married non-Hispanos.[5]

Similar in-depth studies of cross-cultural marriages are lacking for other areas of the Southwest. Still, some writers offer intriguing theories about mixed unions that need to be substantiated
and expanded by further research. James Officer, for example, has
suggested that cross-cultural marriages in Tucson helped establish
amiable relations between Hispanos and Anglos following American acquisition of the region in 1853. In later years, descendents of
these mixed unions linked the two ethnic groups and "helped maintain good relations . . . in Tucson down to the present day."[6]

Mixed marriages may have muted ethnic hostility in other areas
of the Southwest as well. Carey McWilliams suggests that the few
hundred American and European entrepreneurs who infiltrated California during the 1820s and 1830s became "hispanicized Anglos,"
marrying daughters of the California elite, joining the Catholic
Church, hispanicizing their names, and accepting Mexican citizen-
ship.[7] But the assimilation of these men into Hispanic society was

incomplete; at the time of American conquest, Anglo Americans enthusiastically supported the new regime and encouraged their Hispanic in-laws to collaborate with the invader. Moreover, Anglo sons-in-law imparted subtle lessons in Americanization through their wives—daughters of such elite families as the Yorbas, Sepúlvedas, Bandinis, and Picos—and these ethnic alliances assured limited cultural fusion.[8] Research is sparse concerning cross-cultural marriages in California for later years; Leonard Pitt points out, however, that marriage alliances in southern California contributed to a mixed cultural elite that was still evident in the 1880s.[9]

Few scholars of the Southwest, then, have systematically studied cross-cultural marriages. And only Dysart concentrates on Hispanic women and the role they played in mixed unions. For all areas of the Southwest, detailed information is needed concerning the frequency of intermarriage, the social class of spouses, and the tensions and stresses accompanying these unions. To shed light on these and other factors, this chapter will focus on intermarriage in nineteenth-century New Mexico, emphasizing the assimilation process and the nature of social change as it affected Hispanic women. To a limited extent, women who intermarried became culturally uprooted because of the physical mobility of Anglo husbands. By focusing on New Mexico, a territory having the largest Spanish-speaking population in the Southwest in 1846, it will be possible to establish a basis for comparison with other areas.

At the time of American conquest, an estimated 60,000 Spanish-speaking settlers—four-fifths of all Spanish-speaking people in the Southwest—resided in New Mexico.[10] The Anglo-American population was considerably smaller. After Mexico achieved independence and opened its borders to foreigners in the 1820s, Anglo merchants and adventurers began trickling into the territory so that by the 1850s there was an Anglo population of between 500 and 1200 people.[11] Arriving without wives or relatives, many early Anglo settlers married into the territory's elite Hispanic families. Two daughters of the wealthy Jaramillo family, for example, married respectively Charles Bent, first Anglo governor of New Mexico, and Christopher "Kit" Carson, famous fur trapper and explorer. Henry Connelly, a Kentuckian who became well known as a merchant and later as Civil War governor of New Mexico, married into the influential Perea family, while Charles Beaubien of French-Canadian heritage married a daughter of the prominent Lovato family.[12] These marriages tied an intruding foreign population to the ruling class of New Mexico and smoothed transition to American rule.

At the time of American conquest, New Mexico was a highly stratified society in which a small wealthy class (*ricos*) controlled social, economic, and political power. Most New Mexicans were illiterate and poor (*pobres*), subsisting in small rural villages or working on large ranches. Many were held in debt peonage, which meant virtual labor for life to a wealthy land owner.[13] After American takeover, Hispanic elites were forced to share political and economic power with Anglos, but Hispanos continued to be powerful in politics and business into present times.[14]

The first significant influx of Anglos in the American era came during the Civil War, when more than two thousand Union soldiers—members of the California Column—marched from the Pacific Coast to New Mexico to help expel Confederates who had invaded the territory. More than three hundred California veterans remained in New Mexico after their discharge, adding significantly to the Anglo population.[15] Following the war, New Mexico experienced steady population growth, partly as a result of high birth rates but also because a slow but steady trickle of Anglo-American immigrants turned into a vigorous stream after railroads entered the territory in 1879.[16]

Perhaps the most distinctive characteristic of the small Anglo community in New Mexico through the 1870s was its sex-ratio imbalance. Anglo men typically arrived in New Mexico without wives or families, and in early territorial days an Anglo woman was a rare sight. This sex imbalance encouraged unions between Anglo men and Hispanic women, though other factors also contributed to the high frequency of interethnic marriages. Despite cultural and physical differences, for example, the predominant Hispanic culture had no sanctions against mixed marriages, and many Hispanic families welcomed Anglos into their homes, thus filling a void for the newcomers caused by loss of intimacy and family life.[17] In addition, potential barriers to intermarriage were eliminated due to the isolation of Anglos from more restrictive eastern mores. Nonetheless, Anglo Americans were color-conscious and generally chose lighter-skinned women for mates. But this practice paralleled the Hispanic custom of equating lighter skin with higher social class.[18] Certainly differences in skin color did not prevent social intermingling and intermarriage; socially isolated Anglo men welcomed friendships and social contacts within the Hispanic community.

It is true that European and American visitors to New Mexico in the early years were highly critical of Hispanic society, although they reserved their harshest judgements for lower-class customs and mores. These observers frequently recorded in letters and diaries the alleged sins as well as virtues of New Mexican women. Many criticized the women's attitudes about marriage vows and their general moral laxity; others were shocked by their immodest attire.[19]

Opinions varied regarding the physical attractiveness of Hispanic women. A twenty-nine-year-old private stationed in New Mexico during the Civil War expressed distaste for Mexican women whom he described "as black as the ace of spades and ugly as sin." But other troopers agreed with the soldier-correspondent who listed the "sunny smiles of the Castilian beauties" as one of the pleasures to be enjoyed in the small town of Mesilla.[20] Moreover, Hispanic women were universally praised for their kindness and hospitality.[21] Although Anglos viewed their society as superior to that of Hispanos, the many Anglos who married New Mexican women indicated their need and regard for the latter qualities.

Because Anglo migration to New Mexico during territorial days was preponderantly male, cross-cultural marriages occurred almost exclusively between Hispanic women and Anglo men. From early days of Spanish settlement, however, interethnic unions had characterized New World society. Many Spanish conquistadores legally married Indian women while others took them as mistresses. The presence of Spanish-speaking mulattoes in the colonial Southwest reflects similar unions between blacks and Hispanos.[22]

In post-Civil War New Mexico, cross-cultural unions other than between Anglo men and Hispanic females were rare, although some of the most prominent Hispanic men in territorial New Mexico were married to Anglo women, as for example, Miguel A. Otero and J. Francisco Chávez, each of whom served as territorial delegate to Congress.[23] Occasionally Spanish-speaking men of lesser status wed Anglo women or lived in informal relationships with Indian women. Census returns also reveal other interethnic unions. In the small mining community of Silver City, for instance, there resided in 1880 a Chinese laundryman who was married to an Hispanic woman and also an Hispanic laundress who had wed a black man.[24] Still, throughout the nineteenth century, cross-cultural marriages most frequently occurred between Anglo men and Spanish-speaking women.

Nancie González correctly stated more than a decade ago that during the early years after American conquest "intermarriage between Anglo men and Mexican women was apparently quite common and not restricted to any particular social class."[25] Manuscript census schedules for 1870 and 1880 indicate that the overwhelming majority of married Anglo men residing in the territory were married to Hispanic women. Census data for 1870 for three small towns in sprawling Doña Ana County in southern New Mexico testify to the frequency of mixed unions. In the town of Las Cruces, 90 percent of married Anglo men were married to Hispanos; in Mesilla, 83 percent; in Doña Ana, 78 percent. A decade later percentages had declined to 69 percent and 50 percent for Las Cruces and Mesilla respectively, while Doña Ana—a small Hispanic community inhabited by only four married Anglo males—now registered 100 percent.[26]

In the territorial capital of Santa Fe, where large numbers of Anglos resided in 1870, 63 percent of Anglo family men were united in mixed marriages. On the other hand, the mining town of Silver City, inhabited mainly by unattached Anglo males, recorded a low percentage of married men wed to Hispanos—33 percent in 1870 and 23 percent in 1880.[27]

Data concerning military personnel also support the contention that cross-cultural marriages were not uncommon. Most soldiers who arrived in the territory during the Civil War were bachelors, and many who settled in New Mexico after mustering out of the service married Hispanic women. To cite but three examples: Lt. John E. Oliphant of New York married Helena Martínez in Las Cruces one month prior to his discharge; Pvt. Patrick Higgins, an Irishman, married a fourteen-year-old Hispanic girl in a Catholic ceremony at Mesilla two years before he mustered out of the service; and Lt. Albert J. Fountain, stationed at Fort Fillmore, fell in love with sixteen-year-old Mariana Pérez and married her while he was still a soldier.[28]

Nearly two hundred California veterans are listed in the 1870 New Mexico census; over half lived as single men or in households lacking women of marriageable age. Of the eighty-nine who lived in households that included their wives or women of marriageable age, ten were married to Anglo women, while seventy-nine were married to or living with Hispanic women.[29] These figures tend to support an observation made by a Santa Fe resident that in the years immediately after the war "so few of the Americans were married . . . that a married man was an exceptional man."[30] Yet the typical veteran who did marry, wed a Spanish-speaking woman.

Although many Anglo men who journeyed to New Mexico in the 1820s and the 1830s married into elite Spanish families, military records and census returns indicate that mixed marriages in subsequent years were not limited to upper-class members. Among the laboring and artisan class who entered mixed unions were farm laborers, carpenters, blacksmiths, miners, butchers, cooks, and numerous small farmers. The women who married these men frequently came from humble surroundings. Margarita Estrada performed housework in private homes and local hotels before marrying a small Lincoln County farmer. Felipa Montoya worked as a servant in a private residence in Belen before she wed a stage coach driver. María Baca was a laundress at Fort Craig during the Civil War and later married an Anglo rancher and farmer. Not infrequently these women were left destitute upon the death of their husbands. Cruzita Apodaca, a case in point, took in washing and ironing to maintain herself after her blacksmith-husband, Joseph D. Emerson, died in Socorro.[31]

For many New Mexican women, a rise in social status accompanied marriage to an Anglo. The latter generally—but not always—had more money to spend than his Hispanic counterpart and usually was better educated. Because income and literacy rates provide indirect means to assess opportunities for socioeconomic mobility, data from selected areas can shed light on this aspect of interethnic unions.

In one rural precinct bordering the Tularosa River in southern New Mexico, the average Anglo and Hispanic settler reported modest wealth in 1870. Oral tradition handed down through several generations of Tularosa dwellers affirms that when the area was settled in the 1860s, all the settlers—Anglo and Hispanic alike—were poor. The 1870 census tends to confirm this observation. Although Perfecto Armijo, a local merchant, listed his personal assets at three thousand dollars, the vast majority of Hispanos either failed to declare assets or claimed personal assets below three hundred dollars.

Anglo men living in the precinct who had Spanish-speaking wives tended to have assets in excess of five hundred dollars.[32]

Educational levels in territorial New Mexico were abysmally low; the vast majority of Hispanic men and women could neither read nor write. New Mexican women who formed cross-cultural unions with Anglos generally were slightly better educated than their sisters who married endogamously. Literacy data from Santa Fe in 1870 shows that in Precinct Three, sixty-two percent of women in mixed unions were illiterate compared to eighty-seven percent who married Hispanos. In Precinct Four, the figures were seventy-four percent and eighty-four percent respectively. But a great educational chasm separated men whom Hispanic women chose to marry. Only eight percent of Anglo men who had intermarried in Precinct Three, and nine percent in Precinct Four, were totally or partially illiterate, while the percentages for married Hispanic men were seventy-two percent and sixty-nine percent respectively. If sociologists are correct in citing ability to read and write as an index of power and social standing, it is apparent that women who married into the Anglo community enhanced their opportunity for social and economic mobility.[33]

One prime factor affecting rates of intermarriage was the degree of social contact between members of different ethnic groups. Upper-class Hispanic women were less restricted than their nonelite sisters in seeking opportunities to establish social relationships with Anglo outsiders. From the days of earliest contact, social intercourse was common between Anglo men and the Hispanic elite. They exchanged visits, attended the same parties, and danced at the same bailes. Social life in Santa Fe during territorial days has been described as "a hybrid product" of a joint upper-class society.[34]

Lower-class Spanish-speaking women, nonetheless, had the opportunity to establish social relationships with Anglo newcomers. Small towns adjacent to military posts staged frequent dances where local women fraternized with soldiers. One lonely trooper reported that dances were fine amusements as "the Mexican gals are very gay."[35] Then, too, women employed as camp laundresses had ample opportunity to mingle with the troops. Because there were so many "loose women" hovering around military camps, an order issued during the Civil War stated that only married women be employed as laundresses. At least one Hispanic laundress thereafter entered into a written contract with a soldier that they live together as man and wife, though they were not officially married. Upon being discharged three years later, the soldier tore up the contract, left his "wife," and went off to Texas.[36]

The lives of some military laundresses reflected the easy morality characteristic of Hispanic society that shocked Anglo visitors in early territorial days. Describing New Mexico in the 1850s, U.S. Attorney W. W. H. Davis lamented that "probably there is no other country in the world claiming to be civilized, where vice is more prevalent among all classes of the inhabitants. . . . The standard of female chastity is deplorably low, and the virtuous are far outnumbered by the vicious."[37]

In Hispanic culture, an official system of morality demanded formal marriages, but folk practices accepted informal unions that church and state officials reluctantly tolerated. Moreover, social class shaped standards of morality. A double standard in upper-class society demanded legal marriage and chastity for women but allowed men to keep mistresses and flaunt their sexual prowess. In lower-class society, the double standard merged with folk custom that sanctioned greater sexual freedom for women.[38]

Evidence of informal unions and easy morality is scattered in a number of sources—local legislative records, church documents, census schedules, and military pension files. The territorial legislature occasionally enacted laws that legitimatized the offspring of unmarried parents, as in the case of Juana María Gonzáles and John F. Collins, former territorial Indian superintendent and owner of the *Santa Fe Gazette*.[39] Moreover, local priests recorded in baptismal records that certain children were "natural" rather than legitimate offspring of their parents.[40]

Although researchers must use manuscript census schedules judiciously, these records can provide leads for untangling community attitudes toward sex and morality. The fact that certain enumerators in 1880 described the relationship between the head of household and a woman as husband and wife did not necessarily mean that the two had been formally married. The accuracy of the relationship rested to some degree on the moral perspective of the enumerator. Most enumerators—Anglo and Hispanic alike—made infrequent use of the word "mistress" in defining a woman's relationship to the head of household, but the census taker for the predominantly Anglo mining town of Silver City repeatedly made use of that term, revealing his more puritanical approach to informal unions.[41]

Upon the deaths of military men, wives and other survivors became eligible for federal pensions. In the course of investigating their claims, federal agents recorded personal histories of many Hispanic women, and these files contain rare insights into intimate relations. Testimony by Hispanic women reveals that some had borne children out of wedlock prior to their marriage to Anglo husbands. Felipa Montoya, to cite one example, stated that she had never married prior to her marriage to a soldier in the California Column, although she had given birth to four children; two children shared the same Hispanic natural father, while two different Hispanos fathered the remaining two children.[42]

Several veterans of the California Column entered into common law marriages with Hispanic women after they left the service. One old soldier later stated in a deposition that after the war "it was very common for ex-soldiers and Mexican women to live together years before marriage and in many instances not marry until the law suggested."[43] The Dutchman Linklain Butin of Pinos Altos lived for seven years in such an arrangement with his wife Candelaria, who gave birth to two children during those years. When the old soldier became seriously ill in 1876, he and Candelaria were legally married though Linklain died a few days after the marriage. Several years later, when Candelaria applied for a widow's pension, she testified that "we had all the time we were living together intended to get married but kept putting it off thinking to be married by a Catholic priest[.] But we seldom saw one and we never had any spare money to go to one until finally he was taken sick[.] So we were married while he was on his death bed by the justice of the peace so that our children might not suffer from our failure to do so."[44]

When Butin and other members of the California Column arrived in New Mexico, they discovered a society that differed from theirs in language, customs, and mode of living, and these differences had considerable bearing on the nature of cross-cultural marriages. The traditional center of life in territorial New Mexico was the isolated village with its patron saint standing guard over the health and wealth of the community. Margaret Mead has stated succinctly that "to be Spanish American is to be of a village."[45] It was from the village that an individual gained identity, rather than from a larger national or cultural entity, and an intricate webb of kinship fused village members into a cohesive and supportive folk society.

To be Hispanic American, again quoting Margaret Mead, "is to belong to a familia."[46] Spanish culture valued large families, and in New Mexico extended families, consisting of parents, children, and a wide circle of relatives, were common. The familia did not reside always under the same roof but frequently consisted of several households in proximity that together functioned as a unit.

The Hispanic family was patriarchal in structure; authority of the father—and of the oldest male—was unquestioned. In return, the patriarch owed loyalty to the family and was responsible for its welfare. This paternalistic and authoritarian institution demanded submissiveness in women who were regarded by males as irrational, childlike, and in need of strong discipline. The appropriate role for a woman was as housekeeper and mother because her interests centered on producing children and caring for the family. Although census records reveal that some Hispanic women worked outside the home, chiefly as laundresses, servants, and occasionally as teachers, there was no basic alteration in prescribed sex roles throughout the nineteenth century. Women were family oriented and expected to stay at home.[47]

Despite other differences, Anglo and Hispanic societies were both masculine oriented and each assigned subordinant roles to women. Submissiveness in Hispanic wives suited Anglo men since this behavior was also prescribed in Anglo society. Unfortunately, diaries, letters, and journals written by Hispanic women are rare, making it difficult to assess the impact that interethnic marriages had on Hispanic women. To pose one important question, did marriage to an Anglo male force Spanish-speaking women to alter role expectations? Based on available evidence, the answer apparently is no. The vast majority of Hispanic women who married Anglo men cared for children and households.[48] It should be noted, however, that although Anglo men expected women to be submissive, they also valued women as helpmates and companions. These Anglo-oriented values may have placed subtle pressures on women to modify traditional behavior and indeed may have increased their power and independence.[49]

Although the quality and essence of family life within a cross-cultural marriage cannot be restructured with absolute certainty, it is possible to speculate on what it meant to be an Hispanic woman married to an Anglo man. Interethnic marriages tend to break down cultural differences and to cause partial assimilation of one or both partners into their spouse's society. Researchers have pointed out, however, that ethnic identities are hardy things, difficult to erode, and, certainly, New Mexico proved to be no melting pot.[50] Still, Hispanic women who married Anglo husbands experienced subtle pressures for change that women who married in the traditional manner did not encounter. And although the first foreigners to enter New Mexico in the 1820s may have blended into Hispanic society, newcomers who arrived following annexation toiled to reestablish social institutions and the amenities that they had known in former homes. Rather than being assimilated into Hispanic society, Anglo husbands became agents for social change.

Possibly the greatest strain many women endured in cross-cultural marriages was their physical removal from village and familia. Nineteenth-century American society was extremely mobile; pioneers moved from one section of the country to another to exploit natural resources and to build new careers in distant and oftentimes unsettled regions. Anglo men who migrated to the territory and subsequently married Hispanic women were themselves examples of this mobile society, and their restlessness continued in New Mexico. Their Hispanic wives frequently found themselves in regions distant from former homes when they accompanied husbands to isolated ranches, raw mining camps, and even to regions outside the territory. These women were often separated not only from Hispanic friends and relatives but oftentimes from female companionship as well.

Silver City, which emerged in 1870 as a rough mining camp in southwestern New Mexico, illustrates the isolation all women experienced who followed husbands in their search for quick wealth. When the census was recorded for that year, the camp had a population of eighty people, the overwhelming majority of whom were Anglo males. Two Anglo-American women accompanied their husbands to the mines, while four Hispanic women resided there, one of whom was married to an Anglo miner. Conditions were similar in the nearby mining camp of Ralston where in 1870 six Hispanic women were living with Anglo men in nuclear households. The camp was devoid of Anglo women.[51] In both camps Hispanic women were deprived of the rich religious life and kinship ties that animated and strengthened traditional society.

Some Spanish-speaking wives followed Anglo husbands beyond the borders of the territory. Yeneca Montoya married her Anglo husband in 1865 in the small town of Sapello forty miles east of Santa Fe; at the time of her death thirty-two years later she was living at Tascosa, a lawless town in the Texas Panhandle. Children born to Juana Barela testify to the mobile life that she led following her marriage to miner John Van Order at Silver City in 1879. Her first child was born in Clifton, Arizona, her second in Chihuahua, Mexico, and the following two in El Paso, Texas, and Morenci, Arizona. Juana herself died in 1910 at Solomonville in Arizona territory. Occasionally Hispanic women accompanied their soldier-husbands eastward after leaving the service. Tersita Vigil of Las Cruces, for example, married Capt. Thomas P. Chapman in 1864 and subsequently moved with him to Iowa and then Nebraska where they settled on a homestead. Following his death in the seventies, Tersita returned to New Mexico.[52]

Like other frontier women, Hispanic wives who moved to sparsely populated regions commonly were left to fend for themselves when Anglo husbands were absent for long periods of time. This was true of women who lived in the small agricultural community of Mimbres, some twenty miles northeast of Silver City, since the men of that community frequently journeyed to distant mines or to the county seat to attend district court.[53] Although the town had a total population of 180 in 1870 and had ceased to exist as a viable community by the following decade, its brief history illustrates conditions affecting assimilation in cross-cultural marriages. Mimbres was inhabited in 1870 by fifty adult Hispanic women, forty-three adult Hispanic men, five adult Anglo women, and forty-one adult Anglo men. Fourteen of the latter were married to Hispanic women while five had Anglo wives. Some Mimbres women who had intermarried may have had relatives among the town's Hispanic population, but the large number of Anglos undoubtedly had a stronger Americanizing influence on women of mixed marriages than on those who had married endogamously.[54]

In Mimbres, as elsewhere, the ethnic tendency to congregate meant that Anglo men frequently socialized with other Anglos, and their Hispanic wives therefore came into greater contact with non-Hispanic values. Moreover, at least fourteen Mimbres residents had served in the California Column, and they retained their identity as "Column Men" or "California boys" for the rest of their lives. This unique martial bond strengthened the Anglo community and to some extent neutralized the lack of familial ties among Anglos, as for example, when Helena and John E. Oliphant chose Josiah Hull, a former soldier in the California Column, as a godparent for their youngest son, rather than choosing, say, an Hispanic relative. Moreover, several former soldiers, including Oliphant, persuaded relatives to join them in New Mexico, thus providing further reinforcements for the Americanization of their families.[55]

The ethnic tendency to club together is vividly reflected in settlement patterns as disclosed in manuscript census returns. Census enumerators were instructed to list adjacent households consecutively, and even allowing for errors of omission their tabulations reveal the ethnic composition of a community or district. To cite but one example, about 640 individuals resided in Precinct Four of Lincoln County in 1870. Seventeen were adult Anglo men, ten of whose names are listed seriatim in the census of that year. Of the ten Anglos living in close proximity, five were married to Hispanic women and one to an Anglo woman. Since households in this rural precinct were widely dispersed, Hispanic women in mixed marriages were more likely to have Anglos rather than Hispanos for their nearest neighbors. In addition, the five Anglo-Hispanic families lived in nuclear households, bereft of additional Hispanic relatives who might have counterbalanced the Americanizing influence on Spanish-speaking wives and their children.[56]

Anglos not only settled in proximity, they jointly worked to change New Mexico society so that it more closely resembled that found in more settled portions of the United States. Anglo men married to Spanish-speaking women helped spearhead the drive for public education that arose in the territory in the 1870s and 1880s, although some sent their children east for schooling, a procedure greatly accelerating the process of assimilation. In addition to tax-supported education, Anglo men sponsored public lyceums, organized musical and theatrical events, joined fraternal lodges and veterans organizations—all of which served as vehicles for community improvement as well as forums for political discussion. Clearly, substantial numbers of Anglo men who wed New Mexican women formed primary social and fraternal ties with other Anglos, thereby exerting pressure upon their families to assimilate into

Anglo society. Thus, Hispanic wives frequently participated in fraternal activities organized by their Anglo husbands. By 1890, for example, a ladies' auxiliary of the Grand Army of the Republic had been formed in Las Cruces. All but two of its forty-two members were either Anglo women or Hispanic wives and daughters of Anglo men.[57]

Husbands also placed pressures on Hispanic wives to adopt Anglo-American health practices. One army sergeant stationed at Fort Craig had the post doctor attend his Hispanic wife during pregnancy. When she went to nearby La Mesa to be among her family for final delivery, her husband insisted that the post doctor continue to see her at the family home.[58]

Although large numbers of mixed marriages endured until the death of one partner, some ended in divorce. Divorce was not very common in the Spanish Southwest because of strong religious sanctions against it, and, although no statistical study has been made, available evidence indicates that Hispanic women who married Anglo men were more likely to experience divorce than New Mexico women married within the Hispanic community. Some divorces came after Anglo husbands abandoned their Hispanic wives. Francisca Taylor of Mesilla, for example, was granted a divorce from her husband after the courts judged Robert Taylor guilty of "Cruelty and Abandonment."[59]

A second woman abandoned by her Anglo husband was Rosario Catanach. The daughter of a Kentucky-born father and an Hispanic mother, Rosario had married David Catanach in 1867 at the age of fifteen. Over the next fifteen years, Rosario gave birth to thirteen children, including three pairs of twins. Living in Santa Fe, Rosario experienced a mental breakdown after the premature birth of her last child during the spring of 1881. One son James reported that David deserted his wife a few months after her illness and subsequently went to Lincoln County where he established a ranch. A second son John believed the cause of separation was his father's hard drinking—"he would be drunk for a week at a time"—rather than his mother's breakdown. A third son Archibald felt that the separation was caused by his grandparents; they took Rosario to their home after she became ill, claiming that David was not providing her proper care. Although Catanach was granted a divorce in 1885, he subsequently deeded property he

owned in Santa Fe to Rosario and her children. He later left the
territory and never again saw his children.[60]

If divorce was more common among women who intermarried, so too was the potential for internal stress during times of
ethnic conflict. One of the most notorious lawless episodes in New
Mexico's history involved the Socorro vigilantes who split the town
of Socorro into two armed camps pitting Anglos against Hispanos.
In 1880 Socorro was a thriving community of about 1300 people
located on the Rio Grande seventy miles south of Albuquerque.
Gold and silver had been discovered in nearby mountains, and the
town was full of prospectors and drifters looking for new
opportunities.

The tragedy that led to violent ethnic conflict occurred Christmas Eve 1880 when three brothers by the name of Baca, nephews
of the leading Hispanic merchant in the city, killed the editor of
the local newspaper. The machinery of the law was in the hands of
Hispanos, who backed the powerful Baca family in protecting the
brothers. Subsequently, a vigilante group was formed by Anglo
members of the community, headed by Col. E. W. Eaton, veteran
of the Civil War who was himself married to an Hispanic woman.
The vigilantes held daily meetings, and membership became prac-
tically compulsory for Anglos of any standing in the community.
The 1880 census for Socorro lists the names of 109 Anglo men, ten
of whom were married to Anglo women and sixteen married to
Hispanos. Unfortunately a complete vigilante membership list is
unavailable so that it becomes difficult to assess the impact of Hispanic wives on vigilante membership. The fact that Colonel Eaton
led the vigilantes, however, indicates that ethnic loyalties of Hispanic wives had minimal effect in determining actions of their Anglo husbands. But undoubtedly ethnic conflict placed a terrible strain
upon Hispanic women and their children.[61]

Despite conflicts and tensions, marriage to an Anglo started
the process of assimilation for Spanish-speaking women and their
off-spring. The degree of Americanization that occurred varied according to local circumstances and personalities of husband and wife.
Some wives adopted an Anglo mode of living but retained Spanish customs, becoming bicultural in the process. Others took up
certain external features of American culture but, for all intents and
purposes, remained wedded to the traditional folk society.[62]

Scarcity of literary and oral sources, however, complicates efforts to understand the process of assimilation, and manuscript census schedules, though revealing much about household organization and residential practices, shed very little light on the degree to which individuals have accepted an alien culture. One key to the assimilation process rests with the second generation. What happened to the children of mixed marriages? Hispanic influences were undoubtedly great in early years of childhood, as parents generally had children baptized in the Roman Catholic Church and selected godparents from Hispanic friends and relatives. In many instances, households included one or more members of the mother's family.[63] At the same time, however, children underwent a variety of experiences that aided assimilation into Anglo society. Spanish was not universally spoken in the home, and it is probable that many children of mixed unions learned English as their first language.[64] Also helping to assimilate children into their father's ethnic group were attendance at schools, visits by Anglo relatives, and the presence of English-speaking neighbors.[65]

Choice of marriage partners by the second generation no doubt strengthened identification with either the mother's or the father's ethnic group. After sifting through countless marriage and baptismal records, one discovers that no single pattern emerged in New Mexico, as it did in San Antonio, relative to marriage patterns among children of Anglo-Hispanic unions. The majority of children born of intercultural marriages who can be traced in church and civil records in one county—Doña Ana—married into Hispanic society. This appears to be true of upper-class children as well as those born into families of modest means.[66] However, variations are many.

Children of mixed marriages frequently married individuals who were themselves the products of cross-cultural unions, while numerous families of mixed ancestry had sons and daughters who married into each of the ethnic groups. María Silva and David Wood of Las Cruces, for example, produced at least one daughter who married an Hispano as well as a son and a daughter who each married offspring of mixed unions. Francisca Lujan and Henry Cuniffe, on the other hand, raised at least three daughters who married Anglos, while a fourth daughter married the Hispanic sheriff of Las Cruces. In few families did all sons and daughters marry into Anglo society, whereas several families can be located whose children married entirely within the Hispanic ethnic group.[67]

Cross-cultural marriages occurred in all areas of the Southwest, bringing changes to the lives of many Hispanic women and accelerating the rate of Americanization. A decade ago, a prominent scholar challenged western historians to focus their research on the meeting of cultures in the West, to analyze and define the dynamic interaction between different peoples, as a means of providing new and fruitful insights into the settlement of the American West.[68] To understand fully the role that mixed unions played in this process, detailed studies for each major settlement area are needed. In addition, oral histories must be collected from families resulting from intermarriages. In this manner it may be possible to develop clearer perceptions of the quality of mixed marriages and to assess more carefully the tensions placed on Hispanic women who entered such unions.

Scholars generally agree that by the beginning of the twentieth century some degree of Americanization had been experienced throughout the Spanish Southwest. As one recent interpreter of this region has stated, "by a process of accretion, American ways made inroads."[69] When further studies of mixed unions are completed, it will probably be apparent that these marriages played a significant role in this process and that the New Mexico experience was reflected in varying degrees throughout the Southwest.

Notes

1. See Rodman W. Paul, "The Spanish-Americans in the Southwest, 1848–1900," in *The Frontier Challenge: Responses to the Trans-Mississippi West,* ed. John G. Clark (Lawrence: University of Kansas Press, 1971), 32–34. The best overviews of Hispanic societies in the Southwest, emphasizing their diversity, are Carey McWilliams, *North from Mexico: The Spanish-Speaking People of the United States* (New York: Greenwood Press, 1968); Matt S. Meier and Feliciano Rivera, *The Chicanos, A History of Mexican-Americans* (New York: Hill and Wang, 1972); Paul, "The Spanish-Americans in the Southwest."

2. See for example Leo Grebler, Joan W. Moore, and Ralph Guzman, *The Mexican American People: The Nation's Second Largest Minority* (New York: Free Press, 1970), 405–6; Frank G. Mittelbach, Joan W. Moore, and Ronald McDaniel, *Intermarriage of Mexican-Americans,* Mexican-

American Study Project, No. 6 (Los Angeles: University of California, 1966), 1, 5. Quote is from Husuf Dadabhay, "Circuitous Assimilation Among Rural Hindustanis in California," *Social Forces* 33 (December 1954): 141. Although there are many definitions for the term assimilation, here it means to become more like the contact group.

3. Mittelbach, Moore, and McDaniel, *Intermarriage,* 45.

4. Few studies have been completed on intermarriage in the nineteenth century. Most sociologists have focused their research on twentieth-century intermarriages. But see conference paper by Richard M. Bernard, "Intermarriage Patterns Among Immigrants and Natives of Wisconsin, 1850–1920" (paper presented at the Ninth Annual Conference on Social-Political History, 1976).

5. Jane Dysart, "Mexican Women in San Antonio, 1830–1860: The Assimilation Process," *Western Historical Quarterly* 7 (October 1976): 370–72. Such was not the case in rural and isolated regions along the lower Rio Grande, however, where, according to Jovita Gonzáles, descendants of Anglo-Hispanic families attended school in Mexico and merged into Hispanic culture. Jovita Gonzáles, "Social Life in Cameron, Starr, and Zapata Counties" (Master's Thesis, University of Texas, Austin, 1930), 69–70.

6. James Officer, "Historical Factors in Inter Ethnic Relations in the Community of Tucson," *Arizoniana* 1 (Fall 1960): 13–14. For a recent study of intermarriage in northern New Mexico that stresses the fact that intermarriages contributed to, or were signs of, amiable relations between Hispanos and Anglos, see Rebecca McDowell Craver, *The Impact of Intimacy: Mexican-Anglo Intermarriage in New Mexico, 1821–1846,* Southwestern Studies, No. 66 (El Paso: Texas Western Press, 1982).

7. McWilliams, *North from Mexico,* 90.

8. McWilliams, *North from Mexico,* 90–91; Leonard Pitt, *The Decline of the Californios: A Social History of the Spanish-Speaking Californians, 1846–1890* (Berkeley & Los Angeles: University of California Press, 1966) 110, 125.

9. Pitt, *Decline of the Californios,* 267–68.

10. McWilliams, *North from Mexico,* 52. Estimates of the number of Hispanos in the Southwest may need to be refined. See Oscar J. Martínez, "On the Size of the Chicano Population: New Estimates, 1850–1900," *Aztlan* 6 (Spring 1975): 43–67.

11. Robert W. Larson, *New Mexico's Quest for Statehood, 1846–1912* (Albuquerque: University of New Mexico [UNM] Press, 1968), 71.

12. James M. Lacy, "New Mexican Women in Early American Writings," *New Mexico Historical Review* [NMHR] 34 (January 1959): 50; Ralph Emerson Twitchell, *The Leading Facts of New Mexican History,* 5 vols. (Ce-

dar Rapids, Iowa: Torch Press, 1912), 2:273, 391. María Ignacia Jaramillo was the common-law wife of Charles Bent.

13. Paul, "Spanish Americans," 36. Communities in northern New Mexico lacked class stratification, however, and were characterized by equalitarian relations among residents. See Paul Kutche, ed., *The Survival of Spanish American Villages,* The Colorado College Studies, No. 15 (Colorado Springs: Colorado College, 1979), 15–17.

14. For a summary of the political and economic development of New Mexico until statehood, see Howard R. Lamar, *The Far Southwest, 1846–1912: A Territorial History* (New York: W. W. Norton and Co., 1970).

15. Darlis A. Miller, "A Civil War Legacy: Californians in New Mexico" (Ph.D. dissertation, UNM, 1977), 60.

16. Lamar, *Far Southwest,* 107.

17. Miller, "Civil War Legacy," 19. Oral history records that shortly after American takeover (and presumably after the Taos uprising of January 1847), relations between the people of Taos and Anglo soldiers were very friendly because the Americans provided protection against hated Indian raiders. "Then it was that many friendships were begun which resulted in the marriage of some of these soldiers with Spanish families, making for mutual appreciation" (Lorin W. Brown, *Hispano Folklife of New Mexico: The Lorin W. Brown Federal Writers' Project Manuscripts* [Albuquerque: UNM Press, 1978], 64).

18. Dysart, "Mexican Women," 367–68.

19. Beverly Trulio, "Anglo-American Attitudes Toward New Mexican Women," *Journal of the West* 12 (April 1973): 299–39; W. W. H. Davis, *El Gringo: or New Mexico and Her People* (1857; reprint ed., New York: Arno Press, 1973), 221–22.

20. Miller, "Civil War Legacy," 38–39.

21. Lacy, "New Mexican Women," 41. See also Robert C. and Eleanor R. Carriker, eds., *An Army Wife on the Frontier: The Memoirs of Alice Blackwood Baldwin, 1867–1877* (Salt Lake City: University of Utah Library, 1975), 59; Martha Summerhayes, *Vanished Arizona: Recollections of the Army Life of a New England Woman* (Glorieta, N. Mex.: Rio Grande Press, 1970), 144.

22. Francisco Terán, "The Conquistadors' Ladies," *Américas* 28 (February 1976): 12–18; Jack D. Forbes, "Black Pioneers: The Spanish-Speaking Afroamericans of the Southwest," *Phylon* 27 (Fall 1966): 233–46.

23. Carolyn Zeleny, *Relations Between the Spanish-Americans and Anglo-Americans in New Mexico: A Study of Conflict and Accommodation in a Dual-Ethnic Situation* (New York: Arno Press, 1974), 319; Tibo Chavez, "Colonel Jose Francisco Chavez, 1833–1904," *Rio Grande History* 8 (1978): 7.

24. U.S., Department of Commerce, Bureau of the Census, *Tenth*

Census of The United States, 1880, Grant County, New Mexico, Population Schedules, National Archives (NA) Microfilm No. T 9, reel 1.

25. Nancie L. González, *The Spanish-Americans of New Mexico: A Heritage of Pride* (Albuquerque: UNM Press, 1967), 80. Recent scholarship states erroneously that "intermarriage was not a common phenomenon, but rather restricted to marriages between *ricos* and Anglos designed to serve their common economic and political interests" (Alvin R. Sunseri, "Anglo Attitudes Toward Hispanos, 1846–1861," *Journal of Mexican American History* 3 [1973]: 77).

26. Thirty-three Anglo males resided in Las Cruces in 1870; eighteen were married to Hispanic women, and two were married to Anglo women. In 1880 sixty-one Anglo males resided there; eighteen were married to Hispanic women, and eight to Anglo women. Thirty-eight Anglo males resided in Mesilla in 1870; nineteen were married to Hispanic women, and four to Anglo women. Ten years later, sixty Anglo males resided in Mesilla; twelve were married to Hispanos, and twelve to Anglos. In 1870 eleven Anglo males lived in the village of Doña Ana; seven were married to Hispanic women, and two had married Anglo women. In 1880 six Anglo males lived in Doña Ana; four were married to Hispanic women, but none was married to an Anglo. U.S., Department of Commerce, Bureau of the Census, *Ninth Census of the United States, 1870,* Doña Ana County, New Mexico, Population Schedules, NA, Microfilm Publication 593, reel 1; *Tenth Census, 1880,* Doña Ana County. Mixed marriages were identified by place of birth in conjunction with surnames of spouses.

27. *Ninth Census, 1870,* Santa Fe County, reel 4; *Ninth Census, 1870,* Grant County, reel 1; *Tenth Census, 1880,* Grant County, reel 1.

28. John D. Oliphant and Patrick Higgins, Pension Application Files, Civil War Series, Records of the Veterans Administration, Record Group (RG) 15, NA; Arrell Morgan Gibson, *The Life and Death of Colonel Albert Jennings Fountain* (Norman: University of Oklahoma Press, 1965), 23.

29. Miller, "Civil War Legacy," 338.

30. Lycurgus D. Fuller, Pension Applicaiton Files, RG 15, NA.

31. For occupations of men who intermarried, see entries for New Mexico in the 1870 and 1880 census. For women mentioned in this paragraph, see respectively Pension Application Files for Henry C. Brown, Allen Buchanan, Henry Hays, and Joseph D. Emerson, RG 15, NA. During the 1860s, Vincenta Fresquez escaped from peonage to live with an Anglo soldier in Las Cruces. She was later arrested by the sheriff of Doña Ana County and returned to her master, Cristobal Ascarate of Mesilla, to repay a debt contracted by her mother. Ascarate forced Vincenta to work with a chain fastened to her leg (Testimony of Sergeant John W. Carey, 20 April 1864 and Testimony of Vincenta Fresquez, 21 April 1864, Let-

116 *Darlis A. Miller*

ters Received by the Office of the Adjutant General, Main Series, 1861–1870, RG 94, NA Microfilm Publication M-619, roll 284).

32. *Ninth Census, 1870,* Lincoln County, precinct four, reel 2.

33. But see Harvey J. Graff, *The Literacy Myth: Literacy and Social Structure in the Nineteenth-Century City* (New York: Academic Press, 1979). Percentages were computed from data recorded for precincts three and four, Santa Fe County (*Ninth Census, 1870*).

34. Zeleny, *Relations Between the Spanish-Americans and Anglo-Americans,* 315. For a good discussion of conditions affecting rates of intermarriage, see Robert K. Merton, "Intermarriage and the Social Structure: Fact and Theory," in *The Blending American: Patterns of Intermarriage,* ed. Milton L. Barron (Chicago: Quadrangle Books, 1972), 15.

35. Ernest Marchand, ed., *News From Fort Craig, New Mexico, 1863: Civil War Letters of Andrew Ryan, with the First California Volunteers* (Santa Fe: Stagecoach Press, 1966), 72.

36. Henry Hays, Pension Application Files, RG 15, NA. Laundresses and their soldier-husbands lived in a highly stratified military society. A wide gulf separated commissioned officers from all other military personnel, and this caste system extended to wives and children. Because of the nature of their work, Anglo and Hispanic laundresses at frontier posts had ample opportunity for social intercourse, and social isolation from officers' wives generated a unique female world where ethnic differences had less impact than social class.

37. Davis, *El Gringo,* 220–21.

38. Woodrow Borah and Sherburne F. Cook, "Marriage and Legitimacy in Mexican Culture: Mexico and California," *California Law Review* 54 (May 1966): 960–61.

39. "An Act for the Legitimation of Juana Francisca Collins, daughter of John F. Collins and Juana Maria Gonzales," 25 December 1869, Records of the Territorial Legislative Assembly, Territorial Archives of New Mexico [TANM], State Records Center and Archives [SRCA], Santa Fe, reel 4.

40. Baptismal Books, San Albino Church, Mesilla, N. Mex.

41. *Tenth Census, 1880,* Grant County, reel 1.

42. Allen Buchanan, Pension Application Files, RG 15, NA.

43. Linklain Butin, Pension Application Files, RG 15, NA.

44. Linklain Butin, Pension Application Files, RG 15, NA. A former private in the California volunteers declared that he had three natural children by an Hispanic woman whom he later married after obtaining a divorce from his previous wife. See Edwin L. Elwood, Pension Application Files, RG 15, NA.

45. Margaret Mead, ed., *Cultural Patterns and Technical Change* (New York: New American Library, 1955), 152.

46. Mead, *Cultural Patterns,* 153.

47. For discussion of Hispanic families, see Mead, *Cultural Patterns,* 153–57; Dysart, "Mexican Women," 366–67; R. Griswold del Castillo, "La Familia Chicana: Social Changes in the Chicano Family of Los Angeles, 1850–1880," *Journal of Ethnic Studies* 3 (Spring 1975): 42–43; Robert Staples, "The Mexican-American Family: Its Modification Over Time and Space," *Phylon* 32 (Summer 1971): 179–92. For a more optimistic view of women's independence, see Janet Lecompte, "The Independent Women of Hispanic New Mexico, 1821–1846," *Western Historical Quarterly* 12 (January 1981): 17–35.

48. This conclusion is based on pension application files of the California veterans who married Hispanic women as well as census returns for counties of Doña Ana, Grant, Lincoln, Santa Fe, and Socorro.

49. For corroboration of this point in the field of literature, see Cecil Robinson, *With the Ears of Strangers: The Mexican in American Literature* (Tucson: University of Arizona Press, 1963), 84, 93.

50. Ithiel de Sola Pool, "Plural Society in the Southwest: A Comparative Perspective," in *Plural Society in the Southwest,* ed. Edward H. Spicer and Raymond H. Thompson (Albuquerque: UNM Press, 1972), 323; Marc Simmons, *New Mexico: A Bicentennial History* (New York: W. W. Norton and Co., 1977), 164.

51. *Ninth Census, 1870,* Grant County, reel 1. Ralston had a population of 174, which included eighteen Hispanic men and eleven Hispanic women (six of the latter were married to Anglos).

52. For women mentioned in this paragraph, see the Pension Application Files of Theodore Briggs, John Van Order, and Thomas P. Chapman, RG 15, NA.

53. See for example, John E. Oliphant, Pension Application Files, RG 15, NA. Oliphant, who was living in Mimbres with his wife Helena Martinez in 1870, had been gone a month prospecting and working in the mines at Ralston before he returned home and subsequently died of an unknown illness.

54. *Ninth Census, 1870,* Grant County, reel 1.

55. John E. Oliphant, Pension Application Files, RG 15, NA. Oliphant's children were sent east to live with Anglo relatives after their father's death.

56. *Ninth Census, 1870,* Lincoln County, reel 2.

57. Miller, "Civil War Legacy," 339–43, 346–51; Phil Sheridan Post Day Book, Grand Army of the Republic, p. 41, Branigan Library, Las Cruces, N. Mex. It has not been possible to identify the ethnic origin of all auxilliary women married to Anglo men.

58. See statement of Robert A. Christian, 19 March 1866, Southern District of New Mexico, Department of New Mexico, Records of the

United States Army Continental Commands, 1821–1920, RG 393, NA.

59. Civil and Criminal Records (1878–1881), Doña Ana County Records, Doña Ana County, N. Mex., 339.

60. David N. Catanach, Pension Application Files, RG 15, NA; Civil and Criminal Records (1884–1885), Doña Ana County Records, 45; Deed Book R, Santa Fe County Records, SRCA, 410.

61. *Tenth Census, 1880,* Socorro County, reel 3; Chester D. Potter, "Reminiscences of the Socorro Vigilantes," ed. by Paige W. Christiansen, NMHR 40 (January 1965): 23–54. Eventually, one Baca brother was hanged by the vigilantes, one was killed trying to escape jail, and one was acquitted in a court of law.

62. Margarita Romero, "descendant of the great dons of Spanish New Mexico," who married Robert Taylor, a young railroad engineer, exemplifies those Hispanic women who functioned effectively in both Anglo and Hispanic cultures (George Fitzpatrick, "Doña Margarita: Symbol of Lifestyle Now Gone," *Albuquerque Journal,* 14 November 1976. This is not the same Robert Taylor who abandoned his wife.). Dolores Fields and Alvina Walters of Tularosa, on the other hand, are examples of those women who remained tied to traditional Hispanic culture (Interview with Antonio Candelaria, 31 May 1977, Las Cruces, N. Mex.).

63. See *Ninth Census, 1870,* and *Tenth Census, 1880;* Baptismal Books, San Albino Church, Mesilla, N. Mex.

64. See family history compiled by Arthur R. Gurule, December 1977, New Mexico State University (in possession of the author); Brown, *Hispano Folklife,* 8.

65. Census records for the city of Las Cruces indicate that the majority of school-age children of mixed marriages were attending school (*Ninth Census, 1870,* Doña Ana County, reel 1, and *Tenth Census, 1880,* Doña Ana County, reel 1).

66. In addition to sources already cited, the following were utilized in tracing cross-cultural marriages in Doña Ana County: Doña Ana County Church Records (Marriages and Baptisms), Microfilm Collection, Church of Jesus Christ of Latter-day Saints, Salt Lake City, Utah; Marriage Records, 1870–1921, Doña Ana County Records.

67. Diversity characterized marriage patterns in the third generation as well. Grandchildren of mixed unions on occasion married into the opposite ethnic group as did their own mother or father, the offspring of the original mixed union. Leopoldo Reinhard of German extraction, for example, married Francisca Montes; their daughter May wed Horace Hickerson, also of German descent. The Hickerson's daughter Pauline subsequently married Felipe López. But the reverse also occurred. A son of Mariana Pérez and Albert J. Fountain wed an Hispano, while a child of this new union married into the Anglo community.

68. Jack D. Forbes, "Frontiers in American History and the Role of the Frontier Historian," *Ethnohistory* 15 (Spring 1968): 203–35.

69. Simmons, *New Mexico,* 164.

Mimbres bowl depicts woman carrying wood, ca. 1000, Mimbres Valley, southwestern New Mexico. (Courtesy E. L. Bowen, Bowen Collection, *Maxwell Museum, University of New Mexico, Albuquerque, New Mexico.*)

Carrying water at Santo Domingo pueblo, 1848. Etching from W.H. Emory, *Notes of a Military Reconnaissance, from Fort Leavenworth, in Missouri, to San Diego, in California* (New York: Long, 1848).

Theresita Suaso returning from the river with a tub of laundry, wearing a low-cut blouse, short skirt, and rebosa, 1853. Watercolor by Alexander Barclay. (*Courtesy Bancroft Library, University of California, Berkeley, California.*)

Susan McSween Barber, Lincoln County rancher. *(Special Collections, University of Arizona Library, Tucson, Arizona.)*

Living in a *jacal* near Las Cruces, 1900. *(Rio Grande Historical Collections, New Mexico State University Library, Las Cruces, New Mexico.)*

Dance at Fort Stanton, ca. 1880. *(Rio Grande Historical Collections, New Mexico State University Library, Las Cruces, New Mexico.)*

Apache on the Mescalero Reservation, ca. 1889. *(Rio Grande Collections, New Mexico State University Library, Las Cruces, New Mexico.)*

Women of the Amador Family, Las Cruces, ca. 1900. *(Rio Grande Historical Collections, New Mexico State University Library, Las Cruces, New Mexico.)*

Maud Frost Otero and Miguel Otero, Jr. Otero was the son of an Anglo mother and Hispanic father; Maud Frost was his second Anglo wife. *(Special Collections Department, University of New Mexico General Library, Albuquerque, New Mexico.)*

Refugee Mexicanas at El Paso, 1911. *(Rio Grande Historical Collections, New Mexico State University Library, Las Cruces, New Mexico.)*

Hondale Tomato Cannery, Luna County, ca. 1920. *(Deming-Luna Mimbres Museum, Luna County Historical Society, Deming, New Mexico.).*

Nina Otero-Warren campaigning, 1923. *(Bergere Family Collection, Photo No. 21252, New Mexico State Records Center and Archives, Santa Fe, New Mexico.)*

Navajo at Laguna Pueblo, ca. 1935. *(Photo by T. Harmon Parkhurst, Museum of New Mexico, Santa Fe, New Mexico.)*

Winnowing in Chimayo, ca. 1920. *(Prudence Clark Collection, Menaul Historical Library, Albuquerque, New Mexico.)*

Threshing grain with goats, near Santa Fe, ca. 1920. *(Museum of New Mexico, Santa Fe, New Mexico.)*

Drying chile, Chamita, ca. 1940. *(Museum of New Mexico, Santa Fe, New Mexico.)*

Firing pottery, Acoma Pueblo. *(Museum of New Mexico, Santa Fe, New Mexico.)*

Plastering adobe. *(Photo by Mildred Crews, Museum of New Mexico, Santa Fe, New Mexico.)*

Paring fruit, Roswell, New Mexico. *(Rio Grande Historical Collections, New Mexico State University Library, Las Cruces, New Mexico.)*

Two women on their homestead, San Augustine Plains, 1939. *(Rio Grande Historical Collections, New Mexico State University Library, Las Cruces, New Mexico.)*

Gina Allen drives tractor on Las Cruces family dairy in the 1940s. *(Rio Grande Historical Collections, New Mexico State University Library, Las Cruces, New Mexico.)*

"Family under rainbow," gum bichromate print on fabric with added stitching, 1971, 16" x 20", by Betty Hahn. *(Photo courtesy of the artist.)*

"Chicago Family: Aunt," polacolor II, 1979, 20" x 24", by Betty hahn. *(Photo courtesy of the artist.)*

Carmen Freudenthal (center) leads Las Cruces women in campaign for property rights with puppet show, 1958. *(Rio Grande Historical Collections, New Mexico State University Library, Las Cruces, New Mexico.)*

⇐ 5 ⇒

Foragers,
Army Women,
and Prostitutes

Darlis A. Miller

For many years, scholars ignored the role of women in the history of the American West. It seemed easy to justify this omission by pointing out that women, after all, were not fur trappers, miners, explorers, cowboys, merchants, military commanders, politicians, railroad builders, or Indian traders, and therefore presumably unessential in developing the West.[1] Indeed, traditional western histories have focused upon male-dominated industries and institutions, such as the open range cattle industry and the frontier army. Several scholarly books in fact document the importance of the Army in settling the West; many record the heroics and pathos of troopers and warriors engaged in deadly wars. A few articles and monographs have even been written about army dependents and female camp followers, but, for the most part, the story of the frontier army is told from the perspective of its officers and enlisted men.

Social historians are fortunate that some frontier soldiers spent their working hours copying a seemingly endless stream of letters and orders into post and district letterbooks that are now housed in public archives. By carefully reading military records, it is possible to describe experiences of western women that heretofore have remained hidden from view. The records show, for example, that

New Mexico women made direct economic contributions to the frontier army as independent forage agents and as partners in family-operated agencies. The records also reveal important dimensions of military society that officers and their wives skimmed over or omitted in their memoirs and diaries. Despite differences in class and race, for example, all garrison women lived in a highly regulated military society where they were expected to observe codes of conduct appropriate to their rank. Servants and laundresses, as well as officers' wives, who violated these codes were ejected from military posts. Moreover, sexuality was a constant source of tension in these communities where men far outnumbered women. The tremendous sex imbalance, in fact, may explain why the nineteenth-century ideal of the "lady" played such a powerful role in military society. According to this concept, true ladies were pious, pure, submissive, domestic, and essentially asexual.[2] This ideal image of ladies served at least two functions on army posts: it reinforced perceived differences in class (so essential to proper functioning of the army), and it created an invisible shield around officers' wives to deflect sexual advances and protect them from aggression.

By focusing upon women, then, much can be learned about the military and about nineteenth-century society in general. To further our understanding of women's roles in relation to the army, this chapter will examine women's contributions as government forage agents and then focus upon women as members of the garrison-communities in which officers and enlisted men lived their daily lives.

Even though civilian forage agencies figured prominently in the army's western operations, few historians have discussed their importance and no one has recognized that—in New Mexico at least—the agencies were primarily family enterprises, the wife's contributions being as important as those of her husband. Because the army traveled widely throughout the territory, the quartermaster's department contracted with civilians to establish agencies along well-traveled roads as well as in isolated regions where government animals could be fed and sheltered and where officers and enlisted men could find accommodations. Army officials regarded agencies as crucial to operations in the field. Small detachments of troops frequently left posts at a moment's notice, and their success against Indian foes depended upon speed, which in turn depended upon agents furnishing a steady supply of forage for army animals.[3]

A quartermaster's circular issued in 1869 listed some of the duties and responsibilities of agents. They were required to furnish forage "in such quantities as may be needed," receiving in exchange one and three-fourths cents per pound for hay and four to six cents per pound for corn, oats, and barley, depending upon the location of their agencies. They were required to furnish without further remuneration meals to expressmen, corrals for government animals, and fuel to army teamsters and small detachments of soldiers. They were also required to furnish bed and board for officers who stopped at their stations "upon reasonable charges to the said Officers."[4] In addition, the army expected agents to promote the general interest of the United States by protecting government property, recovering stolen or stray animals, taking care of sick animals and indisposed government employees, providing soldiers and employees with means of cooking their meals, and circulating supply advertisements for the quartermaster's department.[5]

The number and location of agencies in New Mexico varied from year to year depending upon military strategies, but most villages on well-traveled roads claimed at least one. Between Fort Craig and Albuquerque, for example, agencies were established in San Antonio, Socorro, Lemitar, Sabinal, Belen, and Los Lunas. New Mexicans competed fiercely and went to considerable expense to secure agencies by building new corrals and comfortable quarters for men and officers, digging wells to provide water, and stockpiling grain and hay.[6] Although it is no longer possible to determine their annual profits, the records show that some agents received substantial incomes during months of intense troop activity. John Ward, agent at San Antonio in Socorro County, received over three hundred dollars for forage fed to public animals during June and July of 1872, and Ramon López, agent at San José in the Fort Union forage district, was paid nearly five hundred dollars for forage issued in December 1874 and January 1875.[7] Indeed, these sums were only a small part of the money that the army pumped into the local economy through these agencies. During a seven-month period ending 30 June 1876, the chief quartermaster requested $49,000 for purchasing fuel and forage from government agents.[8] And the army considered the agencies sufficiently important to investigate carefully complaints of inadequate compensation. At times when grain and fuel became scarce in New Mexico, the quartermaster frequently increased rates to prevent agents from resigning.[9]

The majority of government agents in New Mexico were married men, who in partnership with wives provided services requested by the quartermaster's department.[10] Some men supported their applications for agencies by stating they were family men and thus able to provide better accommodations for officers and their families. Moses Sachs of Belen stated succinctly: "Having a family, I can keep the agency more comfortable for others."[11] Other government documents testify to the value of "women's work" in maintaining a successful agency. Louis Trauer, a single man, resigned his agency in Los Lunas when he found it impossible to employ a cook. Although some wealthy married agents, such as Tularosa resident Patrick Coghlan, hired male cooks, most relied upon the culinary talents of their wives to accommodate military officers and government employees. That the army recognized the importance of the women is clearly revealed in a letter written by army surgeon William B. Lyon supporting the application of Martin L. Hickey for the agency at Mesilla. Hickey himself had been unwell for several months, but Lyon believed that Mrs. Hickey—whom he described as "a notable housewife"—would successfully manage the agency. "Mrs. Hickey sets an excellent table," he noted, "and is now possessed of every facility for accommodating guests and animals."[12]

Several married forage agents also managed hotels, and their wives contributed to both enterprises. Typical of couples who operated both hotels and agencies were Socorro residents Desideria and Joseph Kinsinger. A native New Mexican, Desideria was about thirty-six years old with a twelve-year-old daughter living at home at the time Joseph obtained the agency. In Colfax County, Mary and W. W. Boggs ran a boarding house in conjunction with their government agency. Although Mary had no children residing at home, she kept busy providing services to transient military personnel and thirteen male boarders.[13] Some women, like Dolores Duper of Las Cruces, acquired the necessary skills to carry on these businesses after the death of their spouses. Duper reopened the Montezuma Hotel in 1884 following her husband's death and after having "every room thoroughly cleaned, whitened, and put in perfect order." She offered her guests modest terms, an excellent table, and convenient corral accommodations. By late the following year she was listed among Doña Ana County's wealthiest taxpayers.[14]

At least a dozen New Mexican women, most of whom were widows carrying on family enterprises, acquired agencies in their own names. Quartermaster officers appeared quite willing to designate widows as agents, possibly because they knew from previous business transactions that the women would provide the necessary services. Louisa Frenger, who was appointed agent in Socorro in 1877 after the death of her husband, received endorsement by the quartermaster at Fort Craig, who wrote: "Mrs. Frenger will no doubt keep as good a station in the future as she has done heretofore and her appointment as agent is strongly recommended."[15]

Agencies were awarded to women whenever their appointments appeared to be advantageous for the army, as in the case involving Martin and Ellen Koslowski, who owned a ranch on the Santa Fe Trail twenty-seven miles from Santa Fe. During the Civil War, their house and property had served as a hospital for Union troops following the battle at Glorieta Pass. After the couple separated in 1877, the quartermaster revoked Martin's appointment as forage agent, replacing him with Ellen who retained possession of the house and corrals.[16]

Among widows with some prior experience in managing hotels and agencies were Augustina Castillo Davis, Josefa Ortiz de Clark, and Esther Martin, whose husbands had entered New Mexico during the Civil War with the California Column. Upon being discharged, the men soon married and together with their wives they established hotels and government forage agencies—the Davises in Mesilla, the Clarks in Plaza Alcalde, and the Martins at Aleman on the Jornada del Muerto.[17] Newspaper articles hint at active involvement of all three women in these family enterprises. Upon being widowed in the seventies, Augustina, who was in her thirties and childless, Josepha, twenty-five with at least one child, and Esther, thirty-nine with five children, were named government forage agents and each continued to own and operate a hotel. Josefa Clark retained her agency for two years after the death of her husband, Louis, but upon marrying José Salazar in 1878 she requested that government transactions thereafter be made in the name of her husband. Consequently Salazar was appointed agent at Plaza Alcalde in place of Josepha.[18]

Esther Martin received more attention from the territorial press than any other female forage agent. These contemporary accounts document the working partnership that existed between Esther and her more famous husband Jack leading to their financial success. In 1867, they moved to Aleman, a resting spot midway on the Jornada. The following year Jack successfully sank a well on their property, thus providing much needed water to travelers on the overland road between Santa Fe and Mesilla. It was this feat that earned him the sobriquet "King of the Jornada" and the gratitude of territorial boosters and travelers. At Aleman the Martins operated a hotel, a stage station, a government forage agency, a post office, a dairy, and a small cattle ranch.[19] The Las Cruces *Borderer* noted in 1872 that Esther's "skill as a housewife had made Jack Martin's station on the Jornada famous for its excellent meals and clean soft beds." Another newspaper reported that she had sole charge of the dairy. Like many agencies, however, Martin's was located in a dangerous area, and in January 1872 the family temporarily moved to nearby Fort McRae fearing an Indian attack.[20]

The Martins expanded their business enterprise in 1876 when they purchased the popular Exchange Hotel in Santa Fe, leaving the Aleman property in the hands of a resident-manager. Jack died suddenly a year later. In lamenting his passing the local press gave credit to both Jack and Esther for the success of their hotel. Esther remained briefly in Santa Fe as proprietress of the Exchange but soon returned to Aleman to manage the ranch and forage agency. When she left Aleman permanently to take up residence in Mesilla in 1881, the Santa Fe *Daily New Mexican* described her as "probably the best known woman in New Mexico."[21]

Like Esther Martin, Ellen Casey was an experienced businesswoman by the time she became a forage agent following the death of her husband Robert in 1875. Together they had established a ranch on the Rio Hondo in Lincoln County, and prior to his death Ellen handled some official correspondence relating to his government agency. Ellen ran the agency in her own name for at least four years, and like many other agents she agreed in 1877 to supply forage and fuel to the army on credit while congressmen debated passage of an army appropriation bill.[22]

For other women, running a forage agency was their first venture into the world of business. This was true for Gertrude Hobby, who prior to the 1880 census had moved from Texas to San Lorenzo in Grant County with her husband A. M. Hobby and her two teenage sons by a previous marriage. A. M. Hobby died soon after being named a forage agent, and Gertrude in April 1881 notified the chief quartermaster in Santa Fe that she was ready to carry on the business. Somewhat apologetically she added: "Pardon this very unofficial letter as I am ignorant in such matters, this being my first attempt at business of any kind."[23] There was nothing apologetic or timid, however, about the way she managed the agency. She received nearly three hundred dollars for forage issued during May and June, but when business subsequently declined she wrote to military authorities claiming that so few military trains stopped at her agency that it did not afford her a living "at the price we pay for our supplies." She therefore boldly requested permission to purchase subsistence stores from the army, a privilege many sought but few received. "As Government agents are we not working for the government," she asked, "and thus would we not be entitled to buy our supplies from the Commissary?"[24] The records do not reveal whether her request was granted.

Like most men and women who operated government forage agencies, Gertrude Hobby left no diary and few letters. Most agents were not among New Mexico's political and social elite. They were ordinary people, some more wealthy than others, whose names and activities were recorded in only a few extant documents. These limited sources, however, clearly make visible some heretofore hidden economic contributions of New Mexico women to the frontier army—many as partners in family enterprises, a handful as widowed entrepreneurs. Nineteenth-century census takers described their work as "keeping house"; in reality they not only kept house but they also performed valuable services for the United States army.

In spite of their contributions, women forage agents had only limited contact with army personnel in the military District of New Mexico, which in 1870 included 1,598 men distributed among ten army posts.[25] But even at an isolated post like Fort Wingate near the Arizona-New Mexico border, other women worked hard to maintain stable family lives and were in daily contact with army men. Although few in numbers, women played special roles in these military communities—some as wives of officers, civilian employees, and enlisted men, others as servants and laundresses, and still others as prostitutes living marginal existences on the edge of military reservations.

Army regulations officially recognized only laundresses among the garrison's women; all others, including officers' wives and dependents, were regarded as camp followers, a term loosely applied to male and female civilians who traditionally moved with the troops. Since the commanding officer of a post had complete control over camp followers, the lives of women residents were nearly as restricted and limited as those of soldiers. Post commanders also had authority to banish from their bachelor communities any woman they believed was undesirable or disruptive to good military order. In addition, a rigid military class system sharply divided the garrison's women, just as it did officers and enlisted men. Social custom prevented officers' wives from fraternizing with laundresses, servants, or wives of enlisted men, even though they experienced similar difficulties in adjusting to life at the frontier posts.[26]

The number of women residing on a post depended on its function and size. In 1870, only thirteen adult women lived at Fort Selden, a moderate-sized post built to protect settlers in the Mesilla Valley. The higher-status women consisted of two officers' wives, Sophia Clendenin and Mary Williams, and Teodora Ott, the Hispanic wife of the local hotelkeeper. The working class women, comprising an equal number of Anglos and Hispanos, included four enlisted men's wives (two employed as laundresses and one a hospital matron), wives of two civilian employees, two servants, one laundress who lived alone, and one cook employed at the hotel.[27]

In contrast, at least sixty-two adult women lived at or near Fort Union, a much larger post serving as the district's supply depot. The quartermaster's department here employed over one hundred male civilians, mostly single men working as teamsters, carpenters, blacksmiths, watchmen, and laborers, but at least eighteen lived on the post with their wives. Among higher status women were four officers' wives, all Anglos, and Viviana and Manuela Moore, the Hispanic wife and eighteen-year-old daughter of William H. Moore, the wealthy post trader. It is not possible to identify social class for all garrison women; wives of highly paid civilian bookkeepers and clerks may have been welcomed into the small social circle of the officers' wives. Among working class women, however, were eight cooks (one Hispano, one black, and six Anglos), five laundresses (one Indian and four Hispanos), one Hispanic and one Anglo domestic servant, and one Hispanic seamstress. At least eight Hispanic working class women were listed in the census as "keeping house" for Anglo and Hispanic laborers who had surnames different than their own, indicating either that they were living in common law marriages or that they chose to retain their maiden names upon marriage.[28]

In 1870, most military posts in New Mexico had at least one

officer's wife in residence. A total of eighteen wives resided at six posts selected as being representative of New Mexico's garrisons— Forts Bayard, Selden, and Stanton in the south, Fort Craig in the center, and Forts Union and Wingate in the north. Fifteen of the women had been born in the East, two in Texas, and one in England. Half were between the ages of eighteen and twenty-eight, the other half between thirty and thirty-five. Since older women lived at most posts, they could initiate the young army brides into the social complexities and physical hardships of garrison life. Possibly as a consequence of the hardships, families tended to be small; six households were childless, nine had only one child, two had two children, and only one contained as many as three children.[29]

Among the young wives living at Fort Stanton in 1870 was twenty-two-year-old Frances A. Boyd, who had married her lieutenant-husband at age nineteen and now had a one-year-old daughter, Mabel. Many years later Frances published her memoirs, thereupon joining a small fraternity of army women whose published diaries and reminiscenses provide significant information about daily life in the American West. At least four other members of this writing fraternity spent part of their army careers in New Mexico: Eveline M. Alexander, Alice Blackwood Baldwin, Lydia Spencer Lane, and Marian Russell. As young brides, they rapidly adjusted to the hardships of military life and most fell in love with the army way of life. Only one, however, Marian Russell, had grown up in the West, and only she made her home there after severing connections with the service.[30]

Most women who wrote about their army experiences had been raised in sheltered eastern households and were unprepared for life on the frontier. But with courage and apparent good humor, they shared with their husbands a multitude of hardships: wretched quarters, inadequate diets, poor health facilities, frequent moves, low salaries, and the monotony of living in isolated garrisons. They were not subject to the hard outdoor work of most farm women, however, and many employed servants to help them cook, clean, and launder. This allowed time for sewing, buttermaking, preserving food, tutoring children, nursing the sick, entertaining officers and friends, and writing in journals and diaries. By and large these women were well-educated, articulate, and intellectually curious about the West and its people.[31] The written accounts of Frances Boyd, Alice Baldwin, and other officers' wives

add greatly to our knowledge of everyday life in army garrisons
and about conditions in post-Civil War New Mexico. They also
underscore the rigid caste system that characterized military society and the special need these women felt for female companionship.

Like many pioneer women, Alice Baldwin was several months
pregnant when she crossed the Great Plains in 1867. She gave birth
to her first child at age twenty-two in Trinidad, Colorado, while
enroute to her husband's post at Fort Wingate. During her one-
year stay in New Mexico, Baldwin moved with her husband's command from Old to New Fort Wingate in northwest New Mexico.
Both posts were isolated, and social amenities were limited. Baldwin later recalled that life at the old fort was monotonous: "No
social functions ever were held."[32] Although local Hispanic families were friendly and Hispanic women worked as company laundresses, Baldwin's female social circle was restricted to a few other
officers' wives. After moving to the new post, she made friends
with some Navajo women, but her companions for horseback rid-
ing, fishing, picnicking, and other social activities were limited
to officers and their wives.[33]

Army women who lived at posts close to towns expanded their
social circles to include community women. Frances A. Boyd spent
one happy year at Fort Stanton where officers' families exchanged
social functions with residents of Lincoln. In 1873, Boyd moved
with her husband to Fort Bayard in southwestern New Mexico, a
less desirable post because of its remoteness and lack of suitable
quarters. There were few "ladies" at Bayard, but Boyd soon made
friends in Silver City, an hour's drive from the fort. Visits there,
she recalled, "were a very pleasant feature of our life."[34] She failed
to describe other women living at Fort Bayard, but in 1870 there
were seventeen adult women on the post—three officers' wives,
wives of two post traders, six women married to soldiers, four married to civilians, and two black servants.[35]

Although petty jealousies sometimes created friction among
officers' wives, most relied upon each other for emotional and physical support. They nursed ailing friends and helped bury those who
died in remote frontier outposts. In this highly regimented male
society, they sought female companionship and established intimate female friendships. Marian Russell, who was the only Anglo
woman living at Fort Bascom in 1865, made friends with the Dorsett family living a few miles away. She later recalled: "I saw as

much of Mrs. Dorsett as I could, for I was so lonely."[36] Frances
Boyd wrote in her memoirs: "At each post I formed devoted at-
tachments to some woman, and were the love experienced for them
all and their perfections to be described, this book could contain
little else." And a few pages later, she added, "I would like the
ability to describe one beautiful friend who was my constant companion at that time."[37]

The published memoirs of army women generally present an
attractive picture of military society. They describe strong-willed
women attempting to establish polite Victorian society with its
masked balls, picnics, and fishing parties in isolated and desolate
environments. The memoirs give only a brief glimpse, however,
of officers' wives who did not enjoy army life but rather found
its constraints a heavy burden. Nor did the army women write
about sexual tensions or violations of Victorian morality that seemingly threatened the solidarity and integrity of their upper-middle
class world.

Military documents, however, record the fate of some officers' wives, like Charlotta Buffum and Mrs. John Conline, who
suffered severely for their apparent failure to conform to Victorian
and military codes of conduct. A native of New Jersey, Charlotta
joined her officer-husband in New Mexico shortly after the close
of the Civil War. During the next decade, the Buffums established
a home at a number of frontier army posts. Twice during these
years, Charlotta went east for medical treatment, suffering from
an "internal disease" that prevented sexual relations with her husband. While living at Fort Tularosa between 1872 and 1874, she
received constant treatment from military doctors and for nearly a
year rarely left her quarters.[38] In 1876 the Buffums took up residence at Fort Selden and employed an enlisted man, William Vanstan, as cook and servant. When Lt. Buffum was ordered to Fort
Stanton later in the year, forty-year-old Charlotta remained behind
and soon became intimate with Vanstan. The affair came to an
end three months later when Lt. Buffum's superior officer, Capt.
Charles Steelhammer, took Charlotta to Fort Craig to await return of her husband. Steelhammer had heard that relations between
Charlotta and the servant were open to criticism, and later he ac-
cidently came into possession of a love letter written by Vanstan
and addressed to "My darling Lottie." By the time Lt. Buffum

reached Fort Craig, Vanstan had admitted adultery with Charlotta and was lodged in the guardhouse.[39]

What followed was an example of the army closing its ranks against scandal and perpetuating a double standard that tolerated officers' transgressions but demanded immediate punishment of wayward wives. Charlotta broke two taboos: she committed adultery and she was intimate with an enlisted man. Either breach in conduct seemingly justified punishment; even though the army viewed the second as the greater threat to military discipline, Capt. Steelhammer ejected the Buffums from Fort Craig expressing Victorian abhorance for the "fallen woman" and the need to separate good women and bad. He ordered Lt. and Mrs. Buffum off the post by 2 p.m. because he "could not harbor Mrs. [Buffum] another night under his roof as he would not subject his wife to meeting Mrs. [Buffum]." Furthermore he intended to prevent his household from having "social intercourse with people I know to be morally diseased."[40] He then advised Lt. Buffum to send Charlotta east on the next stage to save the lieutenant's military career and to take up his new assignment at Fort Wingate without her. When Buffum ignored this advice, choosing instead to defend his wife of twenty-two years and prefering charges against Steelhammer for conduct unbecoming an officer, a scandal threatened the regiment. Army officials ordered an immediate investigation, and although enlisted men at Forts Craig and Selden talked openly of the affair, official recording of papers in the case was omitted to avoid further publicity. At Fort Wingate, Charlotta signed an affidavit denying intimate relations with Vanstan, but, nonetheless, allegations against her were substantiated. Following advice from fellow officers, Buffum resigned from the service, and he and Charlotta left the territory.[41] Nothing is known of Charlotta's remaining years, but surely if she ever recalled her days in the frontier army it was with distress and pain rather than with the warmth and love that Lydia Lane and Frances Boyd expressed in their military memoirs.

A second officer's wife whose conduct displeased army authorities was Mrs. John Conline, who in 1877 was ordered removed from Fort Garland, Colorado—then part of the military District of New Mexico—on grounds that she was insane and therefore disturbing the order and quiet of the post. There were no charges of sexual impropriety against Mrs. Conline; rather her primary of-

fense was conduct unbecoming a lady. Indeed her behavior at Fort
Garland violated many precepts of polite military society.

The trouble started in October 1876 when Mrs. Conline left
the post and went to nearby La Veta for an abortion. There she
spoke openly against the post's medical officers who had refused
to perform the operation. Upon her return to Fort Garland, she
used "unladylike and violent language," disputed her bill with the
commissary sergeant, and made daily visits to the laundresses' quarters where she gossiped about officers. It was rumored that she talked
to soldiers on guard duty and had chased one laundress with a gun.
At least two officers later testified that she appeared before them
with her clothing in disarray or in a state of partial nudity. A sergeant stated that she arose nude to unlatch the door for him, returning subsequently to her bed. After Mrs. Conline implied to
garrison residents that the post commander, George Shorkley, had
fathered one of the enlisted men's children, Shorkley decided to
stop her "scandalous" behavior. He first confronted her husband
Lt. Conline, who said that he could not be held responsible for
what his wife might do or say. Two New York physicians, Conline claimed, had judged her insane; a third had said that she might
benefit by going west. Subsequently the post surgeon conducted
an investigation, and as a result of his report Gen. John Pope, commanding the Department of the Missouri, ordered Lt. Conline to
remove his wife from Fort Garland on grounds that she was insane. By this date, however, the lieutenant had reversed his former stand and now defended his wife's conduct, denying that she
was insane. Conline subsequently preferred charges against the post
commander and surgeon for conduct unbecoming officers in their
investigation and persecution of Mrs. Conline. Since the lieutenant faced being court martialed for disobeying orders, however,
he soon arranged for Mrs. Conline to return East.[42]

Mrs. Conline's case can best be understood in light of
nineteenth-century medical practices, whereby physicians tended
to diagnose female deviant behavior as insanity or a form of nervous disorder. Officers at Fort Garland reflected this same tendency,
agreeing that Mrs. Conline was not of "sound mind" but rather
was "subject to fits of emotional insanity," which, they believed,
accounted "to some extent for the eccentricity of her actions."[43]
The post trader thought she was "devilish" rather than insane, however.[44] It is likely that these officers would judge any woman as

unbalanced or insane who so blatantly violated Victorian propriety. A final statement issued by an investigating officer suggests this possibility: "The investigation shows that Mrs. Conline has, to certain extent disturbed the peace and quiet of the Post, it further shows, that whether insane or not the conduct of Mrs. Conline at times had not been such as is to be expected from a Lady."[45]

In sharp contrast to the army's treatment of Mrs. Conline was its treatment of Lt. Conline who escaped punishment for his scandalous behavior by pleading insanity at a court martial. Charges against the lieutenant included an attempt while intoxicated to break into the room of Kate Holland, a laundress at Fort Garland, and being drunk and disorderly in the town of Del Norte, where he became involved in a saloon brawl and then ordered his men to burn down the town. It was the Del Norte incident that led to the court martial trial. Since his actions were reported in the Denver *Rocky Mountain News,* they became a scandal in the eyes of army officials. The district commander, believing that Conline had disgraced the service, tried to get him dismissed, but the errant lieutenant remained on active duty and honorably retired in 1891.[46]

Erratic behavior by Mrs. Conline was sufficient to have her removed from the post; her husband's behavior, equally improper, failed to bring about his dismissal. The army's double standard as applied to the Conlines excused ungentlemanly behavior from an officer but not unladylike behavior from an officer's wife. Although many officers were court martialed for conduct unbecoming an officer, transgressions by officers frequently were tolerated if their behavior was not totally outrageous and did not lead to public scandal. This is clearly shown in the instructions issued by an army inspector to the commanding officer at Fort Craig to investigate rumors that officers there were keeping mistresses within the garrison. "Whatever an officer may do in a town or city," the inspector wrote, "keeping a woman within the limits of the chain of sentinels is considered conduct unbecoming an officer."[47]

Not only do military documents reveal the underside of officers' society, but they also shed light on the lives of working class women. Some officers' families in New Mexico hired Hispanic women as cooks and servants, but many families imported either white or black domestics from eastern and southern states. Because they went to considerable expense to hire female servants, officers tried in various ways to control their movements. Army officials at Fort Union, for example, tried in 1866 to stop servants from "jumping their contracts," accepting employment for higher wages with officers who had not borne the expense of transporting them to New Mexico. Both female and male servants who left their employers were to be immediately ordered off the post.[48] Despite this order, the post surgeon a year later complained that servants were forgetting their positions, leaving their employers to lounge around the post, and espousing "high notions" of their rights. He recently had discharged his own "servant girl" who had become insolent and "got the impression that she was a lady" after receiving attentions from male civilian employees. In a letter to army officials, he warned: "If officers in this matter of servants are not protected by some definite system there is little or no use in bringing female servants to this territory when according to my experience they are spoiled by outside influence of a deleterious nature." Reflecting his own class interests and undoubtedly speaking for many officers, he expressed the opinion that obedience in an officer's household was as important as in official relations with enlisted men.[49]

In diaries and memoirs, officers' wives wrote sparingly about female servants, commenting upon the inadequacies of some and expressing gratitude for the industry and loyalty of others. Many writers recalled that it was difficult to retain female servants because they frequently married civilian employees or enlisted men soon after arriving in the West.[50] Undoubtedly most female servants who married and settled in New Mexico lived full and meaningful lives, but military records document the unhappy fate of others. A black servant, for example, left in charge of children at Fort Craig while the parents were away, was raped by an unknown assailant. An officer later euphemistically reported that the woman died afterwards from a "broken heart."[51]

An investigation was ordered into circumstances surrounding the death of another black servant, Emma Beeks, who died at Fort Union in 1879. In many respects, her background was typical of other black women who traveled west as officers' servants. Born in Georgia, Beeks at the time of her death was thirty-five-years-old, unmarried, and employed as a domestic servant in the household of Assistant Surgeon Carlos Carvallo, having worked as an officer's servant the previous eight years. At Fort Union, she had quarters in laundresses row, where she was in contact with other black women working on the post. After performing an autopsy, Carvallo announced that Beeks' death was caused by a bungled abortion; a sharp pointed needle or other instrument had punctured the wall of her vagina, causing infection and loss of blood. Margaret Berry, a black woman employed as hospital matron, testified that Beeks had taken wild tansy steeped in whiskey, a well-known abortifacient, to which—Carvallo believed—borax was added. Berry also claimed that Beeks had aborted an unwanted pregnancy the previous June. The surgeon suspected that Berry had assisted in the fatal abortion, a suspicion that seemed confirmed by Berry's son-in-law, who stated that "she had produced abortion on her own daughter (his wife) and that she would do so again every time he made her pregnant." After Carvallo produced evidence showing that Berry had stolen some of the dead woman's clothes and had caused other disturbances in the laundresses' quarters, she was expelled from the military reservation.[52]

Although tragic and painful, Emma Beeks' death sheds light on the private world of nineteenth-century women. Lillian Schlissel has noted that "much of the woman's world was omitted from written accounts," as even in diaries women failed to comment upon childbirth, family planning, and unwanted pregnancies.[53] Information about abortion, however, was readily available to nineteenth-century literate women, and some scholars believe that abortion was more common among middle and upper class women because of high prices charged by abortionists. Abortion, nonetheless, was practiced by women of all classes; Emma Beeks' case provides evidence that lower class women without written traditions shared information about abortions and assisted each other in self-abortions.[54]

The expulsion of Margaret Berry from Fort Union also reflected the army's continuing distrust of black women who lived on military bases after the Civil War. Black soldiers now helped to garrison the western posts, and most post commanders viewed black women as potential troublemakers, though their services were in demand as laundresses and servants. Indeed, at isolated posts where black enlisted men chafed under orders of unsympathetic white officers, the presence of a small number of black women contributed to explosive situations, such as developed at Fort Cummings in 1867. Black soldiers there held many grievances against officers, but their mutinous conduct stemmed directly from an affair involving a black woman, Mattie Merritt, employed as a servant by Lieutenant William E. Sweet. An investigating officer later reported that she was "a favorite among the men of the company, and the object of some jealousy between the sergeants." The explosion erupted after officers questioning Merritt about the theft of a large sum of money forced her to "strip to her shift" and later tried to send her off the post. Several angry black soldiers thereupon seized their arms and forcibly prevented her removal. Although the mutiny was short-lived and Merritt was reinstated in Lt. Sweet's household, her guilt never having been established, several enlisted men were arrested for taking up arms and threatening their officers.[55]

The following year at Fort Craig, the commanding officer issued two orders limiting the movements of black women. The first, issued 29 June 1868, stipulated that all black women residents, either married or single, who had the opportunity for employment on the post or elsewhere and failed to take it were to be sent to the end of the railroad by the next returning train. The second, dated 15 July, was even more restrictive, ordering all black women back to "the states" who were not employed on the post as servants or laundresses.[56]

For the maintenance of good order, the army tried to limit the number of all civilians living on army posts—male and female, black and white. Women received special attention because army officials assumed that unattached women contributed to discipline problems among the troops. At times post commanders issued orders restricting women residents to authorized laundresses, their daughters, and members, guests, and servants of officers' families.[57] The number of laundresses residing on a post varied according to its troop strength. In the mid-sixties four washerwomen were allotted to each company, which meant that a single laundress might be washing for twenty-five men though frequently she washed for more. In 1870, six company laundresses washed for over two hundred enlisted men at Fort Bayard, and at Fort Wingate, where it was difficult to secure the services of laundresses, one woman in 1871 washed for over ninety men, employing two Navajo women to aid her.[58]

Women from all ethnic groups worked as laundresses, and in exchange for backbreaking labor, they received a daily ration (food for one day), lodging, fuel, medical attention, and cash payment from individuals for whom they washed.[59] Laundry rates varied from post to post, but those at Fort Union in 1870 were typical. Laundresses there received one dollar a month from enlisted men, five dollars a month from officers, and three dollars a month for each additional member of the officer's family.[60] Laundry bills were deducted from soldiers' salaries at the pay table, but officers sometimes delayed paying their bills, creating hardships for laundresses and their families. Bridget Macklin, a laundress at Fort Wingate, finally requested aid from the post commander in collecting a bill from a lieutenant amounting to $185.[61] Laundresses like Macklin generally lived in the most wretched quarters on a post. Their quarters at Fort McRae were described as *jacales,* crude, mud-covered huts that were "entirely unfit for dwellings."[62]

Modern-day writers find it difficult to assess the true character of company laundresses, primarily because military men left contradictory descriptions of them. Major General E. O. C. Ord described laundresses as "honest married women, wives of the best soldiers," but other officers depicted them as camp terrors, a rough lot that frequently engaged in fisticuffs.[63] More recently an investigator has identified laundresses as a prostitute group, who supplemented their meager salaries by gratifying the sexual urges of enlisted men.[64] But this portrayal of army laundresses as prostitutes is probably inappropriate for women who washed at New Mexico's army posts.

Some laundresses undoubtedly carried on illicit liaisons with soldiers, and others created disturbances by harboring "women of bad character" in their quarters. A laundress by the name of Mrs. Charles was ejected from Fort Union for sheltering disreputable women. Another woman who sold her sexual services, Lucy Jane Fuller, entered New Mexico in 1862 as a laundress attached to the California Column. Soldiers politely referred to her as the wife of Private L. D. Fuller, but she also was known as "Adobe Mary."[65]

During the Civil War, the commanding general of New Mexico made an effort to employ only married women as laundresses by instructing post commanders to issue rations to laundresses only if they could produce marriage certificates. Women who could not obtain this evidence suffered. A sympathetic officer reported the plight of Mrs. Antonio Sandoval, who after several years of marriage had children between the ages of three and twelve but no certificate of marriage. Mrs. Sandoval was known as "a good and diligent laundress"; without her ration she would have experienced difficulty feeding her family.[66]

Despite Adobe Mary and other women of questionable reputations, army laundresses in New Mexico more accurately resembled General George A. Forsyth's characterization of them as "good, honest, industrious wives" rather than a prostitute group.[67] For example, of twenty-one laundresses employed in 1870 at Forts Bayard, Stanton, Craig, and Selden seventeen were married to soldiers, one was married to a civilian, one was a soldier's daughter, and two were unmarried. Typical of the married laundresses were the six employed at Fort Craig, whose ages ranged between seventeen and thirty-eight years. Three had children living at home, including the two oldest laundresses, M. Thacker and Maria Rourke, both Irish women, who had two and five children, respectively.[68] Eva Frazelle, a married laundress at Fort Union, revealed some of the special hardships borne by enlisted men's wives when she wrote requesting the District Commander to allow her husband to return to the post. She was about to be confined for childbirth and had no one to bring her rations or fuel since the other laundresses had accompanied the soldiers to Cimarron. Unlike officers' wives, she was too poor to hire help.[69] Possibly more unmarried women became laundresses later in the century as the army made it increasingly difficult for enlisted men to marry. Without careful documentation, however, there is no way of knowing how many supplemented their incomes by selling sexual services to soldiers.

Prostitution flourished, however, near most army posts at off-reservation "hog ranches" and gambling dens. One of the most notorious settlements in New Mexico where prostitutes encountered soldiers was Loma Parda, only five miles from Fort Union. Army officials referred to it as "a festering nuisance" and as "a resort for thieves, murderers and bad men and women of all kinds."[70] Similar epithets were hurled at Leasburg near Fort Selden and Central City near Fort Bayard, both favorite haunts of prostitutes and bored, lonely soldiers. An 1875 report described Central City as a "Mexican village . . . consisting of a number of adobe shanties, inhabited by gamblers, saloon keepers, and prostitutes, all of whom prey upon the soldiers and support themselves mainly therefrom."[71] Prostitutes also congregated in the small town of Ancon, located on a portion of the Fort Craig reservation leased to a local farmer in the mid-1860s. As business picked up and more and more enlisted men visited the prostitutes, the army intervened and ejected the women from the reservation.[72]

Very little is known about New Mexico women who engaged in commercial sex; rarely are they identified as prostitutes in the manuscript censuses. They undoubtedly led hazardous lives, as their many sexual contacts subjected them to venereal diseases, risk of pregnancy, and physical violence.[73] It is fair to assume that these women were among New Mexico's poor, and indeed many carried on business in unglamorous surroundings—sometimes in crude jacales, sometimes in caves in bluffs that overlooked a post. Since their soldier-clients also were poor, prostitutes accepted payment in government rations, arms, clothing, and other articles that had practical use or could be resold. One officer estimated that the government suffered a loss of fifty or sixty dollars a day because of illegal exchanges between soldiers and inhabitants of Leasburg.[74]

While some officers accepted prostitution as a necessary evil, the army nevertheless attempted to control soldiers' access to off-reservation villages like Leasburg and Loma Parda. Not only did these settlements facilitate commerce in stolen government property, they also contributed to venereal diseases, drunkenness, and desertion, all of which sapped the strength of the frontier army. Army Inspector Nelson H. Davis acknowledged that it was "difficult to prevent men from visiting such places," but he believed that conditions would improve if officers rigidly enforced discipline and kept soldiers busy drilling and working in the garrisons.[75]

Perhaps the most notorious attempt by the army to control prostitution and the traffic in government property occurred in 1852 when military authorities raided caves, bawdy houses, and grog shops in the neighborhood of Fort Union. Several men captured in the raid were taken to Santa Fe to stand trial by civilian authorities, but two prostitutes, Jesusita and Dolores, were placed in Fort Union's guardhouse. Shortly thereafter, the post commander decided to punish the two women according to provisions set forth in a territorial law pertaining to pimps. He ordered the prostitutes publicly flogged, their hair cut off, and then drummed off the post to the blare of martial music.[76]

Other attempts to control prostitution occurred in the mid-1860s when military authorities at Fort Selden placed the town of Leasburg off limits to soldiers. They undoubtedly agreed with Inspector Davis, who described the town as "a curse and a nuisance to the Post—a resort for Gamblers, Whiskey shops, low dances, prostitutes, and murderers."[77] At least seven soldiers had been killed in drunken brawls in Leasburg during an eighteen-month period ending 1 December 1866. During these months, the town at its peak had a population of two hundred people and four saloons and dance halls. Despite military prohibitions, soldiers continued to visit Leasburg's prostitutes, most of whom were transients, arriving in time for soldier's payday and departing soon after the money dried up. But the town must have presented a dismal appearance even at its peak, as some prostitutes reportedly worked out of a dilapidated wooden building having neither windows nor doors.[78]

Women who sold sexual services to officers attained a better standard of living than the prostitutes inhabiting the broken-down buildings of Leasburg. Descriptions of higher status prostitutes in New Mexico, however, are rare. But all available information suggests that women who became officers' mistresses nevertheless lived precarious lives. One prominent New Mexican officer kept a mistress at Fort Garland during the Civil War, next to quarters inhabited by his wife. When he left the post for a trip to Conejos, he posted a sentinel at night outside his mistress' quarters. This blatant disregard for military propriety led to an investigation and the officer's subsequent dismissal from the service, although later he was reinstated as an officer in the New Mexico volunteers through intervention of territorial politicians and military leaders.[79] Nothing further is known about his mistress, but her fate may have been similar to that of another woman who was ejected from Fort Stanton because of her relationship with Associate Surgeon Michael Hillary. Hillary claimed that the woman was his servant, though he habitually slept with her. Enlisted men testified that in the field Hillary's black servant cooked and "waited" upon him and that on one occasion Hillary issued orders to a non-commissioned officer while he (Hillary) and she were lying in bed. Before the surgeon could be tried on charges of conduct unbecoming an officer and a gentleman, he resigned from the service.[80] It is unlikely that either of the above women established long-term liaisons with the officers, and in exchange for short-term luxuries they suffered the uncertainties associated with life built on sexual barter.

Although few in numbers, washers, foragers, servants, prostitutes, and ladies all played special roles in the frontier army. As forage agents, women met needs that were essential to the army's mobility, but, like so much of "women's work," their labor received little official recognition. Other women residing on military posts fulfilled roles as laundresses, servants, and as wives of officers and enlisted men. Although a rigid class system divided these women, they endured many of the same hardships: crude quarters, harsh climates, inadequate health care, frequent moves, monotonous garrison routine, and separation from friends and relatives. Many garrison women also had children to raise, and most worried about pregnancy and giving birth in primitive surroundings. All lived in a masculine-oriented society where they were subject to strict military rule and to the dictates of post and district commanders.

Officers' wives, then as now, experienced special problems. They were expected to create genteel family lives for their husbands under difficult conditions, entertain the posts' elite on limited budgets, and sacrifice personal desires for their husbands' military careers. Army protocol dictated that they comport themselves as well-bred ladies despite the fact that they lived untraditional lives, traveling from one isolated outpost to another, enduring many of the same hardships that all soldiers endured, and becoming in the process more resilient and independent than if they had stayed at home.

The limited number of women on military posts contributed to sexual tensions, entangling men and women in relationships that violated military and Victorian codes of propriety. Like American society at large, the military observed a double standard that frequently tolerated the sexual transgressions of officers but not those of officers' wives. Wives who deviated sexually from the code were expelled from military society. Working class women also established illicit liaisons with soldiers. And because commercial sex inevitably interfered with military discipline, army authorities attempted to control soldiers' access to prostitutes who inhabited villages found on the edge of most military reservations. Even though the nineteenth-century Indian-fighting army was a male-dominated institution, women performed valuable services for its officers and enlisted men and in the final analysis contributed to its western mission.

Notes

1. T. A. Larson, "Women's Role in the American West," *Montana, the Magazine of Western History*, 24 (Summer 1974): 4.

2. For the nineteenth-century ideology of ladies, see Barbara Welter, "The Cult of True Womanhood: 1820–1860," *American Quarterly*, 18 (Summer 1966): 151–174.

3. McDermott to Inman, 9 March 1867, District of New Mexico, Chief Quartermaster, Letters Sent, Records of the United States Continental Commands, 1821–1920, Record Group 393, National Archives, Washington, D. C. (Dist. NM, CQM, LS, RG 393, NA).

4. Circular No. 3, 26 June 1869, enclosed in Myers to Flum, 23 March 1874, Dist. NM, CQM, Letters Received (LR), RG 393, NA. See also Myers to Stevenson, 31 August 1872, Dist. NM, CQM, LS, RG 393, NA.

5. Report of N. H. Davis, 9 April 1867, Hudson to Belcher, 10 January 1877, Dist. NM, CQM, LR, RG 393, NA.

6. Hall to Little, 26 October 1867, Sayre to Ludington, 4 August 1868, Dist. NM, CQM, LR, RG 393, NA; Bean to Chief Quartermaster, 9 July 1876, Dist. NM, LR, RG 393, NA Microfilm Publication M–1088, roll 27 (M–1088).

7. Engle to Chief Quartermaster, 4 July, 4 August 1872, Smith to Chief Quartermaster, 12 February, 6 March 1875, Dist. NM, CQM, LR, RG 393, NA.

8. Platt to Chief Quartermaster, 22 January 1876, Dist. NM, LR, RG 393, M 1088, roll 27.

9. See, for example, Ludington to Vroom, 13 May 1868, Dist. NM, CQM, LS, RG 393, NA.

10. In 1881, the quartermaster's department compiled lists of individuals who had served as forage agents in New Mexico. To verify that most forage agents were married, I selected agents from four counties (Doña Ana, Socorro, Valencia, and Colfax), a total of fifty-one agents, and attempted to locate their names either in the 1870 or 1880 census. Eighteen agents could not be located and had probably left the territory by 1880. Of those whose names appear in the census, twenty-nine were married and four were single. Even if all the unlocated agents were single, the fact remains that the majority of agents were married. A random sampling of agents from other counties also supports this conclusion. See Reports from Post Quartermasters at Forts Bliss, Craig, Stanton, Bayard, Wingate, and Union to Chief Quartermaster dated, respectively, 18 March, 27 March, [n.d.] March, 28 March, 31 March, 14 March 1881, Dist. NM, CQM, LR, RG 393, NA; U. S., Department of Commerce, Bureau of

the Census, *Ninth Census of the United States, 1870,* New Mexico, Population Schedules, NA Microfilm Publication M–593, rolls 893–897 *(Ninth Census, 1870,* M–593) and *Tenth Census of the United States, 1880,* New Mexico, Population Schedules, NA Microfilm Publication T–9, rolls 802–804 *(Tenth Census, 1880,* T–9).

11. Sachs to Spurgin, 10 February 1868, Dist. NM, CQM, LR, RG 393, NA.

12. Trauer to Myers, 2 December 1872, Dist. NM, CQM, LR, RG 393, NA; Lyon to Acting Assistant Quartermaster, 30 January 1878, Dist. NM, LR, RG 393, M–1088, roll 32. John G. Bourke described as excellent the meal he received at a government forage agency near San Ildefonso in 1881. It was prepared by the wife of the forage agent and her black companion, Rosie. See "Bourke on the Southwest," ed. by Lansing B. Bloom, *New Mexico Historical Review,* 12 (January 1937): 66–74.

13. *Tenth Census, 1880,* Socorro and Colfax Counties, New Mexico, T–9, rolls 802, 804.

14. Las Cruces *Rio Grande Republican,* 22 March 1884, 1 August 1885. By 1884, the army had discontinued forage agencies in New Mexico. Therefore, although Duper probably helped with her husband's agency at an earlier date, she managed only the hotel after his death.

15. Endorsement on Ayers to Belcher, 2 June 1877, Dist. NM, LR, RG 393, M–1088, roll 24.

16. McFerran to Hammond, 11 November 1863, Department of NM (Dept. NM), CQM, LS to the Chief Quartermaster General, RG 393, NA; Belcher to Acting Assistant Adjutant General, 21 August 1877, Dist. NM, LR, RG 393, M–1088, roll 30.

17. Darlis A. Miller, *The California Column in New Mexico* (Albuquerque: University of New Mexico Press, 1982), 116–122.

18. Miller, *California Column,* 116–122; Las Cruces *Borderer,* 8 May 1872; Santa Fe *Daily New Mexican,* 3 February 1873, 17 January, 10 March, 14 September 1877; Ortiz de Clark to Belcher, 17 May 1878, Dist. NM, LR, RG 393, M–1088, roll 33.

19. Miller, *California Column,* 116–118.

20. *Borderer,* 8 May 1872; *Daily New Mexican,* 22 January 1872, 30 April 1874.

21. *Daily New Mexican,* 12 January 1877, 10, 22 March 1877, 10 February 1881; Clark to Chief Quartermaster, 4 November 1878, Dist. NM, CQM, LR, RG 393, NA.

22. Enclosure in Hennisee to Chief Quartermaster, 10 March 1874, Casey to Belcher, 18 June 1877, Acting Assistant Quartermaster to Chief Quartermaster, 22 January 1879, Dist. NM, CQM, LR, RG 393, NA. Ellen Casey's activities are discussed more completely in the essay on Lincoln County women.

23. *Tenth Census, 1880,* Grant County, New Mexico, T–9, roll 802;

Hobby to Lee, 29 April 1881, Dist. NM, CQM, LR, RG 393, NA; Stiles to MacKenzie, 23 November 1881, Dist. NM, LR, RG 393, M–1088, roll 44.

24. Walker to Chief Quartermaster, 17 June, 7 July 1881, Dist. NM, CQM, LR, RG 393, NA; Hobby to MacKenzie, 31 January 1882, Dist. NM, LR, RG 393, M–1088, roll 45.

25. Position and Distribution of Troops, 1870, Secretary of War, 41 Congress, 3d session, *House Executive Document No. 1, pt. 2* (serial 1446), 68–71.

26. See Patricia Y. Stallard, *Glittering Misery, Dependents of the Indian Fighting Army* (San Rafael, California: Presidio Press, 1978), 11–54; John R. Sibbald, "Army Women of the West," *The American West*, 3 (Spring 1966): 56–67; Darlis A. Miller, "The Frontier Army in the Far West: 1860–1900," 12, in *The American West*, ed. by William D. Rowley (St. Louis: Forum Press, 1980).

27. *Ninth Census, 1870,* Doña Ana County, New Mexico, M–593, roll 893.

28. *Ninth Census, 1870,* Mora County, New Mexico, M–593, roll 894. Clerks in the quartermaster's department in Santa Fe played active roles in the town's political and social life. The sixty-two women included thirty-four Hispanos, one daughter of an Hispanic mother and Anglo father, twenty-five Anglos, one Indian, and one black. Sixty-two is a conservative figure for the number of women who lived at or near Fort Union. Since the 1870 census does not clearly distinguish between residents at the post and those in the surrounding countryside, I began counting garrison women when I positively identified the name of a post resident.

29. *Ninth Census, 1870,* New Mexico, M–593, rolls 893–897. Census takers frequently made errors in recording the place of birth. Frances Boyd, an officer's wife, is listed in the census as being born in California but her birthplace was New York City.

30. Mrs. Orsemus B. Boyd, *Cavalry Life in Tent and Field* (1894; reprint ed., Lincoln: University of Nebraska Press, 1982); Sandra L. Myres, ed., *Cavalry Wife, The Diary of Eveline M. Alexander, 1866–1867* (College Station: Texas A & M University Press, 1977); Robert C. and Eleanor R. Carriker, eds., *An Army Wife on the Frontier, The Memoirs of Alice Blackwood Baldwin, 1867–1877* (Salt Lake City: University of Utah Library, 1975); Lydia Spencer Lane, *I Married a Soldier; or, Old Days in the Army* (1893; reprint ed., Albuquerque: Horn and Wallace, Publishers, Inc., 1964); Marian Russell, *Land of Enchantment, Memoirs of Marian Russell Along the Santa Fe Trail as Dictated to Mrs. Hall Russell* (1954; reprint ed., Albuquerque: University of New Mexico Press, 1981).

31. See Stallard, *Glittering Misery,* 15–52; Sandra L. Myres, "Romance

and Reality on the American Frontier: Views of Army Wives," *Western Historical Quarterly,* 13 (October 1982): 409–427; Boyd, *Cavalry Life,* v–xiv.

32. Carriker, *An Army Wife,* 59–68. Quote is on p. 68.

33. Carriker, *An Army Wife,* 71–82.

34. Boyd, *Cavalry Life,* 164–171, 206, 211–234. Quote is on p. 214.

35. *Ninth Census, 1870,* Grant County, New Mexico, M–593, roll 893.

36. Russell, *Land of Enchantment,* 109.

37. Boyd, *Cavalry Life,* 222, 231.

38. Buffum to Swaine, 19 January 1877, Dist. NM, LR, RG 393, M–1088, roll 31.

39. Steelhammer to Blair, 6 January 1877, Dist. NM, LR, RG 393, M–1088, roll 30; Blair to Swaine, 12 January 1877, Dist. NM, LS, RG 393, NA Microfilm Publication M–1072, roll 5 (M–1072).

40. Buffum to Swaine, 19 January 1877, Dist. NM, LR, RG 393, M–1088, roll 31; Steelhammer to Swaine, 28 December 1876, Dist. NM, LR, RG 393, M–1088, roll 30.

41. Steelhammer to Blair, 6 January 1877, Dist. NM, LR, RG 393, M–1088, roll 30; Blair to Steelhammer, 2 January 1877, LS, RG 393, M–1072, roll 5; Affidavit of C. H. Buffum, 18 January 1877 and Swaine to Blair, 3 February 1877, Dist. NM, LR, RG 393, M–1088, roll 31.

42. Mrs. Conline's story can be followed in: Shorkley to Whittemore, 7 February 1877, Fort Garland, Post Records, LS, RG 393, NA; Conline to Assistant Adjutant General (AAG), Dept. of Missouri, 8 September 1877, Conline to Acting Assistant Adjutant General (AAAG), NM, 22 January 1877, Shorkley to AAG, NM, 1, 29 January 1877, and Post Surgeon's Report, 26 January 1877, Dist. NM, LR, RG 393, M–1088, roll 29; Whittemore to AAAG, NM, 19 February 1877, Dist. NM, LR, RG 393, M–1088, roll 31.

43. Post Surgeon's Report, 26 January 1877, Dist. NM, LR, RG 393, M–1088, roll 29.

44. Whittemore to AAAG, NM, 19 February 1877, Dist. NM, LR, RG 393, M–1088, roll 31.

45. Whittemore to AAAG, NM, 19 February 1877, Dist. NM, LR, RG 393, M–1088, roll 31. See Ann Douglas Wood, " 'The Fashionable Diseases': Women's Complaints and Their Treatment in Nineteenth-Century America," in *Clio's Consciousness Raised, New Perspectives on the History of Women,* eds., Mary S. Hartman and Lois W. Banner (New York: Harper and Row, 1974), 1–22; Welter, "Cult of True Womanhood," 156; Richard A. Cloward and Frances Fox Piven, "Hidden Protest: The Channeling of Female Innovation and Resistance," *Signs,* 4 (Summer 1979), 651.

46. AAAG, NM, to Wade, 6 August 1877, Dist. NM, LS, RG 393, M–1072, roll 5; Shorkley to Hatch, 12 July 1877 and Charges and Speci-

fications preferred against First Lieutenant John Conline [September 1877], Dist. NM, LR, RG 393, M–1088, roll 30; [Hatch] to AAG, Dept. of Missouri, 27 September 1878, and Hatch to Adjutant General, Washington, 5 August 1879, Dist. NM, LS, RG 393, M–1072, roll 6; Frances B. Heitman, *Historical Register and Dictionary of the United States Army* (1903; reprint ed., Urbana: University of Illinois Press, 1965), vol 1, 321.

47. Wallen to Rigg, 17 March 1863, Dept. NM, LS, RG 393, M–1072, roll 3.

48. Chris Emmett, *Fort Union and the Winning of the Southwest* (Norman: University of Oklahoma Press, 1965), 323.

49. Peters to Hewley, 13 November 1867, Dist. NM, LR, RG 393, M–1088, roll 9.

50. See, for example, Boyd, *Cavalry Life,* 192–193; Lane, *I Married a Soldier,* 141; Stallard, *Glittering Misery,* 66.

51. Letter of Bankhead, 6 October 1871, Dist. NM, Registers of LR, RG 393, NA Microfilm Publication M–1097 (M–1097), roll 2.

52. Carvallo to Post Adjutant, 15, 18 March 1879 and Quartermaster's Notification of Death, 12 March 1879, Fort Union, Post Records, LR, RG 393, NA.

53. Lillian Schlissel, *Women's Diaries of the Westward Journey* (New York: Schocken Books, 1982), 82.

54. James C. Mohr, *Abortion in America, The Origins and Evolution of National Policy, 1800–1900* (New York: Oxford University Press, 1978), 95, 106.

55. Evans to AAAG, NM, 27 April 1868, Dist. NM, Inspector, LS, RG 393, NA; Lee Myers, "Mutiny at Fort Cummings," *New Mexico Historical Review,* 46 (October 1971): 337–350. Myers states that Merritt was employed as servant for Lt. Henry F. Leggett, rather than Lt. Sweet as is stated in Evans' report dated 27 April 1868.

56. General Orders No. 31, 29 June 1868 and General Orders No. 37, 15 July 1868, Fort Craig, Post Records, General Orders, RG 393, NA.

57. See, for example, General Orders No. 12, 10 July 1866, Fort Stanton, Post Records, General and Special Orders, RG 393, NA.

58. DeForrest to Pfieffer, 28 February 1863, Dept. NM, LS, RG 393, M–1072, roll 3; Hartwell to AAG, Dept. of Missouri, 3 June 1871, Dist. NM, LR, RG 393, M–1088, roll 14; *Ninth Census, 1870,* Grant County, New Mexico, M–593, roll 893.

59. Stallard, *Glittering Misery,* 59.

60. Anne M. Butler, "Military Myopia: Prostitution on the Frontier," *Prologue,* 13 (Winter 1981): 248.

61. Letter of Whiting, 30 July 1868, Dist. NM, Registers of LR, RG 393, M–1097, roll 2.

62. Endorsement on Bradford to Post Commander, 10 February 1871, Fort McRae, Post Records, LR, RG 393, NA.

63. Stallard, *Glittering Misery*, 63–64.

64. Butler, "Military Myopia," 247–250.

65. Emmett, *Fort Union*, 350; Miller, *California Column*, 26.

66. Bergmann to Bell, 17 August 1865, Fort Bascom, Post Records, LS, RG 393, NA.

67. Quote is in Stallard, *Glittering Misery*, 63.

68. *Ninth Census, 1870*, New Mexico, M–593, rolls 893–897.

69. Frazelle to Granger, 19 December 1875, Dist. NM, LR, RG 393, M–1088, roll 24.

70. Davis to Cutler, 29 January 1865, Dept. NM, Inspector, LS, RG 393, NA; McFerran to Cutler, [date unclear] May 1865, Dept. NM, CQM, LS, RG 393, NA.

71. War Department, Surgeon General's Circular No. 8, *A Report on the Hygiene of the United States Army with Descriptions of Military Posts* (Washington: Government Printing Office, 1875), 247.

72. Willis to Montoya, 13 March 1865, Fort Craig, Post Records, LS, RG 393, NA; Carleton to Commanding Officer, Fort Craig, 21 April 1866, Dist. NM, LS, RG 393, M–1088, roll 2.

73. For an interesting account of prostitution in a mining town, see Marion S. Goldman, *Gold Diggers and Silver Miners, Prostitution and Social Life on Comstock Lode* (Ann Arbor: University of Michigan Press, 1981).

74. Tilford to Hunter, 26 February 1868, Fort Selden, Post Records, LS, RG 393, NA.

75. Report on Fort Bayard, 8 November 1872, by N. H. Davis, Records of Inspector Generals, RG 159, NA. Cf., Butler, "Military Myopia," who argues that the army made no serious attempt to regulate prostitution, but rather created policies that encouraged and endorsed it (pp. 234–250).

76. Emmett, *Fort Union*, 140–145.

77. Tilford to Hunter, 30 March 1868, Fort Selden, Post Records, LS, RG 393, NA; Endorsement on letter written by Day, 17 December 1866, Dept. NM, Inspector, LS, RG 393, NA.

78. Duncan to DeForrest, 12 November 1866 and Day to Davis, 15 December 1866, Fort Selden, Post Records, LS, RG 393, NA; Day to Tilford, 22 September 1867, Dist. NM, CQM, LR, RG 393, NA.

79. Gillespie to Cutler, 18 February 1863, Regimental Papers, First Cavalry, Volunteer Organizations of the Civil War, New Mexico, Records of the Adjutant General's Office, RG 94, NA.

80. Monahan to McKee, 13 May 1867 and Russell to DeForrest, 22 July 1867, Fort Stanton, Post Records, LS, RG 393, NA.

⇛ 6 ⇚

The Women of Lincoln County

1860–1900

Darlis A. Miller

From the nearly deserted mining town of White Oaks, twelve miles northeast of Carrizozo, eighty-three-year-old Susan McSween Barber wrote in a letter dated 23 November 1928: "I am now in this place, White Oaks, still trying to do business and am very old but supple."[1] This perseverance in spite of age and previous misfortune was characteristic of Barber throughout her entire life. One of New Mexico's most successful women ranchers from 1881 to 1902, she was a key figure in the Lincoln County War and witnessed the violence that surrounded the death of her husband Alexander McSween during the 1870s. A similar firmness of character helped many other Lincoln County women to survive—and even to flourish—in the crude, frontier environment of nineteenth-century southeastern New Mexico.

Settled by Hispanic and Anglo farmers in the 1850s, Lincoln County has become one of the best known counties in the West, primarily because of the Lincoln County War and other violent episodes that punctuated the county's early history. Modern-day writers have focused on this violence, ignoring topics that would lead to a better understanding of the lives of pioneer families who lived there. To shed light on their experiences, this chapter will focus on nineteenth-century Lincoln County women, primarily Hispanic and

Anglo women, giving special attention to their economic contributions to family and community.

The sources for reconstructing the history of these women are limited. They consist primarily of manuscript census returns, deed books, probate records, a few newspaper accounts, military records, a handful of oral histories, two memoirs written by Anglo women, and secondary accounts authored by Eve Ball and James D. Shinkle. This description of Lincoln County women, therefore, is necessarily incomplete. Nonetheless, by careful analysis of the sources, it has been possible to sketch the central patterns of these women's lives.

At the end of the Civil War, Americans entered an era of exploitation and expansion. Eastern states experienced rapid industrial and urban growth while western states and territories filled with miners, railroad workers, farm and ranch families, and other westward traveling Americans. New Mexicans migrated internally during these years and established new homes and farms in promising agricultural locations. Some became pioneer settlers in Lincoln County which was carved out of eastern Socorro County in 1869. The county seat was located at Rio Bonito, also called Las Placitas, but shortly renamed Lincoln. Boundary changes in 1878 enlarged the county so that it stretched across the entire southeast quarter of New Mexico. It is uncertain when the first colonists of European descent found their way to the rich bottomlands of the Bonito, Ruidoso, and Hondo rivers. Authorities generally agree, however, that permanent settlement became possible after Fort Stanton was established on the Rio Bonito in 1855. Not only did the garrison offer protection against Mescalero Apaches who were resisting encroachment on their lands, but also it provided a market for surplus crops raised by local farmers.[2]

By 1860 two hundred seventy-six people resided at Rio Bonito, located nine miles southeast of Fort Stanton. Although sources are not available for a full description of this early settlement, census returns provide information about its composition. This was a mixed community of one hundred ninety-three Hispanos, sixty-six Anglos, fourteen children of Hispanic mothers and Anglo fathers, one male and one female Indian servant, and one six-year-old black girl residing with an Anglo farm family. Living in the community were seventy-seven Hispanic women (seven of whom were married to Anglo men), six daughters of mixed marriages, and nineteen Anglo women (nine married women and their daughters). All but seven women were living in some kind of family relationship, either as wife or daughter to a male head of household, whereas at least sixty-eight adult men were living as single men, many working as herders, teamsters, and laborers for more prosperous farm families. Two of the above seven women, fifty-year-old Nepomucena Silvestre and her twenty-five-year-old daughter Barbara, were living together, supporting themselves as seamstresses. One Hispanic woman, Manuelita Miller, lived alone although she was married to Canadian-born William Miller who was working as a laborer on a nearby ranch. Although women comprised only thirty-eight percent of the population, the gender imbalance—a ratio of seventeen men to ten women—was much less than that found in some parts of the West.[3] The ratio of men to women in Colorado in 1860, for example, was thirty-four to one; in Arizona in 1870 it was four to one.[4]

The majority of Rio Bonito women, Hispanic and Anglo alike, lived in farm families, their families either owning a farm or the male head of household laboring for other farm owners. The twenty-five farms listed in the 1860 agricultural census ranged in size from sixty-five acres to six hundred acres and in value from two hundred dollars to nine thousand dollars.[5] Some men classified as laborers undoubtedly owned small plots of land on which they raised subsistence crops, although this acreage was not recorded in the agricultural census. The most substantial farm in Rio Bonito was owned by H. M. Beckwith and his Hispanic wife Refugia, who claimed one hundred acres of improved and five hundred acres of unimproved land valued at nine thousand dollars. In 1860, they owned nine horses, four mules, fifty cows, twenty-eight oxen, sixty beef cattle, and twenty-two hogs. During the preceding year they harvested sixty bushels of wheat, six hundred bushels of corn, forty bushels of beans, two hundred fifty bushels of Irish potatoes, and fifty tons of hay, and they manufactured one hundred pounds of butter.[6]

Refugia Beckwith was among the women who soon fled the new settlement. Confederate troops invaded New Mexico in 1861, and shortly thereafter Union soldiers evacuated Fort Stanton, firing the buildings and destroying surplus supplies. Shorn of military protection, Rio Bonito settlers packed their belongings and left for settlements in the valleys of the Rio Grande. Col. Christopher

Carson and the New Mexico volunteers, however, reoccupied the post in the fall of 1862, and their successful campaign against the Mescaleros encouraged settlers to return.[7] By late December, Carson reported that settlements were springing up rapidly on the Rios Bonito and Ruidoso and that a large quantity of wheat had already been planted. Military officials believed that the country near Fort Stanton contained some of the best grazing and agricultural lands in the territory, and they encouraged settlers to raise more crops in order to reduce the cost of forage and subsistence stores.[8]

Many women who settled along the Rios Bonito and Ruidoso came from the villages of Manzano, San Acacio, and Belen. Among families who migrated from Manzano, a small settlement on the eastern slope of the Manzano Mountains, was that of Geralda and Gregorio Herrera, who moved to Las Placitas (Lincoln) soon after their marriage in 1860. In August of the following year, Geralda gave birth to a daughter, Lorencita. Unfortunately, Gregorio was killed a few days later, and Geralda returned to Manzano where she placed her baby daughter in the care of an aunt, Trinidad Herrera. Sometime later, Geralda, Trinidad, and Lorencita moved back to Las Placitas where the latter married José D. Miranda in 1877.[9] Among members of the Miranda family who had migrated to Lincoln County from the Rio Grande village of San Acacio, located about fifteen miles north of Socorro, was twelve-year-old Prudencia Miranda, a cousin of the above José. Prudencia crossed the Gallinas Mountains in a wagon drawn by oxen with her parents in 1862. That expedition eventually consisted of fifteen wagons as several other families joined the Miranda party seeking protection against possible Indian attack.[10] Still other Lincoln County women had their origins in the Rio Grande village of Belen. Dolorita Aguilar Carbajal was born in Belen in 1807 and moved by ox-drawn wagon to Lincoln County in 1870 with her husband and several children.[11]

These women were members of families attracted to the fertile agricultural and fine grazing lands along streams flowing out of the White Mountains. By June 1866, three hundred Hispanos and five Anglos were living along the Rio Bonito where they were cultivating crops of corn, wheat, and beans and herding about five hundred head of sheep, goats, and cattle. Forty Anglos and eighty Hispanos were raising similar crops and herding a small number of cattle along the Ruidoso and Hondo rivers.[12]

The main factor retarding further agricultural development, however, and further immigration by women, was continued opposition by the Mescalero Apaches. Although the Mescaleros had been forcibly removed to the Bosque Redondo Reservation along the Pecos River early in 1863, they remained under military surveillance only a short time before they quietly slipped away to continue their traditional way of life in the mountains of southeastern New Mexico and northern Mexico.[13] Even during the Bosque Redondo Reservation period, however, about one hundred Mescaleros remained at large, threatening to dislodge white settlers from their newly established homes. In May 1863, a party of Indians raided farmers on the Ruidoso, killing one man, driving off his stock, and then boldly entering Las Placitas and driving off more stock. By September some of the families along the Ruidoso had deserted their farms; others near Fort Stanton were so destitute of food that they were described as being "almost in a starving condition" and the post's commander was authorized to issue them provisions.[14] Three years later over seventy Rio Bonito men appealed to General James H. Carleton, commander of troops in New Mexico, for protection from Mescalero raiders. The settlers were poorly armed and would have to leave if left unprotected: "Some of us have slings, some have bows without arrows and others who are the best armed have firearms but no ammunition."[15] Carleton gave assurances that he would do all he could to aid settlers in opening the region "to civilization," and the army later established pickets at Nesmith's mill on the Ruidoso and at the junction of the Bonito and Ruidoso rivers. But the raids continued, and farm families living in unprotected areas became more and more discouraged.[16]

Despite the fact that most settlers in the 1860s lost stock in Indian raids, the fertile countryside continued to attract new residents, and the female population slowly increased.[17] By 1870 the population of Lincoln County was 1,803, including 1,465 Hispanos, 270 Anglos, 54 children of Hispanic mothers and Anglo fathers, and 14 blacks. Women now represented forty-one percent of the population, and the sex ratio was fourteen men to ten women. Among the Hispanic population the sex ratio was almost even, for living in the county were 687 Hispanic women (47% of the Hispanic population), but only twenty-three Anglo women (9% of the Anglo population). Taking each ethnic group as a unit and excluding daughters of mixed marriages, the ratio of men to women in the Hispanic community was eleven to ten and that in the Anglo community was one hundred seven to ten. The twenty-three Anglo women consisted of thirteen married women and their daughters. Five Anglo women were soldiers' wives employed as laundresses at Fort Stanton, and two were officers' wives. Approximately forty-three Hispanic women were married to Anglo men, representing about twelve percent of the married Hispanic women. Twenty-five daughters of mixed marriages and five black women also resided in the county. Anglo women, then, were only three percent of the total female population.[18]

Although few Anglo women resided in Lincoln County, most shared with Hispanic women the common experience of living in farm families. Most Hispanic and Anglo women established homes, became mothers, and cared for families on farms. They also were economic producers, contributing to whatever economic success their families attained. Roughly eighty-one percent of Hispanic and Anglo women lived and worked on one of the 368 farms listed in the Lincoln County 1870 agricultural census. Many of the farms were small affairs; ninety percent contained less than fifty acres, thirty-one percent less than twenty acres.[19]

Typical of the different types of farms were those of the Flores, the Miranda, and the Baca families. Abrana Flores and her husband Ramon owned a small farm near the town of Lincoln. The Floreses farmed twelve improved acres and owned one horse and three hogs. In 1869 they harvested twenty-four bushels of wheat and one hundred seventy-five bushels of corn, the grain being valued at $300. Thirty-two-year-old Leonarda Miranda and her husband José cultivated a more prosperous farm in the same vicinity. They claimed forty acres of improved land valued at $500. They owned two horses, two milk cows, eight oxen, and seven hogs, and in 1869 they had produced eighty bushels of wheat and five hundred bushels of corn valued at $1,500. One of the most successful farm families in the town of Lincoln was that of Juana and Saturnino Baca, who owned one hundred acres of improved and two hundred twenty acres of unimproved land valued at $6,000. They owned three horses, one milk cow, four oxen, and five hogs. During 1869 they produced $1,450 worth of grain—thirty bushels of wheat, five hundred bushels of corn, two hundred bushels of oats, and one hundred seventy-five bushels of barley. Farms in Lincoln County generally were larger and more productive than those, say, in Socorro and Santa Fe counties, and in only two counties, San Miguel and Taos, did the total value of all farm production in 1869 exceed that of Lincoln County.[20]

It is difficult to know just what these farm households of Abrana, Leonarda, and Juana were like, but primitive living conditions generated a rough kind of equality among farm families who clearly exhibited social and economic differences. Some poorer residents lived in jacales, simple structures made of posts stuck in the ground and plastered with mud.[21] Most of the farm houses, however, were flat roofed adobes with hard-packed dirt floors. Barbara Jones's first home in the Hondo Valley was described as a crude hut of logs, poles, and earth with a blanket covering the door opening.[22] Ellen Casey's first home near the junction of the Ruidoso and Hondo was more spacious if not more elegant: a two room adobe dwelling, the rooms fourteen by sixteen feet, with dirt floors and dirt roof.[23] Helena Anne Coe, soon after her marriage, moved into one of the first houses built in the Ruidoso Valley, consisting of a single room twenty by forty feet, with a dirt floor, flat dirt roof, no windows, and a single door.[24]

Some women also remembered a tradition of cooperation among women in the early stages of community building. Looking back on her early years in Lincoln, Lorencita Miranda recalled that "[people] helped each other with their work. If someone was building a home, neighbors would help build it. If wheat was being cut, everyone would gather to help . . . . Women friends would help their neighbor when they had a bunch of men to feed . . . . Many people that were poor and had small crops, received food in payment when they helped their neighbors."[25] Hispanic residents also welcomed Anglo newcomers, helping them to build homes, fence fields, construct acequias and teaching them methods of irrigation. When Barbara Jones entered her new home at Picacho, ten miles east of the Ruidoso and Bonito junction, she discovered a generous supply of food prepared by women of the village. Hispanic women later taught Jones to prepare chiles and to use a metate and mano to grind corn. The women also exhanged healing lore; the Hispanic women taught Jones to gather herbs and Jones freely shared her medicines. After moving near Fort Stanton, Jones established friendly relations with some Mescalero women. She treated their sick babies and exchanged food for buckskin, from which she made jackets and gloves for her family and neighbors.[26]

Women also shared the dangers of childbirth. Sources on this topic for Lincoln County are limited to statements by Anglo women, who expressed fear at being alone at childbirth. The surgeon at Fort Stanton handled some maternity cases, and Barbara Jones served as midwife to Hispanic neighbors. On one occasion, Jones herself gave birth with only her teenage son in attendance. Undoubtedly there were other noted midwives in the small Hispanic communities. Primitive medical knowledge, however, could not prevent tragedies: Barbara Jones's son Sam married in succession two Gordon sisters and each died in childbirth.[27]

Most of the women were young frontier mothers. The 1870 census demonstrates that the average household in Lincoln County, like any newly settled area, contained very few children. In the precinct that included the town of Lincoln, the majority of Hispanic women who were listed as heads of household (there were twelve) or who lived with husbands, lived in residences containing one child or none. The women with no children living at home included one woman married to a carpenter, one married to a herder, two married to laborers, seven living alone, eight married to miners, and twenty-five married to farmers. The majority of the twenty-five farm women were between the ages of seventeen and twenty-five and were married to farmers who were among the least prosperous in Lincoln County. Only a few households in the precinct listed as many as six children living at home. Many factors undoubtedly combined to produce small families, but of major importance was the youthful nature of this precinct. Roughly sixty-five percent of Hispanic women were under the age of twenty-five and less than eight percent were forty-five or over.[28]

Lincoln precinct contained several families that were related. Women's kinship networks can be traced through census data and probate records combined. Citing one example, probate records reveal that three farm families residing in adjacent residences—the Farmers, the Montoyas, and the Aguilars—formed the nucleus of an extended family. Sixty-two-year-old Luz Montoya and her seventy-year-old husband Rafael lived alone. To one side lived their thirty-six-year-old daughter María Aguilar and her husband Nestor. On the other lived María's twenty-three-year-old daughter Gabina Farmer, her husband James, and baby son. A short distance away lived Luz's thirty-three-year-old son Ramon Montoya, who was living alone with his wife. Still further removed but in the

same precinct lived Luz's thirty-two-year-old daughter Pabla Syl-
van, her husband, and five children.[29] In this sparsely populated
region where in 1870 farm land remained relatively easy to acquire,
the emphasis may have been for sons and daughters to leave home
as soon as possible to establish their own households.

Most women worked hard to maintain families and to assure
the success of family enterprises. Although sources describing wom-
en's work are more complete for Anglo women than Hispanic
women, these accounts make clear that women who migrated to
New Mexico in the 1860s acted as partners with their husbands in
economic production. Take the case of Ellen Casey. The Casey
family bought property on the Hondo, six miles east of the junction of the Rios Bonito and Ruidoso, which included good farm
land and a grist mill. Robert Casey supervised operations of the
mill and rented much of the farm land to Hispanic neighbors for
half the crops. In addition to the familial tasks of cooking, making
clothes, knitting, and taking care of children, Ellen Casey manufactured butter and cheese, raised chickens, harvested a large garden, supervised the grist mill when Robert was away, and provided
meals and lodging to travelers. She sold her surplus vegetables, butter, and cheese to the post trader at Fort Stanton.[30] Ellen's daughter Lily learned "to ride, rope, brand, and perform the various
functions of a cowboy," and she assumed major responsibility in
caring for the Casey cattle.[31] Several daughters of Anglo settlers,
in fact, could ride, round up stock, tame broncos, and generally
made good cowhands. In addition, Anglo women acquired certain
skills needed to survive on the frontier. They learned to shoot, drive
teams of oxen, and some traveled alone across the countryside carrying shotguns for protection.[32]

The economic tasks performed by Hispanic women were also
essential for the survival of their families. Like Ellen Casey, they
cooked, made clothes, took care of children, washed and ironed
clothing (using roots of amole for soap), and provided food and
lodging to travelers. They also whitewashed houses, hauled wood
and water (the latter in ollas balanced on their heads), ground corn
and wheat on metates, and gathered herbs for medicines and plants
for dyes.[33] It is also likely that Hispanic men of Lincoln County
took major responsibility for clearing the fields, digging ditches,
and preparing soil for planting and that women and children aided
in planting, harvesting, and herding domestic animals.[34] Family

histories indicate that in the early twentieth century young girls
cared for goats and hogs, milked cows, and helped cut hay and that
women made cheese and butter for sale, planted apple trees, and dug
ditches for irrigation.[35] One Lincoln County woman recalled that
as a young girl prior to 1920 she plowed, planted, brought in stock,
and helped cut wood.[36] These women undoubtedly were carrying
on a tradition of hard outdoor work that was inherited from their
nineteenth-century ancestors. And like Anglo women, Hispanic
women learned to ride horses and care for animals. Prudencia Miranda was such a good horsewoman that she participated with men
in the sport known as *correr el gallo,* "running the cock," in which
competing riders raced to capture a rooster that had been buried
alive with only its head remaining above the surface of the ground.[37]

These women who labored on family farms were described in
the 1870 census as "keeping house." Only a few Lincoln County
women were listed as having other occupations; they included eighteen laundresses, five seamstresses, three domestic servants, two
housekeepers, one waitress, and one cook. Eight laundresses—four
Anglos and four Hispanos—were employed at Fort Stanton; the
three domestic servants were black women also working at Fort
Stanton, probably for officers' wives. Mary Emmons was the cook,
who with her husband James, operated a hotel in the third precinct. It is not clear from the census how many Lincoln County
women had other women working for them. Several women who
were married to laborers and described as "keeping house" must
have taken in washing and ironing for wealthier women, as Sophie Poe reported happening in the early 1880s.[38]

Violence, the activity for which Lincoln County in the seventies is best remembered, undoubtedly affected all women regardless of class. Men, women, and children shared the danger of living
in a region fought over by antagonistic groups: Indians and whites,
Hispanos and Texans, cattlemen and cattle rustlers, the Murphy-
Dolan and the McSween-Tunstall factions. Part of this lawlessness
stemmed from the growth of the cattle industry in Lincoln County;
thieves proliferated as quickly as the herds. Texas cattlemen first
trailed their cattle into the Pecos area in the mid-1860s to take advantage of markets at Forts Sumner and Stanton. The Pecos Valley and its tributaries had some of the finest grazing in the territory
with natural grasses standing "belly deep to a horse." Attracted by

the lush ranges, entrepreneurs like Joseph C. Lea established permanent ranches along the Pecos in the 1870s, contributing to the county's population growth.[39]

The violence that afflicted the county was widespread and not limited to any one area. And although the majority of families survived the decade intact, they experienced the uncertainties associated with living in communities where law and order virtually disappeared. Some families packed their belongings, left crops standing in the fields, and fled the area to escape the terror. Several men and some women lost their lives, others were wounded, and still others were endangered in these deadly encounters.[40] Not only did survivors grieve for murdered spouses and children, but they also experienced economic hardships brought about by the death of family providers.

But Lincoln County women were not passive witnesses to wanton deeds of violence; they fought back and carried on with whatever resources they had. The experiences of Susan McSween, Juana Baca, and a delegation of village women illustrate this point. During the height of the Lincoln County War, Susan McSween chose to remain with her husband and his supporters during the five days that the McSween residence came under heavy gunfire. On the fateful fifth day, she left her burning home in order to appeal to the commanding officer at Fort Stanton to intervene and save lives. Later she unsuccessfully sought revenge in the courts against her husband's enemies and then went on to build a new career for herself as a rancher.[41] Juana Baca, wife of Saturnino Baca who had gained the enmity of the McSween faction, was left unprotected when, soon after the killing of Alexander McSween, a military guard was withdrawn from the Baca residence. Juana, however, refused an invitation to move onto the military reservation for protection until after she and the family had cared for crops that were being harvested.[42] Finally, during these dangerous months, two women living in San Patricio were raped by outlaws. A delegation of village women thereafter traveled to Fort Stanton with a petition signed by twenty-seven mothers asking "in the name of God and the Constitution" that soldiers be sent to protect them from further abuse.[43]

Despite the violence, by 1880 Lincoln County had a population of 2,512, an increase of thirty-nine percent over the previous decade.[44] There were now more Anglo women in the population,

which included 1,525 Hispanos, 857 Anglos, sixty-six children of
Hispanic mothers and Anglo fathers, fifty-nine blacks, three Indians, and two Chinese.[45] But inspite of a dramatic increase in the
number of Anglo women, women as a whole represented only
thirty-eight percent of the population, and the sex imbalance was
slightly more pronounced than in 1870, sixteen men to ten women,
indicating that men were increasing at a faster rate than women.
The female population now consisted of 718 Hispanos, 203 Anglos, twenty-seven daughters of mixed marriages, eleven blacks,
and one Indian married to an Hispanic man from Mexico. Over
sixty-five percent of Anglo men and women resided in the Fifth
Precinct, which encompassed the cattle region bordering the Pecos, and in the new mining districts of White Oaks and Nogal northwest of Lincoln. The majority of Anglo men in the mining districts
were living as single men, although several had wives living elsewhere in the United States. As in 1870, the ratio of men to women
in the Hispanic population was eleven to ten; the ratio in the Anglo population had dropped to thirty-two to ten. Only twenty-
three Hispanic women were now married to Anglos, representing
about eight percent of married Hispanic women.[46] This build-up
in the Anglo population, from fifteen percent of Lincoln County
residents in 1870 to thirty-four percent in 1880, foreshadowed the
heavy influx of Anglo families into southeastern New Mexico that
occurred around the turn of the century.

The number of black women also increased slightly. Increase
in black population was due to the stationing of black soldiers at
Fort Stanton. Eight black women resided at or near the post, two
employed as laundresses and one as a servant in the commanding
officer's household. Kentucky-born Sarah Williams was "keeping
house" for her three daughters and sergeant-husband, the only black
married couple living in the county. One twenty-seven-year-old
black woman, whose occupation was not recorded in the census,
lived with Clara McVeigh, a white woman who later in the decade
was licensed to sell liquor near the post.[47]

The Hispanic population in Lincoln County experienced little
growth in the decade of the seventies, increasing only by thirty-
one females and twenty-nine males. Families tended to be slightly
larger in 1880 than in 1870 and the population older. In the town
of Lincoln, about forty-one percent of Hispanic women who were

married or heads of household lived in families containing one child
or none; about forty-four percent lived in families containing two
to four children. Only three families listed as many as seven children. Fifty-six percent of Hispanic women in Lin-
coln were under the age of twenty-five, and thirteen percent were
forty-five and over.[48] Families living in Lincoln, San Patricio, Picacho, and other predominantly Hispanic villages probably were becoming more interrelated as their children intermarried. One woman
recalled that by the early twentieth century almost everyone in San
Patricio was related.[49]

Census returns conceal the economic contributions of Anglo
and Hispanic women, most of whom continued to live and work
in farm and ranching families. Returns also underestimate the total
number of farms, thereby giving a misleading picture of agriculture and family life in Lincoln County. The sixty farms listed in
the 1880 agricultural census would indicate a precipitous decline in
the number of farms as well as in total agricultural production. A
decade of lawlessness and intrusion by large cattle herds, as well as
the army's inability to consume local grain surpluses, may account
for a small decline in local farming.[50] It seems likely, however, that
the census taker failed to record many small farms, since in 1890
the census listed 303 farms, only slightly fewer than the 1870 figure. Probate and other county records support this conclusion. The
1882 will of José Alberto Sedillo, for example, indicates that he
and his wife María owned forty acres of land in Lincoln, on which
they probably raised sufficient crops for subsistence, yet he is listed
in the 1880 census as a laborer.[51]

The 1880 census returns seem, therefore, to provide information primarily about the more successful farms, such as that owned
by Josepha and José Montaño, who also operated a dry goods store
in Lincoln. The Montaños owned 319 acres of improved land, on
which they raised corn and beans, and one acre of vineyards. They
also owned five horses, three mules, ten oxen, one hundred beef
cattle, ninety sheep, three hogs, forty chickens, and several milk
cows. They valued their farm at $4,000, their livestock at $4,000,
and their farm production in 1879 at $6,000.[52]

On rare occasions newspaper editors described some aspects
of the woman's importance on farms such as these. One of the more
successful farming operations in Lincoln County was that oper-

ated by Catherine and Charles Fritz on their Spring Ranch eight miles below Lincoln on the Rio Bonito. They claimed ownership of 940 acres, including 400 acres of improved land on which in 1879 they raised 3,900 bushels of corn, 320 bushels of oats, 660 bushels of wheat, and 50 bushels of beans. They owned a variety of domestic animals, including fifteen oxen, fifteen milk cows, three hundred beef cattle, and one hundred chickens. In one twelve-month period, they harvested 250 bushels of apples, manufactured 520 pounds of butter, and collected 1,100 dozen eggs. Their farmland and buildings were valued at $15,000, livestock at $5,000, and farm products at $4,000. When Catherine Fritz died in January 1884, the editor of the Las Cruces *Rio Grande Republican* applauded her industry: "Under her care, [the Fritz] ranch grew to be one of the finest in the county, and she was among the first to establish a dairy and to promote fruitgrowing."[53]

As the century progressed, class distinctions also became more noticeable in Lincoln County. By excluding small land owners, the 1880 agricultural census provides a short list of the most prosperous Anglo and Hispanic farm families. Tax assessment and probate records also indicate disparities in wealth among residents. The wealthiest individual taxpayer in San Patricio was José Analla, who in 1898 was assessed $120 in taxes on 320 acres of land, his improvements, and 2,400 sheep and goats. When his estate was probated following his death in 1899, it was revealed that he owned over 10,000 sheep, most of which were rented to others on shares. His wife Dulces and his four daughters were among those who inherited this wealth.[54]

Among the few estates of Lincoln County women probated in the nineteenth century was that of María Gertrudes Herrera de Chávez, who died at Raventon northeast of Carrizozo in 1892. Her property included 160 acres of land valued at two dollars an acre, 1,453 sheep, seventy goats, twenty-two chickens, wearing apparel and gold earrings valued at two hundred dollars, and a variety of household goods and furnishings. The total estate, valued at $4,313, placed Herrera de Chávez in an economic class above that of most Hispanic women.[55]

Account books of merchants also document disparities in wealth. As one would expect, wealthy women were more likely than poor women to purchase ready-made clothes, canned fruits, perfume, jewelry, and other accessories. Well-to-do Hispanic wom-

en in 1890 paid $45 for silk dresses, $8.50 for hats, $3.50 for slip-
pers,$1.75 for corsets, 75¢ for gloves, and 50¢ for bustles. These
women also purchased gingham, calico, linen, manta, sateen, silk
lace, silk thread, buttons, and ribbons for manufacturing their own
clothes. By the end of the century, numerous Lincoln County
women owned sewing machines, although the majority continued
to lack finances to purchase one.[56]

Daughters of prosperous families also attended boarding schools
even though public and private schools were available locally. Nearly
one year after the death of her mother, twelve-year-old Matilda
(Tillie) Fritz entered the Academy of the Visitation conducted by
the Sisters of Loretto in Las Cruces. Board and tuition for a ten-
month term was two hundred dollars, clearly beyond the means
of most Lincoln County families. Instruction in piano, guitar, drawing and painting cost extra. Mid-way through the first term, Tillie's father died, and she subsequently enrolled in the Academy at
Santa Fe, where tuition fees were equally high, to be near a brother
who attended St. Michael's College.[57]

Whether rich or poor, Hispanic and Anglo women who were
widowed shared the experience of learning to function in society
without their husbands. By living in kin-related communities, Hispanic widows—more so than Anglos—could rely upon relatives
to cushion the economic and personal shock of widowhood. Among
the county's Hispanic population, there were more widows than
widowers in 1880. The census listed forty-five Hispanic widows
as heads of household, many of whom had children living at home,
and twenty-one widows who were residing in other households.
In several cases, a widowed daughter lived with her widowed
mother; some widows lived alone, including eighty-five-year-old
Anna Benavides of Lincoln. The census listed only five Anglo widows as heads of household and four Anglo widows residing in other
households.[58]

Widows like Ellen Casey and Bonifacia Brady continued to
manage family enterprises after the death of their husbands. Robert Casey was shot and killed by a former employee in 1875.
"Largely because of the indomitable courage of Ellen E. Casey,"
one scholar observed, "the family remained a solid working unit."[59]
The six Casey children ranged in ages from eighteen months to
fifteen years, and Ellen kept the older ones busy planting, herding
cattle, and working on the property. She also supervised the Casey

store and grist mill, delivering flour as far away as Seven Rivers on the Pecos. During the height of the Lincoln County War, she remained on the ranch, although the older children went to Texas to escape the violence. She tried to remain neutral but, as her daughter noted, "it was hard." The location of their ranch, wrote Lily Casey Klasner, "caused both sides to put up with her as men went back and forth on expeditions and forays. Both sides annoyed her by searching the house and premises for someone hiding."[60] When peaceful times returned in the 1880s, Ellen Casey received final patent to the family homestead, signed at least one government contract to deliver hay at Fort Stanton, and continued to manage the Casey property.[61] Bonifacia Brady, whose husband also died after being shot on the main street of Lincoln during the Lincoln County War, continued to care for her eight children (the oldest was about fifteen years old) and to cultivate the 320 acre family farm, one of the most valuable in Lincoln.[62]

Other widows rented their cattle and sheep on "partido" (shares) to local ranchers. One woman leased eleven head of high-grade cattle for five years, receiving at the termination of the lease double the number of cattle. Another leased her entire stock of cattle (amount unknown), stipulating that at the end of the five-year lease she would receive the original stock plus half the increase.[63]

Still other widows were left in difficult circumstances and relied upon family and community for economic survival. At age sixty-six, newly-widowed Margarita Estrada Brown lived in San Patricio with a son who supported her. Because she applied for a Civil War widow's pension, her personal history has been preserved, providing a rare glimpse into the life of a Mexican citizen who migrated to Lincoln County as an adult and subsequently outlived two husbands. Margarita Estrada was born in the state of Chihuahua in 1844, and at age twenty-five and single she moved to El Paso, Texas, where she supported herself by doing housework. She made subsequent moves to Las Cruces, where she worked in a hotel, and to Tularosa, where she taught school and married her first husband, Juan Torres, who died around 1881. After being widowed a little over a year, she married a Civil War veteran by the name of Henry C. Brown, a widower who was farming along the Ruidoso. They lived together on the "Brown Ranch" for several years until he began seeking medical attention at soldiers' homes. About a year before he died in 1908, he took up residence in the soldiers' home in Los Angeles, sending Margarita a small sum of money every three months. By this date, Margarita was blind and almost totally dependent upon her son.[64]

As one would expect, widows from prosperous families had greater economic security than Margarita Brown. But these widows also experienced economic difficulties when delays occurred in settling estates. One woman, whose husband's property was appraised at ten thousand dollars, went into debt for one year to support herself and child before funds from the estate were made available to her.[65] Much time was consumed in inventorying large estates and in assuring equitable division of property.

New Mexico's inheritance laws in the nineteenth century seemed to have confused and delayed settlement of estates. These laws decreed that upon death of a spouse, one-half of the community property that remained after payment of common debts would be set aside for the surviving husband or wife. From about 1865 until 1884, the law further stipulated that if the decedent died intestate, the decedent's half of the community property as well as his or her personal property (now called the estate) would be divided equally among the decedent's children, except when the estate amounted to more than $5,000; then the surviving spouse would receive one-fourth of the estate, the remainder to be divided equally among the children. In case the decedent left a will, the law was even more complicated and more confusing. In general it appears that from one-fifth to nearly one-half of the decedent's estate would be used to cover legacies, after which division of the estate would follow the same rules as for intestate. In 1889, the $5,000 provision was dropped and inheritance laws were simplified. The law now stipulated that the decedent's half of the community property and his or her personal property could be disposed of by will, or in absence of will, would be distributed one-fourth to the surviving spouse and the remainder in equal shares to the children.[66]

Delays occurred even in settling small and uncomplicated estates. José Miranda, who lived at Junction Plaza near modern-day Hondo, died intestate in 1880. He and his wife María owned one hundred sixty-two acres of land, valued at about nine hundred dollars. The Rio Bonito flowed through the property, dividing it into two unequal sections. West of the river were forty-four acres of good bottomland; east of the river were thirty-six acres of bottomland and eighty-two acres of hilly land. The heirs agreed that the two sections, though of unequal size, were of equal value, but final division of the property was not completed until 1890. The widow received one-half of the community property (forty-four acres west of the river), and Miranda's eight children received equal portions of land east of the river, amounting roughly to four and one-half acres of bottomland and ten acres of hilly land. Occasionally, when only a small amount of land comprised the estate, children relinquished their claims and allowed their widowed mother to use the property as long as she lived.[67]

Not only complex laws but complex family patterns could cause difficulty. Schisms appeared in some families when heirs believed that the division of property was unfair. This was especially true when a decedent had children by more than one wife. One rancher in San Patricio who died intestate near the turn of the century left a valuable estate of sheep, cattle, horses, wool, promissory notes, and ranch equipment. His heirs included his third wife, their four children, and six children from two previous marriages. The estate remained unsettled for years, some heirs accusing the estate's administrator—the eldest son of the decedent—of mismanaging the estate and improperly dividing the property.[68]

Sometimes a widow believed that provisions in her husband's will were unjust and rejected its benefits in hopes of obtaining increased benefits from other legal sources. When Charles Fritz died in 1885, leaving a valuable estate in land and personal property, he bequeathed his real estate to his four sons and one daughter to be divided equally among them. He also stipulated in his will that his personal property should be divided equally among his second wife Amelia and the above five children. He instructed his sons to give Amelia a good home and provide for her wants as long as she remained single. Amelia, however, surrendered benefits given to her in the will in lieu of her dower right, and she asked that the homestead she occupied at the time of Fritz's death (the valuable Spring Ranch) be included as part of the dower. Under community property laws, the recently-married Amelia probably had no claim to the Fritz real estate, since Charles undoubtedly claimed it as his personal property at the time of their marriage. By invoking the common law concept of dower, Amelia hoped for a share of the land, as dower "consisted of a life estate in one-third of all the lands" which the husband possessed during marriage. This was the "interest of the surviving widow" and could not be set aside in the will of the deceased husband. The concept of dower added to the confusion surrounding nineteenth-century inheritance laws and was abolished in New Mexico in 1907. Amelia apparently settled her claim out of court, as the Fritz children subsequently purchased her interest in the estate, formed a corporation to manage Fritz's cattle grazing along the Rio Felix, and divided among themselves the Spring Ranch property on the Rio Bonito.[69]

Amelia Fritz left Spring Ranch and settled in the town of Lincoln, where she first opened a millinary store and later a hotel. Other county women—some probably widows like Amelia—also embarked upon commercial careers during the 1880s. The only record that remains of these female-owned enterprises is a list of business licenses issued to the proprietresses. Six women took out licenses to run hotels, three to retail merchandise, four to retail liquor, one to operate a gaming table, and one—Rosa Esperanza de Emillio—to peddle merchandise from a two-horse wagon. Only one woman—Ellen Casey—had obtained a business license in the previous decade.[70]

The increase in licenses issued to women reflected the county's growth in population, which reached 7,081 in 1890, an increase of one hundred eighty-two percent. This remarkable growth resulted primarily from increased migration of Anglo families and the expansion of the cattle industry. Many immigrant families came from Texas, which caused one newspaper correspondent to remark: "You cannot go ten miles on any road without seeing the covered wagons [of Texans] with from six to sixteen tow headed children aboard."[71] Texas women brought with them a tradition of hard farm work. Texas-born Nellie Branum recalled that soon after her family arrived in Lincoln County, her father went to work as a blacksmith at Fort Stanton while her mother and older sister plowed, planted crops, made adobes for the family house, and built a rock fence around the property.[72] Other Texas women recalled similar work experiences.

As population increased throughout New Mexico, farm families such as the Branums brought thousands of acres of land under cultivation. Governor Edmund G. Ross, who described this process in his 1887 annual report, noted that Anglo and Hispanic farmers alike were adopting improved methods of agriculture, discarding "the wooden plow, the sickle, the thrashing stockade, and the winnowing fork" in favor of improved machinery.[73] Family ranches also increased in size. In 1890 Lincoln County officials reported that 126,721 head of cattle and 56,584 head of sheep were grazing on county ranges. Although at this date it is not possible to determine the full extent of female ownership, some of these animals were owned and managed by women. Most women worked as partners with their husbands. Hispanic women in partnership with husbands routinely accepted legal responsibility for livestock taken on shares. A few women entered partido arrangements in their own names. Mrs. M. H. Lutz signed a contract with José Analla of San Patricio in 1895 whereby she would receive from Analla two thousand ewes on shares for five years. She agreed to return the same number of ewes at the end of the contract and to deliver to Analla each October during the life of the contract two pounds of wool for every sheep.[74] Newspapers give tantalizing glimpses of some women who owned cattle. A Mary Sepulver, for example, published a notice in the *New Mexico Interpreter* stating that she was sole owner of certain stock ranging in Lincoln County. Other women who owned cattle published their brands in local newspapers.[75]

Among the most famous of New Mexico's women ranchers was Susan McSween Barber, whose ranching activities deserve much more recognition than they have received by historians. Born in 1845, Susan E. Hummer grew up near Gettysburg, Pennsylvania. She married Alexander A. McSween in Atchison, Kansas in 1873 and moved to Lincoln two years later where Alexander established a law practice. Her role in the Lincoln County War is vividly portrayed in *Maurice Garland Fulton's History of the Lincoln County War* and need not be recounted here. In this and other secondary accounts, Susan McSween emerges as a strong and courageous woman. Two years after the death of her husband, she was living in Lincoln and managing a one-hundred-sixty acre farm, on which she raised corn and kept an assortment of farm animals.[76]

Susan took her farm property into a second marriage partnership when on 20 June 1880 she married George B. Barber, a Lincoln County surveyor and later a prominent local attorney.[77] It is obvious from land records that the couple worked in partnership to acquire the land that later became the cornerstone of Susan's cattle enterprise. In fact, the Barbers were typical nineteenth-century entrepreneurs, acquiring land in widely scattered areas that showed potential for economic growth and development: White Oaks, South Spring River near Roswell, and Three Rivers west of the White

Mountains. In November 1879, while still a widow, Susan had entered a claim under the Timber Culture Act to one hundred sixty acres of land near South Spring River, adjoining property owned by Pitser M. Chisum. In the same area, she subsequently entered a claim to and patented three hundred twenty acres under the Desert Land Act and purchased from Sebrian Bates, a former black employee of the McSweens, one hundred sixty acres which he had acquired under the Homestead Act. Within ten years, she relinquished the Timber Culture claim and sold for a nice profit the remaining four hundred eighty acres.[78]

Rather than developing the South Spring property near the Chisum headquarters, Susan and George Barber established a cattle ranch in the western foothills of Sierra Blanca at Three Rivers, twenty miles north of Tularosa. By 1888 Susan claimed ownership to 1,158 acres of Three Rivers land; this included four hundred acres that George patented January 1883 under the Desert Land Act.[79] Susan later said that in 1881 she constructed a dam across Three Rivers (a mere stream) and a half-mile ditch to convey water to her property; apparently these were the first improvements on the ranch.[80] Susan further stated that after the Barbers located their ranch on public domain, and in order "to economize their resources," George returned to Lincoln to open a law office and she took charge of the ranch, having absolute control of its management. "She planned and superintended the construction of all the buildings on the place, designated the location of the fences, corrals, and all the necessary works of this character, at the same time overseeing the cowboys, masons, carpenters and farm hands."[81] While improvements were being made for the cattle ranch, she also had men at work improving another portion of the land for a farm, on which she would raise grain, vegetables, fruit trees, and berries. By the turn of the century, Susan was recognized as one of the most successful fruit growers in Lincoln County.[82]

The cattle ranch prospered under Susan's management and attracted the interest of eastern investors. Indeed, she was building her ranch during the cattle industry's boom period, when many eastern and foreign capitalists were investing in western ranches. In January 1887 Susan sold for an undisclosed sum one-half interest in her Three Rivers property to John Rugee and Emil Durr of Milwaukee, Wisconsin. Although the new partnership never incorporated, it took the name "Three Rivers Land and Cattle Company" and employed Susan as general manager. Five thousand head of cattle soon grazed on the company's ranges. For tax assessment purposes, the company's cattle were valued at $49,000 in 1891.[83]

In writing about Susan's success, a newspaper correspondent declared that she had rendered a valuable service to ranchmen "by demonstrating the fact that cowboys can be gentlemen." He claimed that guns had been "entirely dispensed with" on her ranch and that cowboys working there "wear clean shirts, take off their hats when they come into the house, wash their faces, comb their hair, and put on their coats when they come to the table, and otherwise respect the customs of civilization."[84] By insisting that her employees behave as gentlemen, Susan was conforming to the stereotyped image of western women as the chief civilizing agents who tamed the frontier. In this case, however, it was not the mere presence of a woman that influenced male behavior, as the image makers would have us believe, but rather Susan's power as an employer to hire and fire.

In September 1891, Susan filed suit for divorce in District Court, claiming that George had failed to support her during the marriage and that he had abandoned her the previous March. About the time the divorce became final in 1892, the local press reported that Susan drove between seven hundred and eight hundred head of cattle from her ranch to the railroad at Engle, from which point they were shipped to feed lots in Kansas. Later she traveled east, where she was described in the New York *Commercial Advertiser* as "one of the most remarkable women of this remarkable age." The reporter described with some journalistic license her Three Rivers home: "a low, whitewalled adobe building . . . covered with green vines and fitted out with rich carpets, artistic hangings, books and pictures, exquisite china and silver, and all the dainty belongings with which a refined woman loves to surround herself."[85]

Susan Barber purchased the half interest of Rugee and Durr in 1901 and then sold the ranch and what remained of the cattle—about three hundred head—to Monroe Harper in 1902 for $32,000. It was Monroe Harper and not Susan Barber, as some authors have claimed, who sold this property in 1915 to Albert B. Fall, a key figure in the Teapot Dome Scandal.[86]

During the years that she managed the cattle ranch, Susan Barber acquired real estate in the communities of Tularosa, Nogal, and White Oaks. The mining camp of White Oaks, in fact, was barely two years old when both she and George secured inexpensive town lots from county officials. Starting in 1887, Susan began purchasing additional lots, undoubtedly for speculation since increased amounts of gold were being extracted from the mines. The Barbers maintained a residence at White Oaks, in addition to the ranch house at Three Rivers, and for a few years George had his law office there. After the divorce, Susan continued to maintain the White Oaks residence and moved there permanently after selling the Three Rivers Ranch.[87] By this date the mines had played out, the railroad had bypassed White Oaks, and the once-thriving community had begun its permanent decline. Always the businesswoman, Barber tried late in life to interest oil men in her White Oaks properties but with little success. She died there in 1931—her savings almost depleted—at age eighty-six.[88]

For two decades prior to 1900, White Oaks was a bustling mining community, and its residents considered themselves as progressive community-builders rather than as struggling pioneers. In 1888 White Oaks boasted a population of eight hundred people (making it the largest town in the county), eight mercantile establishments, two weekly newspapers, three hotels, both a public and a private school (whose teachers were frequently young single women from the East), two meat markets, three physicians, three law offices, and a dentist.[89] Although many single men resided there in the early years, the town soon filled with families who would boost civic improvements.

From extant newspapers, it is clear that women played active roles in the community's economic life. Although two hotels had male proprietors, their wives prepared the meals and helped maintain the buildings. The barber's wife repaired and cleaned clothes for her husband's customers. The community's principal butter manufacturer was a woman. At least three women established dressmaking and millinery shops, and at least one ran a boarding house. The postmaster was Ella G. Timoney, who also sold books and stationery from her stand in the post office building. The White Oaks *New Mexico Interpreter* in 1891 was edited by Mrs. A. L. McGinnes, who employed another woman as a typesetter. Although the total number of women engaged in these and similar economic activities remained small, residents viewed their work as important to the community and as proper occupations for women.[90]

By 1900, women had achieved a stable and important place in

Lincoln County—women now comprised forty-five percent of the population. Law and order prevailed in most communities, settlers and Indians lived at peace, and the Anglo population equaled that of the Hispanic.[91] Railroads made it convenient for Lincoln County residents to exchange visits with eastern relatives. A few Anglo women had sufficient funds to tour Europe and Japan. Lincoln County women also became active in national movements. Some farm women joined local Farmer's Alliances, spoke at meetings, wrote letters to newspaper editors, and served as alliance officers. Several White Oaks women formed a chapter of the Women's Relief Corps, a national organization established in 1882 to assist the Grand Army of the Republic and to aid widows and orphans of Union veterans.[92]

Many women of Lincoln County grew to adulthood during the last four decades of the nineteenth century, coping with frontier conditions that required them to perform hard outdoor farm work, tasks customarily defined as men's work. Working as partners with husbands to maintain households and to enlarge family incomes, their economic roles were valued by their families and communities. And although the women of Lincoln County differed in class and ethnic background, crude and dangerous living conditions fostered cooperation and broke down some of their differences.

Without a doubt, Lincoln County women were productive and hard working. It is open to question, however, how much their lives were influenced by the nineteenth-century upper-class ideology of "true womanhood," which dictated that proper ladies should be pious, pure, submissive, and domestic, confining their energies to nurturing a family within the privacy of their homes. This ideology presents a passive image of women that does not reflect the behavior of most Lincoln County women. Nevertheless, wealthier women exhibited in their Victorian wearing apparel and household furnishings an awareness of "female propriety." And women like Susan Barber who engaged in male-dominated industries did so in a manner that acknowledged a proper code of conduct for female entrepreneurs. In defending her career as a rancher, Barber once remarked: "I never did anything on that ranch that was uncouth or unbecoming a lady."[93] Women in Lincoln County undoubtedly internalized some Victorian ideals, but most of them lived lives of steady toil, caring for families and farms, doing outdoor labor when necessary, and engaging in other enterprises for economic survival.

Important questions remain unanswered about these pioneer Lincoln County women. Were their daily lives as restricted as those of women living in eastern rural villages? Or did the frontier communities of Lincoln, San Patricio, and White Oaks allow for greater individual freedom and variation? We may never have the correct answers to these questions, but if historians will listen to what the twentieth-century descendents of these women care to tell them, perhaps more precise estimates can be made about the quality of life among nineteenth-century western women.

Notes

1. Barber to Dilton, 23 Nov. 1928, Old Lincoln County Courthouse, Lincoln, N.M.

2. William A. Keleher, *Violence in Lincoln County, 1869–1881* (reprint; Albuquerque: University of New Mexico Press, 1982), xxiii; Robert N. Mullin, ed., *Maurice Garland Fulton's History of the Lincoln County War* (Tucson: University of Arizona Press, 1968), 13–15; Cecil Bonney, *Looking Over My Shoulder, Seventy-Five Years in the Pecos Valley* (Roswell: Hall-Poorbaugh Press, Inc., 1971), 57–62.

3. U.S., Department of Commerce, Bureau of the Census, *Eighth Census of the United States, 1860,* Socorro County, N.M., Population Schedules, National Archives (NA), Microfilm T–7, roll 158. Hispanos comprised seventy percent of Rio Bonito's population, Anglos twenty-four percent, and children of mixed marriages five percent.

4. T.A. Larson, "Women's Role in the American West," *Montana, The Magazine of Western History* 24 (Summer 1974): 5.

5. Rio Bonito, Socorro County, N.M., Agricultural Schedules of the Eighth Census of the United States, 1860, State Records Center and Archives (SRCA), Santa Fe, N.M. (hereafter Agricultural Schedules, 1860). The average size of farms in New Mexico in 1860 was 278 acres; the average value was $532. *Ninth Census of the United States, 1870,* vol. 3 (Washington: Government Printing Office, 1872), 341, hereafter *Ninth Census, 1870;* U.S., Bureau of the Census, *Historical Statistics of the United States, Colonial Times to 1970,* Bicentennial Edition (Washington: Government Printing Office, 1975), pt. 1, 463 (hereafter *Historical Statistics).*

6. H. M. Beckwith, Socorro County, Agricultural Schedules, 1860.

7. Robert W. Frazer, *Forts of the West* (Norman: University of Oklahoma Press, 1972), 103; Murphy to DeForrest, 11 June 1866, District of New Mexico, Letters Received, Records of the United States Continental Commands, 1821-1920, Record Group 393, NA, Microfilm M-1088, roll 3 (hereafter Dist. NM, LR, RG 393, NA, M-1088); Santa Fe *Weekly Gazette,* 27 Dec. 1862.

8. Santa Fe *Weekly Gazette,* 27 Dec. 1862; Carleton to Brady, 27 April 1865, Fort Stanton, Post Records, LR, RG 393, NA, Washington, D.C. (hereafter PR, LR, RG 393, NA).

9. Mrs. Lorencita Miranda, 5 May 1939, WPA Files, SRCA.

10. Elerdo Chávez, 7 July 1939, WPA Files, SRCA.

11. Daniel Carabajal, 23 Jan. 1939, WPA Files, SRCA.

12. Murphy to DeForrest, 11 June 1866, LR, Dist. NM, RG 393, NA, M-1088, roll 3.

13. Robert M. Utley, *Frontiersmen in Blue, The United States Army and the Indian, 1848–1865* (reprint; Lincoln: University of Nebraska Press, 1981), 236–237, 246.

14. Smith to Cutler, 20 May, 28 August 1863, Fort Stanton, PR, Letters Sent (LS), RG 393, NA; DeForrest to Smith, 5 August 1863, Department of New Mexico, LS, RG 393, NA, Microfilm M-1072, roll 3.

15. Romero to Carleton, 18 March 1866, Dist. NM, LR, RG 393, NA, M-1088, roll 4.

16. Carleton to Romero, 8 April 1866, Dist. NM, LS, RG 393, NA, M–1072, roll 3; Santa Fe *Weekly Gazette,* 23 May 1868.

17. Kautz to Townsend, 24 Jan. 1872, Fort Stanton, PR, LS, RG 393, NA.

18. U.S., Department of Commerce, Bureau of the Census, *Ninth Census of the United States, 1870,* Lincoln County, N.M., Population Schedules, NA, M–593, roll 894. (hereafter Lincoln County, Population Schedules, *Ninth Census, 1870,* NA, M–593). In 1870, eighty-one percent of the Lincoln County population was Hispanic, fifteen percent Anglo, three percent the children of mixed marriages, and one percent black. Approximately 355 Hispanic women were married.

19. Lincoln County, N.M., Agricultural Schedules of the Ninth Census of the United States, 1870, SRCA. The average size of farms in New Mexico in 1870 was 186 acres; the average value was $404. *Ninth Census, 1870,* vol. 3, p. 341; *Historical Statistics,* p. 463.

20. Lincoln County, Agricultural Schedules, 1870; *Ninth Census,* 1870, vol 3, 358, 208–209.

21. Sophie A. Poe, *Buckboard Days* (reprint; Albuquerque: University of New Mexico Press, 1981), 196.

22. Eve Ball, *Ma'am Jones of the Pecos* (Tucson: University of Arizona Press, 1969), 12.

23. Lily Klasner, *My Girlhood Among Outlaws,* ed. by Eve Ball (Tucson: University of Arizona Press, 1972), 41.

24. Wilbur Coe, *Ranch on the Ruidoso, The Story of a Pioneer Family in New Mexico, 1871–1968* (New York: Alfred A. Knopf, 1968), 71.

25. Interview with Lorenzita [sic] Miranda by Nan Boylan, 1953, copy of transcript made available by Nora Henn, Lincoln County Historical Society, and Rio Grande Historical Collections, New Mexico State University (hereafter Lorenzita Miranda interview, 1953).

26. Ball, *Ma'am Jones,* 21–23, 27, 33–35, 41–42, 57. See also Coe, *Ranch on the Ruidoso,* 12.

27. Ball, *Ma'am Jones,* 29, 226; Coe, *Ranch on the Ruidoso,* 72; Poe, *Buckboard Days,* 209–211.

28. Lincoln County, Population Schedules, *Ninth Census, 1870,* NA, M–593, roll 894. Individuals are listed in the 1870 census according to household, but no relationship is recorded for people living in the same household. Women and children are listed beneath a male head of household, and where the surname for a woman has been deleted in preference for a straight line, it is assumed that she carried the same surname as the man and that they were husband and wife. It is not always possible, however, to claim a husband-wife relationship as sometimes unmarried daughters remained at home to "keep house" for their widowed fathers. Whether one includes or excludes the families where relationships are in doubt, the fact remains that in over half the households where women of marriageable age were living with male heads of household, one child or none lived at home.

29. Lincoln County, Population Schedules, *Ninth Census, 1870,* NA, M–593, roll 894; María de La Luz Torres, Probate Records, Lincoln County Courthouse, Carrizozo, N.M.

30. James D. Shinkle, *Robert Casey and the Ranch on the Rio Hondo* (Roswell: Hall-Poorbaugh Press, Inc., 1970), 59; Klasner, *My Girlhood Among Outlaws,* 45–51.

31. Klasner, *My Girlhood Among Outlaws,* 48.

32. Ball, *Ma'am Jones,* 32, 107, 169, 176, 192; Coe, *Ranch on the Ruidoso,* 78, 123; Klasner, *My Girlhood Among Outlaws,* 68; Shinkle, *Robert Casey,* 44; Bonney, *Looking Over My Shoulder,* 158–161.

33. Poe, *Buckboard Days,* 207–208, 218; Klasner, *My Girlhood Among Outlaws,* 43–45; Mrs. Orsemus B. Boyd, *Cavalry Life in Tent and Field* (reprint; Lincoln: University of Nebraska Press, 1982), 172; Ball, *Ma'am Jones,* 42; Lorenzita Miranda interview, 1953.

34. See Frances Leon Swadesh, *Los Primeros Pobladores, Hispanic Americans of the Ute Frontier* (Notre Dame: University of Notre Dame Press, 1974), 179.

35. Family history compiled by D. Sanchez, Nov. 1977, New Mexico State University (in possession of the author).

36. Information provided by Lynda A. Sanchez concerning her mother-in-law, in letter to author, 20 June 1983.

37. Lorenzita Miranda interview, 1953. W. W. H. Davis, *El Gringo; or New. Mexico and Her People* (reprint, New York: Arno Press, 1973), 188.

38. Lincoln County, Population Schedules, *Ninth Census, 1870,* NA, M–593, roll 894; Poe, *Buckboard Days,* 207–208.

39. See James D. Shinkle, *Fifty Years of Roswell History, 1867–1917 (Roswell: Hall-Poorbaugh Press, 1964), 4–8, 18, 26, 40–42.*

40. For the Lincoln County War, see Keleher, *Violence in Lincoln County* and Mullin, *Maurice Garland Fulton's History of the Lincoln County War.* For the Horrell War, see P. J. Rasch, "The Horrell War," *New Mexico Historical Review* 31 (July 1956): 223–231. See also Santa Fe *Daily New Mexican,* 30 Sept. 1873, 27 Jan. 1874, 19 Jan. 1875, 4 May 1877; *Grant County Herald* (Silver City), 8 June 1878; Dudley to Devins, 15 August 1878, Dudley to Acting Assistant Adjutant General (AAAG), 28 Sept., 16 Nov. 1878, 15 Feb. 1879, Fort Stanton, PR, LS, RG 393, NA; Gardner to Dudley, 18 August 1878, Lyon to Post Adjutant, 1 Oct. 1878, Fort Stanton, PR, LR, RG 393, NA.

41. Mullin, *Maurice Garland Fulton's History of the Lincoln County War,* 249–269, 303–330, 345–349, 356–367.

42. Mrs. J. Baca to Dudley, 22 August 1878, Fort Stanton, PR, LR, RG 393, NA.

43. Dudley to AAAG, 6 July 1878, 15 Feb. 1879, Fort Stanton, PR, LS, RG 393, NA.

44. U.S., Department of Commerce, Bureau of the Census, *Tenth Census of the United States, 1880,* Lincoln County, N.M., Population Schedules, NA, Microfilm T–9, roll 802 (hereafter Lincoln County, Population Schedules, *Tenth Census, 1880,* NA, T–9). The author's count of individuals listed in the 1880 Lincoln County population schedules is one less than the official population listed for Lincoln County, 2,513. See *Tenth Census of the United States, 1880,* vol. 1 (Washington: Government Printing Office, 1883), 72 (hereafter *Tenth Census, 1880).*

45. In 1880, Hispanos comprised sixty-one percent of Lincoln County's population, Anglos thirty-four percent, children of mixed marriages three percent, and blacks two percent. The author's count of black residents (59) is one less than the official count (60) listed for Lincoln County. See *Tenth Census, 1880,* vol. 1, 402. Twitchell states that of Lincoln County's 2,513 inhabitants, 2,303 were native to the territory. This is in error. The Census Bureau recorded 2,303 residents as native to the United States, including 1,515 born in the territory. Some historians have used Twit-

chell's figure to represent the number of Hispanos in Lincoln County. My figure for the Hispanic population includes those individuals born in Mexico as well as those born in New Mexico. Ralph Emerson Twitchell, *The Leading Facts of New Mexican History* (Cedar Rapids: The Torch Press, 1917), vol. 3, 129; *Tenth Census, 1880,* vol. 1, 521.

46. Two hundred sixty-nine married Hispanic women lived in Lincoln County. (This figure excludes widows.)

47. Lincoln County, Population Schedules, *Tenth Census, 1880,* NA, T–9, roll 802.

48. Lincoln County, Population Schedules, *Tenth Census, 1880,* NA, T–9, roll 802.

49. Family history compiled by D. Sanchez, Nov. 1977, New Mexico State University (in possession of the author).

50. Darlis A. Miller, "Civilians and Military Supply in the Southwest," *Journal of Arizona History* 23 (Summer 1982), 132–133.

51. *Eleventh Census of the United States, 1890, Agriculture* (Washington: Government Printing Office, 1895), 166 (hereafter *Eleventh Census, 1890); Contracts and Agreements C,* p. 77, Lincoln County Courthouse, Carrizozo, N.M. The Census Bureau accounted for an apparent reduction in number of farms reported for New Mexico in 1890 by stating there had been a failure "to enumerate a considerable number of small farms belonging to Mexicans." See *Thirteenth Census of the United States, 1910,* vol. 7 (Washington: Government Printing Office, 1913), 148.

52. Lincoln County, N.M., Agricultural Schedules of the Tenth Census of the United States, 1880, SRCA (hereafter Agricultural Schedules, Tenth Census, 1880). The average size of farms in New Mexico in 1880 was 125 acres; the average value, $1,091. *Tenth Census, 1880,* vol. 3, 25; *Historical Statistics,* p. 463. The census listed the Montaños as owning 300 milkcows, but this figure is probably in error. Dairies of this size were seldom found so far from large urban areas.

53. Lincoln County, Agricultural Schedules, Tenth Census, 1880; *Rio Grande Republican,* 19 Jan. 1884. In addition to the farm women, the 1880 census lists among Lincoln County women one Anglo and eleven Hispanic servants, three Hispanic laundresses, two Hispanic cooks, one Anglo saloon keeper, and one Anglo actress.

54. Tax Assessment Records, Lincoln County, 1898, SRCA; José Analla, Probate Records, Lincoln County Courthouse, Carrizozo, N.M.

55. María Gertrudes Herrera de Chávez, Probate Records, Lincoln County Courthouse, Carrizozo, N.M.

56. See Account Book, 1890, James J. Dolan Store, Lincoln, N.M. On sewing machines, see *Report of the Governor of New Mexico to the Secretary of the Interior, 1895* (Washington: Government Printing Office, 1895), 18.

57. Charles Fritz, Probate Records, Lincoln County Courthouse, Carrizozo, N.M.; *Rio Grande Republican,* 26 Sept. 1885.

58. Lincoln County, Population Schedules, *Tenth Census, 1880,* NA, T–9, roll 802. There were twenty-six Hispanic widowers, seventeen living as heads of household and nine residing in other households. There were twenty-two Anglo widowers, sixteen listed as heads of household and six residing in other households.

59. Shinkle, *Robert Casey,* 136.

60. Klasner, *My Girlhood Among Outlaws,* 173, 188; Shinkle, *Robert Casey,* 88, 112, 123–126.

61. Shinkle, *Robert Casey,* 66–67; Endorsement on Cavenaugh to Chief Quartermaster, 31 Oct. 1884, Dist. NM, LR, RG 393, NA, M–1088, roll 55.

62. Lincoln County, Agricultural Schedules, Tenth Census, 1880, SRCA; Dudley to AAAG, 13 July 1878, Dist. NM, LR, RG 393, NA, M–1088, roll 34.

63. See *Contracts and Agreements C,* 222, 385, Lincoln County Courthouse, Carrizozo, N.M.

64. Henry C. Brown, Pension Application Files, Civil War Series, Records of the Veterans Administration, RG 15, NA.

65. Jefferson D. Grumbles, Probate Records, Lincoln County Courthouse, Carrizozo, N.M.

66. *Compiled Laws of New Mexico, 1884,* (Santa Fe: New Mexican Printing Co., 1885), sections 1410–1414; *Compiled Laws of New Mexico, 1897* (Santa Fe: New Mexican Printing Co., 1897), sections 2030–2031.

67. José Miranda, Probate Records, Lincoln County Courthouse, Carrizozo, N.M.

68. José Analla, Probate Records, Lincoln County Courthouse, Carrizozo, N.M.

69. Charles Fritz, Probate Records, Lincoln County Courthouse, Carrizozo, N.M. Similar to dower, the husband held a right in his wife's property known as curtesy: "a life estate in all of the wife's lands, provided that a child had been born to the marriage capable of inheriting the land." Arie Poldervaart, *New Mexico Probate Manual* (Albuquerque: University of New Mexico Press, 1961), 82.

70. Records of the Territorial Auditor, Licenses, Lincoln County, Territorial Archives of New Mexico, SRCA, microfilm, roll 50.

71. *Eleventh Census, 1890, Population,* pt. 1, 241; *Rio Grande Republican,* 1 August 1885. Eddy and Chaves Counties were carved out of eastern Lincoln County in 1889, but the 1890 census failed to recognize this division, counting their residents as part of Lincoln County.

72. Nellie Branum, [date unclear], WPA Files, SRCA; Lincoln County Pioneer Stories, WPA Files, SRCA.

73. *Report of the Governor of New Mexico to the Secretary of the Interior, 1887,* (Washington: Government Printing Office, 1887), 8–9.

74. *Eleventh Census, 1890, Agriculture,* pp. 258, 299; *Contracts and Agreements D,* 18–19, 67–68, 74–75, 136–137, 151–158, 172–173, Lincoln County Courthouse, Carrizozo, N.M.

75. *Nogal Nugget,* 19 July 1888; *New Mexico Interpreter* (White Oaks), 31 July 1891.

76. Mullin, *Maurice Garland Fulton's History of the Lincoln County War,* 249–278; *Lincoln County News,* 9 Jan. 1931; Lincoln County, Agricultural Schedules, Tenth Census, 1880, SRCA. Documents in the P. J. Rasch Files, Old Lincoln County Courthouse, Lincoln, N.M., indicate that Susan's maiden name was Hummer and not Homer, as stated in her obituary.

77. Susan E. Barber and George B. Barber Divorce Records, SRCA.

78. *Deed Record C,* 175–176, *Deed Record F,* 315–316, *Deed Record I,* 555–557, *Patent Record C,* 60, 178–179, Lincoln County Courthouse, Carrizozo, N.M.; U.S., General Land Office, Registers of Lands in the Office at La Mesilla, Timber Culture, microfilm copy, University of New Mexico, Special Collections.

79. *Patent Record C,* 58, *Deed Record I,* 154–155, *Deed Record K,* 445–446, Lincoln County Courthouse, Carrizozo, N.M.

80. *Water Rights A,* 30, Lincoln County Courthouse, Carrizozo, N.M.

81. *Lincoln County Leader* (White Oaks), 28 July 1888.

82. *Report of the Governor of New Mexico to the Secretary of the Interior, 1900* (Washington: Government Printing Office, 1900), 387.

83. *Deed Record I,* 154–155, Lincoln County Courthouse, Carrizozo, N.M.; Tax Assessment Records, Lincoln and Doña Ana Counties, 1891, SRCA. As a married woman, Susan Barber purchased land in her own name. But when selling land, her husband's signature appears along with her own on the deed of sale.

84. *Lincoln County Leader,* 28 July 1888.

85. Susan E. Barber and George B. Barber Divorce Records, SRCA. Newspaper accounts are found in Keleher, *Violence in Lincoln County,* 160.

86. *Bill of Sales Record D,* 403–404, 446, 448, *Deed Record T,* 215, 218–222, *Deed Record U,* 80–84, Lincoln County Courthouse, Carrizozo, N.M.; *Deed Record Five,* 137–139, Otero County Courthouse, Alamogordo, N.M. A correspondent for the *Roswell Register* (11 July 1902) reported that Barber sold her ranch for $35,000.

87. *Deed Record A,* 39–40, *Deed Record H,* 290, 429, 432, *Deed Record J,* 247, 297–298, 306–309, 457–458, Lincoln County Courthouse, Carrizozo, N.M.; *New Mexico Interpreter,* 21 Sept. 1888, 15 Nov. 1889, 2 Jan. 1891, 10 July 1891; *Lincoln Republican* (Lincoln), 8 July 1892.

88. Barber to Fulton, 2 July 1928, 1 August 1930, Maurice Garland Fulton Collection, University of Arizona Library, Tucson, Arizona.

89. *Lincoln County Leader*, 11August 1888. For a delightful view of early White Oaks residents, see Morris B. Parker's *White Oaks, Life in a New Mexico Gold Camp, 1880–1900* (Tucson: University of Arizona Press, 1971).

90. *Lincoln County Leader*, 2 June 1888, 1 March 1890; *New Mexico Interpreter*, 14, 21 Sept. 1888, 20 Feb., 3, 24 April, 8 May, 31 July, 2, 30 Oct. 1891; *Contracts and Agreements D*, 33, Lincoln County Courthouse, Carrizozo, N.M.

91. *Report of the Governor of New Mexico to the Secretary of the Interior, 1895* (Washington: Government Printing Office, 1895), 56; *Twelfth Census of the United States, 1900, Population*, pt. 1 (Washington: U.S. Census Office, 1901), 513.

92. *New Mexico Interpreter*, 3 June 1887, 30 Oct. 1891; *Lincoln County Leader*, 19 May 1888, 1 Feb., 19 July 1890; *Nogal Nugget*, 1, 28 June 1888; *Rio Grande Republican*, 1 May 1891. Department Commander for all chapters of the Women's Relief Corps in New Mexico was Maggie M. Rudisille of White Oaks, who in 1890 attended the national convention in Boston.

93. Barber to Fulton, 24 March 1926, Maurice Garland Fulton Collection, University of Arizona Library, Tucson, Arizona.

⇐7⇒

Canning Comes
to New Mexico

Women and the
Agricultural Extension
Service
1914–1919*

Joan M. Jensen

In 1919, Alice Corbin Henderson summed up a report on the work of New Mexico women during World War I by referring to the "English, Spanish, and Indian speaking women who met over the canning kettle."[1] It was a striking image that reflected the hopes of some Anglo women that the women of the three cultures could find a common space and work together. But what was the reality behind such an image? Assuming for the moment that a canning kettle might have been an appropriate place to meet for women in a predominately rural state, was it possible?

For Henderson, as for other fighters of the home-front war, canning had been a part of the war effort. Canning was also an essential element of the Country Life Movement, however, the rural component of the progressive reforms of the early twentieth century. Already well underway when overtaken by war, the Country Life Movement had as its goal keeping farm families on the farm and, if possible, encouraging urban families to return to the land. The reformers who led the movement—primarily white Pro-

*Reprinted by permission of the regents of the University of New Mexico and the editor of the *New Mexico Historical Review*.

testant professional groups dedicated to an orderly transition to industrial capitalism—were worried that rural conditions would drive yet more farm folk into the chaotic cities, thus further compounding the social conflict there. Statistics gathered by rural life reformers showed farm families to be culturally isolated, badly overworked, and receiving miserably low incomes. Many families seemed to be loosing ownership of their land and facing tenancy or urban migration. To alleviate these alarming conditions, reformers formulated projects to improve farm management both in the fields and in the home. One of the domestic reforms was to train women to can more efficiently. Hence, the image of the women meeting over the canning kettle was more than just one of homefront effort, it symbolized an ideal of the Country Life Movement.

Like many other important types of work performed by rural women, canning is difficult to trace historically. Because the teaching of canning methods became a part of government policy after the establishment of the Agricultural Extension Service in 1914, however, it is possible to test Henderson's assertion, at least in part, through an analysis of the introduction of canning into New Mexico by the extension service. According to home demonstration agents, canning was a crucial skill, for once having acquired it a rural woman could provide a nutritious diet for her family as well as save money for the farm household.

Reflecting the country life reform ideas of the Progressive era, agents saw their job as raising the level of rural life by making farming more efficient—in home and field. While the program for teaching women and girls in rural areas included cooking and sewing as well as food preservation, canning seemed an especially important skill in the survival of rural family farms, for the process allowed hard-earned cash to remain within the farm economy. According to agricultural experts, each jar of vegetables or fruit that the farm women canned meant an increase in farm income and profits for the household. The introduction of new skills in food preparation resulted in the spread of the canning kettle in New Mexico from 1914 to 1919. Government policy did not, however, join women at the canning kettle as Henderson claimed.

Canning, the process of preserving foods by sealing and then heating the contents of jars, was introduced into the United States in the early nineteenth century. Invented by the Frenchman Nicholas Appert, whose 1810 treatise on canning was soon published in the United States, the process quickly replaced older methods of preserving vegetables with salt brine or vinegar. Glass jars and covers were introduced soon after—the Mason screw cap dates from 1858—and American women were soon on the road to liberation from old methods and subordination to the new. The practice spread slowly because of the cost of jars and caps and because of the time and effort demanded by cold pack canning. Middle-class women in Eastern states were the first to adopt the practice, and by the turn of the century canning was fairly widespread among the Euro-American population, providing an inexpensive and varied diet for the rural and urban family. Canning also moved west, but as late as the 1920s, Ruth Allen found in her study of Texas women that most Hispanic and black women did not home can, nor did many poor Anglo women because of the expense and the work involved. Many of the poor women worked for wages and bought commercially canned food. The situation in New Mexico was somewhat different than in Texas, but the limited use of canning was similar.[2]

Into the 1930s, most Native American and Hispanic women in New Mexico used drying rather than canning as their principal method of food preservation. Therefore, few of these women would have met English-speaking women over the canning kettle during 1917 and 1918. Rather they worked with women of their own cultures preserving foods in ways that had been perfected and respected over long periods of time. Drying was an inexpensive and efficient way to preserve food, and it formed the center of domestic food technology of Hispanic and Indian women. Native American methods were by far the most complex, including techniques for processing hundreds of varieties of plants. The women of each tribe had their regional crops and variations on processes that scholars now believe date back to the very dawn of human existence. Although much of the early technology of processing was lost because ethnologists did not recognize the importance of women's prehistoric food strategies, records still exist for tribes in New Mexico because they continued to use traditional food preservation techniques late into the twentieth century.[3]

A particularly detailed account of Navajo food preservation practices was made by the anthropologist Emma Reh in 1939. Although at that time Navajo food consumption habits were changing rapidly, she was able to record in detail the food preservation methods of the older women. This account gives some concept of the persistence of these traditional methods among Indian women.[4]

Corn was still the main staple that women dried, shelled, and hung in sacks in their hogans, to be cooked later in water or milk. Women also made green corn into tamales, then baked, dried, and stored them in sacks to cook with meat or milk. Some corn they dried on the cob and stored in bottle-shaped underground pits eight to ten feet deep and four to five feet across, closed on top with logs, bark, and earth. Often the women stored more than a one-year supply of corn. Melons were the main fruit women preserved, by peeling, wilting, cutting circularly in long strips, hanging them to dry, and then winding the strips into balls for storage, to be boiled later. Squashes they boiled before peeling, wilting, cutting in long strips, drying, and winding in balls. Hard shelled squash, and sometimes watermelons, they stored like corn in pits. Pumpkin seeds were dried and toasted. Wild seeds and greens were gathered, boiled, dried, and stored in sacks or pails in hogans. Dried Huaa (a spinach-like plant) they preserved in concentrated form through boiling several times, drying into hard black chunks, and then storing in sacks. Navajo women told anthropologist Reh that three pounds of Huaa concentrate would last three weeks when cooked with meat. Women also sliced surplus meat thin, salted it, and dried it on the line. Usually in winter and in the spring women made goat cheese. By the end of summer, a Navajo woman's hogan was hung with lard pails, sugar sacks, containers of wild seeds, dried greens, squash seeds, peach pits, bags of dried roasted corn, hardened green tamale dough, and wads of dried squash and melon strips. Not every woman had sufficient preserved food to feed her family for the winter but what she had was nourishing. If she had no blanket to trade for food needed, the family could always go to a neighbor's hogan to eat.

Navajo women seldom purchased processed food. Traders introduced canned tomatoes, peaches, and corned beef around 1910; they added sardines and canned milk in the 1920s, and jams, jellies, and peanut butter in the 1930s. Even at the end of the 1930s, when class differences were beginning to be noticeable among the Navajos, the poor rarely bought these goods. At any rate, most women still preserved large quantities of food throughout the 1930s and also carried on a brisk trade with Hopis for dried peaches and other foods Hopi women had preserved. While some of the new consumer foods provided important nutrition—especially sardines and peanut butter—the overall effect may have been to lower the nutrition of Navajos at a time when their own native food supplies were dwindling.

There was one main exception to the rule that Navajo women still relied primarily on dried food. While women on reservations followed traditional food preservation methods that emphasized drying, daughters were being taught to can at boarding schools. During the years before World War I, Navajo families were forced to send at least one child to boarding schools where missionaries and government employees taught daughters the white women's ways—including how to preserve food. At the McKinley County School for Navajos, for example, matrons apparently taught the young girls to can in 1918, though there was little chance that they would use these skills on the reservation. It was, however, part of the national program to replace traditional skills of the Indian woman with skills that would make them more dependent upon the Euro-American culture and occupy the place women were assigned in that culture.[5]

The systematic teaching of canning to women on reservations and to women living in pueblos did not get underway for a decade after World War I. Fabiola Cabeza de Baca Gilbert was the first demonstration agent to be assigned to the Pueblos in the 1930s. Probably a few bilingual Pueblo women canned before the 1930s, but the records of the Agricultural Extension Service before 1920 made no mention of even considering teaching Indian women in the pueblo villages of northern New Mexico. The Indian woman, whether Tiwa, Tewa, Navajo, or Apache speaking, was probably uninterested in the canning kettle or in meeting there her sisters from Hispanic and Anglo cultures.[6]

At first glance, it seems that Hispanic women were also unlikely to be involved in the reality of the canning kettle. Fabiola Cabeza de Baca Gilbert wrote in the *Journal of Home Economics* in 1942 that the extension service first reached Hispanic women in rural areas of New Mexico in 1929 and that the first Spanish bulletins on canning were issued in 1930. Until then, she pointed out, Hispanic women, like Indian women, used traditional drying methods.[7]

The Hispanic tradition of preserving food through drying is well known. Dried corn, chile, onions, beans, and meat were win-

ter mainstays of New Mexico villages in all parts of the state. Hispanic women relied on solar energy for much of their processing.
They used flat-topped roofs and trees, strung chiles in ristras and
sliced beef and dried it at their winter *matanzas* (butcherings). Maria Duran, who lived in the southern New Mexico village of San
Miguel, remembers growing chile on the family *sembrado* (plot of
land). She recalled years later: "We would roast green chile outside, peel it, and put it out to dry on the bark of the tree. We would
clean the bark real good and put it there to dry. We called it chile
pasado."[8] Other women remember hanging roasted chiles on lines.
Summer squash was also dried, giving women an abundance of
meat and vegetables to which they added goat cheese and roasted
corn, cane juice, and pinons gathered from the mountains. While
much less varied than the native American diet, traditional food
processing, particularly drying, enabled the Hispanic woman to feed
her family nourishing meals year round.[9]

This pattern, drying until 1929 and then a rather rapid adoption of canning by Hispanic women, is confirmed by a study of
the extension circulars published between 1915 and 1919. These
circulars do not indicate that 60 percent of the women of the state
were Hispanic and Spanish-speaking or that there was any inten-
tion of including this majority in the outreach program. Only two
pictures of girls' clubs show non-Anglos, one of Indian girls at the
Albuquerque Indian School in 1915 and one of the girls in the "Old
Mesilla Sewing Club" in 1918. One Spanish surnamed woman,
Gertrude Espinosa, is listed as working with the boys' and girls'
clubs. The impression given is that Hispanic women were not
reached and that girls were taught only to sew.[10]

Despite this lack of published evidence, oral histories, while
sometimes difficult to date, confirm the importance of canning to
some Hispanic women and indicate that canning could possibly have
been more common than published sources indicate. In *Las Muj-
eras,* Ida Gutierrez remembers: "At the end of every summer my
mother would can the fruits and the vegetables for the next year.
She had this extra wood stove that she put outside because it got
so hot. She'd build up a big hot fire, and then she'd take the corn,
the *chiles,* the peaches, and the tomatoes and she'd put them in jars
and boil them in a big kettle." Although her remembrances probably date from the 1930s, others by Jesusita Aragon clearly date from
the period around World War I. Aragon remembers living on a

farm near Trujillo in northern New Mexico: "We used to can everything, so in the winter we don't have to buy anything." The oral histories are an additional clue that at least some Hispanic women were canning before the 1930s.[11]

The annual reports submitted to Washington by the New Mexico Agricultural Extension and microfilmed by the National Archives in the 1950s offer additional evidence that Hispanic women were part of the extension outreach program during the war years from 1917 to 1918. Afterwards, the program was drastically curtailed and once more confined primarily to Anglo women until the 1930s when the service again expanded and became part of the New Deal policy to save farms through increasing the preserving of food for home use. The question of reaching the Hispanic majority came up frequently in the reports of the Agricultural Extension Service from 1914 to 1919. These references give a picture of the limitations of the service in teaching Hispanic or "Mexican" and "native" women, as the agents referred to them. Records also indicate that many women were contacted, especially in 1918. Reports reflect the agents' perspective but are nonetheless noteworthy glimpses of the lives and attitudes of rural women.

The New Mexico Agricultural Extension Service began in 1914 as a part of the cooperative extension formed in each state under the federal Smith-Lever Act. Under this legislation, using federal and state matching funds, extension agents were to carry into rural areas the methods of agricultural experiment stations, the United States Department of Agriculture, and the most progressive farmers. The legislation sought to diffuse practical information on subjects relating to agriculture and home economics to the American people. Because the extension service was to be conducted by land grant colleges, the young Agricultural College at Las Cruces in New Mexico would be in charge of developing a program of field demonstrations, publications, and other educational projects.[12]

As a typical piece of progressive legislation, the Smith-Lever Act provided for a dual gender program. Home demonstration agents were to work out programs for women and agricultural agents to develop programs for men. Both were to develop youth programs as well. While men and women would be coordinate in rank, the records of the New Mexico Extension Service reveal a pattern that was probably widespread in most states. Women's work received a smaller amount of funds, fewer women than men were hired, and at lower salaries. As late as the 1960s, only a third of New Mexico county agents were women. In the 1930s, the proportion was usually smaller. In 1924–25, for example, less than 25 percent of the agents were women, and the highest paid woman received the salary of the lowest paid male. Women were not only underpaid but overworked because their small numbers necessitated traveling much of the time. The additional pressure of war work brought on the illness of several agents, including one whose doctor ordered her to take a six-week vacation to recover. At that time there were no disability payments, paid sick leave, or paid vacation.[13]

The home demonstration staff consisted of just one woman in November 1914, Dora Ross. Undaunted by her lack of colleagues, Ross planned an ambitious project for rural women to study poultry raising and marketing, to make and market handwork, and, most important, to teach methods of economical and rapid preserving of fruits and vegetables. She expressed the goal of the home economics extension office in the first circular published six months after the service began. The purpose was to organize women into cooperative groups to make "a more profitable, cultured, pleasant, and attractive country life." The women agents were to carry "the practical and scientific wisdom to every farm woman."[14]

The programs that Ross worked out during her single year as agent revealed how much the extension program was the daughter of progressive reformers who saw scientific housekeeping as a way to raise the status of the occupation of homemaking. Tura A. Hawk, who headed the New Mexico agents in 1918, expressed this concept clearly when she stated the object of the agents was the instruction in home economics and approved household practices "in order that the home may be made more convenient and its surroundings more attractive and that the profession of home-making may assume its proper place among the high callings of our national life."[15]

Circular No. 7, published in December 1915, best displayed the scope of the programs. In "Study and Program Outlines for Home Maker's Association," Ross listed the study topics as cookery, meats, sanitation, bread, beauty in home surroundings, cake making, kitchens, modern conveniences, diet, recreation, aesthetics, dietetics, public schools, meals, and—of course—canning. Ross planned a mother-daughter canning project, instruction of chick raising, and a home-building contest. In 1916, the study program under Ross's successor, Gail Ritchie, even included suggestions for "a Baby week campaign," care and feeding of the sick, laundry and other items, as well as the favorite—canning. The ambitious women promised to make available Cornell College reading lists for study programs for women's clubs. The circulars so busily prepared during the first two years, slavishly copied plans worked out by agents in the East. The projects strongly reflected the interests of the country life advocates in raising rural life to the level of city life by encouraging adoption of home economics. Only in this way, the reformers believed, could rural women achieve the status of urban women.[16]

From the establishment of the New Mexico Agricultural Extension Service in 1914, the staff officials realized that their success in a bilingual state depended upon their ability to recruit bilingual agents. A. C. Cooley, in his state leader report for 1915, admitted they were having difficulty reaching the Hispanic majority. "It is almost impossible to find properly trained Mexicans capable of filling a county agent's position," he wrote, "and it seems equally as hard to find an American who speaks Spanish and understands the Mexican people." Ross, in her report for 1915, also noted the difficulty in organizing a population that seemed scattered and transient and where "only a minority of the population . . . are being served by the extension worker who speaks no Spanish."[17]

Agricultural agents who spoke Spanish were soon hired for the predominantly Spanish-speaking counties. Some county commissioners stated in their agreements that agents must be Spanish speaking. By the end of World War I, there were numerous Hispanic agents and several bilingual Anglo agents. The problem was not as easily solved with home demonstration agents, because there was only one, and it seemed to be assumed that the one must be Anglo and not necessarily Spanish speaking. By 1916, however, agent Ritchie was hoping to get an assistant who might help make demonstrations in Spanish. At the end of June 1916, Ritchie reported she was still trying to find ways to assist "the native women in making their home life pleasanter but just what course is best to pursue has not yet been decided."[18]

The war finally galvanized the extension service into expanding its outreach to Hispanic women. That happened, however, only because federal and state legislation passed following the declaration of war in early April 1917 appropriated huge sums of money to the Agricultural College for agriculture programs. In less than six weeks, work more than doubled and, as state leader Cooley reported, "There was a sudden right-about-face in attention to food production and conservation." The service hired twelve temporary home demonstration agents in June 1917. One of them was Gertrude Espinosa of Santa Fe. In 1917, Espinosa became assistant in club work, and a second Spanish-speaking woman, Sara Van Vleck, was added as home demonstrator in February 1918. These two women provided the main services to Spanish-speaking women with the part-time assistance of Spanish-speaking male agents.[19]

From the beginning, county agents felt the burdens of working in a state like New Mexico. The Anglo population was a mixture of migrants from many states and foreign countries who seemed transient and unstable. Many farmers knew little about irrigation and dry land farming. Families had paid exorbitant prices for their land and now, dissatisfied and discouraged, they wanted to sell and get out. Thousands more had come for their health. Real estate sharks and grafters seemed to abound. People needed to have faith in the country, wrote one agent, and get the "home-making spirit." Like other Anglos before them, some agents had little respect for the Hispanics who were stable and had learned not to demand more than the land could produce with simple tools. Hispanics, Cooley wrote at the end of 1915, had some of the best land but still farmed "in a very primitive way." Agents were determined to reach the Hispanic population and improve their "primitive methods of farming."[20]

It was difficult at first for agents to understand why farmers should not wish immediately to accept their advice. "The Spanish speaking people were hard to work with in boys and girls clubs," wrote one, "as they do not understand the work and are naturally suspicious of every new movement." As agents came to know their constituents better, a few began to analyze the reasons for the suspicions of the Hispanic community. Hispanics did not trust outside people because of past bad experiences. "In no place where the majority of the farmers are Mexicans," wrote R. C. Stewart, agricultural agent for Bernalillo County, "can one begin to show results with less than a year's work. These people have often been unfairly treated by the better educated classes and are therefore skeptical of anyone who tries to work with them, until they come to know him, and something about the work that is being undertaken."[21]

Next to trust, an inability to invest in new tools was probably the most important reason why Hispanics did not respond as quickly as Anglo farm families to suggestions. Whether new devices for spraying insects or glass canning jars, Hispanic families could not immediately experiment with new equipment that might not work. Rather, they waited for someone else to take the risk. They were much more likely to invest their meagre resources in new equipment once a method was proven successful. Still, trust must certainly have been the key element, for the Hispanic agent in San Miguel County reported organizing Hispanic farmers there with no difficulty.[22]

What the Hispanic agents did naturally because of their shared culture, Anglo agents often had to learn by trial and error. The experience with the boys' and girls' clubs was perhaps the best example of this fact. The organization of rural boys and girls into project clubs was a major part of the extension outreach program. In fact, the federal government considered the training of farm children so important that by 1916 the Las Cruces headquarters county agents had been ordered to spend one-fourth of their time organizing young people. This was far more time than that devoted to the organizing of adults. The influence of this early organizing effort nation-wide can best be seen in the figures of the United States Department of Agriculture. By 1914, more than 270,000 rural girls were already enrolled in clubs. By 1930, 41 percent of all rural girls were being reached by extension agents. By 1938, 63 percent of all New Mexico youths eleven years or older were enrolled in clubs, a majority of them girls. By the end of 1918, 5000 New Mexico youths were already in clubs.[23]

Actually, some 1000 boys and girls had already been organized in 40 rural clubs by 1913, but according to the first annual report of the agricultural extension office, these early clubs had "not been a great success." Under the new service, agents and a state-wide club leader worked through teachers to spread the club concept and to enroll local volunteer leaders to work with the young people during the summer months when most teachers returned to their homes. Eventually, many areas obtained additional appropriations from county commissions or school boards to hire summer organizers. The volunteer system continually caused problems for county agents, and those who were able to find funds for paid organizers seemed the most successful in maintaining the interest of the new club members.[24]

Agents had particular problems in Hispanic communities because the general distrust was transferred to the club organizers. Once agents discovered that they must explain the clubs to the parents before proceeding, things became easier. This was quite different from Anglo communities where the agents often organized the children first in the schools, and the students then helped interest their parents in extension projects. There were a few exceptions. In Old Mesilla, for example, the Anglo teacher in 1917 organized seventeen Spanish-speaking girls into a club that did outstanding needlework, canned, and even gave a concert to win an award as champion club in the state. In the town of San Miguel, just south of Las Cruces, Señora Rodriguez, described by the agent as the "most cultured and influential lady in town," became club leader. The distrust may have reflected an alienation from schools that frequently had Anglo teachers, some of whom spoke no Spanish, but close supervision by Hispanic parents of children seemed to be the crucial element.[25]

While meetings with parents helped clear the way for enrolling young Hispanic people in the clubs, the distrust persisted. During the war, it even increased in some areas. Catherine Pritchett, who worked in Socorro County in 1918, found: "At San Juan and La Joya the parents persist in the belief that the government had some sinister motive and that the children after finishing a course are to be taken from them." In Sierra County, parents thought club work would make children liable to military service.[26]

The problem of hiring sufficient Spanish-speaking demonstrators and club workers was never solved during the war. Valencia County commissioners had stipulated that a Spanish-speaking woman be employed as soon as possible, yet at the end of 1918, the home demonstration leader reported it had been impossible to hire one. The service tried to recruit Puerto Ricans and Mexicans and were turned down by their one Spanish-speaking applicant because the salary was too low. The service did think it best for Hispanics to have "workers of their own race"; in fact, Anglo women did urge families to plan for more education for girls, who seldom had more than primary education, but the service could only urge Spanish-speaking girls to finish high school and then take home economics classes. Since social and economic conditions made this difficult, the urgings were unlikely to be successful.[27]

This meant that not only young farm daughters but also their mothers could not be reached to teach them canning. Still important contact occurred. Although some daughters were learning English in schools, many still could not read and write English. A majority of all the women did read Spanish, however. Therefore translations began on the county level rather early, and agents adjusted to women's needs. In Socorro, the home demonstration agent reported in 1917: "The natives practice canning very little, but as a result of the meetings and demonstrations many were induced to can and dry products that in the past had gone to waste." Espinosa translated club circulars on cooking, sewing, and poultry into Spanish as well as instructions for keeping records so that mothers could understand the club movement. She spoke to groups of parents before organizing their sons and daughters and also gave demonstrations. In 1918 alone, agents gave 162 demonstrations in Spanish in seven counties and visited more than 300 homes of Hispanic women.[28]

Agents and demonstrators also adjusted their methods of giving demonstrations. Hispanic women, unlike Anglo women, did not feel at home in school houses or public buildings. They also preferred meeting without Anglo women. "It is not possible to combine demonstrations for English and Spanish-speaking people even when they can all be reached by one language," wrote one agent, "because the Spanish-speaking people will not come to a meeting called for both. They are very retiring and can best be reached in small groups." At Sandoval, agents gave successful demonstrations at a farmer's picnic. Usually, however, they gave demonstrations at homes. Wrote one agent: "to reach the native women especially it is necessary to lay aside much of the formality of presentation that might otherwise accompany demonstration work."[29]

Virtually no written descriptions exist of these small meetings where Spanish-speaking demonstrators introduced Hispanic women to canning. One glimpse came from an agent who wrote of Van Vleck's canning demonstrations in Valencia: "It is interesting to visit Mrs. Van Vleck in her work and see the native women come with black shawls over their heads, roll their cigarettes and smoke as they stand about the table where the demonstrator is working." Many Hispanic women did learn to can during the war years. In

Valencia, where Van Vleck distributed 10,000 tomato plants to women, Hispanic women busily canned the entire crop. If they did not literally meet English-speaking women over the canning kettle, Hispanic women did can large quantities of vegetables during the war years where demonstrators reached them. They were eager to learn and adopt new ideas when agents adapted methods to their needs.[30]

The home demonstrators, however, reached far more of the female Anglo minority than the Hispanic majority, thus making it appear that Anglo women took up canning more enthusiastically than did Hispanic women. Yet responses from Anglo women varied widely, usually depending on their previous experience. In San Juan County, for example, home demonstration agent Eva Fuchs discovered five Mormon women who canned 1,000 quarts a season. Mormon women were prodigious canners, staging neighborhood bees in Utah where they canned collectively, and agents obviously had little to teach them. Other women resented the agents' claim to expertise. In Curry County, the older women told the agent: "[we] economized all our lives; what is the use to study Home Economics?" Elsewhere, women responded enthusiastically to the agent's demonstrations. At Alto in Lincoln County, where women knew nothing of canning, they came eagerly over long distances to learn.[31]

Early demonstrations went forward rapidly under the guidance of the home economics agents. During her year as demonstrator, Ross estimated traveling 17,978 miles, addressing almost 7,000 men and women at 162 meetings, distributing 2,370 bulletins and circulars, answering 445 letters, giving 102 demonstrations, visiting 60 farm homes, writing 43 articles for publication, aiding 32 organizations, and making 30 telephone calls. These early public demonstrations attracted many Anglos who considered them entertaining. When Ritchie took over in 1916, she organized three-day sessions in Chavez, Colfax, Eddy, and Torrance counties, as well as demonstrated and lectured in school houses and small home groups. Agents conducted most demonstrations with middle-aged women, and even though almost all had been to school, as one agent reported, "these have in most cases gotten out of the way of studying from books or taking instructions as given in public schools so the information given to them must be made very concrete. It is the aim of the demonstrator always to make herself one of the group of women among whom she is working and to try to see the problem from their standpoint."[32]

Despite the shared Anglo language and culture, demonstrators found that organizing clubs through the schools was the best way to interest parents in their work. Agricultural agents seemed to welcome the emphasis on club work. Wrote one: "it is much easier to work with willing, active and susceptible young minds than with set, old and indifferent ones." Thus the establishment of clubs was not an independent work but one integrally related to teaching the women in a community.[33]

The Extension Service initially organized eight types of clubs: gardening, poultry, pig, calf, rabbit, field crops, cooking, and sewing. Agents apparently rigidly separated these clubs by sex, though club workers seldom mentioned the sex of members in each club. Through 1916, agents enrolled boys in gardening, field crops, rabbit, calf (only one of each of these clubs existed in 1916), and pig clubs. Catherine Pritchett was the only demonstrator to question this sexual segregation in writing. "I have had occasion to wonder why girls are not included as members of pig clubs," she wrote in 1918, "I believe they would have more stick-to-itiveness than their brothers." Such gender consciousness seldom surfaced, however. Neither girls nor women received much help for their agricultural production needs through the extension service. One exception seemed to be poultry clubs that were open to boys and girls and where the majority may have been girls. In 1916, poultry clubs were the most frequently organized (39), although sewing clubs outdistanced them in numbers enrolled (364 to 313). The highest producers in the poultry clubs that year were 4 girls who raised turkeys and chicks. Since poultry raising was a common way farm women earned income in New Mexico at the time, these clubs must have been an important source of information for farm women.[34]

New Mexico reported no separate canning clubs in 1916, as did Arizona, for example, which enrolled 313 girls in 23 canning clubs. Agents did give club demonstrations in canning in the canning season of 1915 and reported that letters indicated "an awakened interest in home canning," but organization of girls into canning clubs did not make much headway until the war years.[35] Then work in canning by girls expanded rapidly as the New Mexico Council of Defense took up the problem of food preservation. The Council set aside funds to hire additional home economics specialists to preach the gospel of food conservation and mobilized women all over the state to help encourage the prospect. Additional funding enabled the extension service to add twelve women to supervise demonstrations and transferred Espinosa to full-time club work. By the end of 1917, girls were being enrolled in canning clubs and demonstrators reported that they canned 2,438 quarts of fruit and vegetables, at an average estimated value of 33 cents per jar and cost of 9 cents per jar. During 1918, girls in 78 canning clubs produced more than 16,000 quarts of food.[36]

That year saw a great flourishing of the canning activities by young women and the beginning of a folklore about their amazing feats. These "canning stories" featured both young girls and women as their heroines. Young May Cribb of Roosevelt County, for example, was reported as doing all the home canning and showing her neighbors how to cold pack after joining a canning club at the Benson School house. At a statewide Mother–Daughter Congress held in Albuquerque in June 1918, teams of girls put on canning demonstrations in Spanish and English. Although some parents forbade their children to participate in club projects, generally the enthusiasm of the young people helped agents interest mothers in extension work. A Clovis demonstrator reported that county women and girls there preserved 15,000 quarts of food in 1918.[37]

Agents depended on clubs and schools in New Mexico to reach women because there were no rural women's organizations that agents could use to further their organizing efforts. The state had few farm organizations of any kind when agricultural extension began in 1914 although the Agricultural College had conducted Farmer's Institutes. State leader Cooley reported in 1915: "The work is so new to the people here that it was thought a county organization or farm bureau would be more of a hindrance than a help, so no effort was made to perfect an organization in the county before placing an agent."[38]

Home demonstrators did call on urban women's clubs for support in club extension work. Ross clearly hoped for some sort of urban-rural alliance that would enable her to utilize organized urban women to reach unorganized women. In southern New Mexico, Ross visited clubs at La Union and Anthony and began a county federation of women. In Colfax, the agent interested county commissioners in club work by having the women's club request a paid club leader. The county commission subsequently hired a Raton

High School domestic science teacher for $75 a month to conduct club work. During the war, women's clubs and the Women's Auxiliary of the State Council of Defense joined hands to promote preservation of food, and wherever women's clubs existed they rallied patriotically to the call to can.[39]

As the agricultural agents began to organize the male farmers, they usually ignored women. Most male agents organized the men first; female agents waited until the men were organized before beginning to organize the women. There was considerable diversity in how the women were to be organized as demonstrated by the experience from Doña Ana, Colfax, and Curry counties.[40] Curry County early established a goal of organizing 600 men and women into a Farm Bureau. In Curry County, women were economically active, raising many chickens and turkeys for the market, and these activities may have affected their early consideration. "Women are responsive," wrote the agent, "are glad to be permitted to belong to the Farm Bureau organization and are willing to act as local demonstrators."[41]

In Colfax, an energetic agent who worked with the women's club to obtain successful passage of a Clean Milk Ordinance also organized women. Although the men organized first as the Colfax County Farm and Live Stock Bureau, this agent quickly formed a woman's committee and established local units in all parts of the county. She set up special meetings for men and women where information about common agricultural interests could be shared and special meetings for women where prenatal and child care were a part of the program. Here too, agents treated women as a separate group within the organization, and as having special interests. There was, however, an attempt to make them an active if separate part of the organization.[42]

In Doña Ana, women apparently played an important role in organizing the County Farm Bureau. H. H. Brook, county agent, wrote: "The ladies are very willing and anxious to help and are going to be a strong factor in making the Farm Bureau a success." With the support of the Women's Auxiliary of the State Council of Defense, the Farm Bureau took over county food conservation while the auxiliary operated in Las Cruces. The group planned exchanges of local products between country growers and city women, helped get one of the Farm Bureau's five rooms set aside as a "Ladies Rest Room" for farm women, and generally tried to carry out

Ross's vision of a rural-urban coalition of organized women. Yet, even in Doña Ana, women in the Farm Bureau were not conceived of as mutual economic partners in agricultural production but as women contributing through their "home" work and men through their "farm" work. As in other counties, those women who conceived of or practiced direct agricultural production must have found themselves in an anomalous position, uncomfortable in the male groups and uninterested in the female groups.[43]

There is no breakdown by sex of the 2,693 Home Bureau members who had joined the ten clubs formed in New Mexico by the end of 1918. It seems likely that women were a small minority since agricultural agents still considered furthering home demonstration and club work a small part of their responsibilities. Home economics agents planned to take up canning demonstrations as a major project in 1919, but staff cuts reduced the twelve demonstration agents to four, the state Defense Council closed its offices, and federal funding also declined. It is difficult to tell if women could have done better had they organized independently. Such individual organizations never seemed an option. Both male and female agents expected rural women to be part of the male dominated organizations. Farm Bureaus were not involved directly in politics. Farmers were intensely political in most areas of New Mexico, but Farm Bureaus, established by and with support of federally and state funded extension agents, were far different from the earlier populist or socialist farmer's organizations. The government may not have explicitly developed Farm Bureaus in opposition to these more radical farmer's groups, but they did make it possible for the government to introduce agricultural reform without radical political change. As such, Farm Bureau organizing was very much a part of the progressive search for political order in the early decade of the twentieth century.[44]

War brought the climax of the first phase of agricultural extension work among the women of New Mexico just as the women's suffrage movement was also reaching its high tide of political influence. Women suffragists clearly envisioned meeting Hispanic women at the ballot box as well as at the canning kettle, but the imagery of the progressive women's movement had been cast in the ideology of motherhood and domestic science, thus the canning kettle was not so much a contradictory image as one that would help strengthen the bonds of womanhood across cultures. Indian women were always poorly integrated into the movement, but there were more than token efforts to join Hispanic and Anglo women together, at the ballot box as well as over the canning kettle. The first statewide Mother-Daughter Congress had demonstrations in Spanish as well as English, and while only a few Hispanic and even fewer Indian women were involved in the canning process, the image seemed appropriate to the new upsurge in female leadership. The impulse to meet as women was partly a result of the exclusion of middle-class women from male organizational activities in the progressive era and partly women's attempt to find a constituency among their gender.[45]

Almost concurrently with the flowering of canning in the summer of 1918 came the outbreak of influenza in New Mexico. It brought a sobering reminder of the divisions among women, for Hispanic and Indian women suffered far more than did Anglo women. Historians are still not sure why. Rural poverty was apparently intensified by the war, for although commercial farmers made money selling needed foodstuffs, subsistence farmers did not. A two-year drought beginning in 1916 brought severe wheat shortages in some areas of New Mexico. Cattle owners were able to ship out cattle and trim losses, but dry farming crops were a failure and shortages drove up food prices.[46]

Agents reported the devastation in their annual reports. "In our Spanish-American sections people died by the hundreds," reported Van Vleck. In Valencia County, she wrote, the epidemic of Spanish influenza has been very bad; "many of the native people's condition was very bad and many deaths . . . resulted." She and other demonstration agents helped the Red Cross by establishing soup kitchens.[47] Four agricultural agents died, three of them Hispanic, and several demonstration agents became ill. After the first two weeks in September, the state government banned all public gatherings, and most home demonstration agents returned to Las Cruces to complete office work.

Demonstrators did not speculate in their reports how availability of food or nutrition might have affected the Hispanic population. There are hints, however, that grain shortages might have affected rural resistance to disease. One report noted the inability of demonstrators to reach the really poor Hispanic women in the summer of 1918 and noted that many people suffered "on account of their inability to change their food habits." Another agent reported that as the shortage of wheat became acute in summer 1918, merchants began stocking soybean flour as a substitute, but Hispanic women did not know how to use it. The agent then set up demonstrations and reported: "It was necessary to teach the use of this product before there could be any sale."[48]

How can this slender evidence be evaluated? It is possible that had demonstrators been able to work more extensively in Hispanic areas and had a more flexible training program developed that Hispanic women might have coped more successfully with the drastic changes in food supply the war created. There were probably many reasons why more Hispanics than Anglos died, but nutrition was certainly a factor in making one part of the rural population more resistant than another. Since no rural relief existed, the rural poor suffered disproportionately.

Hispanic women, on the other hand, also avoided some of the conflicting messages that the Country Life Movement brought to rural Anglo women through canning. In the early nineteenth century, urban middle-class women often subscribed to a doctrine of spheres, that women's sphere was domestic; man's sphere public. In practice, many middle-class women carved out a considerable range of acceptable public action but the idea that "domesticity" was the only proper sphere for women was widespread in both the settled East and on the western frontier. Still, farm women had always done work wherever and whenever necessary, whether in the home, the barnyard, or the field. Farm women were contributors to the farm economy not only through their domestic work and food preservation, but also through participating in food production. Yet this role as food producer received relatively little attention from agricultural extension agents. These agents hoped to raise the status of rural women by introducing "domestic science" to them. Agents assumed a woman's place was in the home being a skilled, efficient homemaker. In doing so, however, agents provided a model of work for girls and women that was not functional for poor women and farm families if they were to survive on the land.[49]

In providing this model of "domesticity," agents undermined the very goal they had of keeping farm families on the farm. Farm women could not both meet the needs of survival and the ideals for women of the Country Life Movement. Agricultural agents focused on how to make the male farmer more agriculturally productive but without the female farmer also becoming more agriculturally productive, the farm families could not survive, much less reverse the trend of rural impoverishment. Thus, the federal, state, and county governments all subscribed to a rural policy that encouraged women in the home to help absorb the costs of an agricultural sector increasingly dependent on commercialization and on national markets while giving them only limited tools with which to deal with those changes. Through education, agents sought to make the farm wife more self-sufficient at the very time her husband was being taught to become more dependent on commercial agriculture. The pattern was most clear in Anglo families by 1919. It had only a limited influence on Hispanic families before the 1930s when the New Deal would take up and expand the ideals to Hispanic and native American farm families. The canning kettle, then, can be seen as a symbol of sisterhood but also of an essential but separate sphere within the male-dominated rural culture.[50]

Ironically, as reformers brought education for domesticity to rural women, urban women were abandoning many of their previous practices regarding food preservation. The per capita output of commercial canneries which had remained almost constant between 1899 and 1909, began to rise during the very decade that rural women were being encouraged to can a greater amount of their food supply. Ruth Schwartz Cowan has remarked of the urban middle class that by the mid-1920s "home canning was on its way to becoming a lost art." As urban schools shifted the emphasis in economics to consumerism, rural reformers preached the doctrine of scientific homemaking with greater enthusiasm and with the financial support of the federal government. A similar movement was taking place with the southern rural white population. And because southern states would not match federal funds for black programs, private philanthropy rather than the federal government took the same message to black children through industrial teachers such as the Jeanes teachers. "Corn and tomato" clubs provided the equivalent of boys' and girls' gardening and canning clubs.[51]

Even in rural areas, the canning kettle was an outmoded symbol even before Henderson chose it for New Mexico women in 1919. The open canning kettle had already largely been replaced by cold pack canning. The pressure cooker had been introduced and would spread rapidly after 1919. Still, the image lingers, a powerful symbol of the ideal of sisterhood, the witches' caldron transformed into a canning kettle, emblem of a common culture, around which women could meet and learn from one another.

Notes

1. Alice Corbin Henderson, "The Women's Part," *New Mexico Blue Book, 1919* (Santa Fe: Office of the Secretary of State, 1919), 97.

2. Thomas Cooper, *A Treatise of Domestic Medicine* (Reading, Pa.: G. Getz, 1824), contained Appert's treatise of 1810 on preserving. For canning in Texas, see Ruth A. Allen, "The Labor of Women in the Production of Cotton" (Ph.D. diss., University of Chicago, 1933).

3. Adrienne L. Zihiman, "Women as Shapers of the Human Adaptation," in *Woman the Gatherer,* ed. Frances Dahlberg (New Haven: Yale University Press, 1981).

4. Emma Reh, "Navajo Consumption Habits," 24 October 1939, File 121.31, box 1, RG 81–87, Soil Conservation Service, Special Collections, New Mexico State University (SC, NMSU).

5. Report of Assistant State Demonstrator, 1918, Elizabeth Koger, New Mexico College of Agriculture and Mechanic Arts, State College, Agricultural Extension Service, Annual Reports, New Mexico, National Archives, Microcopy T876, Reel 2 (NMCAAES, Annual Reports).

6. "Women's Work, Mescalero Apache Indian Reservation," box 1, RG 81–109, Soil Conservation Service, SC, NMSU; Maryann Abkemeier and Laura Robertson, *Stand Against the Wind: A Biographical Sketchbook of New Mexico Women* (Albuquerque: Wahili Enterprises, 1977), 46.

7. Fabiola [Cabeza] de Baca Gilbert, "New Mexican Diets," *Journal of Home Economics* 34 (November 1942): 668.

8. Joan M. Jensen, *With These Hands: Women Working on the Land* (Old Westbury, N.Y.: Feminist Press, 1981), 121.

9. Fabiola Cabeza de Baca Gilbert, *The Good Life: New Mexican Food* (Santa Fe: San Vicente Foundation, 1949), 5–22.

10. NMCAAES, Circular 13 (December 1915); 35 (March 1918).

11. Nan Elsasser, Kyle MacKenzie, and Yvonne Tixier y Vigil, *Las Mujeres: Conversations from a Hispanic Community* (Old Westbury, N.Y.: Feminist Press, 1980), 67; Fran Leeper Buss, *La Partera: Story of a Midwife* (Ann Arbor: University of Michigan Press, 1980), 21.

12. Donald B. Williams, *Agricultural Extension: Farm Extension Services in Australia, Britain and the United States of America* (Carlton, Victoria: Melbourne University Press, 1968), 22–25.

13. Lloyd E. Blauch, *Federal Cooperation in Agricultural Extension Work, Vocational Education, and Vocational Rehabilitation* (1933; reprint, New York: Arno, 1969), 198; Fred W. Alber, "County Commissioners' View of Extension: A Study in New Mexico," (Master's thesis, Colorado State University, 1967), 32, 45. County commissioners also rated home economics lowest in educational objectives on a scale of five. Salaries and numbers for 1924–25 are in box 34, UA78–43, Agricultural Extension Service, Budget Folder, SC, NMSU.

14. Helen D. Crandall, "Twenty-Five Years of Home Demonstration Work in New Mexico," typescript, box 34, UA78–43, Agricultural Extension Service, SC, NMSU.

15. Tura A. Hawk, "Demonstration in Home Economics, April 11, 1918," Folder, Extension Work in New Mexico Since 1914, box 34, UA78–43, Agricultural Extension Service, SC, NMSU.

16. NMCAAES, *Circular* 7 (December 1915); 14 (December 1916). For the country life movement, see William L. Bowers, *The Country Life Movement in America, 1900–1920* (Port Washington, New York: Kennikat Press, 1974); Mabel Carney, *Country Life and the Country School: A Study of Agencies of Rural Progress and of the Social Relationship of the School and the Country Community* (Chicago: Row, Peterson, 1912); and Liberty Hyde Bailey, *The Country-Life Movement in the United States* (New York: Macmillan, 1911), 85–96.

17. A. C. Cooley, State Leader Report for 1915 and Demonstration Work in Home Economics in First Annual Report of the Extension Division, 1914–1915, NMCAAES, Annual Reports, NA T876, Reel 1.

18. Home Economics Report for Year Ending June 30, 1916, NMCAAES, Annual Reports, NA T876, Reel 1.

19. A. C. Cooley, Third Annual Report for the Year Ending June 10, 1917, NMCAAES, Annual Reports, NA T876, Reel 1.

20. Second Annual Report of the State Leader for New Mexico, 1915 and Semi-Annual Report of County Agents, Jan. 1–June 30, 1915, NMCAAES, Annual Reports, NA T876, Reel 1.

21. Summary of County Agriculturalists work in Doña Ana County, 1916, Narrative Report of County Agricultural Agent from Bernalillo County, R. C. Stewart, 1916, NMCAAES, Annual Reports, NA T876, Reel 1.

22. Report for San Miguel County, in Fifth Annual Report for Year Ending Dec. 31, 1918, NMCAAES, Annual Reports, NA T876, Reel 1.

23. "25 Years of 4-H Club Work," U.S., Department of Agriculture, Extension Service, *Circular* 312 (1939): Figures 1, 4, 6.

24. W. T. Conway, Annual Report, 1914, NMCAAES, Annual Reports, NA T876, Reel 1.

25. Boys' and Girls' Club Work, Annual Report, 1917; Monthly Re-

ports of Agents for 1917, San Miguel; Boys' and Girls' Club Work Annual Report, Year Ending Dec. 31, 1918, Doña Ana, NMCAAES, Annual Reports, NA T876, Reel 1.

26. Boys' and Girls' Club Work Annual Report, Year Ending Dec. 31, 1918, Socorro, Sierra, NMCAAES, Annual Reports, NA T876, Reel 1.

27. Second Annual Report, County Home Demonstration Work in New Mexico for Year Ending Dec. 1, 1918, NMCAAES, Annual Reports, NA T876, Reel 2.

28. Fourth Annual Report of County Agent Work, Dec. 31, 1917, Fourth Annual Report of Cooperative Extension Work, Year Ending June 30, 1918, NMCAAES, Annual Reports, NA T876, Reel 1.

29. Fourth Annual Report of Cooperative Extension Work, Year Ending June 30, 1918, NMCAAES, Annual Reports, NA T876, Reel 1.

30. Monthly Report of Home Demonstration Work, 1918, NMCAAES, Annual Reports, NA T876, Reel 2.

31. Report of State Leader of Home Demonstration Agents, October 1917, NMCAAES, Annual Reports, NA T876, Reel 2.

32. Third Annual Report of County Agent Leader for Year Ending Dec. 31, 1916, NMCAAES, Annual Reports, NA T876, Reel 1.

33. Third Annual Report of County Agent Leader for Year Ending Dec. 31, 1916, NMCAAES, Annual Reports, NA T876, Reel 1.

34. Annual Reports of Boys' and Girls' Club Work Year Ending Dec. 31, 1918, NMCAAES, Annual Reports, NA T876, Reel 1. While gardening might have been open to both sexes, only boys are mentioned in the records.

35. First Annual Report of the Extension Division, 1914–1915, NMCAAES, Annual Reports, NA T876, Reel 1.

36. Boys' and Girls' Club Work, Annual Report, 1917, 1918, NMCAAES, Annual Reports, NA T876, Reel 1.

37. Second Annual Report, County Home Demonstration Work, Year Ending Dec. 1, 1918, NMCAAES, Annual Reports, NA T876, Reel 2; Annual Reports, Boys' and Girls' Club Work, Year Ending Dec. 31, 1918, NMCAAES, Annual Reports, NA T876, Reel 1.

38. A. C. Cooley, State Leader Report, Annual Report, 1915, NMCAAES, Annual Reports, NA T876, Reel 1.

39. Demonstration Work in Home Economics, First Annual Report of the Extension Division, 1914–1915; Semi-Annual Report, Jan. 1–June 30, 1915, NMCAAES, Annual Reports, NA T876, Reel 1.

40. Second Annual Report, County Home Demonstration Work, Year Ending Dec. 1, 1918, NMCAAES, Annual Reports, NA T876, Reel 2.

41. Annual Report, County Home Demonstration Agent, Jan. 1, 1918–Dec. 1, 1918, NMCAAES, Annual Reports, NA T876, Reel 2.

42. Annual Report of State Leader of Home Demonstration Agents, 1918, NMCAAES, Annual Reports, NA T876, Reel 2.

43. Fourth Annual Report of Cooperative Extension Work, Year Ending June 30, 1918, NMCAAES, Annual Reports, NA T876, Reel 2. Similar sex role ideology has lessened the effectiveness of agricultural extension programs more recently in developing nations. See Kathleen A. Staudt, "Women Farmers and Inequities in Agricultural Service," *Rural Africana* 29 (Winter 1975–76): 81–94, and "Class and Sex in the Politics of Women Farmers," *Journal of Politics* 41 (May 1979): 492–512.

44. Robert W. Larson, *New Mexico Populism: A Study of Radical Protest in a Western Territory* (Boulder: Colorado Associated University Press, 1974); James R. Green, *Grass-Roots Socialism: Radical Movements in the Southwest, 1895–1943* (Baton Rouge: Louisiana State University, 1978). For socialism in New Mexico, see an unpublished paper by David Hutchinson, "A Note on Socialism in New Mexico," Special Collections, NMSU.

45. For attempts at Anglo-Hispanic cooperation see Joan M. Jensen, " 'Disfranchisement is a Disgrace': New Mexico Women and Politics, 1900–1940," *New Mexico Historical Review* [NMHR] 56 (January 1981): 5–35.

46. For a review of the effect of the epidemic on one Native American community, see Pam Bunte and Richard Stoffle, "The 1918 Flu Epidemic and Southern Pacific Territorial Re-arrangement," Paper presented at the Annual Meeting of the American Society for Ethnohistory, Colorado Springs, 1981. Also see Richard Melzer, "A Dark and Terrible Moment: The Spanish Flu Epidemic of 1918 in New Mexico," NMHR (July, 1982): 213–36.

47. Annual Report of State Leader of Home Demonstration Agents, 1918, NMCAAES, Annual Reports, NA T876, Reel 2.

48. Fourth Annual Report of Cooperative Extension Work, Year Ending June 30, 1918; Annual Report of State Leader of Home Demonstration Agents, 1918, NMCAAES, Annual Reports, NA T876, Reel 2.

49. Concepts of domesticity are explored in Kathryn Kish Sklar, *Catharine Beecher: A Study in American Domesticity* (New Haven: Yale University Press, 1973), and Julie Roy Jeffrey, *Frontier Women: The Trans-Mississippi West, 1840–1880* (New York: Hill and Wang, 1979).

50. Robert H. Wiebe, *The Search for Order, 1877–1920* (New York: Hill and Wang, 1967), and Ellis W. Hawley, *The Great War and the Search for a Modern Order: A History of the American People and Their Institutions, 1917–1933* (New York: St. Martin's, 1979), explore these concepts but do not apply them to rural policy.

51. Margaret G. Reid, *Economics of Household Production* (New York: J. Wiley and Sons, 1934), 55; Ruth Schwartz Cowan, "Two Washes in the Morning and a Bridge Party at Night: The American Housewife Be-

tween the Wars," *Women's Studies* 3 (1976): 160–61; James D. Anderson. "Northern Foundations and the Shaping of Southern Black Rural Education, 1902–1935," *History of Education Quarterly* 18 (Winter 1978): 371–97; Lance G. E. Jones, *The Jeanes Teachers in the United States, 1908–1933* (Chapel Hill: University of North Carolina Press, 1937).

⫷ 8 ⫸

"I've Worked,
I'm Not Afraid of Work"

Farm Women
in New Mexico
1920–1940

Joan M. Jensen

These words of Edna Gholson of Quay County, New Mexico, in many ways symbolize the history of farm women in New Mexico during the two decades from 1920 to 1940. The work of farm women has always been visible, known, and talked about in rural areas. Any farm woman can give a detailed description of the work she and her neighbors perform in the farm house, farm yard, farm field, and farming community. It is only historians who have had difficulty translating that oral tradition into a written account. Because New Mexico has been rural longer than most states, women have been absent from most written accounts of New Mexico history. Rural women's history is accessible, however, through census material, agricultural extension records, and especially through oral history. These sources make the twentieth century history of New Mexico farm women particularly rich for those historians who take the time to look for it.

This chapter describes the work of New Mexico farm women in family and community. It is confined primarily to the Hispanic and Anglo majority. Although Native American women have had a long, rich agricultural history, as other chapters in this book testify, their history has also been separate in many ways. Their history deserves special skills of analysis and is available through separate sources for the most part. For these reasons, the Native American minority, which numbered less than six percent of the population in 1920 and lived scattered through McKinley, San Juan, Sandoval, and Valencia counties is not discussed here. Nor are black women, an even smaller, more urban group that numbered less than two percent of the population. The intercultural perspective here presented, then, is that of the almost equal numbers of Hispanic and Anglo females who together composed the 85 percent white majority of the state in 1920. Of these 306,000 females, almost 78,000 were twenty-one years or over, and 64,000 of them rural. Members of this rural adult female population and the changes in their lives over twenty years are the focus of the following study.[1]

This study takes as its direct focus farm women in Bernalillo, Doña Ana, Union, Rio Arriba, Santa Fe, Taos, and Valencia counties. Anglo women were represented heavily in the counties of Bernalillo, Doña Ana, and Union, although only Union was almost entirely Anglo. Rio Arriba, Santa Fe, Taos, and Valencia were predominantly Hispanic with small Anglo minorities. Doña Ana is located in the south, Valencia and Bernalillo in central, and Santa Fe, Rio Arriba, and Union in the northern part of the state. These counties give regional and ethnic representation. In addition, oral and family histories from women of a number of other counties describe similar conditions and attitudes of farm women, and agricultural extension documents from 1921, 1925, 1930, 1935, and 1939 describe the activities of farm women. Together, the oral histories and written records provide rich documentation of the work farm women performed in the economic and cultural survival of family and community. Although divided by ethnicity and sometimes by class, these farm women shared a common history as they worked in the valleys, plains, and mountains of New Mexico.

The primary bond of unity among these Anglo and Hispanic women was poverty. The majority of each group was desperately poor, not only by contemporary standards but also by middle class standards of the time. As frustrated extension agents found, many women were so poor they could not afford the few cents necessary for patterns, hat frames, or material to complete clothing projects. For this reason, extension agents in most areas concentrated on food preservation, labor intensive work that could provide necessary food for the whole family and which required equipment that could often be purchased collectively and used cooperatively. Pressure cookers and glass containers, although still expensive for impoverished farm families, were within the reach of most. Growing food and preserving it, increasingly became an important summer task for large numbers of Hispanic and Anglo farm women.[2]

All New Mexico farm women were affected by certain grim economic facts of life in the two decades between 1920 and 1940. Bounded on each end by a world war that affected agriculture and family intensively, these decades were primarily ones of economic depression and change for the entire farm population of the United States. The adjustment to changing world and domestic markets after World War I, the depression that spread out from urban areas, combined with one of the worst droughts in the history of the Southwest, left thousands of farm families with little hope for changing their lives. Hard times were not new to most New Mexican farm families, whether homesteaders who had so recently and so optimistically dotted the eastern plains with their sod and frame homes and windmills or Hispanic farmers who held small irrigated plots along the Rio Grande. All had already suffered hard times. What they lost in these depression years was primarily the hope that hard work could make a good life for their families on the land. It was hard to look forward and to expect better times. Without that hope many sold out, moved to town, or became tenants and farm laborers on the land of other farm families.[3]

The life styles honed by poverty, nevertheless, gave these farm families great survival skills. Labor exchange, barter, a common rural socio-economic status gave people a feeling of shared experience. There were few wealthy farm families at whom rural people could direct their anger. Simple life styles were the rule even for most ranch and farm families that had wealth in land. While there were growing class divisions in the state, these were masked by urban-rural rifts. The wealthy most often lived in town or out of state, appearing occasionally in communities or, as one commentator wrote, in the offices of extension agents in their "white linen suits." Conflict occurred during these years but it usually took the form of conflict against outsiders who attempted to extend control into rural areas. Open violence flared occasionally but usually the community majority united against the outsider. The representatives of these outside interests held their tongues, for the most part, and bided their time.[4]

In addition to a type of class homogeneity, farm women also benefited from federal and state agencies expanded or established to meet the crisis of the depression and drought of the early 1930s. In addition to dealing with new conditions, officials tackled old problems like rural health, hazards of water supply, environmental dangers of soil erosion from over grazing, and isolation of farm women. The actions of state extension agents and federal officials, while sometimes bungling and inappropriate, eventually provided an impressive rural service infrastructure. Rural women were better organized in many ways by the end of the 1930s than their urban sisters. There was a community spirit of cooperation which, while unequal in different areas, increased during the 1930s. Welfare, government jobs and loans, extension clubs, and projects all had their pitfalls. But when officials could operate effectively with their rural constituency, helping them meet their needs, the agencies provided a network of support that rural people had not experienced previously in American history. Some contemporary commentators noted the great gains by the wealthy elite from federal funding. Hugh G. Calkins, for example, observed that in the Mesilla Valley of southern New Mexico, the wealthy farmers had received most of the $675,000 in payments under the Agricultural Adjustment Act. Nevertheless, middle class farm families in the Mesilla Valley also gained from the assistance of state and federal programs. Poor farm families, who did not have enough money to keep their land, received federal relief.[5]

For rural women, the family remained central to their lives in a peculiar way, for most of their work was performed within the family on family owned farms. The rules for this circumstance were embedded so deeply in family law and custom that many may not have consciously considered them or possible alternatives. For that reason, a review of family law that encompassed community property law in New Mexico is fundamental to understanding women's relation to agriculture.

Research on the history of family law in New Mexico is still relatively new but the general outlines are clear. Hispanic women had enjoyed the rights of community property under Spanish and Mexican law but these rights were diminished under American rule and the adoption of common law procedures. The property rights of Hispanic women should not be romanticized, however. Like women under common law, New Mexico women forfeited most of their civil rights upon marriage. Married women were subordinate to their husbands under Mexican law. While a woman had a legal right to retain separate title to property brought into a marriage and had a legal right to one half of the property accumulated after marriage, her husband, as legal head of the family, had management and control of property during marriage. She could lose her property rights for adultery or if she entered the church. Community property laws gave the family, not the individual woman protection. Marriage was a legal partnership under Spanish and Mexican law with each partner owning one half of the acquired property but one partner, as a legal commentator remarked, had "larger power than the other." A woman had a legal right to control of her property only at her death unless her husband died first. The husband could dispose of his property at will; the wife, except for small gifts to the poor, only with the consent of her husband. Before 1907, however, women did have the right to dispose of their separate property and one half of the community property by will.[6]

In 1907, the New Mexico legislature passed statutes modeled on California family law. Under the new law, a woman could not dispose of her property by will. This meant that her property passed automatically to her husband. She had no right to make a will or determine who would receive her property. Although California changed its law in 1923, New Mexico retained the old California law until the 1970s. In 1919, the courts held that a wife did not forfeit community property because of adultery. Moreover, an Eddy county ranch woman, bringing suit in this case, and having admitted adultery, was found by the courts to have a right to one half of a ranch valued between $100,000 and $200,000. The court held the husband had tried to defraud the woman by offering her a settlement of $4,000 and ordered the lower courts to divide the property equitably. But a loyal wife had little legal power. To be single, widowed, or divorced gave farm women their only legal equality.[7]

Given the property structure of family law, married farm women theoretically had little control over the property that they owned as marital partners. How this law worked out in practice, however, has not yet been studied by historians. The law gave farm widows considerable power; it may also have given farm wives more power in practice than the theory indicates. But farm women in their oral histories complain of husbands as "partners" who uprooted the family when they decided to move, and as "manag-

ers" of the partnership who ran families into debt, leaving women
no alternative but divorce or acquiesence. The experiences of Florence Hill of Carlsbad and Edna Gholson of Tucumcari are relevant
here. Both husband managers ran up debts for the partnership.
Hill found out only after her husband died that he had run up debts
for another woman. She worked to pay for his funeral expenses
but refused to pay his debts. She had to support her children by
keeping house for a wealthy neighbor. Gholson had a partner whose
problem was drinking. After her divorce, she paid off $900 in debts
in one year on her own by taking in boarders.[8]

Divorce was less common in Hispanic than in Anglo families
in the 1920s and 1930s. Equal division of land among children by
Hispanic fathers remained common, however, and when a husband died without a will the courts divided his community property equally among the children. Such equal partition gave daughters
a stake in family property and increased their control; it also increasingly divided the farm land. By the 1930s, land owned by Hispanic families in counties like Rio Arriba and San Miguel averaged
three acres per family. While land was plentiful and communal grazing lands available, equitable partition had strengthened the families. As Anglo land owners gradually took over communal grazing
lands, such farms could provide only subsistence. Cash incomes
had to be sought, usually by the males in the family, in off-farm
employment. This trend began in Hispanic families before World
War I and accelerated at the end of the war in 1918. Works Progress Administration accounts of the 1930s noted, for example, that
in Cordova men came back from the war reluctant to take over the
farming that women had managed while they were gone. Women
continued to plant the fields while men left the community to work
at nonagricultural jobs for six to eight months. The men's incomes
went to buy new tin roofs and new automobiles while the wom-
en's subsistence farming provided for basic family needs.[9]

Thus the increasingly small irrigated farms of Hispanic families and the larger dry land farms of the Anglos both led to a large
number of subsistence farms where women took care of the farms
while men sought off-farm labor for much of the year. By 1920,
the homesteading boom of the first two decades was over and families were already moving to town. The rural population in New
Mexico had increased by 67 percent in the decade from 1900 to
1910, almost the same percentage as the urban population, which

increased by 70 percent. In the next decade, the homesteading boom over, rural population increased by only five percent. The total number of farms dropped by sixteen percent.[10]

In 1920, farm women lived on less than 30,000 individual farms in New Mexico. In the previous decade, the amount of land in farms had doubled and the average size and value increased over 100 percent. Overall, farms under 20 acres decreased by almost 20 percent, farms from 10 to 175 acres decreased by almost 30 percent, farms from 175 to 500 acres by seven percent. Farms over 500 acres, on the other hand, increased by 337 percent, from less than 4 percent to over 20 percent. Almost 50 percent of the farms were 50 to 500 acres, and about 30 percent were under 50 acres. Ownership was still 86 percent but tenancy more than doubled between 1910 and 1920, and mortgaged farms increased from 5 to 25 percent. Women owned about 5 percent of owner farms, ran 2 percent of managed farms, and worked less than 2 percent of tenant farms. The farms controlled by women were small and poor.[11] In other words, women held few farms singly and small farms operated in conjunction with husbands were decreasing in number and becoming more heavily mortgaged.

During the next two decades the number of farms gradually increased again to the 1910 number but the average size increased very little. Of the 41,000 farms that existed in 1935, almost half of them reported crop failures and the value of farm lands was lower in 1940 than in 1920. By 1935, half of the operators had off-farm work. As the depression worsened, fewer farmers hired labor. Only 14 percent of the farms had hired labor by 1935. Increasingly, the work was done by family labor, a trend that continued to 1940. Families still labored with little mechanization. Two percent of farms had tractors in 1920 but twenty years later only 15 percent of the 34,105 farms had them.[12]

By 1940, a 67 percent majority of New Mexico women were still rural. Almost half of these 84,000 farm women (46 percent) lived on farms under 50 acres and over three-fifths (65 percent) on farms under 175 acres worth just over $4,000 each. Over a third of the farms were subsistence farms, producing primarily for use items that totaled less than $200 per year. Almost two-fifths (39 percent) were semi-subsistence, producing less than $250 for use and sale each year, while almost three-fourths (73 percent) were living on family farms that produced less than $1,000 worth of products to use or sell. Thus, by 1940 three out of every four farm women worked on these small family farms where there was virtually no cash to spend on consumer goods.[13]

The gender division of labor on these small New Mexico farms was never strict. While census statistics do not describe the division of labor, both extension records and oral histories reflect the extensive work performed by women on the farms of New Mexico. On subsistence farms, both small Hispanic farms and homesteading farms, women worked outside most of the year. In the counties of Rio Arriba, Taos, and Santa Fe, the farm work of women, like men, was heaviest in the summer. They planted gardens, hoed and weeded, harvested, and then preserved, usually outside in the yards. In counties where chile was the main cash crop, they picked and strung, dried and marketed it. In Rio Arriba, for example, merchants handled over 60,000 strings of chile a year, usually offering credit. Strings of chiles translated into necessities at the markets. In 1939, Rio Arriba women produced not only enough food for their families for all year and bartered chiles, but also sold $2600 worth of food, $2459 worth of eggs, and several hundred dollars worth of handicrafts.[14]

Should their fields not produce enough, women picked at neighbors on shares, or canned on shares. The Home Demonstration Agent reported from Rio Arriba that women who had poor chile crops helped neighbors hoe and irrigate, pick and string, in return for enough food to feed their families. She estimated that labor exchange saved people at least $200 a year. An additional 150 people exchanged food—peaches for apples, chile for beans and potatoes. At the stores they bartered chile and eggs for sugar, coffee, citrus fruit, and a few other food luxuries. In other parts of New Mexico homesteaders did much the same thing. Edna Gholson remembered working for a neighbor picking tomatoes, carrots, cucumbers, and green beans, washing them and preparing them for market in return for vegetables that she stayed up all night canning. The next morning she would be in the fields picking again.[15]

Hispanic women in northern New Mexico also plastered their own homes in fall and exchanged their labor for cash and in kind payments. Women bartered skillfully. In fall, they also helped thresh and took responsibility for hand winnowing. Relatives and neighbors performed this task cooperatively. Grace Pritchett who taught at Placitas boarded in a household where the mother came to the home of her daughter to help winnow. They poured the wheat from one pan to another to winnow it, then washed and spread it on clean tarps to dry. Women kept small flocks of chickens, and whenever possible a cow or goat for family milk. Men were frequently gone at off-farm work in the 1920s. When men returned, they concentrated mainly on growing fodder crops for animals, and on growing beans and corn. A surplus of beans might also be traded at the stores or in specific communities such as Mountainair, where families went to trade. The cash of the male usually went to purchase his necessities, equipment for the farm, and building supplies. The woman's income provided food and clothing for the family. Farm women may have preferred credit at the local market to cash purchase, for credit, like barter and labor exchange, gave women some control over the products of their work. Despite the cultural differences of homesteading women, the subsistence economy made their working lives similar to those of Hispanic women. Men hired out on larger farms for harvest, worked on the railroads, on road construction, or at any other day labor they could find. Women remained on the farms, tending animals, raising vegetables, preserving food, and developing a crop to provide credit or cash for the necessities of the family.[16]

Although buttermaking had been a traditional way of bringing in cash in other regions, women soon found that this was not true in many parts of New Mexico. Stella Hatch, for example, on arriving near Sand Hills, New Mexico, took a batch of butter to a nearby store, fully expecting to get the traditional credit. The store keeper told her they had no market for butter but he could use lard. "I was shocked," she said, "I had never heard of anyone not wanting to buy butter." She had just rendered some lard, however, so she returned with it to get her needed credit. The experience of Hatch was probably typical of the experiences of other Anglo women settlers. Most women produced butter and lard for use but only a few marketed it. Lard had a ready sale as few Hispanic families raised hogs, but wanted lard for cooking. Lucille Tatreault of Mesilla Valley remembered selling lard to Hispanic neighbors.[17]

Some women did sell dairy products. When Stella Hatch moved to the Mesilla Valley, she sold butter there—fifteen to sixteen pounds a week. Tatreault also found a market for butter in Las Cruces. Edna Gholson remembered selling cream from their dairy near Tucumcari in the 1920s. Doña Ana had a dairy project in 1921 where four families sold two pounds of butter a week at seventy-five cents a pound and made $78 a year. Extension records mention dairying principally as a male occupation, however. Some girls enrolled in extension clubs to raise dairy cows in 1921 and the female tradition of dairying must have lingered on in practice but males received most support for managing commercial dairies. Extension reports reflect little support for market production of butter by farm women.[18]

Poultry raising more likely occupied women in New Mexico. Here again, the practice seems to have been regional and shifting. The extension agent in Union, Edith Hurley, for example, reported that in 1921 on her suggestion families had marketed 105,856 dozen eggs and 9468 chickens for an income of $35,000. Hurley reported "the farm flock a very profitable part of the farming operation" and that she found "nearly all of the ladies and many of the men interested in poultry." Florence St. John marketed eggs in El Paso from a flock started with 15,000 chicks. Later she sold eggs to stores and restaurants in Las Cruces. She and her husband found the income from chickens more steady than that from cotton, which they also raised. Florence Hill remembered raising turkeys in Chaves County for the Kansas market. Another farm woman remembered sending turkeys from Roosevelt County to Los Angeles in dry ice. She cleared $500 one year. On small farms in Bernalillo County, women were well known for their expertise in poultry. Mrs. J. G. Gentry headed the Bernalillo Poultry Association in 1925. Other women appear in the records as poultry experts.[19]

But developing a poultry business was beginning to require a market expertise that farm women had not needed traditionally. Egg merchants in cities were picky. They wanted eggs that kept in warm weather. This meant eggs could not be fertile so hens had to be kept from roosters. Pure bred chickens, fed with animal feed, culled regularly, and kept in well built poultry houses was what extension agents recommended. In 1925, New Mexico imported into the state one half of the poultry products consumed. Still, hundreds of New Mexico women did develop poultry businesses. The high cost of feed during the drought of the 1930s seems to have driven many of these small poultry keepers out of business. By 1936, 70 percent of eggs used in the counties of Bernalillo and Valencia were shipped in from outside the county. By 1939, the town of Santa Fe was importing most of its eggs from Kansas City. Yet

credit at markets for chickens and eggs as well as the bartering of
eggs with neighbors persisted through the period.[20]

In the north, Hispanic women relied on chile as their main
cash and credit crop. As urban areas developed, rural women found
a ready market for red chile. They picked and strung chile, then
hung it on the walls of their adobes to dry. A crop was often estimated by the number of strings produced. Relatives and neighbors gathered at harvest time to work at stringing *ristras*. Merchants
accepted strings for credit at their stores. One could buy almost
anything with a ristra. Women also ground chile, which stores then
marketed. When the Farm Security Administration estimated income for loans, they carefully noted the number of "strings" of
chile produced the year before, along with beans, corn, and wheat.[21]

In northern New Mexico, there was also a revival of handcrafts for sale, a movement in which farm women participated.
Indians had been creating handcrafts for tourists since the late nineteenth century. The Spanish colonial handcraft revival dated from
the early twentieth century. Wood and tin work, and textiles were
the main handcrafts revived. Women participated most frequently
in the textile revival.[22]

Extension agents kept careful records of the value and amount
of handicrafts sold by Hispanic families, for they saw the artisan's
work as a way to supplement subsistence on small farms in the
heavily populated northern counties. Unfortunately, this handcraft
market was geared to tourism for the most part rather than to mass
urban consumption. It also usually depended on local marketing.
When tourists did not tour, as extension agent Felix Armijo reported from Rio Arriba in 1939, many people could not sell their
wares.[23]

Families in several northern villages were successful in sup-
plementing their income by selling handcrafts. In one of these villages, Chimayo, east of Española, families had long depended upon
income from male migration to work in sheep camps, lumber mills,
mines, smelters, and railroads, as well as from weaving. This weaving dated back to the nineteenth century and Chimayo blankets
had gained income and fame for the community. In the 1920s,
women from Chimayo took the weaving skills to Cundiyo, about
26 miles north of Santa Fe. There over half of the families were
weaving blankets by the 1930s. But neither at Chimayo nor Cundiyo could the expert weavers bring in enough money to provide

a sufficient income for families. Most also depended on tourists who came to their villages. When no tourists came, their income shrank.[24]

For villages that could not depend on tourists, the Santa Fe artisan's market was of some assistance. From 1934 to 1940, a group of Santa Fe philanthropists established what they called the "Native Market" to provide an outlet for artisans. Curio stores and a few factories that featured Spanish colonial crafts were flourishing by the early 1920s, and a revival of Spanish New Mexican folklore, architecture, and crafts was in full swing. Author Mary Austin and artist Frank Applegate founded the Spanish Colonial Arts Society in 1925. Concha Ortiz y Pino established the Colonial Hispanic Crafts School at Galisteo in 1929. The Normal School at El Rito began offering craft classes in 1930 and Santa Fe schools under supervisor Nina Otero-Warren soon began offering similar courses. The federal government added its support and funding for vocational training in the arts. For urban Anglos and artists, the arts revival was tinged with a romantic conservatism about preserving the "native" past. For farm families, it was a way of modernizing to survive agricultural hard times.[25]

In 1934 a wealthy Anglo, Leonora Curtin, subsidized the opening of the Native Market, an outlet for only the best quality crafts. The market was an important outlet for yarn, weaving, and colcha, traditional wool embroidery that many northern Hispanic women still loved to produce. In the early 1930s, Santa Fe already had a sizeable Anglo artists' community. By 1936, Santa Fe had been "discovered" by the eastern artistic elite. That year *Vogue* magazine carried an article on the Native Market. The Native Market operated at a loss, however. Rural people found it difficult to use hand skills to compete in an industrial economy. When federally subsidized programs like the WPA and the National Youth Administration offered rural people reasonable wage rates, most quickly abandoned the poorly paying craft work. Women found fewer opportunities in federal work and thus continued to combine crafts with their subsistence farming longer than males. When they had opportunities, young women also moved to the city to obtain better paying jobs.[26]

Still, like canning, handicrafts helped rural families to survive the deepest trough of the depression. A report of Rio Arriba agriculture extension agent Armijo showed that, even with a decline in tourism, women and men produced and sold $5700 worth of weavings in 1929. Santa Fe women continued to provide the main outlet for rural handcrafts. They organized craft fiestas and the women's exchange market, as well as the Native Market.[27]

Produce markets as well as craft markets underwent a revival in the 1930s. In the 1920s, children usually had the task of selling surplus garden produce by the roadside. Fruit or vegetables piled in old cans, and a farm child, were the main ingredients in this marketing of surplus. As automobiles became more popular in the 1930s, urban dwellers often combined inexpensive touring with food purchases. The number of automobiles, even on farms, increased rapidly in New Mexico in the 1920s and 1930s. To a people frustrated by long distances, the automobile seemed a necessity. The number of automobiles on farms more than doubled between 1920 and 1940, from 6018 to 15,731. Farmers could now more easily bring produce to town while townspeople could also more easily fetch their own country produce. Rural people took advantage of both.[28]

Roadside stalls became a common sight in the 1930s, replacing the child and pail. Farm families built attractive stalls, farm women began to organize and staff them. Bernalillo County was developing roadside markets by 1930. In 1930, extension agent Armijo reported from Rio Arriba that farm families had sold $3000 worth of farm products during the last season at roadside markets. This was an important source of additional cash. In Bernalillo County, farmers also brought their produce in to Albuquerque where they established a farmer's market in 1939. There the extension agent helped raise money and organize the market. Farmers near Albuquerque began to increase their truck farming with a ready market for their produce.[29]

For rural people to survive economically this market production had to be combined with subsistence farming and the cash brought in by males either from off-farm work or the raising and selling of animals and field crops. The records kept by the Farm Rehabilitation agents provide some idea of the rural economy in northern New Mexico in the late 1930s. The federal agents made most loans to Hispanic farm families who owned only a few acres although farm families with larger acreage were also eligible. By 1940, work for wages, most of it off-farm work, was bringing in almost fifty percent of the income of these families. Grants from the federal and state governments were bringing in another third.

Income from produce and livestock accounted for about one fourth. Of the off-farm income, mining was by far the most profitable for the families but income from daughters who taught school was the second most profitable. Teaching brought in more money than any of the male occupations, including sheep herding. To have a farm daughter who taught was to have a substantial income in times when farm products could supply little to families.[30]

While subsistence farming doomed families to a minimal economic level, it none the less provided security. Through it, families could hold on to the small acreage they still owned. This was particularly true in the 1920s when men brought in cash from other work. This reliance on subsistence farming and commitment to it was one of the factors that deeply separated thousands of Hispanic farm families and the Anglo experts who most often staffed the extension offices. Time and again, Anglo agents would report that Hispanic families seemed unwilling to change, rooted in traditional ways, sometimes appearing almost inexplicably opposed to sound and reasonable concepts of commercial agriculture.[31]

The conflict over the Middle Rio Grande Conservancy District was the most visible and violent confrontation between traditional and modern values in which farm women were involved. Almost as soon as extension agents went into Valencia County in 1914 and saw the conditions that existed on the irrigated farms there, they dreamed of reclamation. Deforestation in the north in the first two decades of the century had caused silting of the river. Intensive irrigation had resulted in waterlogged acres. By 1920, agricultural agents estimated that 60,000 acres of land in four counties were unusable. It seemed logical and progressive to support schemes for a conservancy district that would develop productive, commercially viable farms.[32]

Urban businessmen apparently saw the plan as one from which they could profit as bond holders of the money that would be raised to finance the project. Farmers owning land benefiting from the project would be taxed to pay for the capital and interest. Farmers would increase their productivity and their income and thus be able to pay increased taxes. Everyone would be happy.[33] Unfortunately, no one consulted with the farm families who were to be benefited by the scheme. The state legislature accepted petitions to establish the project from Albuquerque businessmen outside the farming areas, set up a conservancy district with the legal right to tax, and approved the sale of bonds.[34]

By the time engineers had their machinery in place to lay down drainage culverts, angry farmers had organized. They stopped the engineers, tore up the culverts, disarmed the attorney general, and kicked and pushed the directors of the project when they arrived at the confrontation. Officials called for the national guard and Governor Richard Dillon quelled the uprising by arranging for a moratorium on payment of taxes. Farms over twenty acres would have three years; farms under five acres would have five years before beginning tax payments for the improvements. By that time, they could have increased production to pay taxes levied on their farm land. The project went forward among extreme hostility from the farm families. An Anglo extension agent who had enthusiastically supported the project found farmers hostile to him. "The situation even got so bad, that many farmers when visited by the County Agent, were not even friendly, sometimes very bitter and unfriendly, and at times refused to talk or have any business with the County Agent," R. S. Conway reported from Valencia County in 1930. His work absolutely at a standstill, he soon left the county.[35]

After the moratorium expired in 1934, the farmers refused to pay. Although few foreclosures occurred, much land changed hands. The state dared not move to foreclose lest they encourage open warfare. But many farmers grew discouraged and sold out. Between 1934 and 1936, Anglo ownership of land in the conservancy district rose by seven percent. As one report concluded, Hispanic farmers would soon disappear and be replaced by Anglo commercial farmers.[36]

A similar dispossession of Hispanic farm familes had already taken place in the Mesilla Valley as a result of the building of the Elephant Butte Dam. There Hispanic men and women became the laborers for new cotton farms in the 1920s. The change had taken place with little overt conflict, however, a condition that led state officials to believe that similar changes could be effected in the Middle Rio Grande Conservancy District. Despite the opposition of the Valencia farmers, this second dispossession took place. The refusal of many farmers to pay back taxes simply led to a federal assumption of state obligations. Federal funds eventually rescued the project financially and allowed its completion.[37]

In the north, similar antagonism might have flared under the crushing impact of drought and depression. In these counties, however, Hispanic farmers had firm political control and there were no conservancy plans. County commissioners appropriated money for extension agents with the proviso they be Hispanic. In Rio Arriba county, Fabiola Cabeza de Baca arrived in 1929 to begin a successful decade of work among Hispanic women and agent Armijo found Hispanic families willing to work with him on changes. Both de Baca and Armijo reported good relations with the farmers, a willingness on the part of Hispanics to experiment. Both exhibited understanding of how to work with these families. Armijo reported after de Baca's first year that her work had influenced the whole community favorably, men as well as women, and made his work much more successful.[38]

De Baca was 35 when she arrived in Rio Arriba County as agent. Born in Las Vegas, New Mexico, her mother died when she was five, and she went to live on her grandparents' hacienda, some miles from Las Vegas. Then she studied with the Sisters of Loretto and began teaching in a small rural school. She spent some time in Spain, some time on her grandparents' ranch, and then returned to school to receive her degree in Home Economics from the agricultural college in Las Cruces. After training 10 weeks in San Miguel, she began work in August 1939. For the next ten years, she sent lengthy reports back to headquarters in Las Cruces describing her work with Hispanic women—a unique record of the lives of rural women.[39]

De Baca's reports on her work in Rio Arriba and Santa Fe counties are important both for what they tell us about the women and for what they document about the effectiveness of Hispanic agents in working in predominantly Hispanic communities. They also indicate the importance of work with women for the success of the extension program as a whole. De Baca concentrated on food because that seemed most important to the families and to the survival of their subsistence farms. De Baca gave demonstrations in women's homes, organized youth clubs, located club leaders among teachers and mission workers, organized clubs for adult women, and began a home economics column in the newspaper *El Nuevo Mexicano* that featured translations of recipes. Before long, she had helped Dixon women organize their own club house and helped county health officials start two clinics.[40]

De Baca's work accomplished the changes the extension service wished without creating tension and hostility. The women provided support for the changes men wished to make because they understood how their own work could change to benefit themselves and their families. When the depression of 1932–1933 and drought of 1933–34 nearly decimated northern farm communities, the work of de Baca bore fruit.

The drought hit farm families before there were federal programs. The state responded as best it could. In Rio Arriba and Santa Fe counties, field crops failed and there was not enough fodder for animals. Many weakened animals could not survive the second year of the drought, and by that second year families were in danger not just of losing animals but of starvation itself. By this time, extension agents had already started counseling families to concentrate their energies on family gardens. They helped provide seeds. De Baca expanded and intensified her training in canning both vegetables and meat. When the federal government finally arrived with its program to purchase cattle, families were ready to butcher and can the healthiest of the starving animals.

No Rio Arriba families had pressure cookers when de Baca arrived in 1929 and only a few had them in Santa Fe and Taos. By 1935, thousands of pressure cookers existed in Rio Arriba, Santa Fe, and Taos counties. Families bought them cooperatively and shared them. Men put their cash earnings toward buying these tools for women. In 1935, extension agent J. W. Ramirez reported that the previous year "would have been one of the worst calamities ever experienced had it not been for timely financial aid from the Agricultural Drought Service and the food preservation program." Taos and Santa Fe county families survived for the same reasons. Better than 90 percent of the farm families there preserved enough food for the following year. Prodigious canning on subsistence farms allowed the rural population to remain on the land and to feed itself during one of the severest droughts and depressions in New Mexico history. The survival of Rio Arriba, Santa Fe, and Taos farm families during these years was the best example of how state and federal agencies working in concert with, instead of against the wishes of a rural community, could provide crucial services.[41]

Pressure cookers, which spread so quickly through Rio Arriba, Santa Fe, and Taos counties in the early 1930s, are perhaps the best material objects with which to trace the transfer of technology to farm women during the 1920s and 1930s. Pressure cookers became a necessary tool for most farm women, and one they most commonly purchased and used. Other types of household technology—washers, irons, refrigerators—had to wait electrification that reached rural families slowly and unevenly. Of technological systems desired by rural women, water was the most important. Sewing machines were too expensive for many families during the 1920s. Pressure cookers, water systems, and sewing machines, however, are the three technologies that best reflect changes in farm women's physical lives during these years.[42]

Pressure cookers were just being introduced in the wealthier farm families at the end of World War I. The pressure cooker was a considerable time saver for women who needed to can, for it greatly reduced the time required to process canned vegetables, according to one account from five hours to 80 minutes. It also offered greater insurance that the processed vegetables would be safe when canned in home kitchens. The extension service published bulletins that explained use of pressure cookers in English in 1925 and in Spanish in 1931.[43]

The problem for most farm women was not unwillingness to use new technology but inability to accumulate the cash to purchase it. Pressure cookers sold for $18 in 1921, an amount of money that women seldom spent on household tools. Doña Ana County, where there were many wealthier farmers and a great deal of educational work by the college extension agents, led the way in cooperative purchase of pressure cookers. In 1921, agents reported the importance of acquiring cookers in Doña Ana and arranged to purchase them in quantities for $13.50 each. At least 265 women bought them that year. So many women now owned them, reported the agent, that demonstrations were no longer needed. By 1939, the agent reported that almost all farm families had them. Thereafter, pressure cookers were seldom discussed in reports from Doña Ana County.[44]

Cooperative canning provided a solution for many farm women who could not afford their own pressure cookers. Agents helped set up community canneries. Maud Doty helped set up a successful community cannery in Bernalillo County in 1925 where women installed steam canning equipment with a 500 quart a day capacity and tinned everything from peaches to whole beef. During 1934, the federal government set up a canning project in Taos County to provide work for community women. That year women canned over 12,000 cans for the Federal Emergency Relief Administration to distribute to needy families in addition to cans for their own home use. Agents estimated women filled 43,000 number two tin cans in the first eleven weeks of operation and eventually 110,000 cans and jars. The Resettlement Administration also budgeted money in Bernalillo County in 1935 to purchase canning equipment for many women who had never canned before. In Rio Arriba, federal funds helped women buy jars and pressure cookers. There women preserved food in over 46,000 containers in 1939.

Canning then, even for women who could not afford their own pressure cookers, was the main technological change for rural women in New Mexico during these years. While urban women were acquiring indoor plumbing, electricity, and such appliances as irons, these rural women were still devoting their time and acquiring technology to preserve food. While most farm women in New Mexico had pressure cookers by the end of the 1930s, few yet had electric irons, because as late as 1945 only one third had electricity. Urban women, meanwhile, were using electric irons and buying most of their food in cans.[45]

Water systems were more costly to acquire and much more rare than food preservation tools during this period. The Doña Ana home demonstration agent reported proudly in 1921 that she was helping a ranch family to install an entire demonstration bathroom. The cost for supplies alone was $120, a sum that few but the wealthiest could afford. In Curry County, the home demonstration agent reported the importance of a kitchen water supply for her farm women and the industriousness of one woman in acquiring a system. Here too, even with labor supplied by the family, the system cost the woman $90 for the tank and water pipes. Most farm women still carried their own water as they recalled in oral histories. For those fortunate few who got even partial running water, the saving in time and effort was impressive. The home demonstration agent who reported on the Curry County system noted that the farm woman had previously walked an estimated 260 miles a year bringing water from the well to her kitchen. Of almost 30,000 New Mexico farms in 1945, only 28 percent had running water. That meant 72 percent of all farm women still carried their water.[46]

Sewing machines were less expensive than water systems and less dependent upon males for installation although women might be dependent upon men for repairs. Clothing construction remained one of the most gender defined of all farm tasks. Young men never joined clothing clubs while it was the most popular among young women. Yet, the use of clothing construction equipment that cost money made little headway because farm women felt they could not spend money on clothing. The home demonstration agent in Taos County reported that women there "found it difficullt to get even the price of a commercial pattern," then selling for a few cents. When hat making became popular in early 1920s, and times were good in Union County, women there were able to order wire hat frames from the dime store for 10 to 35 cents and delightedly made summer hats from dried corn shucks. Even before the depression deepened in the 1930s, demonstration agents reported that neither girls nor women could afford to purchase sewing supplies in counties like Otero, for "the people have hardly had enough to eat." Flour sacks were a necessity for sewing projects. Remodeling and maintaining older clothing became the focus of much of the women's attention. Two hundred Doña Ana County women reported making an average of two garments and remodeling ten during 1921. They pooled their scraps in a "community bag."[47]

No easily obtainable statistics exist for sewing machine purchases in New Mexico. Non-electric sewing machines sold for anywhere from $30–$80 in 1930 mail order catalogs. Farm families frequently ordered from these catalogs because towns were so widely dispersed and roads still largely unimproved. In fact, home sewing became a necessity even for women who had never sewed previously, because mail order clothes were unsatisfactory and towns so difficult to get to. Most farm women sewed their own clothes but even foot powered treadle machines were not common. The operation of sewing machine clinics in Doña Ana in 1921, and a record of 292 home repairs there, indicates that middle class farm women in some counties had sewing machines. But these clinics did not appear in the north until late in the 1930s. In 1939, San Miguel County women had few sewing machines and only one girl could afford to purchase material for a sewing project. By the late 1930s, however, young girls were showing a much greater interest in sewing, perhaps because so many were considering moving to urban areas to find work.[48]

Rather interestingly, creative hand work does not show up in most communities. Agents trained in home economics tended to discourage creative work of this sort because they felt farm women needed to concentrate on practical skills. Still the impulse to create beautiful and not necessarily functional items existed among some farm communities. De Baca mentioned the large number of Hispanic women who enjoyed doing colcha embroidery and other needlework during the three months a year they did not work outdoors. She wished the extension service had listed it as a project so that clubs could work on it. Here was a missed chance to combine the creative interests of women with support for a marketable product. An agent visiting the isolated village of Pilar in Taos County in 1921 mentioned seeing "oceans of crocheting and other fancy work" in the homes of Hispanic women she visited. Quilts do not show up in records of the counties selected for this study except in Union County in 1935 when the agent reported club women making 115 quilts. Where a quilt tradition existed, it probably came in with the homesteaders from Oklahoma and Texas. But women there were such hard working pioneers that they may not have had time to sew quilts, at least not the magnificent quilts that older women produced later when freed from incessant work and absorbing poverty.[49]

Technology benefited a few women during these decades but organizing probably benefited them more. To facilitate their work in reaching women, agents encouraged women to form clubs to decide what they needed. To the extent that these clubs benefited poor women and women of different ethnic groups, and agents oriented their work to the needs of these women, the clubs provided an important forum for farm women. In clubs, they met, exchanged joys and laments, and received support from each other.

Organizing was not always dependent on agents. In counties like Union, for example, older farm organizations with hundreds of men and women members were in existence when agents arrived. Home demonstration agent Edith Hurley reported 250 Farm Bureau members in 1921 with "the ladies . . . as much, or more interested in all lines of work as the men." Two women and three men assumed leadership in organizing the Farm Bureau there and it flourished in the eastern part of the county. In some areas agents skillfully pulled farm women together into organizations, where they found new strength together. Sometimes club women, like Bernalillo club women in 1921, used their organizational strength politically to maintain county financial support for home demonstration agents. The state narrative for Bernalillo County read:

"There was some doubt about the work's being continued in Bernalillo County for the coming year, and a great deal of pressure was brought to bear on the commissioners by the women of the county, and some of the men, as well as the Director of Extension. . . . The rural women are working to save the work." In Union County, on the other hand, the agent reported, "the new County Commissioners have the reduction mania and there is some danger of the work being cut out. The women are making every effort to hold it." Women there failed to convince male county commissioners to fund a female home demonstration agent even though they continued to fund a male agricultural extension agent.[50]

Some clubs welcomed agents; some operated successfully aloof and separate; some crumbled without the agent's support. The two decades saw impressive organizing among woman, however. By the end of the Depression large numbers of rural women in New Mexico were not only organized for the first time but also organized more effectively than many urban women. Women organized in Farm Bureau clubs, in rural women's clubs, and in extension clubs. Each offered rural women important experience.

Farm Bureau women were among the first to organize. The Doña Ana Farm Bureau was one of the largest and strongest units in the state and women in that county were probably the best organized. Farm Bureau membership was by family but members soon learned that the gender division of labor and special gender concerns of women made it more comfortable for them to meet separately. The disadvantage of separate groups was that it segregated women from meetings where important farming skills were learned and shared by men. The advantage was that separate locals gave women space and time to be by themselves to discuss their needs away from the men. Farm Bureau women in Doña Ana formed women's locals in every community. They discussed and planned their projects, and told agents what they wanted of them. They provided a strong support network for almost 300 members by 1925. Women helped raise money to establish a "Rest Room" for farm women in the Temple of Agriculture, furnished it, and used it in turn, to raise money for other projects. Doña Ana Farm Bureau members provided experience for community leadership and needed service for women.

The main criticism that can be made is that the Farm Bureau apparently did not extend its base deeply into the poorer Anglo or

Hispanic farming communities. Farm Bureau members remained composed primarily of Anglo women from medium sized farms. Their organization gave these average farm families important leverage in the community. Nina Griffin later remarked that farm women were better organized than Las Cruces women in the 1930s. Moreover, when federal programs promised assistance to communities to modernize, these rural women led the way. Griffin remembered wanting paved roads and working with other farm women to raise money to pay for materials when the Works Progress Administration offered free labor.[51]

Elsewhere, Farm Bureau organizations seemed to rise and fall. For a while, Valencia County boasted the only Farm Bureau in central New Mexico. Then during the conservancy conflict, it disintegrated. The agent there, who had begun to organize the Farm Bureau, soon found that he was doing all the work. Farm families simply refused to cooperate and the agent let it fold. Union County had a flourishing Farm Bureau for a few years. By 1934, however, that county's Farm Bureau was also gone. In other areas, Farm Bureaus were never formed. Men formed marketing associations for themselves, such as the Bean Growers Association, which left women out; or farmers remained unorganized.[52]

Where no Farm Bureau existed, women organized rural women's clubs. These clubs apparently never federated. One once affiliated with the State Federation of Women's Clubs but the agent sadly noted that they were moving away from home economics. Most simply had an independent club that rose and fell with the fortunes and interests of community women. These clubs took names that reflected the names and attitudes of their communities: the Bluewater Food Club in Valencia County, Volcanic Canning Club of Union County, the Miercoles Club in Bernalillo County. The clubs usually concentrated on family and community affairs, and left few records but those by extension agents. Extension agents worked extensively with these clubs, asking them to make plans for projects and to decide what information they needed from agents. Agents did demonstrations, showed films, suggested new projects, and acted as outside catalysts.

Eventually agents began to organize women into Extension Clubs that could function throughout the county. Taos had 500 members in 23 of these clubs by 1935. In these clubs, although the agents assumed more responsibility, they attempted to have farm

women do most of the organizing. De Baca was especially successful in organizing Rio Arriba women who had little experience
with formal community organizing. She wrote in one report: "Outside of dances, Church festivals, and weddings, they never get together for social activities." But the women responded to her
organizing activities. "It has been a change in their lives to get together once a month regularly," de Baca wrote. "They may not
have accomplished very much materially, but they have gained much
spiritually. It has started them to think along the social side of life."
When one woman pleaded being too busy, another retorted: "If
we have an excuse to leave our work for one day a month, we
ought to take advantage of it even if it is only to get away from the
work." For these women it was a rest, as one said, "from the daily
routine of house and outdoor work."[53]

Whatever the club, farm women joined most often when clubs
gave farm women new skills and encouraged them to share their
own. Clubs provided important psychological support as well. One
Colfax County farm woman recalled later joining a homemakers
club after having a nervous breakdown. Other women remembered
grabbing up small children and escaping to meetings where they
simply enjoyed each other's company, laughing, joking, and swap-
ping experiences. "I just picked up my baby and went," recalled
Frances Mathews of Colfax County.[54]

As social organizations rather than economic organizations,
clubs could do little to change the patterns that were making it increasingly difficult for subsistence farms to survive. Hispanic women
in many counties were already moving off farms and into urban
neighborhoods. Or they were continuing to live in villages but increasingly dependent on off-farm work. For these women, the clubs
had little to offer.

Still, with the help of agencies and agents, their own hard work
and resilient spirits, many women did survive as farmers and kept
their families together on the land through hard times. Looking
back on that experience, some things seemed particularly fortunate to the survivors. The fact that most families suffered about
equally, that they usually could get enough food, that their children respected the hard work of the parents and understood that
the work the family performed together was necessary for survival
were among those mentioned later in oral histories. Women worked
hard but they took pride in their work, whether in field or farm

house. "Yes, I *was* busy," recalled sharecropper Ellen Grubbs Reaves. "And if you think I didn't work, you just wasn't there," exclaimed Edna Gholson when she remembered her hard work boarding highway workers to feed her family and pay debts. But perhaps Nona Berry captured the positive feelings that farm women must have often felt, after they had worked long and hard at tasks they could perform skillfully when she asked, "Did you ever take a fine baking of bread out of the oven and felt like you had done real well?"[55]

During these decades women's work on the farm was essential and crucial for the survival of farm families. Told from documents and from their own oral remembrances, women's history gives a fuller picture than what has been traditionally termed agricultural history. It is proof that agricultural history must give way to a true rural history in which women and men are represented in the full context of their lives on the land.

Notes

1. Population statistics from U.S., Department of Commerce, Bureau of the Census, *United States Census of Agriculture: 1945* (Washington, 1946), Vol. 1, Part 30, New Mexico and Arizona, 1–14.

2. Joan M. Jensen, "Canning Comes to New Mexico and Arizona: Agricultural Extension Service, 1914–1919," *New Mexico Historial Review,* 57(1982): 361–386.

3. Joan M. Jensen, "Farm Women in New Mexico, 1900–1940," in Robert Kern, ed., *Labor in New Mexico: Strikes, Unions,* and *Social History Since 1881* (Albuquerque: University of New Mexico Press, 1983), 61–81 has an overview.

4. Hugh B. Calkins, "Reconnaissance Survey of Human Dependency on Resources in the Rio Grande Watershed," (Mimeographed, USDA, Soil Conservation Service, Region Eight, Regional Bulletin No. 33, Conservation Series, No. 6, Dec. 1936), 116.

5. *Ibid.*

6. Theodore E. Jones, II, "Community Property—Power of Testamentary Disposition—Inequality Between Spouses," *Natural Resources Journal,* 1(1967): 645–649; Robert Emmet Clark, "Management and Control of Community Property in New Mexico," *Tulane Law Journal,* 26(1952): 324–343.

7. *Barnett* v. *Barnett,* 9 N.M. 205 (Oct. 1897).

8. Oral histories of Edna Gholson and Florence Hill in Working Lives of New Mexico Women Project, Rio Grande Collections, New Mexico State University. Hereafter cited as WLNMW, NMSU.

9. Lorin W. Brown, *Hispanic Folklore of New Mexico: the Lorin W. Brown Federal Writers' Project Manuscripts* (Albuquerque: University of New Mexico Press, 1978): 190–191.

10. U.S., Department of Commerce, Bureau of the Census, *Farm Population of the United States* (Washington, 1926), 210–211, Tables 77, 78.

11. U.S., Department of Commerce, Bureau of the Census, *Fourteenth Census of the United States Taken in the Year 1920* (Washington, 1922), Vol VI, Part 3, Agriculture, 199–203.

12. U.S., Department of Commerce, Bureau of the Census, *United States Census of Agriculture: 1945* (Washington, 1946), 1–14.

13. *Ibid.*

14. Home Demonstration Agent Fabiola Cabeza de Baca, Annual Report for Rio Arriba and Santa Fe Counties, 1939, New Mexico College of Agriculture and Mechanical Arts, State College, Agricultural Extension Service, Annual Reports, New Mexico, National Archives, Microcopy T876, Reel 22. Hereafter cited as NMCAAES.

15. *Ibid.;* Oral history of Edna Gholson, WLNMW, NMSU.

16. Grace Pritchett, *The Road Goes This Way and That Way* (St. Paul, New Mexico: Brawn, 1981), 12–13.

17. Oral histories of Lucille Tatreault and Stella Hatch, WLNMW, NMSU.

18. State Administration Reports, 1921, NMCAAES, Reel 4, reported some cheese making but no buttermaking. Doña Ana County, Home Demonstration Agent, Annual Narrative Report, 1921, NMCAAES, Reel 4, reported that women made cheese and butter for home use only and that dairies exported milk to El Paso.

19. *Ibid.* Union did not turn out to be a major poultry region, however. By 1924, farm families were producing only for use. Union County, County Agent Annual Report, 1924 and Bernalillo County, County Agent, Annual Report, 1925, NMCAAES, Reel 7. Oral histories of Florence St. John, Lucille Tatreault, Florence Hill, WLNMW, NMSU.

20. State Administration Reports, 1925, Poultry, and Bernalillo, Annual Report, Home Demonstration Agent, 1935, Santa Fe County Annual Report, 1935, Reel 17, and Santa Fe, Annual Report, Home Demonstration Agent, 1939, NMCAAES, Reel 22.

21. Farm Security Administration, Rehabilitation Loan Application, National Archives, Record Group 96. Hereafter cited as NA, RG.

22. Sarah Nestor, *The Native Market of the Spanish New Mexican*

Craftsmen: Santa Fe, 1933–1940 (Santa Fe: The Colonial New Mexico Historical Foundation, 1978), 3–4.

23. Annual Report, Rio Arriba, Felix Armijo, 1939, NMCAAES, Reel 22.

24. Descriptions of weaving and economic conditions at Chimayo and Cundiyo are in Farm Security Administration, NA, RG 96.

25. Nestor, *Native Market,* 11–20.

26. *Ibid.,* 31–32.

27. Home Demonstration Agent, Annual Report, 1939, Santa Fe and Rio Arriba, NMCAAES, Reel 23.

28. U.S., Department of Commerce, Bureau of the Census, *United States Census of Agriculture: 1945,* Vol. 1, Part 30, 4.

29. Bernalillo County, Home Demonstration Agent, Annual Report, 1930, 1935, NMCAAES, Reels 12, 17.

30. Joan M. Jensen, "Farm Families Organize Their Work: New Mexico, 1900–1940," Paper presented at the New Mexico Family and Community Conference, Albuquerque, New Mexico, July 15, 1983.

31. Comments were frequent from some Anglo agents. See, for example, State Administration, Reports, 1921, and Bernalillo, Annual Report, 1935, NMCAAES, Reels 4, 17.

32. Valencia, Annual Report, County Agent, R. S. Conroy, 1930, NMCAAES, Reel 12; Brian McDonald, John Tysseling, Michael Browde, and Lee Brown, *Case Studies in the Development of New Mexico Water Resources Institutions: the Middle Rio Grande Conservancy District and Urban Water Pricing* (New Mexico Water Resources Research Institute, Technical Competition Report, Project N. 1345640, 1981), 10.

33. *Ibid.,* 13–14.

34. *Ibid.*

35. Valencia County Agent, Annual Report, 1930, NMCAAES, Reel 12; Calkins, "Reconaissance," 58. Conroy was gone from Valencia County by 1935.

36. *Ibid.*

37. McDonald, et al, *Case Studies,* 43–47.

38. Rio Arriba County, Narrative Report, Extension Agent, F. A. Armijo, 1930, NMCAAES, Reel 12.

39. Oral history of Fabiola Cabeza de Baca Gilbert, NMSU.

40. Rio Arriba and Santa Fe Counties, Home Demonstration Work, 1930, Fabiola Cabeza de Baca, NMCAAES, Reel 12.

41. Santa Fe County, Annual Report, 1935, J. W. Ramirez, Taos County, Annual Report, 1935, NMCAAES, Reel 17.

42. Rio Arriba and Santa Fe Counties, Home Demonstration Work, 1929, Fabiola Cabeza de Baca, Santa Fe County, Home Demonstration Work, Fabiola Cabeza de Baca, 1930, NMCAAES, Reel 12. Report of

Home Demonstration Agent Work in New Mexico for the year ending Nov. 30, 1921, Mary B. Richardson, NMCAAES, Reel 4.

43. *Ibid.,* Doña Ana County, Home Demonstration Agent, Annual Report, 1939, NMCAAES, Reel 22. Grace B. Luna, *Canning Club Work* (Extension Circular 83, March 1925) and Fabiola C. de Baca, *Boletin de Conservar* (Extension Circular 106, May 1931).

44. Bernalillo County, Home Demonstration Agent, Annual Report, 1925 and 1935, Reels 7, 17; Taos County, Annual Report, 1934, Reel 16, NMCAAES.

45. Some women in eastern New Mexico and perhaps elsewhere did have access by 1929 to gas irons. Joan M. Jensen and Mary Johnson, "What's in a Butter Churn? Objects and Women's Oral History," *Frontiers,* 7(Fall 1983). Bernalillo County reported two gasoline systems for irons in 1921, Bernalillo County, Home Demonstration Agent, Narrative Report, 1921, Reel 4, and 25 houses with electricity in 1925, Home Demonstration, Annual Report, 1925, Reel 7, NMCAAES.

46. This cost included a hot water tank, bath tub and sink, pipe and drain boards, State Administration reports, 1921, Reel 4, NMCAAES. Bernalillo County reported one power washing machine that year. Quote from Joan M. Jensen, "Recovering Her Story: Learning the History of Farm Women," Paper presented at the National Extension Homemakers Conference, Laramie, Wyoming, August 3, 1983. Oral history of Nina Griffin, Mesilla Valley reported having to carry water a half a block on their farm, WLNMW, NMSU.

47. State Administration reports, 1921, Reel 4; Narrative Report of Mrs. Edith Hurley, Home Demonstration Agent, Union County, 1921, Reel 4; State Administration Reports, 1925, Reel 7.

48. Doña Ana County, Home Demonstration Agent, Annual Narrative Report, 1921, Reel 4, Annual Report, Child Development and Parent Education, 1939, Reel 22, NMCAAES. Sewing machine prices from Sears, Roebuck and Co., *Spring and Summertime Catalog* (1930).

49. Second Annual Report for Year Ending June 30, 1916. Reel 1, NMCAAES contains early disparagement of "fancy work." Rio Arriba and Santa Fe Counties, Home Demonstration Work, Fabiola Cabeza de Baca, 1939, Reel 12, State Administration Reports, 1921, May Report, Reel 4, Union County, Home Demonstration Agent, M. Kathryn Woodbridge, 1935, Reel 17, NMCAAES. Patricia Cooper and Norma Bradley Buferd, *The Quilters: Women and Domestic Art* (Garden City, New York: Doubleday, 1977).

50. Union County, Narrative report of Mrs. Edith F. Hurley, Home Demonstration Agent, 1921, Reel 4, NMCAAES. "History of Extension Work in Union County, 1916–1939," in Union County, Annual Report, 1939, reported 500 members organized in a society of "farmer's

equity," when the agent arrived in 1916. Whether this was populist or socialist is not clear but members assisted the agent. A Farmers and Stockmen Bureau was organized in 1916 and grew rapidly. The Farm Bureau was apparently organized about the same time. Edith Hurley was not retained after 1921 and Union had no Home Demonstration Agent from 1928 to 1933. State Administration Reports, 1921, Bernalillo Narrative Report, Reel 4, NMCAAES.

51. Doña Ana County, Home Demonstration Agent, Annual Report, Sara Van Vleck, 1925, Reel 7; Doña Ana County, Home Demonstration Agent, Annual Report, 1921, Reel 4, NMCAAES. Oral history of Nina Griffin, Mesilla Valley, WLNMW, NMSU.

52. Valencia, County Agent, Annual Report, 1929. Reel 11, 1930, Reel 12; Union, Esther B. Call Report, 1934, Reel 16, NMCAAES.

53. Home Demonstration Work Carried out in Rio Arriba and Santa Fe Counties, 1930, Reel 12, Santa Fe, Home Demonstration Work, 1935, Reel 17, NMCAAES.

54. Jensen, "Recovering Her Story."

55. Oral histories of Ellen Grubbs Reaves and Edna Gholson, WLNMW, NMSU.

56. Jensen, "Recovering Her Story."

⫷ 9 ⫸

The Women of
the Amador Family

1860–1940

Sandra L. Stephens

The women of the Amador family of Las Cruces, New Mexico, have left a rich and poignant legacy in their correspondence—the voice of an upper-class Hispanic family from the territorial and early statehood periods of New Mexico. A 10,000-item collection of their papers is located in the archives of the New Mexico State University Library, documenting nearly a century of the family's history in the Mesilla Valley. The correspondence of family members comprises the bulk of the manuscripts, with a concentration of material between 1880 and 1920. The collection includes letters from friends and business associates, legal and financial documents, and assorted memorabilia. Most of the family's letters are in Spanish.

For several decades the Amador family has attracted attention from local writers. Generally, however, these researchers have considered the family only in terms of its public history—particularly Martin Amador's merchandising business, hotel and livery stables. An examination of the Amador Collection goes beyond the public to the private realm. It focuses on the attitudes of the women of the family. Not only do the personal letters permit the reconstruction of the texture of the family's private life, but also the collection allows the reconstruction of an historical picture of this unique group of upper-class Hispanic women, whose lives spanned the Victorian and Progressive eras in American history.

The history of the Amador family in the Mesilla Valley began in the mid-nineteenth century, when New Mexico was still part of the northern frontier of Mexico. Martin Amador is often cited as coming to the territory from Spain, but among his legal papers are statements by him that he was born in El Paso del Norte in 1840 and lived in Ysleta with his widowed mother, brother, and sister. In 1846, Doña Maria Gregoria Rodela de Amador moved to the town of Doña Ana, where the family lived in the household of José Maria Costales. Members of the family do not appear in the 1850 territorial census but again, information regarding their first years in Doña Ana is contained within Martin Amador's legal papers.[1] His mother remarried in 1847 and the 1860 territorial census shows the family living in Las Cruces with Francisco Telles, Doña Gregoria's husband.[2] The census lists Telles's occupation as a farmer but makes no reference to the mercantile store owned and operated by Doña Gregoria. Researchers for the Doña Ana County Historical Society say this store, established in the 1850s, formed the basis for Don Martin's later merchandising enterprises.[3]

As a boy of six, Don Martin became a citizen of the United States in a public oath-taking ceremony in Doña Ana after American troops occupied the territory in 1846.[4] He remained a resident of Doña Ana County for the rest of his life, marrying Refugio Ruiz of Juarez, Mexico, in the early 1860s and establishing his family in Las Cruces.[5] Throughout its history, the Amador family was related through business, marriage and friendship to prominent families in Mexico, notably the Terrazas-Creel *hacendados* of Chihuahua.[6] Their lives exemplified the ability of families in the border territory to interact with two cultures, resulting in a unique mixture of values and traditions.

Doña Refugio was a very young woman when she came to Las Cruces as a bride, probably no more than thirteen or fourteen years of age. Yet, with the help of domestic servants, she maintained their household and cared for their growing family while Don Martin traveled on business. At the same time she preserved close ties with her friends and relatives in Juarez, showing remarkable strength and independence in managing her life and responding to extended family obligations. Her letters attest to her knowledge of business matters and to the active role she assumed in managing farming enterprises in Las Cruces during her husband's absence. Don Martin expressed his confidence in her ability to manage their family affairs in a will he wrote in 1880, leaving her in charge of all their business and property and praising her as a good wife and a good mother. Both friends and family respected Doña Refugio for her kindness and her gentility, and her daughters' lives bear witness to the strong role model she presented as a capable and gracious woman.

The Amador family held a position of importance in Las Cruces society that reflected Don Martin's enterprising nature and his interest in the development of New Mexico. Early in territorial history he responded to regional commercial needs, working as a subcontractor for the United States government. He supplied United States cavalry troops with hay and grama grass, cut from the base of the Organ Mountains, employing as many as forty men for this job.[7] In the 1870s he opened a freighting business with routes from Santa Fe to Chihuahua and offices in Silver City and Bayard.[8] In Las Cruces, which was the reststop for his wagon train drivers, he established livery stables and a fortress-like hotel to provide services and protection for the teamsters.[9]

Settlement of the region and the coming of the railroads changed territorial business patterns and the need for wagon trains dwindled in the 1880s. Responding to these changes, Don Martin and his sons marketed agricultural products from their farms and handled orders and deliveries from mail order houses. The reststop for teamsters became the Amador Hotel, a social gathering place for the town. Rebuilt in 1885, with a theatre and a gallery, the hotel provided a location for elegant *bailes*, as well as providing services to travelers, until the 1960s.[10]

Martin Amador's interest in the quality of life in Las Cruces extended beyond commercial endeavors. He was not only a prominent businessman and a property owner, but also he was a responsible political figure, holding the offices of Probate Judge and Deputy U.S. Marshal in the Third District. He was active in the Republican Party and testified before the Committee on Territories in the U.S. Senate.[11]

Don Martin's efforts to promote education and to improve the quality of life in Las Cruces were varied. He organized social events to raise money for the Las Cruces school system and served on committees that sponsored cultural events, offering the services of the hotel for these occasions.[12] His deep interest in agriculture in the Mesilla Valley led him to experiment with different methods of farming and harvesting. In 1878, a note appeared in the local newspaper, *El Echo,* commenting on a method Don Martin had devised to use horses in threshing corn, ". . . a vast improvement over the way most in vogue—threshing the grain from the cob with a long stiff pole."[13] Furthermore, in the 1880s, he designed a plow, the Amador Combination Plow, which was adaptable to various sizes of teams and farming requirements.[14] Clearly, Don Martin successfully established himself on the cutting edge of social, political and commercial activities in the growing community, exhibiting characteristics associated with frontier pioneers—inventiveness, ingenuity and resourcefulness.[15]

During a period when Hispanic families in the territory were losing their properties in battles over the legality of their inherited titles, the Amador holdings expanded. Don Martin's business acumen contributed to this financial success and his social, political and commercial activities provided many advantageous contacts. Not to be underestimated as a contributing factor to the family's wealth, although it cannot be documented within the collection, is the possible source of income from Mexican properties that Doña Refugio inherited from her mother. She held these properties in her own name throughout her married life, the traditional right of Hispanic women.[16] Upon the probating of their combined estates in 1907, Doña Refugio's properties as well as Don Martin's New Mexican holdings were successfully transferred to the next generation. All seven of their living sons and daughters inherited significant wealth, in the form of houses, businesses, and ranches.[17]

Not only were Doña Refugio and Don Martin successful and upright members of the Las Cruces community but also, as invitations among their papers indicate, they were accepted in many circles and enjoyed a rich social life. They were frequent guests of prominent families in Las Cruces, Mesilla, El Paso, and Juarez, participating in a wide variety of social and cultural events. Don Martin's name appeared frequently on committees that sponsored dances and artistic programs, along with the names of other prominent families—Armijo, Barncastle, Chavez, Fountain, Freudenthal, and Lohman.[18] Memorabilia and letters in the collection attest to the intimacy of these families' friendships with the Amadors.

As a prominent Catholic family, the Amadors befriended the

Sisters of Loretto who came to Las Cruces in the 1870s to establish the Academy of the Visitation. Together with other Las Crucens they were instrumental in the successful liquidation of a $5,000 building debt by helping Mother Praxedes Carty to organize a fund-raising bazaar in 1880.[19] Mother Rosine Green, who succeeded Mother Praxedes as head of the Academy, was godmother to their daughter Clotilde—another sign of the family's close relationship with the Sisters of Loretto in Las Cruces.

Some of the formal invitations the family received provide interesting comments on attitudes toward historical events in the region. For example, in 1880, they attended a ball honoring General George Buell for services rendered in "ridding this border of the presence of that Great Scourge Victorio."[20] Responding to the impact of settlement on the Apache way of life, Victorio and Geronimo had terrorized the Southwest from 1879 to 1886.[21]

Las Cruces was indeed a territorial frontier, rough and beset with violence in the 1880s, but the financial records of the women of the Amador family, mostly in the form of receipts and itemized lists of purchases, are evidence of their consciousness of style and quality associated with refinement. They shopped by mail from large and prestigious houses in the East, such as Bloomingdale's of New York City.[22] They maintained the services of a dressmaker in Louisville, Kentucky, and receipts of her work show they dressed in elegant and elaborate costumes and had special clothing made for times of mourning and for weddings. One of the most detailed bills in the collection, which may have been for a trousseau for one of the daughters, is filled with items such as silk piping, beaded yokes, and expensive lining for sleeves that illustrate the care for details and the levels of elegance they strove for in their garments.[23]

The fashion consciousness of the family was also apparent in their home. Building preparations for this "fine dwelling" were noted by Martin Lohman in *El Echo* as early as 1870.[24] Completed in 1881, the two story house was seventy feet by forty-eight feet. The ground floor rooms, which were below the level of the street, were used for storage of produce from the Amador farms. The second story, with nine rooms and a large hall, was the residence. Access to the home was provided by a wide porch running the length of the house and connected to the street by a bridge.[25] The carved wooden picketing on the porch and bridge bespoke Don Martin's admiration for the style of houses in New Orleans. The Amador

House, or, the Garden House, as it was called, was famous for its interesting, even lavish furnishings, reflecting not only a Victorian style, but also Don Martin's eye for "collectibles."[26] A rather grand parlor, filled with musical instruments, cabinets and tapestries, was the center of the home. Travels of family members to Mexico City, St. Louis, and Chicago influenced their sense of the fashionable, and the family merchandising business brought them into contact with modern homemaking tools, such as washing machines and sewing machines.[27]

The patterns of the family's life indicate the importance of extended family relationships and inter-familial ties, and theirs was a large family. Of the fifteen children born to Don Martin and Doña Refugio, only eight survived infancy.[28] There were five daughters: Emilia, Maria, Clotilde, Julieta, and Corina. There were three sons: Juan, Francisco, and Martin, Jr. (Martin, Jr. died from consumption in 1889, at the age of twenty.)[29] Neither Juan nor Francisco attained the social stature of their father, yet both followed his pattern of farming and business. Juan's nature was somewhat rebellious and his adult association with his family was marked by periods of alienation. Francisco was closer to the model presented by his father, and it was he who managed the family business as Don Martin's health began to fail near the turn of the century.

The lives of the daughters, especially the three oldest who are best represented in the collection, were deeply entwined with their parents' household. They helped raise their younger brothers and sisters and cared for the business of the household even after their marriages. This arrangement was mutually beneficial, because crises in the daughters' adult lives required their return to the family household in Las Cruces. The prosperity of the Amador family, combined with the tradition of maintaining strong family ties, encouraged interdependency throughout their lives. This pattern is reflected in the disposition of the family estate upon Doña Refugio's death in 1907. Shared ownership of certain valuable property linked the welfare of the brothers and sisters, while individually held property allowed each a certain measure of independence.[30]

The economic success of the family and the very nature of Martin Amador's businesses placed the family in highly public and social roles within the community. Don Martin's goals for his children reflected his commitment to active and responsible participation in New Mexican development. In the will he wrote in 1880 (a will superseded in later life but a valuable indicator of his attitudes at the time) he urged his wife to use his estate to ensure that his children were educated and learned to speak English. He also stressed that he wanted his sons to be educated in "Agriculture."[31] The boys were sent to Catholic boarding schools—the Christian Brothers College in St. Louis and the College of St. Michael in Santa Fe.[32] The girls attended the Loretto Academy of the Visitation in Las Cruces, where a solid academic program was accompanied by religious instruction and training in cultural arts. Many of the daughters of the family's friends in Juarez and El Paso also attended this fashionable school, viewed as something of a physical and cultural oasis in the Mesilla Valley.[33]

The family's wealth allowed the Amador children a wide variety of opportunities for self-development, reflected not only in the schools they attended, but also in their activities. They were able to entertain friends and to attend social functions. They traveled within the area to visit friends and family and to Mexico to spend time with relatives. In 1895, Maria and Clotilde traveled to Mexico City with Mother Praxedes and Mother Rosine from Loretto Academy, where they visited the Shrine of Our Lady of Guadalupe and were received by Doña Carmelita, the wife of President Porfirio Diaz.[34] Julieta traveled to Mexico City in 1915 to visit her aunt, Belen Ruiz de Escobar. An unpleasant episode that she experienced in the revolutionary conditions of the city was reported in a social column of a St. Louis newspaper.[35] In 1893, Emilia and her husband traveled to Chicago to attend the Columbian Exposition. It is possible that she was sent by Don Martin, for his correspondence shows that he hoped to sell the patent on his plow at the fair.[36] Emelia's letters to her family contain delightful accounts of her reaction to the fair and to the city of Chicago. She wrote on stationery decorated with pictures of the Women's Building and the Agricultural Building, citing with pride a prize won by New Mexican wheat and expressing her preference for life in New Mexico. She admired much of what she saw, but concluded, "What a Babylon this is. I prefer Mexican cities."[37]

Music and art lessons were available for the children as well as funds for instruments and supplies. Letters indicate that both Clotilde and Julieta were accomplished mandolin players. Clotilde's name is listed frequently in programs of events at Loretto Academy.

Corina, the youngest daughter, was a painter, and examples of her work appeared on the walls of the Amador Hotel.

The world view of family members extended beyond New Mexico, connected as they were to social and business circles in the United States and Mexico. Comments on national events in both countries appeared in their letters. In particular, Emilia and Maria's letters reflect a keen interest in public events. Emilia noted the Pullman Strike and the presence of troops on the trains in Albuquerque in 1894.[38] She reported many events in Albuquerque such as an assassination in the plaza in 1893[39] and a visit by Porfirio Diaz in 1899.[40] Maria noted the assassination of President William McKinley and the appearance of the first automobile in El Paso.[41] She was keenly aware of the Mexican Revolution, living in Juarez and Parral, Chihuahua, where her husband, Alejandro Daguerre, was a representative for manufacturing firms.[42] Her sympathies lay with the Federal troops and she reported in 1915 that she had helped organize meals for General Rábago's soldiers.[43] In the same year she attended functions in Juarez to raise money for the benefit of refugees. Evidence of the networking among families on both sides of the border during the Revolution appears in requests the family received for help in relocating refugees.[44]

Many kinds of networking broadened the scope of daily interests for the Amador women. The letters they exchanged with a lively and educated group of Catholic nuns provided a channel for news of former classmates and events in other parts of the territory. Clotilde's former teacher, Sister Mary Bernard, frequently encouraged her to continue her music studies and regularly reported conditions of schools where she taught. Her letters help document the development of school systems in New Mexico, including the fact that nuns were hired at times to teach in public schools.[45] The letters of Sister Mary Rosine, Clotilde's god-mother as well as her teacher, are striking for their humorous and thoughtful commentary. She gently teased Clotilde about being the oldest daughter at home after Maria married, calling her "Miss Amador" in honor of her new position in the family. She frequently reported news of the activities of her motherhouse and news of former pupils who were Clotilde's friends. Throughout her letters, she engaged Clotilde with questions and expressons of her own opinions. For example, in 1917, she noted that General John J. Pershing was in pursuit of Pancho Villa and asked Clotilde what she thought of the matter. In 1916, she commented that it was a good sign that the country had not declared war.[46] Because of the close ties maintained with former teachers, the Amador family frequently sent fruit, vegetables, and other gifts to the Sisters, combatting the meagerness that marked their lives in small New Mexico towns. Also, the contact with former teachers provided a model of highly dedicated and independent women.

The Amador Collection, especially the correspondence before 1900, reflects an interest in fancy cards and stationery that was characteristic of the Victorian period.[47] But for the Amador family, letter writing was not just a fashionable activity. It was an important channel of communication, necessary for keeping a flow of news among the members of this active family. Not only did Don Martin and Doña Refugio maintain their relationships with distant friends and relatives through letters, but also they relied on letters to communicate with each other during periods when business matters required Don Martin to travel. Letters were the link between the parents and their sons while Juan and Francisco were attending boarding school. During periods when married sons and daughters lived away from Las Cruces, letters also served to maintain family ties. Both males and females in the family observed the custom of writing cards and letters to each other to mark birthdays, saint's days, and holidays. These occasions meant the exchange of formal expressions of love and recognition—rituals of family life that affirmed bonds of intimacy and conveyed cultural values. Letters served to underscore the family's expectations regarding behavior, as well as to provide news and messages.

The letters of the women of this family reveal a strong commitment to values they considered "civilized" and a strong commitment to family relationships. Taking advantage of the excellent mail service that the railroads provided in the 1880s, they routinely wrote to one another and their friends as often as twice a week. They filled their letters with accounts of family activities, detailed health reports, and expressions of affection. Since purchasing of materials was handled through the family business, they frequently discussed orders and bills in their letters. When Emilia married Jesus Garcia, a deputy sheriff in Bernalillo, she relied on trains to bring letters from her family, flowers and vegetables from the family garden, and her younger sisters to visit in her home in Albuquerque. Likewise, when Doña Refugio made extended trips to

Juarez to visit her sister, she used the mail and train service to stay in contact with her family in Las Cruces.

The letters of Doña Refugio and her daughters show that the three oldest daughters, Emilia, Maria, and Clotilde, were very devoted to their parents and assumed an active role in managing the family home, particularly as their parents' health began to fail at the turn of the century. This devotion to the family may have influenced the ages at which the daughters married and had children. The pattern of all the daughters' lives contrasts with their mother's life. Not only did Doña Refugio marry at the age of thirteen and have fifteen children, but also her child bearing years spanned three decades. Emilia married young, at the age of eighteen, when the family's fortunes and health were high,[48] but she only had two children, one of whom survived.[49] This daughter was born during the fourteenth year of Emelia's marriage. Clotilde, who assumed the position of eldest daughter in the 1890s after Maria's marriage, married Antonio Terrazas when she was twenty-nine years old.[50] None of the six children whom she bore survived infancy.[51] Maria, Julieta and Corina married in their mid-twenties.[52] Maria experienced several miscarriages and had no children.[53] Julieta and her husband, Fabian Garcia, had one child, a son who died in infancy.[54] Corina and her husband, Frank Winslow Campbell, had two children, a son and a daughter.[55] Only one of the Amador children had a large family. Juan and his wife, Mary Woodworth, had nine children.[56] Francisco and his wife, Maria Terrazas (sister of Clotilde's husband, Antonio), had three children.[57] This dramatic change from one generation to the next reflects primarily the particular health problems of this group of women, but also helps explain the transition to Anglo–Victorian fertility patterns.[58]

The subject of health was frequent in the letters of the family and the overall impression is that the family had many problems. The women in particular reported on their health with a startling candor. Their willingness to describe health problems so graphically may be attributed to many factors. First, letter writing probably provided an outlet for their frustration concerning their numerous health problems—miscarriages, infant deaths, epidemics of smallpox, influenza, and pneumonia. Second, this was also a way to exchange remedies and information at a time women in general were making a transition from traditional female health practitioners to medical specialists who were mostly male. And finally, this was an age that defined women's reproductive functions as pathological[59] and labeled women as frail and given to mysterious ailments like "nervousness." Lacking accurate information, these women experienced a great deal of fear and worry[60] which they expressed to each other through letters.

During a time when she herself was ill, Maria described the illness of a friend that had been diagnosed as "female hysteria." The tone of her letter to her mother hints that she thought that she might have the same problem. At that time in 1899, she was managing the household in Las Cruces and recovering from very real problems: weakness, fever, and swelling in her legs. Alejandro was working in Mexico; Clotilde and her mother were visiting in Juarez. The emotional quality of Maria's letters during this period suggest that she was nearly overcome with her responsibilities.[61]

Written records of the women's health problems also exist in the form of drafts of letters to patent medicine companies.[62] The letters describe ailments in great detail and contain poignant expressions of hopes for cures. Like countless others, the Amador women sought help from these companies for a variety of problems: delicate stomach, arthritis and anemia, and in Clotilde's case, the continuing deaths of her children shortly after delivery. Although doctors were available and they could afford their services, the Amador women even used letters to communicate with physicians. Perhaps they were reluctant to seek advice in person in some "delicate" matters or were hesitant after years of dealing with chronic problems. No information exists in the collection to indicate to what extent Doña Refugio and her daughters accepted the traditional care of midwives in the delivery of their children, but due to the large number of miscarriages and infant deaths in this group, the subject of their health care deserves further investigation. Early funeral records for the family do not list the cause of death for infants, but research on infant mortality in the United States suggests the main cause was influenza and pneumonia. The rate of infant death during the first year of life was 10 percent at the turn of the century.[63] The rate in New Mexico was probably much higher.

The emotional and material support that the Amador women derived from their family relationships, particularly in times of trouble, permitted a certain degree of flexibility in response to problems in their adult lives, although the centrality of these relationships required significant amounts of inter-familial cooperation. Clearly, the Amador women did not have to rely on marriage to give them a meaningful place in society and they valued their positions of responsibility within the family home. Clotilde received a proposal of marriage in 1902 at the age of twenty-two,[64] and she was courted by her husband-to-be as early as 1899.[65] Yet, she did not marry Antonio until 1909, two years after her mother died. After her marriage she moved to her husband's ranch in Chihuahua, Mexico. Then, when the turmoil of the Mexican Revolution threatened the safety of the Terrazas family, she returned to Las Cruces to live in the family home. During this period her letters were filled with concern for Antonio's safety and desolation over the deaths of their infant children.[66] Care of her younger sisters was an important outlet for her feelings and defined her days in the absence of her husband. She had been a mainstay in the home in the last years of her mother's life and continued to embrace that role, sharing it from time to time with Maria.

Cooperation within the family was not just between the parents and their children. After her marriage to Jesus, Emilia provided a home for her younger sister, Julieta, for many years. Possibly Albuquerque was regarded as a more healthful climate for Julieta's health problems. (Julieta died at the age of thirty-six from chronic pneumonia.)[67] Later, both Clotilde and Maria helped to care for Emilia's daughter, Maria Paulina, who lived with the family in Las Cruces for the first years of her life. Emilia's letters indicate that she and Jesus experienced some kind of change in their status in the 1890s that influenced the decision to send their infant daughter to live with her grandparents. There are references to the child's delicate health as well as indications that there was tension between Emilia and her father over the decision.[68] Although many questions regarding this situation are not answered in the collection, the important fact is that Maria Paulina lived in the family home for the first years of her life and was dearly loved. Maria, in particular, was devoted to this child. The depth of her affection was reflected in the nurturing care she gave Maria Paulina and also expressed in her generosity to her niece in her will.[69]

Several other sources of emotional support are apparent in the correspondence of these women. Letters from their godparents show that the role of *padrino* (godparent) was a serious one, often providing an individual with a lifelong friend and ally, as well as a person concerned with matters of spiritual development. Affinities among family members and their cousins also provided special friendships in their lives. Clotilde received letters from her cousin, Carlos Escobar, that were full of affectionate teasing and the young man's braggadocio about his life in Mexico City as a student of the Colegio Militar. Carlos sent Clotilde copies of love poems and gossip about friends. In one characteristic letter he sent her an exaggerated apology for not having written that must have seemed slightly blasphemous to her in his use of Christ and Judas as an analogy.[70] Letters from her brother, Francisco, were also indicative of a warm friendship, one that allowed joking and playfulness. They exchanged these letters as teenagers and young adults, despite the twelve-year age difference between Clotilde and Francisco.[71] The letters are particularly poignant in light of the alienation the two experienced after the death of their mother, resulting from differences in their interpretations of Doña Refugio's will.[72]

Within the family, females often assumed the role of intermediary. Both Clotilde and Maria received inquiries in letters from their brothers regarding their parents' moods and attitudes. Some were humorous, as in the case of Francisco's growing a beard;[73] some were serious, as in the case of his asking why his father was dissatisfied with his work.[74] Frequently, the children approached their father through their mother, counting on Doña Refugio to communicate with Don Martin when there was tension or disagreement. The children's cousin, Sister Mary Clotilde, who taught school in Las Vegas, New Mexico, often directed her messages to the parents through the children. It was to Clotilde that she directed her requests that the convent buy fruit and vegetables from the Amador gardens and to Clotilde that she complained when the parents neglected to write to her.[75] Clotilde and Maria's intercession was sought on another level, also. Recognition of their religious piety prompted friends and family to seek remembrance in their prayers in times of trouble.[76]

The women rarely discussed problems and difficulties in family affairs in any detail in their letters. Cryptic references to someone's "disgrace" or "difficulty" appeared, along with brief criticism, usually couched in religious terms of accepting God's will and resigning oneself to suffering in this life. While this absence of detail frustrates efforts to piece together a complete framework of events in their lives, it is consistent with the non-judgmental tone these women generally took in their correspondence. A change can be observed after the death of the parents in the manner in which the daughters expressed their opinions over family problems. With the stress of the thirteen-year-long legal struggle over Doña Refugio's will, the sisters voiced more open criticism of their brothers, and fissures in family loyalties became more obvious in their correspondence.

So far the attitudes of the Amador women have been described mainly in terms of their roles as daughters, sisters and mothers. Although all the women shared a deep sense of family—and Clotilde and Maria expressed frustration in not having their own children—their activities went beyond a closed inner world, characteristic of many women's lives in the Victorian era. They belonged to a busy and prosperous family group, where work and ingenuity brought rewards and prestige in the community and where women traditionally maintained control over their own property. Particularly after the deaths of their parents, they actively engaged in managing their inherited properties and generating income. In the case of Maria and Clotilde, whose husbands' fortunes were limited by the Mexican Revolution, this business activity became increasingly necessary. Their financial papers show they leased their farms and ranches for the production of cash crops such as alfalfa and cotton. Clotilde raised and marketed poultry and Maria cooperated with her brother, Juan, to produce vegetables. As the agricultural depression deepened in the Mesilla Valley during the 1920s and 1930s, the two sisters expanded their efforts to derive income from their property. They rented rooms to students from New Mexico College of Agriculture and Mechanic Arts, leased property for parking lots, and sold some of their lots in downtown Las Cruces for commercial use.[77] Although these activities are indications of the critical nature of their financial situations and a drastic change in lifestyle from their childhood, they are also evidence of their independent natures regarding business matters. Even as married women they paid their own taxes and negotiated leases in their own names.[78]

In particular, Clotilde emerged as a shrewd and even aggressive business woman as her financial difficulties increased. Although the collection does not reveal to what extent Antonio's fortunes were changed by the Mexican Revolution, he lived in Las Cruces with Clotilde from 1911 until his death in 1919. Frequent references to his being ill lend credibility to an assumption that Clotilde was managing their affairs even before he died. Following his death, her papers document a vigorous and determined effort to support herself. She sued the Department of the Interior for damages from the overflow of the Mesilla ditch on the Tres Hermanas farm that she owned with Julieta and Corina.[79] She sued Francisco for her share of settlement money from an Indian depredations case that Don Martin had initiated in 1898, payment finally coming in 1922 for an incident that had occurred in the 1860s.[80] She sued Maria for non-payment of a lease in the 1920s and in the Depression she wrote directly to President Franklin D. Roosevelt to apply for a farm recovery loan.[81] Further evidence of her determination is found in a document from the government Re-employment Service, indicating that she was looking for a job in the 1930s, at the age of fifty.[82]

Maria's legal documents also indicate the critical state of her financial affairs in the Depression. Alejandro died in 1929 and she lost considerable amounts of property before her own death in 1936. Some of her property in El Paso and Las Cruces was sold for non-payment of taxes and some was heavily mortgaged. She deeded property to her younger sister, Corina, and to her brother-in-law, Fabian Garcia, suggesting that some reciprocation for her own needs was negotiated in these arrangements. Upon her death, her estate was sufficiently intact to leave pieces of property and houses to her nieces and nephew.[83]

Although the circumstances of these women's lives were very different in adulthood from those of their parents, they drew, nonetheless, on the qualities and values modeled by their parents. The wills and legal documents of the women are excellent sources for information regarding their attitudes, often confirming personality traits and the nature of relationships only hinted at in their letters. Maria's and Clotilde's wills reflect their religious natures, their concern for social conditions among poor Hispanics, and a concern for education that their father shared. In an early will (1921), written while Maria and Alejandro were hopeful for the success of an automobile manufacturing company that they owned in Mexico, Maria stipulated that her share of this business be used to establish a hospital for the poor, organized by the bishop in El Paso, and a college for boys to be donated to the Franciscans.[84] Clotilde's papers include a will in which she directed that her money be used for the education in the United States of persons "of Spanish birth and Mexican descent." In another will she granted money to her nephew, Martin Campbell, providing that he attend a Catholic college and never marry a non-Catholic.[85] Among Maria's papers are letters indicating that she supported the Cristero[86] movement in Mexico and complied with instructions to use a different name so her donations could not be traced. She participated in a variety of sodalities in St. Genevieve's parish and kept a notebook with names and addresses of people to contact for meetings.[87]

Sadly, the business papers of these women document a fair amount of inter-familial conflict over finances in later years. In particular, their wills reflect the painful break between the sisters and their brothers after the death of their parents. The suspicion and distrust that Maria and Clotilde held for their brothers extended to their brothers' families. Maria died in 1936, still expressing these feelings. She requested that none of her estate go to Juan or Francisco and if they protested, they were to be given ten dollars apiece.[88] Clotilde did not include her brothers in any of her wills, always stipulating that her property go to her sisters and their children. There is a definite hint of matrilineal sentiments in the wills of the Amador family, the members choosing to pass their most valuable property to the next generation through the females. Of course, factors such as husbands dying before wives, more females than males in the family, and bitterness of early quarrels must be considered in this interpretation.

Clotilde's life-long anguish over the loss of her children is also expressed in her will in her directions that she wished a mausoleum to be built for the graves of her six infants, her mother and father, her husband, and her brother, Martin, Jr., who had died at the age of twenty. This mausoleum was never erected and perhaps its absence symbolizes the changes in the Amador family and fortunes, just as the razing of their Garden House in 1962 symbolized the end of an era. Yet, the Amador Collection, tracing the family's history and relationships for so many decades, is perhaps an even more powerful symbol than a monument or a building. As social historian H. L. Perkins says, "It is in the daily talk of ordinary men and women that the real values of a society are felt and heard."[89] The papers of the Amador family, now a public legacy, are a rich source of this daily talk, deserving further study.

This brief examination of the Amador Collection establishes the importance of several voices in the reconstruction of lives within an historical framework. While documenting the influence of the

Amador family in the commercial and social development of the Mesilla Valley, the letters also raise many questions for future clarification: the extent and significance of the family's business and political activities on both sides of the border, the inter-familial conflicts suggested in Emilia and Juan's lives and in the breakdown of loyalties during inheritance litigation; and, perhaps most important, the reasons for the staggering rate of infant mortality within the family.

The letters of the women clearly demonstrate values consistent with both Mexican and American upperclass society in the Victorian and Progressive eras, and their papers reflect shifts in attitude and behavior demanded by changing patterns of agricultural development after the Mexican Revolution and the Great Depression. Future research in the Amador Collection will result in a more detailed picture of this unique, yet representative, family, and will provide further insights into the changing fortunes and responses of Hispanic women of the upper classes.

Notes

1. *Family Papers of Martin Amador,* Rio Grande Historical Collection, New Mexico State University Archives, Box 27, Folder 3, hereafter cited as Amador Papers, RGHC. Each folder contains many letters, unnumbered but arranged chronologically. It is possible that José Maria Costales referred to by Martin Amador is the same man who originally applied for the Doña Ana Bend Colony Grant. He and his household do not appear in the 1850 territorial census either.

2. *1860 Census Population Schedule of New Mexico,* United States Census Reports, Microfilm Publications, National Archives, Roll 158, H 7–7.

3. *Doña Ana County Historical Society Second Annual Banquet Program, January 25, 1968,* "The Amador-Garcia-Adair Building," 9–11.

4. Amador Papers, RGHC, Box 27, #3. This information appears in statements Don Martin made before a Court of Claims, April 6, 1896, Indian Depredation Case #8450.

5. Amador Papers, RGHC, Box 27, #3. Some discrepancies appear in public records regarding the ages of the couple and the year they married. This statement of "the early 1860s" is supported by the 1900 census which records Martin and Refugio as having been married for 39

years. This census also supports a later statement in this article that Refugio was 13 or 14 years old at the time of her marriage. Martin was 10 years older than she.

6. *Hacendado* means landowner in Spanish. The Terrazas-Creel clan held the largest estates in Chihuahua and all of Mexico during the Porfiriato—7 million acres of land and varied enterprises such as mining, milling, and banking. Descriptions of their position in Mexican affairs can be found in Michael C. Meyer and William L. Sherman *The Course of Mexican History* (New York: Oxford University Press, 1979), 459–60.

7. Amador Papers, RGHC, Box 27, #3.

8. Amador Papers, RGHC, Box 27, #1. The 1870 Census lists Martin as a freighter but by the 1880 Census his occupation appears as "Sales and Farmer."

9. Anne E. Kapp and Guylyn M. Nusom, eds., *The Las Cruces Historical Buildings Survey,* (City of Las Cruces: 1982), 114.

10. *Doña Ana Historical Society Third Annual Banquet Program,* January 30, 1969, "The Amador Hotel," 6. The Amador Hotel now houses the main offices of the Citizens Bank in Las Cruces. Several rooms have been preserved and the public is free to visit the building. Furniture and other family belongings are displayed throughout the bank.

11. Amador Papers, RGHC, Box 2, #4.

12. Amador Papers, RGHC, Box 1, #1 and #2.

13. Martin Lohman, "Squibs from El Echo," a 1878 newspaper clipping collection, *Las Cruces History Folder,* RGHC.

14. Amador Papers, RGHC, Box 1, #2.

15. Martin Ridge and Ray Allen Billington, *America's Frontier Story. A Documentary History of Westward Expansion* (New York: Holt, Rinehart and Winston, 1969), 9–10.

16. Amador Papers, RGHC, Box 2, #4.

17. Probate Book Journal 4, p. 605 for Don Martin's final will, Book of Wills and Testaments #4, p. 752 for 1880 will and p. 783 for 1892 will; Will Record #5, p. 173–176 and Probate Book Journal 5, p. 127 for Doña Refugio's will and probate record of her estate, Doña Ana County Courthouse Records, Las Cruces, New Mexico.

18. Amador Papers, RGHC, Box 1, #1.

19. *The Loretto Chimes, Golden Jubilee Number (1870–1920),* p. 12. "Loretto Academy," *Las Cruces History,* RGHC.

20. Amador Papers, RGHC, Box 1, #1.

21. Maurice Garland and Paul Horgan, eds., *New Mexico's Own Chronicle. Three Races in the Writings of Four Hundred Years* (Dallas: Banks, Upshaw and Company, 1937), 214.

22. Amador Papers, RGHC, Box 2, #1.

23. Amador Papers, RGHC, Box 20, #1 and Box 2, #4.

24. Martin Lohman, "Squibs from El Echo," on April, 1878 clippings in folder *Las Cruces History,* RGHC.

25. Laiten L. Camien, "The Amador House," *New Mexico Architect,* (February 1962): 21–6.

26. Lou Lash, "Legend of the Amador House Near End of Colorful Era," *Las Cruces Sun News,* February 15, 1962.

27. Amador Papers, RGHC, Box 2, #5.

28. See footnote 6, p. 4. Wills provide this information.

29. Funeral Records, 1889. St. Genevieve's Parish Records, Las Cruces. A nine-month old son, Reinaldo, also died in 1888. His funeral is recorded, but as in the case of most infants, no cause of death is listed in the parish records. Curiously, letters in the collection indicate Doña Refugio was in Juarez at the time Reinaldo died in Las Cruces. His severe fever is mentioned in letters to her from Don Martin, as well as an outbreak of diphtheria, Amador Papers, RGHC, Box 2, #1.

30. Will Record, #5 op. cit.

31. Book of Wills and Testaments #4, Doña Ana County Courthouse, 752.

32. Amador Papers, RGHC, Box 1, #4.

33. *Loretto Chimes,* school program notes and letters throughout the collection, RGHC.

34. *Loretto Chimes Golden Jubilee Number (1870–1920),* 15, RGHC.

35. Amador Papers, RGHC, Box 5, #3.

36. Amador Papers, RGHC, Box 27, #2.

37. Amador Papers, RGHC, Box 2, #2, (translation from Spanish by author).

38. Amador Papers, RGHC, Box 4, #1.

39. Amador Papers, RGHC, Box 2, #2.

40. Amador Papers, RGHC, Box 2, #3.

41. Amador Papers, RGHC, Box 2, #4.

42. Amador Papers, RGHC, Box 11, #4.

43. William Weber Johnson, *Heroic Mexico. The Narrative History of a Twentieth Century Revolution.* (Garden City, New York, 1968), 165.

44. Amador Papers, RGHC, Box 5, #3.

45. Amador Papers, RGHC, Box 4, #3.

46. Amador Papers, RGHC, Box 5, #4.

47. The collection contains many beautiful examples of period stationery, letterheads, and cards.

48. St. Genevieve's Parish Records, Marriages, 1859–1889, 15.

49. *1900 Census Population Schedule of New Mexico,* Microfilm Publications, National Archives, Roll 1000, No. 7623.

50. Newspaper clippings of the wedding provide a picture of the family's social status, prestige and wealth. Conspicuously absent from the

guest list are Emelia and Jesus Garcia. They do not seem to have been included in family celebrations and the collection does not indicate why.

51. Amador Papers, RGHC, Box 29, #2.

52. St. Genevieve's Parish Records, Marriages, 1907 and 1912.

53. Amador Papers, RGHC, Box 2, #3.

54. *Doña Ana Historical Society Seventh Annual Banquet Program,* January 25, 1973, "Fabian Garcia." Garcia Annex at New Mexico State University is named after Fabian Garcia honoring his work in entymology at the Agriculture College during the early twentieth century.

55. Wills #6, Doña Ana County Probate Court Records, 318.

56. Document 1–582, Doña Ana County Probate Court Records. (Probate of Mary Woodworth Amador's will, 1927).

57. Wills, #8, Doña Ana County Probate Court Records, 319–20. (Will of Maria Terrazas de Amador).

58. Mary P. Ryan, *Womanhood in America from Colonial Times to the Present,* 2nd ed. (New York: Franklin Watts, 1975), 142.

59. See particularly Carroll Smith-Rosenberg, "The Hysterical Woman: Sex Roles and Role Conflict in Nineteenth Century America," *Social Research* 39, no. 1 (Spring 1972) 652–78; John S. Haller, Jr., and Robin M. Haller, *The Physician and Sexuality in Victorian America* (New York: University of Illinois Press, 1974); and Ann Douglas Wood, "The Fashionable Diseases: Women's Complaints and Their Treatment in Nineteenth-Century America," *Journal of Interdisciplinary History* 4, No. 1 (Summer 1973): 25–52.

60. Sara Dalamont and Lorna Duffin, eds, *Nineteenth-Century Woman. Her Cultural and Physical World* (New York: Barnes and Noble Books, 1978), 62–3.

61. Amador Papers, RGHC, Box 2, #3.

62. Amador Papers, RGHC, Box 2, #5 (mother); Box 11, #4 (Maria); Box 5, #3 (Clotilde).

63. Sam Shapiro, Edward K. Schlesinger, Robert E. L. Nesbitt, Jr., *Infant, Perinatal, Maternal, and Childhood Mortality in the United States* (Cambridge, Massachusetts: Harvard University Press, 1968), 3.

64. Amador Papers, RGHC, Box 4, #4.

65. Amador Papers, RGHC, Box 4, #2.

66. Amador Papers, RGHC, Box 5, #2.

67. St. Genevieve's Parish Records, *Funeral Records 1920.*

68. Amador Papers, RGHC, Box 2, #3; Box 4, #1 and 2.

69. Amador Papers, RGHC, Box 30, #1.

70. Amador Papers, RGHC, Box 4, #2.

71. Amador Papers, RGHC, Box 4, #1.

72. Amador Papers, RGHC, Box 28, #1–4.

73. Amador Papers, RGHC, Box 4, #1.

74. Amador Papers, RGHC, Box 4, #2.

75. Amador Papers, RGHC, Box 4, #1–2.

76. Amador Papers, RGHC, Box 4, #2.

77. Amador Papers, RGHC, Box 29, #3 and Box 21, #1 and #3. The financial records of Maria and Clotilde in these folders support the above discussion of their business activities.

78. Amador Papers, RGHC, Box 12, #1.

79. Amador Papers, RGHC, Box 29, #2.

80. Amador Papers, RGHC, Box 28, #4.

81. Amador Papers, RGHC, Box 12, #3.

82. Amador Papers, RGHC, Box 29, #3.

83. Amador Papers, RGHC, Box 30, #1 (1936 will).

84. Amador Papers, RGHC, Box 30, #1.

85. Amador Papers, RGHC, Box 30, #2.

86. Amador Papers, RGHC, Box 22, #1. The Cristero Rebellion was a violent reaction to the implementation of anticlerical articles of the Mexican Constitution under President Calles in the 1920s. For a brief discussion see Michael C. Meyer and William L. Sherman, *The Course of Mexican History,* (New York: Oxford University Press, 1979), 587–590.

87. Amador Papers, RGHC, Box 22, #1.

88. Amador Papers, RGHC, Box 30, #1.

89. H. L. Perkin, "Social History," in *The Varieties of History: From Voltaire to the Present,* ed. Fritz Stern (New York: Vintage Books, 1972), 449.

⇻ 10 ⇺

Women, Pottery, and Economics at Acoma Pueblo

Terry R. Reynolds

In situations of transition from self-contained, agrarian economies to ones dependent on cash and integrated into the Western market system, women often are faced with drastic changes in the definition of their economic role and in their ability to contribute to their households' livelihood. In self-sufficient, agrarian economies women are economic producers: they work in the fields, they tend animals, they process raw materials. Their labor complements that of men in providing for the household. The market system, however, often does not recognize women as economic producers. Rather, men are the producers. They labor outside the home, work for a wage, provide a living. Women cook the food, make the clothing, clean the home, and socialize the children. They maintain the household's way of life while men provide the household's living.[1]

In the transition from a self-sufficient, subsistence economy to one dependent on cash and markets, women frequently find themselves excluded from earning much cash and from participating in the market. Most women in transitional economics must find a way to maintain their economic productivity. Often they do not participate in new productive roles suited to the market place, but rather they are involved in traditional ones modified to fit the new economic situation. Women may try to maintain subsistence agricultural production on their own while their men participate in wage labor, they may modify a traditional productive skill to perform for wages, or they may make a traditional product modified for cash sale. The latter option was tried successfully by many women at Acoma Pueblo in this century as the Acoma subsistence economy increasingly became integrated into and dependent on the cash economy of the United States.

As long as Acoma Pueblo was a self-sustaining community its women were well-integrated into its centuries-old agrarian economy.[2] The lives of the women of Acoma centered on a community situated for centuries on a high, almost inaccessible mesa, sixty miles west of Albuquerque. Women helped Acoma men to plant and to harvest dry-farmed fields in valleys and lowlands for a radius of fifteen or twenty miles around their home mesa. Women also helped to plant and to harvest irrigated fields along the San Jose River twelve miles to the north of the mesa, where two farming villages, Acomita and McCartys, were well-established by the late 1800s. Acoma women, usually with assistance from children, tended the field crops of corn, squash, beans, cotton, and Spanish-introduced grains. Women did much of the gardening that provided such vegetables as chile and onions for household consumption. They raised turkeys and chickens. With their families they helped gather such wild plant products as piñon nuts, prickly-pear cactus fruit, and Rocky Mountain beeweed that supplemented their diet and provided needed sustenance during drought years. Together with men they prepared food for storage and occasionally participated in rabbit hunts. Acoma women processed food and carried water for household consumption, gathered and prepared materials with which they made pottery and baskets, and plastered the walls of buildings and constructed outdoor ovens. Clearly, Acoma women were producers in the economy of their Pueblo.

Men also had productive roles in the Acoma subsistence economy. Not only did they work with women to plant and to harvest field crops, to gather wild plant products, to hunt rabbits, and to prepare food for storage, but also they alone wove cotton and woolen cloth, tanned hides, and built houses. In addition, the men performed tasks taking them away from home for long periods of time. Assisted by boys, they herded Spanish-introduced sheep and goats on ranges far from the Pueblo. These men and boys left their families for weeks at a time. Male hunting groups also spent days hunting deer and antelope.

Acoma women and men, together, were responsible for economic production. Women's and men's activities complemented and supplemented one another. From prehistoric times until the last half of the nineteenth century, women and men both played significant productive roles in the Pueblo's economy.

At the beginning of United States jurisdiction over New Mexico, the economic self-sufficiency of the Pueblo was much the same as it had been in the 1500s when Baltazar de Obregón wrote about Acoma:

> The pueblo has, on its site and settlement, fields of maize, beans, calabashes, tobacco, and cotton. There are also wells and reservoirs. The natives have everything necessary for their wants, even raising food and weaving clothing on their stronghold. Thus they need not have recourse to aid from other places.[3]

Throughout the Spanish and Mexican periods, with brief exceptions, Acoma people lived in relative isolation from the New Mexican Hispanic population.[4] Missionaries introduced grain crops, fruit trees, and livestock to the Pueblo, but they did not greatly affect its economic system beyond increasing the variety in Acoma diet and providing a productive role for men that was a modification of their traditional involvement with animals. They now not only hunted animals, but they also tended them. Acoma trade with Hispanics for European-manufactured objects also had little influence on the Pueblo's economy. For centuries, with other Native American groups, the people from Acoma traded crops, pottery, woven cloth, and tanned hides for salt, hunting and gathering products, and luxury items, such as shell beads from far away.[5] The trade with Hispanics differed little from their traditional exchange.

For much of three hundred years after European contact Acoma's agrarian way of life was self-contained. The Pueblo's population provided most of their own food, clothing, utensils, and housing. Acoma people controlled their own economy. They made all decisions about producing, processing, and dispersing products. In less than one hundred years after coming under United States authority, however, Acoma people could not maintain economic self-sufficiency, nor could they control all aspects of their own economy. This loss of self-dependency and control came about as the result of factors that created problems in their traditional agrarian economy and at the same time changed their expectations and life style.

The Pueblo's economy began to experience difficulties when its land base shrunk. In the late 1700s and throughout most of the 1800s outside encroachment on Acoma territory occurred frequently and reduced significantly the area in which these people could farm, herd, hunt, and gather.[6] Navajos and Apaches attacked Acoma farms and herds. Hispanics and Anglos moved on to Acoma land settling near water resources and grazing their livestock over the range. Laguna Pueblo interfered with Acoma activities on the east. In the 1870s the United States government set the Pueblo's land boundaries, resulting in a drastic shrinkage of its northern and western boundaries. The people of the Pueblo had to rely more and more on the lands and resources nearer Acoma settlements. As Acoma's population grew in the last years of the nineteenth century and the early years of the twentieth century, it put more and more pressure on this land and these resources so that it became increasingly difficult to make a living.

Another important factor in the inability of this Pueblo to remain self-sufficient was the effect of drought on these heavily-used and limited resources. Not only did crops fail, but also livestock ranges deteriorated, especially as livestock numbers increased.[7] By the middle of the drought-ridden 1930s Acoma lands could not grow enough to feed all of the horses, mules, and burros kept for transportation and farming operations. Farming no longer provided all the needs of the Pueblo for crops. At the same time range cover was lost, and the land eroded. Acoma livestock faced a shortage of forage. In 1935–1936 one-third of Acoma groups using land had to purchase feed for these animals.[8]

While Acoma's economic productivity was decreasing because of land loss and drought, Acoma people were coming into direct, prolonged contact with Anglos and their institutions.[9] In 1880 the Atlantic and Pacific Railroad entered Acoma lands. For the first time large numbers of Acoma men had an opportunity to do wage labor. They worked on track crews along the railroad, and they helped lay the original track through Acoma land. The railroad did not provide job opportunities for Acoma women. The railroad provided easier access to Anglo life styles, manufactured goods, and

markets. Traders and tourists who came to Acoma territory provided links through which the Pueblo partially participated in the
cash economy. These outsiders provided goods, markets, and cash.
Over the next half century Acoma people gradually developed a
desire for non-Pueblo goods.

Education programs sponsored by the federal government and
Protestant missions also helped to increase this desire.[10] Although
relatively few Acoma children attended boarding or day school for
any length of time before the 1930s, those who did were exposed
to Anglo foods, clothing, equipment, and concepts. These youth
returned to the Pueblo with new ideas and desires. They often
learned skills most relevant to a market economy. Boys learned
tailoring, printing, painting, machine repairing, woodworking,
blacksmithing, and leatherworking. Girls learned sewing, cooking, housekeeping, beadworking, and pottery making. Many of
these skills could not be used productively by either men or women
in the Pueblo's agrarian economy, and the skills learned by Acoma
women brought only low pay in the cash economy. At the same
time that officials encouraged Acoma men to leave the Pueblo so
that they could be employed using these skills, women were encouraged to remain working at home. This education provided new
economic role definitions for women and men: women were not
economically productive in a cash economy and men were not agriculturally productive in a market system.

For Acoma Pueblo the early, gradual loss of a self-contained
and controlled economy occurred over more than fifty years. In
the 1930s direct government intervention in Acoma's economy facilitated this loss. Like other Indian groups, the Pueblo participated
in projects that pushed Native Americans into greater reliance on
the cash economy of the United States. Beginning in 1933 a series
of government programs provided Native Americans with short-
term wage jobs on or near Reservation lands.[11] In 1935–1936 almost one-third of Acoma men worked in these programs. Almost
no Acoma women were employed for these projects. More Acoma households, however, received a cash income than ever before. They now had opportunities to purchase more consumer
goods. More Anglo goods came to the Pueblo. In addition, in 1935
the United States Soil Conservation Service in cooperation with
the United States Indian Service instituted an eight year plan for
Acoma.[12] The plan put under government control decisions regard-

ing how many head and what kind of livestock could graze, where they could graze, and how livestock products should be marketed. Before this program Acoma people had maintained control over their traditional productive activities although they did not control the prices paid for those products sold in the market rather than consumed, and had little control over the productive activities they performed in either the public or private sectors of the United States economy. With the loss of Pueblo control over livestock production, Acoma moved toward an even greater dependency on the Western market system. At the same time the Pueblo's women had moved towards greater dependency on the traditional agrarian economy as they were excluded from the market system.

By 1935–1936 the economy of the Acoma Reservation was mixed and transitional. It was mixed in that no one livelihood was completely dominant in terms of participation or income. Members of each of the 142 consumption groups on the Reservation engaged in a number of different economic activities (see tables 1 and 2).[13] A consumption group was "a group of people who constantly and habitually fund and share all forms of income, including products of agriculture, products of livestock, and goods purchased from traders."[14] Cultivating fields, raising livestock, producing craft items, doing wage work, and participating in government-sponsored work-relief programs were the most common and important economic activities of group members.

At the same time, Acoma's economy also was no longer wholly self-sustaining. While most consumption groups (96%) contained persons still engaged in the subsistence pursuits of farming, livestock raising, and craft production, most (97%) also contained individuals involved in producing crops, animals, or craft items for cash sale or in working for wages in either the private or public sectors of the United States economy (see table 2).[15] The Pueblo's economy was in transition from a subsistence one to one involved in a market system.

At this point most of the Pueblo's population was residing year around in one of the two farming villages along the San Jose River.[16] Households were scattered in dwellings among the fields. Every family also maintained its own house or had access to a clan house at the old Pueblo of Acoma. The old village was still the center of ceremonial and political life that had been maintained through the centuries, but it was actually inhabited by a very small portion of the population, usually by those involved in the ceremonial-political structure of the community. Others preferred to be near their irrigated fields, near pasture and corrals, and near the railroad and highway providing easy access to Grants and Albuquerque. Families and individuals returned to the old village for ceremonial occasions and duties.

Acoma households often were composed of matrilineal, extended families, that is, of at least three generations of people or two married couples related to each other through women.[17] Households might be composed of two sisters, their spouses, and their children, or of a mother, father, their married daughter, her spouse, and her children. At the old Pueblo, three-story houses with common walls lined three streets on the mesa top. Those living here most often ate and slept on the floor, and they cooked in fireplaces and outdoor ovens. Families residing in farming villages had separate dwellings often containing Anglo furnishings.[18] They had tables, chairs, beds, cupboards, and stoves. Many Acoma people wore some Anglo clothing.[19] Women's dresses or blouses were sometimes manufactured far away. Men wore overalls or jeans and shirts. School children were required to wear Anglo-style clothing.

In 1935–1936, the 1,041 inhabitants of the Acoma Reservation needed cash. With it they purchased livestock feed, some food stuffs, some Anglo-style clothing, some household furnishings and utensils, some Anglo-manufactured equipment, and some livestock.[20] Cash income was achieved in a variety of ways (see table 3). A few consumption groups (8) sold some of their crops. These groups produced a surplus of alfalfa or corn, and they sold part of their harvest to traders. Crops, however, provided less than one-half of one percent of the total cash income at Acoma. Livestock products, lambs, calves, and wool, accounted for almost one-half (44%) of the total income. Acoma craft items such as pottery, silver ornaments, and beaded belts made up an additional 9 percent of the total cash income. Just over one-half (53%) of Acoma's cash was derived from productive activities important in the traditional subsistence economy.[21] The other one-half (47%) came from wage work. While these people were involved in the cash economy, their cash-producing activities often stemmed from their traditional economy. Acoma's economy was in transition, but it had not lost its agrarian base.

In 1935–1936 the degree to which women and men were able

to provide cash for their consumption groups varied widely from their more egalitarian productive activities and contributions in their traditional economy (see tables 4 and 5). Women produced just 13 percent of Acoma's total cash income. Over two-thirds (69%) of this money came from pottery sales and less than a third (31%) from women's wages. Men contributed well over three-quarters (87%) of the Pueblo's cash. Approximately one-half of this money came from the sale of livestock products and the other half (51%) from men's wages. This unequal cash contribution of women and men was due in large part to factors beyond the Pueblo's control. For example, the market value of livestock products derived from men's activities was relatively greater than that of pottery derived from women's activities.[22] Consequently, livestock sales produced a greater income than pottery sales.

Women also had a difficult time doing wage labor. The Acoma Reservation was remote from job markets. Acoma women had to be willing to leave their land and kinsmen to take jobs. Much of the work available to persons without much formal education and skill in the English language involved hard, physical labor. From both Acoma and Anglo points of view, this type of work was better suited to men than to women. Consequently, it was difficult for Acoma women to find jobs. Only 3 percent of the women participated in the wage market as opposed to 21 percent of the men. The jobs they held, with a few exceptions, were performed near or on the Reservation and did not involve much hard physical work. These jobs required the women to have some formal training or to speak English rather well. They worked as teachers, nurses, housekeepers, storekeepers, and tourist guides. Not only was it harder for Acoma women to find jobs, but they also had to have inordinate skills to be employed. In addition, on the average, women who worked earned about fifty dollars less than men doing wage labor (see tables 4 and 5).

It was even more difficult for Pueblo women to be employed in government work-relief programs. Most government projects failed to recognize women as potential cash earners. They provided few jobs women could perform. Most involved hard, physical work or took persons away from the vicinity of their homes. Only 1 percent of Acoma women earned any cash from these programs compared to 31 percent of the men (see tables 4 and 5). When women were employed in a project, they worked shorter amounts of time

and for less money than men. The three women who participated
in these programs earned an average of fifteen dollars each, while
the 105 men who worked earned an average of fifty-seven dollars
each (see tables 4 and 5). The United States government did not
assist Acoma women in entering the job market.

In sum, it was much easier for the men of Acoma to make the
transition to the cash economy than it was for the women. Acoma
men were considered economic producers both in their traditional
economy and in the market economy. They could work in the economic world beyond the Pueblo. But Acoma women were not
viewed as cash earners by either the private or public sectors of the
national economy. If they were to gain a cash income, most women
were forced to achieve it through their traditional productive activities on the Reservation. Many women first entered the market
system through pottery making.

Pottery was something Acoma women had always made. For
centuries they produced vessels for their own use in everyday life,
for trade with other people, and for use in Acoma ceremonial life.
In the twentieth century, as Anglo wares took the place of Acoma
pottery in the everyday life of the Pueblo, Acoma-made vessels
were still an integral part of their ceremonies. Prayersticks were
placed in pottery bowls after the death of an individual. A water-
jar filled with water was broken on the grave of the deceased to
provide a last drink.[23] Pieces of pottery were given as gifts during
ceremonies.[24] Acoma women did not have to revitalize their pottery-
making tradition: it was a well-known skill among the women.
The materials for its production, moreover, were readily available
on Acoma lands. Acoma women controlled its production.

In many ways Acoma pottery was the finest hand-coiled Pueblo
ware made throughout the historic period.[25] Technically excellent,
it was characterized by vessel walls that were very thin, smooth,
and strong. A pure white slip provided a background for complex
geometric designs or abstract plants and animals done in black,
brown, yellow, red, or orange. It was well-fired.

While in the twentieth century there was no revitalization of
pottery making at Acoma, the women changed and developed some
aspects of its design in order better to meet market demands.[26] In
the 1930s, pottery was primarily sold to tourists seeking momen-
tos of their Southwestern travels. During the first two decades of
the century the women began to use yellow-orange and orange

paints for designs in addition to the older black, brown, and red paints. Beginning in the 1930s they also experimented with design elements and color combinations. This experimentation produced designs with single motifs such as an abstract bird copied two to four times around the vessel framed with very simple plant or geometric elements. The women also made vessels designed after articles in the Anglo world such as candlesticks and ash trays. For the tourist, the pieces they made were more often smaller and less well executed than those made for their own use.

The women succeeded in meeting market demands. Since before the turn of the century, they had sold pottery to traders in the tourist business and directly to tourists.[27] In the 1920s and 1930s the women sold to tourists from roadside stands along U.S. 66, in the train station at New Laguna, and along the trail to the old Pueblo on the mesa top.[28] In the 1920s and 1930s, they received twenty-five cents for small pieces and up to five dollars for large water jars.[29]

By 1935–1936, over 60 percent of Acoma consumption groups contained women who made pottery for sale (see table 2). These consumption groups had a cash income of one hundred and twelve dollars less on the average per year than those groups in which women did not make pottery (see table 6), thus they had a greater need for cash income than those without pottery production. They also were larger groups. They contained on the average 7.6 persons while in those groups not making pottery the average was 7.1 persons (see table 7). This difference in group size was due entirely to a larger number of women in pottery-making groups. There were on the average 2.1 women in each pottery-making consumption group and only 1.7 in each group not producing pottery (see table 7). Not only did groups in which women made pottery have a greater need for cash than those groups not making pottery, but also they had more members per group depending on the smaller monetary income. In addition, these groups had a special resource, female labor.

Thus female labor was available to meet the cash needs of consumption groups. In many groups one woman made pottery and the second did not. In some groups, however, two or more women made pottery. These women probably worked together. Pottery making was in many ways a cooperative activity. As a craft it was learned through apprenticeship with older kinswomen teaching younger ones the necessary skills involved.[30] Often Pueblo women divided pottery production tasks with one woman shaping vessels, another polishing them, and still another painting on decorative designs.[31] Any particular piece of pottery might be the product of more than one woman's hand and might have received the benefit of several women's creative ideas.

Over one-third (37%) of all adult Acoma women were involved in pottery production for cash sale in 1935–1936. Over two-thirds (70%) of these women were middle aged, i.e., between 30 and 54 years of age (see table 8). These women were less likely to be involved in intense mothering activities. Some of their children were old enough to help care for the younger ones and to help their mothers in other tasks. These women therefore had time to pursue pottery making and to learn and to practice the skills involved in pottery production.

The amount of cash produced by pottery sales in total, as well as on the average per women making it, was relatively low, ninety-five dollars per woman per year.[32] The economic situation on the Acoma Reservation, however, was not particularly good. These people, who were exploiting a number of different resources and participating in a variety of economic activities, lived on cash incomes that were considerably less than incomes received by other Americans. The standard wage in the mid 1930s for unskilled workers was two dollars a day. Even if only two of the four average number of adults in a Acoma group were employed in unskilled jobs, the total income per group should have averaged about twelve hundred dollars a year from wage labor alone. Yet the average cash income for Acoma consumption groups was only eight hundred and nine dollars per year, not very much money to satisfy the needs of the seven to eight persons in each group.

In a situation with increasing cash demands and low cash flow, even small monetary contributions can be meaningful. Consumption groups in which women made pottery had a 15 percent lower income than those groups not involved in pottery production. Without pottery income these groups would have had one hundred and fifty-four dollars less on the average per year. Pottery also may have fulfilled a cash flow need in that it would have provided money without regard to the time of year, for traders could stockpile it for the tourist season. Livestock and agriculture provided seasonal cash income, and work-relief jobs were short term. Women may have produced pottery and sold it to traders when cash was needed and no other readily-available source could be found.[33] In 1935–1936 Acoma women were able to make enough money from producing pottery to help their consumption groups through periods of need, allowing them to purchase additional food and clothing.

Pottery allowed Acoma women to have an economically productive role in the Western market system, even though they were largely excluded from it. In the 1930s pottery production allowed them to make the transition from their traditional subsistence economy to a cash economy. Pottery, moreover, continued to provide an important transitional income over the following decades.

Today, the women of Acoma still make excellent pottery with more sophisticated and intricate decorative designs than those used in the 1930s.[34] Acoma pottery now is sought by people from around the world. Larger, well-executed pieces sell for hundreds of dollars. Acoma women are acclaimed for their artistry and excellence in pottery. Museum exhibits, popular literature, and awards celebrate the excellence of the modern Acoma potter.[35] Many fine private and public collections of Pueblo pottery contain recently-produced pieces. Yet most of the world fails to recognize an even greater importance of the Acoma pottery-making tradition—its continued value for women's economic survival. As in the 1930s Acoma women today achieve an economically productive role through making pottery for cash sale. They deserve to be recognized as artists, but they, their mothers, and their grandmothers should also be recognized as economic survivors.

Notes

The author wishes to thank David F. Aberle for providing inspiration for this analysis and Sherril B. Selander for assistance in organizing and analyzing numerical data. Whatever shortcomings this analysis contains are the author's responsibility alone.

1. Laurel Bossen, "Women in Modernizing Societies," *American Ethnologist* 2 (November 1975), 587–601; Ester Boserup, *Women's Role in Economic Development* (London: George Allen and Unwin Ltd., 1970); Mona Etienne and Eleanor Leacock, eds., *Women and Colonization: Anthropological Perspectives* (New York: Praeger, 1980).

2. For historic and ethnographic information regarding Acoma women's and men's productive activities, see Leslie A. White, *The Acoma Indians* (Bureau of American Ethnology, Annual Report 47, 1929–1930); Leslie A. White, "New Material from Acoma," *Anthropological Papers* 32 (Bureau of American Ethnology Bulletin 136, 1943), 301–59; James Paytiamo, *Flaming Arrow's People* (New York: Duffield and Green, 1932); Mrs. William T. Sedgwick, *Acoma, The Sky City* (Cambridge: Harvard University Press, 1926); Ward A. Minge, "Historical Treatise in Defense of the Pueblo of Acoma Land Claim," *Pueblo Indians* 3 (New York and London: Garland Publishing Inc., 1974), 121–210; Robert L. Rands, "Acoma Land Utilization," *Pueblo Indians* 3 (New York and London: Garland Publishing Inc., 1974), 213–407; Velma Garcia-Mason, "Acoma Pueblo," *Handbook of North American Indians* 9 (Washington: Smithsonian Institution, 1979), 450–66; Frederic H. Douglas, *Acoma Pueblo Weaving and Embroidery* (Denver Art Museum Leaflet Series 89, 1939); Harold E. Driver and William C. Massey, *Comparative Studies of North American Indians* (Transactions of the American Philosophical Society 47:2, 1957), 363–73.

3. George P. Hammond and Agapito Rey, eds., *Obregón's History of 16th Century Explorations in Western America* (Los Angeles: Westzel Publishing Co., 1928), 28.

4. In 1598–1599 Acoma had an encounter with Hispanics that led to the partial destruction of the Pueblo on the mesa, the torture and killing of some Acoma people, and the capture of others who were forced into slavery. Acoma's population and villages were reconstituted shortly. See Ward A. Minge, *Acoma* (Albuquerque: University of New Mexico Press, 1976), 10–16.

5. For information regarding Acoma-Hispanic interaction, see Rands, "Acoma Land Utilization," 219–71; Minge, "Historical Treatise," 130–73.

6. Minge, *Acoma,* 52–118.

7. Dewey Dismuke, "Acoma and Laguna Indians Adjust their Livestock to their Range," *Soil Conservation* 6 (1940), 130–32; Minge, *Acoma,* 71–4, 83–94.

8. These figures were derived, as all numerical data for Acoma Pueblo in 1935–1936, from the Human Dependency Survey Schedules, Acoma Pueblo, U.S. Soil Conservation Service (Region 8, Albuquerque), Ms 190, Rio Grande Historical Collections (RGHC), New Mexico State University Library, Las Cruces. In September and October of 1936 two employees of the Soil Conservation Service interviewed a member of each Acoma consumption group. Survey information collected included the demographic parameters of each group's membership and data regarding their subsistence and cash-producing activities. This survey examined the

total population of the Acoma Reservation rather than a sample of it. Consequently, the survey was not subject to sampling error although it may have been affected by interviewer inconsistency and by missing information.

9. Minge, *Acoma*, 64–71; White, "New Material," 330.

10. Minge, *Acoma*, 74–82, 94–100; White, "New Material," 331–33; Garcia-Mason, "Acoma Pueblo," 461–93; Sedgwick, *Acoma*, 24–33.

11. Donald L. Parman, *The Navajos and the New Deal* (New Haven and London: Yale University Press, 1976), 32–4.

12. S. D. Aberle, "The Pueblo Indians: Their Land, Economy, and Civil Organization," *American Anthropologist Memoir* 70 (1948), 17–23; Dismuke, "Acoma and Laguna," 130–32.

13. There were 4 additional Acoma consumption groups about which no demographic or economic data was reported. They are deleted from this analysis.

14. It is assumed that the definition of a consumption group was used consistently by the Soil Conservation Service in their interviewing among all Native Americans. This definition was used by interviewers on the Navajo Reservation. Soil Conservation Service, "Report of Sociological Survey, Land Management Unit 8," (1936), 1, J. Lee Correll Research Collection, Native American Research Library, Navajo Nation Library System, Window Rock.

15. To avoid implying an unwarranted degree of accuracy for data collected years ago under unknown conditions by interviewers with unknown skill, all percentages on tables have been rounded to the nearest whole percent, and all dollars have been rounded to the nearest whole dollar.

16. White, *The Acoma Indians*, 28–34; Sedgwick, *Acoma*, 33–4.

17. The consumption group may have been similar to the matrilineal extended family household considered by Eggan to have been the traditional household unit at Acoma. See Fred Eggan, *Social Organization of the Western Pueblos* (Chicago and London: University of Chicago Press, 1950), 232. One of the researchers recorded the kin relationships among members of 19 consumption groups. All 19 groups were composed entirely of kinsmen. Those groups containing more than a nuclear family had members most often related through matrilineal descent. It should be pointed out that consumption groups were not necessarily residential units. In a few groups investigators noted that some members lived and worked in Albuquerque, Santa Fe, Dulce, Winslow, and California.

18. Elsie Clews Parsons, "Notes on Acoma and Laguna," *American Anthropologist* 20 (1918), 178–9; White, *The Acoma Indians*, 29; Sedgwick, *Acoma*, 19–34.

19. Sedgwick, *Acoma*, 24; Parsons, "Notes on Acoma," 168–69.

20. Frank Beckwith, "A Day in Acoma," *El Palacio* 35 (December, 1933), 203; White, *The Acoma Indians,* 29–33; Paytiamo, *Flaming Arrow's People,* 30, 97; Dismuke, "Acoma and Laguna," 130–32; Aberle, "The Pueblo Indian," 17–23.

21. It is likely that piñon nut and firewood gathering for cash sale were minor economic activities. Acoma craftsmen also probably made some craft items from leather and drums for sale. Minge, *Acoma,* 93.

22. Average income per head of sheep at Laguna Pueblo in 1936 from lamb and wool sales was $2.75. In the same year the average calf sale price in northern New Mexico was $15.34. Division of Human Surveys and Planning, "Data and Procedures used in Conversions," U.S. Soil Conservation Service, Ms 190, RGHC. On the other hand, a piece of Acoma pottery brought from 25¢ to $5.00. Ruth L. Bunzel, *The Pueblo Potter* (New York: Columbia University Press, 1929), 5; Beckwith, "A Day in Acoma," 203.

23. White, *The Acoma Indians,* 137; Parsons, "Notes on Acoma," 162–86.

24. John E. Collins, *A Tribute to Lucy M. Lewis* (Fullerton: Museum of North Orange County, 1975), 13; White, *The Acoma Indians,* 33.

25. Alfred E. Dittert, Jr. and Fred Plog, *Generations in Clay* (Flagstaff: Northland Press, 1980), 28, 43–7; Francis H. Harlow, *Historic Pueblo Pottery* (Santa Fe: Museum of New Mexico Press, 1970), 26–30; Betty Toulouse, *Pueblo Pottery of the New Mexico Indians* (Santa Fe: Museum of New Mexico Press, 1977), 26, 43–4, 65–6; Pedro J. Lemos, "Marvelous Acoma and its Craftsmen," *El Palacio* 24 (1928), 234–44; Fredrick H. Douglas, *Modern Pueblo Pottery Types* (Denver Art Museum Leaflet Series 53–4, 1933), 10–11; Bunzel, *The Pueblo Potter,* 5–7, 29–36.

26. Kenneth M. Chapman, "Roadside Shopping," *New Mexico Magazine* 14 (June, 1936), 20–21, 38–9; Dittert and Plog, *Generations in Clay,* 45; Toulouse, *Pueblo Pottery,* 26, 43–4, 65–6, 80–81; Douglas, *Modern Pueblo Pottery,* 10–11.

27. White, "New Material," 328.

28. White, *The Acoma Indians,* 33; Sedgwick, *Acoma,* 17; Beckwith, "A Day in Acoma," 203; Chapman, "Roadside Shopping," 39.

29. Bunzel, *The Pueblo Potter,* 5; Beckwith, "A Day in Acoma," 203.

30. Maxwell Museum of Anthropology, *Seven Families in Pueblo Pottery* (Albuquerque: University of New Mexico Press, 1974), 2–16; Collins, *A Tribute,* 13–18; Bunzel, *The Pueblo Potter,* 60–62.

31. Bunzel suggests that "pottery bees" with women working together on pottery did not take place among Acoma women. Bunzel, *The Pueblo Potter,* 64. Beckwith, however, saw such a group of women working together on pottery during his visit to the old village. Beckwith, "A Day in Acoma," 208. Whether each woman worked on her own vessels

or several women divided up production tasks on each vessel is unknown. The latter situation occurred at other Pueblos. See U.S. Soil Conservation Service, "Phases of Decline and Recovery of Craft," *Tewa Basin Study* I (1939), 54–78.

32. Other Government reports from the same general time period give lower total income for Acoma than the consumption group schedules used in this analysis. See Minge, *Acoma,* 92–3. In 1936 a range management survey also gave different numbers of livestock than those reported in the Human Dependency Survey. See U.S. Soil Conservation Service, "Comparison of Cattle and Sheep Counts by Dependency Survey and by Range Management for Acoma Pueblo," (1936), Ms 190, RGHC. Recognizing that all Government surveys likely include recording bias, as well as estimates in those areas where information was unavailable, this analysis uses data only from the Human Dependency Survey. These Survey schedules are the only known available source of both demographic and economic data for subsistence and cash-producing activities.

33. Traders often gave credit to Indians rather than actual cash payments; however, traders stocked food stuffs, clothing, equipment, and utensils that could be obtained through credit. Credit was given in dollar amounts and prices for goods were in dollars. Native Americans dealing with traders did so within the cash system, not a barter one.

34. Dittert and Plog, *Generations in Clay,* 46–7; Toulouse, *Pueblo Pottery,* 80–1; Maxwell Museum, *Seven Families,* 2–16; Collins, *A Tribute,* 21–4.

35. See Minnie Oleman, "Lucy Lewis: Acoma's Versatile Potter," *El Palacio* 75 (Summer, 1968), 10–12; David L. Arnold, "Pueblo Artistry in Clay," *National Geographic* 162 (November, 1982), 593–605; Maxwell Museum, *Seven Families,* 2–16; Collins, *A Tribute,* 13–18. The latest award to be given to an Acoma potter is the New Mexico Governor's Award. In October, 1983, Lucy M. Lewis received it for excellence and achievement in pottery.

Table 1. Acoma, 1935–1936

Total Population		1,041
Females	501[A]	
Males	523[A]	
Total Number of Adults (16 years and older)		620[B]
Females	279	
Males	341	
Total Number of Children (15 years and younger)		410[B]
Total Number of Consumption Groups		142[C]
Average Number of Persons per Consumption Group		7.3
Average Number of Adults per Consumption Group		4.4
Average Number of Children per Consumption Group		2.9

[A]The number of females and males do not total 1,041, because it is impossible from the data to determine the sex of 17 individuals.

[B]The number of adults and children do not total 1,041, because it is impossible from the data to determine the ages of 11 individuals.

[C]There were 4 additional Acoma consumption groups about which nothing was reported. They do not appear in any tabulations.

Table 2. Acoma's Mixed Economy, 1935–1936

	Percentage of Adults Participating in Activity	Consumption Groups with Percentage of Adults Participating in Activity
ECONOMIC ACTIVITY		
Agriculture	A	94
Sheep	B	43
Cattle	B	58
Crafts		
Pottery	17	63
Other Craft	★	2
Wage work	13	45
Work Relief Programs	17	53

★Percentage equals less than one-half of one percent.

[A]No information is available regarding the number of adults who contributed labor to cultivating fields.

[B]No information is available regarding the number of adults who contributed labor to sheep and cattle raising.

Table 3. Acoma's Cash Income, 1935–1936

ECONOMIC ACTIVITY:	Total Cash Income in Dollars	Percent of Total	Average Dollar Income Per Adult Involved in Activity	Average Dollar Income Per Consumption Group with Adult(s) in Activity
Agriculture	502[A]	*	E	42[F]
Sheep	40,606[B]	36	E	666
Cattle	8,544[C]	8	E	104
Crafts				
Pottery	9,831[D]	9	95	110
Other craft	69	*	23	23
Wage Work	46,001[D]	41	590	719
Work Relief Programs	6,071[D]	5	56	78
Total	111,624	100	E	809[G]

*Percentage equals less than one-half of one percent.

[A]Although 94 percent of the consumption groups cultivated fields, only 8 of them sold crops for cash.

[B]Sheep income is estimated from herd size multiplied by $2.75. This was the average income per adult sheep at Laguna Pueblo in 1936. See "Data and Procedures Used in Conversions," Soil Conservation Service, Division of Human Surveys and Planning (1937), Rio Grande Historical Collections, New Mexico State University Library, Manuscript Collection 190, Box 1.

[C]Cattle income is estimated from herd size, multiplied by .496, which is the percent of calf crop per adult head in the Pena Blanca, Dixon, and El Rito area of New Mexico in 1936, multiplied by $15.34, which was the average income per calf in the same area. See Division of Human Surveys and Planning, "Data and Procedures used in Conversions," U.S. Soil Conservation Service, Ms 190, RGHC.

[D]Income is estimated for some individuals participating in crafts, wage work, and work relief programs. The average cash income per person from a particular activity is calculated from known income and then multiplied by the number of unknown-income persons. This is added to known income for a total cash income estimate for a particular activity.

[E]No information is available regarding the number of adults who contributed labor to cultivating fields and to sheep and cattle raising.

[F]Average calculated only for groups selling crops for cash.

[G]Average calculated only for groups with cash income. Four consumption groups have no known cash income.

Table 4. Participation in Acoma's Cash Economy, 1935–1936 by Adult Women

	Adult Women			
	Total Dollar Income	Percent of Total Income	Percent of Women Involved in Activity	Dollar Income Per Female Participating
ECONOMIC ACTIVITY:[A]				
Sheep	—	—	—	—
Cattle	—	—	—	—
Crafts				
Pottery	9,831	69	37	95
Other Crafts	9	*	*	9
Wage Work	4,350	31	3	543
Work Relief Programs	45	*	1	15
Total Cash Income	14,235			
Percent of Total Cash Income[B]	13			

—No Cases.
*Percentage equals less than one-half of one percent.
[A] Amount of income from agricultural products is very small relative to other activities. It is eliminated from this tabulation.
[B] Percent is calculated on basis of total income minus the $502 received for agricultural products.

Table 5. Participation in Acoma's Cash Economy, 1935–1936 by Adult Men

ECONOMIC ACTIVITY:[A]	Adult Men			
	Total Dollar Income	Percent of Total Income	Percent of Men Involved in Activity	Dollar Income Per Male Participating
Sheep	40,606[C]	42	D	D
Cattle	8,544[C]	9	D	D
Crafts				
Pottery	—	—	—	—
Other Crafts	60	*	*	30
Wage Work	41,651	43	21	595
Work Relief Programs	6,026	6	31	57
Total Cash Income	96,887			
Percent of Total Cash Income[B]	87			

—No Cases.

*Percentage equals less than one-half of one percent.

[A]Amount of income from agricultural products is very small relative to other activities. It is eliminated from this tabulation.

[B]Percent is calculated on basis of total income minus the $502 received for agricultural products.

[C]Livestock raising is a predominantly male economic activity. Women may help in some tasks necessary to this endeavor.

[D]The number of individuals actually participating in this activity is unknown.

Table 6. Acoma Women's and Men's Cash Income, 1935–1936 as Related to Pottery Production

	Total Cash-Earning Consumption Groups[B]							
	Groups with Pottery Production				Groups without Pottery Production			
	Total Dollar Income	Percent of Cash Income	Average Dollar Income Per Group		Total Dollar Income	Percent of Cash Income	Average Dollar Income Per Group	
CASH INCOME:								
Total Income	68,459	100	769		43,166	100	881	
Women's Total[A]	10,437	15	117		3,798	9	78	
Men's Total[A]	57,640	85	647		39,248	91	801	

[A]These totals do not include income from agricultural activities, because women's and men's contributions can not be determined.
[B]There were 4 consumption groups out of the 142 that did not have any cash income. They are not tabulated in this table.

Table 7. Acoma's Consumption Group Size, 1935–1936 as Related to Pottery Production

| | Total Cash-Earning Consumption Groups[A] | | |
	Total Consumption Groups	Groups with Pottery Production	Groups without Pottery Production
Consumption Group Size:			
Average Number of Persons per Consumption Group	7.4	7.6	7.1
Average Number of Adult Women per Consumption Group	2.0	2.1	1.7
Average Number of Adult Men per Consumption Group	2.4	2.4	2.4
Average Number of Children per Consumption Group	3.0	3.0	3.0

[A]There were 4 consumption groups out of the 142 that did not have any cash income. They are not tabulated in this table.

Table 8. Age Distribution of Adult Acoma Women, 1935–1936 as Related to Pottery Production

| | Total Percentage of Adult Female Population | | |
	Total	Potters	Non-Potters
Age Distribution:			
Under 30 years old	43	18	58
30–54 years old	43	70	26
55 years old and over	14	13	15

⇒ 11 ⇐

"Disfranchisement is a Disgrace"

Women and Politics in New Mexico 1900–1940*

Joan M. Jensen

"I hear women are bombarding our two Senators with letters, to Mr. Catron's supreme disgust and he shows discourtesy to our delegation. I have written to you heretofore, the only hope for New Mexico is federal action." So wrote sixty-four-year-old Ada Morley to Anne Martin of the Congressional Union on 15 March 1916, reporting on the campaign to have the New Mexico delegation support passage of the Susan B. Anthony women's suffrage amendment in Congress.[1] Morley wrote this letter to Martin "on the wing" coming back to her Datil ranch in Socorro County after a run up to Albuquerque for "baby week." In the previous month she sent out 100 suffrage notes to friends urging them to write to Senator Thomas Catron supporting suffrage. In one period of five days, the furious lady wrote thirty letters. "I am always and ever on the alert to gain my own liberty. Disfranchisement is a disgrace," she told Martin in a second letter, adding that she had heard one of Susan B. Anthony's "masterly appeals" in Washington, that she was now having the life of the eighteenth century feminist Mary Wollstonecraft read to her, and that she believed writer Charlotte Perkins

*Reprinted by permission of the regents of the University of New Mexico and the editor of the *New Mexico Historical Review*.

Gilman to be Wollstonecraft's reincarnation. "I am happy," she ended the letter.[2]

These letters from Ada Morley, together with other letters in the National Woman's Party Papers in the Library of Congress, indicate the existence of an active women's movement in New Mexico during the early twentieth century. Forgotten in later years when feminism declined, this early movement for women's political rights deserves reanalysis not only as a part of women's history but also as a part of New Mexico's political history, particularly because it illuminates the way in which parties dealt with ethnic and sexual divisions in the population.[3]

Women's political history in New Mexico can be divided into four periods. During the first period, before the 1890s, no organized women's movement existed. During the twenty years from 1900 to 1920, women organized political pressure groups and finally achieved suffrage. In the twenty years after passage of the Nineteenth Amendment women moved into voter and party participation and into state and local office holding. Since 1940 the women of New Mexico, like women of other states, have emerged as active political participants at all levels of government except high elective offices, the last bastion of male political supremacy in a system that men once totally dominated. This chapter focuses on the period from 1900 to 1940 and seeks to answer two questions: Why did women in New Mexico not achieve suffrage until 1920, six years after women in all the other western states had been enfranchised, and what did they do after achieving the vote? To answer these questions, I have used methods from the new political history, including collective biography of political activists and quantitative study of voter participation and office holdings, as well as research techniques from women's history and traditional political history.

Women's history in New Mexico has not yet dealt with women's political participation in the state. In the absence of systematic analysis, fragmentary memoirs have become the main source for assessing the historical significance of women's political activities. Thus, for example, Agnes Morley Cleaveland's judgment of her mother Ada in *No Life for a Lady* has not been questioned. In this book, Cleaveland described her mother as a woman who lived a "shattered dream of becoming a cattle tycoon," a misfit, "tragically miscast" as a range boss bringing up three children after the death of a first husband and the disappearance of a second, her life a "succession of disappointments and failures." Cleaveland dismissed her mother as something of a crank, saying little about her part in the women's movement in New Mexico. Older accounts of women's suffrage in the West omit New Mexico because it was the only western state without woman suffrage in 1914. The official history of suffrage, which the National American Woman Suffrage Association (NAWSA) compiled, did no more than list a few suffrage workers from New Mexico and offer a fragmentary sketch of the ratification battle in 1920.[4]

Political historians have added to this impression that New Mexico women were politically ineffective. Robert W. Larson attributed defeat of women's suffrage before 1920 to the opposition of Hispanic males. Anglo males, he implied, had no choice but to abandon women's suffrage, even after suffragists formed a pressure group during the constitutional convention of 1910. Jack E. Holmes, in his pioneering work in the application of quantitative methods to New Mexico politics, did not even mention women's suffrage or consider sex as a variable in voting trends after 1920 although half the voting universe was female. No one has attempted to reconcile Larson's conclusions with the findings of Billie Barnes Jensen for Colorado, where she found that not enough support existed in Anglo areas to carry suffrage before the 1890s and that one of the strongest suffrage supporters in southern Colorado was a Hispanic politician from Taos.[5]

Once one examines the history of women's political activities, however, several reasons emerge for the delay of women's suffrage in New Mexico. Before 1900, organized support within the Anglo population—either male or female—was insufficient to make suffrage a real issue. NAWSA, the only national organization devoted principally to achieving suffrage, had numerous subscribers to its *Woman's Journal* in Utah during the 1890s but only one in New Mexico. This subscriber, Mamie Marble, reported that the New Mexico legislature, through its "junketing to Colorado," had left no time to consider a bill for women's suffrage. The only evidence of NAWSA activity in 1900 is a mimeographed letter to national political convention delegates asking them to support the Susan B. Anthony suffrage amendment in Congress. By 1910, NAWSA had two women listed on its subscription list for New Mexico. One name had "dead" scribbled after it; the other woman was in a Silver City sanitorium. Hardly the base for an active women's movement.[6]

Not until the emergence of the women's club movement in the late nineteenth century did an organizational structure exist capable of exerting political pressure in New Mexico. By the end of the first decade of the twentieth century, several hundred New Mexico women, apparently almost all Anglo, had organized into nine clubs in which women could work together on civic, educational, and cultural affairs. In 1909, women's clubs federated into a state organization, and one year later the president of the state organization presented a petition to delegates of the state constitutional convention in support of women's right to vote on issues relating to the public schools. That school suffrage petition signaled women's willingness to organize publicly to demand political rights.[7]

The state constitutional convention of 1910 opened a decade of organized suffrage activities. Resolutions introduced into the convention reflected three possible positions on women's suffrage. The most politically advanced resolution provided that equal political rights could not be abridged on account of race or sex. The most conservative statement called for a referendum by all males and females over twenty-one to decide on women's suffrage in the first state election after 1925—fifteen years in the future. The middle position, which organized women supported, stood for immediate partial suffrage in school district elections and women's eligibility to hold public office. Since male voters had already elected women to the superintendencies of public education in Colfax and Roosevelt counties and the territorial governor had appointed a woman to the office of state librarian, some action seemed necessary on office holding as well as suffrage.[8]

Debates in the convention concerning women's suffrage present an opportunity to analyze relative support by Anglo and Hispanic representatives. Unfortunately, only a few memoirs written many years later and fragmentary newspaper accounts remain of that important convention. Of the three published memoirs, just two mention women's suffrage. One simply says members compromised on women's suffrage; the other notes that "the very nature of New Mexico's background was against giving women the voting privilege with men." These vague comments made years later have led historians to conclude that the Hispanic delegates accepted school suffrage in return for protection of their political rights.

A careful analysis of contemporary newspaper accounts does not, however, support the view of two ethnic groups divided over women's suffrage. Instead, accounts indicate a spectrum of attitudes ranging from support of total suffrage by a small Anglo minority to opposition by a few Anglos and Hispanics, with influential leaders from both groups favoring limited school suffrage. Of the sixty-five Anglo delegates, newspapers reported possibly two favoring total suffrage, eleven supporting school suffrage, and two opposed to any suffrage. Newspapers mentioned only two of the thirty-five Hispanic delegates protesting against suffrage, although Solomon Luna, probably the most popular politician in the state, was listed as joining political chieftain Holm Bursum in support of school suffrage. Without the record of roll call votes, one cannot conclude that school suffrage resulted from trading protection of Hispanic rights for women's rights. In fact, the evidence indicates that men compromised on the already limited suffrage that organized women in New Mexico desired.[9]

Primary evidence for this conclusion is the compromise that delegates imbedded clearly in Article VII of the constitution of 1910. While the constitution gave women the right to hold school office as superintendent, director, or member of a board of education, Article VII restricted the right of women to vote for these officials if enough men objected. If a majority of voters presented a petition to the board of county commissioners requesting disfranchisement of the women, a majority of voters favoring the restoration of the franchise had to present a counter petition before women could vote again. No documents remain in the state archives showing how many women did vote or whether this political right was ever taken away (because in county elections both ballots and any petition challenges remained at the county level and were destroyed after thirty days), but this compromise certainly gave women tenuous political rights. In addition, the constitutional compromise protecting the elective franchise of Hispanic males, however that was achieved, made it virtually hopeless to attempt to amend the constitution to give women the vote. Under the new constitution, three-fourths of the voters in each county had to approve amendments to the franchise provisions. Such overwhelming approval was assumed by politicians to be almost impossible to obtain. Women in other western states who achieved suffrage by 1914 had no such provisions to overcome. Thus, as Ada Morley wrote to the Congressional Union, federal action was their only hope.[10]

Amid the celebrations of new statehood, then, a small group of women were dissatisfied with their disfranchisement. At first, some of the club women worked through NAWSA, which attempted to expand its activities in New Mexico between 1912 and 1915. Deane Lindsey, an active club woman and former teacher from Portales, became state chairman. NAWSA offered little incentive for New Mexico women to become politically active, however, because it had begun to focus on state suffrage referendums. These referendums were virtually impossible to win in New Mexico because of the need to obtain a three-fourths majority to amend.[11]

More important than NAWSA for fueling the engine of women's discontent in New Mexico was the National Federation of Women's Clubs (NFWC) with which the New Mexico Federation of Women's Clubs (NMFWC) became affiliated in 1914. Committed to an active campaign on behalf of women's right to public life, the NMFWC joined the vision of a reformed society to an evangelical feminist ideology. "The Feminist Movement," proclaimed the New Mexico club president in 1914, was a "tidal wave of sentiment," a cooperative movement of hundreds of thousands of women committed to a better life for American families through better homes, better schools, better babies, and better citizens." To achieve this, the NMFWC supported an extensive program of legislation. Women's suffrage would make the legislation possible.[12]

Thus, when the Congressional Union sent its first organizer to New Mexico in 1914, New Mexico club women were ready to act. A splinter group under the leadership of Alice Paul that separated from NAWSA in 1912, the Congressional Union (CU), had adopted the militant and sophisticated pressure tactics of the British suffragettes (as the British called their campaigners). Like their political sisters in Britain, CU organizers adapted the strategy of holding the party in power responsible for any defeat of suffrage in Congress and also the tactic of organizing socially prominent women into pressure groups. Organized women in the forty-eight states would then "make a big noise in Washington" to force delegates to support the national amendment and, finally, compel thirty-six state legislatures (the number needed for passage of the amendment) to ratify it. CU leaders additionally expected to mobilize the four million western women who had sufficient votes to threaten the party in power. Although New Mexico women had no votes, CU leaders considered the state important because they assumed organized anti-suffragist opposition would be weaker in the West than in the East and because the New Mexico delegation of three congressmen would be easier to pressure than larger delegations from more populous eastern states.[13] The group of women that the CU pulled together in New Mexico launched its first campaign in late 1915, continued to mobilize during the war, and remained the most active organization during the ratification battle.

Of the four organizers Paul sent to New Mexico between 1914 and 1920, three worked extremely well with New Mexico women. The second organizer, Ella St. Clair Thompson, who arrived in late 1915 liked the New Mexico people very much and was particularly impressed with the women. Letters from New Mexico to national CU officials testified that she, in turn, was well liked. The organizers brought excitement and activity. One young woman wrote from Santa Fe to Thompson after she left: "The old town is as dull and stupid as ever, and it is all I can do to keep from packing my trunk." When the third organizer left in December 1917, another woman wrote that the visit had been like a breath of mountain air and that she was committed to working with the organizer. The personal contact of these representatives was crucial to the organizing of New Mexico women, and only during the last campaign of ratification in 1920 did a CU organizer antagonize New Mexico women. By this time, the tactics of the CU had become much more militant. Members had carried banners that condemned President Woodrow Wilson for not supporting suffrage. Many had been arrested, and some had staged hunger strikes in jail. Militants did alienate more men than did the conservative suffragists, in New Mexico as well as elsewhere, but these militant tactics probably paved the way for the more moderate suffragists.[14] In New Mexico, the worst criticism of the last CU organizer was that she, as one state leader said, "was a Texas Democrat and should not have come into a Republican State."[15] By this time women had begun to move into political parties; bipartisanship was breaking down, and tempers were short in the final push.

The main problem of organizers was identifying local networks and socially prominent women. The first organizer, Mabel Vernon, who arrived in early 1914, began to organize through the New Mexico Women's Christian Temperance Union (WCTU). A

CU organizer spoke at the state WCTU convention in July 1915, and women then began the letter writing campaign that Ada Morley enthusiastically joined. Because the WCTU had relatively little influence among socially prominent women in northern New Mexico, the CU soon shifted its emphasis to club women. Thompson, who arrived in late 1915, spoke before the women's club in Santa Fe, located the most influential women in the town, and then, working through the state federation, she urged clubs to suggest women in different parts of the state to serve on delegations. Once the state network was set up, Thompson planned the type of pageant that the CU had made famous—a mass meeting, a parade, and deputation to Senators Thomas Catron and Albert Fall. In addition, Thompson sent delegations to all political conventions, from the smallest division to the state convention. "Please have as much of a bombardment as possible descend upon Congress from these political gatherings," Paul wrote to Thompson in February 1916.[16] And so the bombardment began.

Once the state network had been set up, Thompson organized the public meeting to climax the work. A president was chosen, and the campaign officially launched. At the meeting, purple, gold, and white bunting along with suffrage flags decorated the hall while speakers explained that the federal amendment was the quickest route to suffrage for New Mexico women. Organizer Doris Stevens summed up the philosophy of the CU: "Congress understands only vigorous and persistent demands and unless such methods are used in dealing with the august body, the amendment will be sidetracked." Later she told a reporter from the Santa Fe *New Mexican*: "We women have been meek too long. It is time to be impatient." Four million women would be voting in the upcoming election, she reminded her New Mexico audience.[17]

Who did these organizers attract to their purple, gold, and white banners? The women who rallied to the CU call were not representative of various regions of New Mexico, ethnic groups, or classes. (See table 1 for numbers of cases and percentages). They were a predominantly Anglo elite centered in Santa Fe, Albuquerque, and other northern cities.[18] Although few of these women gained independence through their personal careers, they had married men among the political and business elite. At a special reception for delegates of the state constitutional convention of 1910, for example, ten women mentioned prominently as presiding or

Table 1. Biographical Characteristics of New Mexico Suffragists

Category	Number	Percent
Ethnicity (N = 107)		
Anglo surname	100	93
Spanish surname	7	7
Residence (N = 68)		
Northern New Mexico	58	85
Marital Status (N = 80)		
Ever Married	60	75
Year Married (N = 24)		
1871–1910	21	88
Number Children (N = 22)		
0–1	3	14
2–3	13	59
4–5	6	27
Length of time in State (N = 27)		
Born in New Mexico	8	30
To State 1871–1890	12	44
To State 1891–1910	7	26
Region From (N = 25)		
New Mexico	8	32
Midwest	10	40
East	4	16
Membership (N = 100)		
Congressional Union	80	80
NAWSA	30	30
NMFWC	25	25
WCTU	9	9
Career Experience (N = 13)		
Artists–Writers	4	31
Teachers	4	31
Political Office	5	39
Church (N = 14)		
Protestant	13	93
Catholic	1	7
Presbyterian	5	36
Status of Family Male (N = 29)		
State Office	12	42
Business/Finance	13	45
Lawyer	8	28
Political Party (N = 25)		
Republican	20	80
Democrat	4	16
Socialist	1	4

attending later joined the suffrage movement. The women attracted to the CU counted among their husbands and male relatives bank presidents, political party leaders, high officials of mercantile businesses, and lawyers who represented railroad and land syndicates. An overwhelming number of the members' husbands identified with the Republican Party, the dominant party in the state. These women were exactly the type of persons whom the CU had hoped to attract with its recruiting.

By far the largest proportion of the New Mexico suffragists had married, more than half of them between 1890 and 1910. Almost one-third were born in New Mexico, but more than two-fifths had immigrated to the state between 1871 and 1890, primarily from the Midwest. More than half had three to five children. Few had graduated from college, but almost one-fourth of the women belonged to a woman's club and nearly 10 percent to the WCTU. Whatever this said for their interests, it did show that the suffrage networks spread through groups of women already organized to effect changes in their communities. They were a combination of young and middle-aged, upper middle-class women, both unmarried and married with children.

Both the WCTU and the NMFWC were almost entirely Anglo, but when Thompson arrived she made efforts to recruit daughters of Hispanic politicians. Although CU records mention only six Hispanic women as participating, these six were key women. Aurora Lucero, daughter of the secretary of state, joined. So too did the three nieces of Solomon Luna, including thirty-four-year-old widow Adelina Otero-Warren, who became the most influential New Mexican woman in the CU. To appeal to a broader constituency, Thompson had leaflets printed in Spanish and English for the mass meeting in October 1915. "They say it is very difficult to get the Spanish ladies out," she wrote to Paul on October 15, "but as I have one on the program to speak *in Spanish,* I think they will come—and their husbands as well." Thompson wrote a speech for Aurora Lucero, carefully emphasizing child welfare in order to convert the Hispanic women, and had the speech translated into Spanish. Even though Otero-Warren was too timid to speak then, she particularly impressed Thompson. The Hispanic women seemed pleased with Thompson's efforts. "I speak a little Spanish—very little—but it helps a lot," she reported to Paul.[19]

But progress was not so smooth in other areas. Ada Morely

wrote in discouragement from Datil that Hispanic voters were against them "solid" and that they needed Spanish-speaking suffrage sentiment. She was not optimistic. Paul refused to give up, however. Instead, she continued to encourage leadership among Hispanic women, asking Otero-Warren to join the advisory council as vice president. When the head of the state group resigned in September 1917, Paul asked Otero-Warren to head the state group.[20] Beginning as a timid woman unwilling to speak in public, Otero-Warren gradually became a political force. Her uncle, Solomon Luna, the powerful and popular head of the Republican Party, had died in 1912, but her father was still active in politics, and other Otero males were moving into influential positions in the Republican Party. In 1917, Republicans appointed Otero-Warren school superintendent in Santa Fe, and in 1918 she defeated a male opponent to retain this elective position. She accepted leadership of the New Mexico CU and was soon skillfully evaluating local tensions among factions. "I will keep out of local fuss but will take a stand and a firm one whenever necessary for I am with you now and always!" she wrote to Paul on 4 December 1917.[21]

Otero-Warren guided the New Mexico phase of the campaign to pry the amendment out of the United States Congress. Complaining that the extra war work in the schools kept her from doing as much suffrage work as she wished, she nevertheless kept the state group intact through the war and resigned from the CU only to become the chair of the women's division of the Republican State Committee for New Mexico. When it appeared the state might not ratify in 1920, Otero-Warren stepped up her Santa Fe political activities, working closely with state Hispanic Republican leaders to get the amendment ratified. On the last day of the struggle, after the Senate had narrowly ratified and the House balked at passing the amendment, she spent three hours in the Republican caucus, reputedly the first woman to ever attend a state political caucus. Writing enthusiastically to Paul in March 1920 that the Republicans had just voted to allow women in the primaries and to be seated at the next convention, she predicted that the women's vote would be a big factor in the next election.[22] Experience with the CU encouraged Otero-Warren to see herself as a politician and to participate in the complex party politics of the time.

Raising the political consciousness of women was a necessary activity of the CU, but mobilizing women to challenge men who controlled the political structure in New Mexico was the ultimate goal. While women in political office might help convince men that women were competent and sufficiently interested in politics, only group pressure could move intransigent politicians to support women's demand for suffrage.

Of the two New Mexico senators, women found Senator Albert Fall the more sympathetic to their cause. Fall invited one delegation to visit his Three Rivers ranch, his wife Emma Morgan Fall served on the original CU committee formed in 1916, and even Ada Morley grudgingly described Senator Fall as "not as dense and obdurate as Catron." Though never an active suffragist, Fall remained a friend to New Mexico women during the nine years he was in office.[23]

Senator Catron opposed women's suffrage consistently during the six years (1911 to 1916) he represented New Mexico in Washington. In 1911, at seventy-one, the stout and aging Catron had achieved the office of his life's ambition, gladly giving up a declining position in state politics for the Senate, where he reportedly spent from one to two hours every morning in the luxurious baths provided for the Senators. Concerned mainly with higher tariffs, a grazing Homestead Act, and military preparedness, Catron not only opposed women's suffrage, he did it with ill humor. "He thinks all we are good for is to stay home, have children, have more children, cook and wash dishes," a suffragist complained bitterly after he rebuffed one delegation.[24] Thompson described Catron once as an "awfully cross old thing" but urged New Mexico women to take him seriously. Even Ada Morley, who advised the CU that Catron controlled New Mexico politics "as a cat does a mouse," that he was "as corrupt, as dishonorable a politician as ever lived," and that it was "creditable to have him as an enemy," nevertheless warned that "you need his vote."[25]

Beginning in 1914, a steady stream of women wrote and visited Catron in Santa Fe and in Washington. Some visits went better than others. Thompson reported in October 1915 that at least "he didn't try to wriggle" because she had people in her delegation he cared for, but Catron would not budge. By February 1916, the women were discouraged. In that month, Deane Lindsey wrote to Morley: "I think Catron has been stormed and stormed about the suffrage matter. The Santa Fe women have written and written."[26] Catron steadfastly remained opposed to the Susan B. Anthony amendment and, as a last salvo, even introduced an anti-suffrage statement in the Senate in February 1917.[27]

Women also believed the single representative from New Mexico, Benigno Cardenas Hernandez, would not move as long as Catron opposed suffrage. Morley, with her usual blunt criticism, claimed that Catron controlled the congressman totally; he "simply put Hernandez in Congress before our citizens knew what was being done." While Catron had influenced the political career of Hernandez, the Hispanic representative was a skilled politician in his own right and had as his campaign manager the husband of an active suffragist. Nevertheless, Hernandez did not openly espouse suffrage as long as the senior member of Congress from New Mexico opposed it.[28]

What specific influence women had in insuring Catron's political decline is difficult to determine, but they certainly helped to make Catron a political liability to the Republicans. Although Catron wanted renomination, Republicans nominated the unpopular but prosuffrage Frank Hubbell in 1916. That year for the first time parties in New Mexico supported the women's suffrage amendment.[29] The CU maintained its nonpartisan stand in the election of 1916; members of the organization opposed Democrats who would not endorse suffrage and refused to campaign for Republicans. Concerned about women's political potential, the Republican Party brought a prominent suffragist from California in 1916 to organize Women's Republican Clubs throughout the state. Dr. Jessie A. Russell, a retired physician, arrived in New Mexico in mid-October for a whirlwind tour. Part of the impetus for the last-minute campaign to win voteless women to the cause was the belief that Frank Hubbell's unpopularity might take the rest of the Republican slate down to defeat with him. To capitalize on the endorsement of suffrage by presidential candidate Charles Hughes and on the network of women already organized into suffrage groups in the state, Republican managers contacted key women and women's clubs to urge them to arrange mass meetings. In addition, these women were encouraged to organize Women's Republican Clubs whose goal was "to aid passage of federal suffrage by aiding the election of Republicans."[30]

Who benefited most—the Republican Party or suffragists—is difficult to determine. The speeches and publicity surrounding Russell's tour certainly popularized the suffrage cause. Russell usually scheduled two meetings in each town, the first to present a non-partisan talk on suffrage or "women in public life" and a second speech later in the day to organize women into Republican Clubs. While the CU had concentrated much of its energies on raising the consciousness of a select few and organizing them to lobby politicians, Russell asked women to participate in a major party structure. Moreover, many men and women attended her Republican-sponsored meetings, thus providing an education for the male voters. Russell saw herself, and the women she spoke to, as part of a "women's movement" and considered her work as involving women never before interested in public matters. She hoped to attract women with Democratic or Socialist preferences to the new Republican women's clubs, but at the same time she wanted to strengthen the nonpartisan suffrage movement. She traveled throughout the state, speaking to university women in Las Vegas, organizing a large meeting for Ada Morley at Magdalena, and taking the message to Gallup.[31]

This initial attempt by Republicans offered women political participation in a major party, even if in separate groups; but it offered women no autonomy and no way to articulate their political needs: the women's movement still held the political lifeline of prospective voters. The Women's Republican Clubs apparently did not help the party much, for both Hubbell and Hernandez were defeated in the Wilson landslide of 1916. The clubs did, however, give the Republican Party a structure through which to organize women voters once they had the vote and thus an edge over the Democrats who did little to organize women during the first twelve years after suffrage.

The 1916 election put two prosuffrage Democrats from New Mexico in Congress. Although the new representative, William B. Walton, promised the CU to vote for the amendment, he later seemed to waver, and Martin sent a hurried note from headquarters urging Otero-Warren to turn up the political heat: "I think he is a little shaky and needs pressure from his constituents." This last-minute pressure steadied Walton so that he voted for the Nineteenth Amendment which passed the House in January 1918. Meanwhile, Andrieus Aristiens Jones from Socorro, who replaced Catron in Congress, moved into the chair of the influential Senate Committee on Woman Suffrage. Jones proved his support by visiting CU militants jailed for their Washington protests and saw the Susan B. Anthony amendment out of committee and on to the Senate floor where he worked for its passage.[32] The Senate voted favorably in June 1919. After fifty years of independent organizing for suffrage, women had finally pried the federal suffrage amendment out of Congress.[33]

The political focus now shifted back to New Mexico where the legislature had to approve the amendment. Suffragists were so confident that the amendment would pass easily in the January 1919 session that the new head of the state CU, now calling itself the National Women's Party (NWP), made the mistake of leaving for California. With Otero-Warren lobbying among the Hispanics, the amendment passed the House easily; but in the Senate a Republican member sidetracked the amendment by substituting a state referendum measure which, as everyone knew, could not pass.[34] This defeat in New Mexico bitterly disappointed both New Mexico women and national suffrage leaders who hoped New Mexico would be one of the first states to ratify. Twenty-two states ratified the amendment in 1919, including Texas and Colorado, but fourteen more were needed, and the women knew the longer the ratification process, the more opposition would organize against passage. NAWSA also increased its activity in the West that fall with a special trip by leader Carrie Chapman Catt to eight states, including New Mexico.

By this time, antisuffragists were labeling suffragists as disloyal Americans and Bolshevik agents. Although most moderate leaders got used to these attacks, Catt felt compelled to spend time refuting claims made by the antis that women would vote socialist once they were enfranchised.[35] As the political right began to organize in the postwar period later known for its "red scare," moderates became distressed about the tactics of the National Woman's Party. Catt believed that the militant activism during the war, especially picketing the president during the war, had cost women precious support. As the crisis deepened surrounding passage of the amendment, the two major suffrage groups found it difficult to work together, in part because leadership believed in different tactics, in part because right-wing spokesmen increasingly attacked the more moderate NAWSA which responded by disassociating itself from the NWP. Intent on keeping the two groups separate, Catt even sent a special emissary to Wyoming to bring that state back into the NAWSA fold after it had strayed into the NWP's camp; she also traveled to the West to recapture other territory lost to the National Woman's Party and to gather support for passage of the amendment. She lobbied at the Governor's Conference in Salt Lake City to gain backing from western governors for ratification. Early in 1920, Arizona and Utah ratified after governors from those states promised support. Governor C. A. Larrazolo of New Mexico promised both NAWSA and NWP leaders passage of the amendment at a special session called for 16 February 1920. If New Mexico ratified as the thirty-second state, only four more would be needed for passage.[36]

Final victory in New Mexico resulted from coalition work by NWP and Republican women. Otero-Warren swung into action in January lining up Republican leaders behind the amendment.[37] When antisuffragists attempted the same tactic that had worked in 1919, introducing a resolution to substitute a referendum for the resolution ratifying the federal amendment, Paul alerted prosuffrage Republican supporters to the plot and warned state NWP leaders that they must be on guard against such moves. A Republican secretary informed Paul of a secret meeting in Washington where at least one leader had been brought to line up Hispanic opposition in return for financial support in the next campaign. In a desperate attempt to block ratification in New Mexico, Republican antisuffragists hoped Hispanics could be convinced that women's suffrage was against their interests and vote it down. Anglo politicians could then blame Hispanic males for the defeat of a law Anglos did not want enacted.[38]

In addition to a last-minute caucus with Republican leaders, Otero-Warren joined Paul in countering a flurry of telegrams from antisuffrage states in the South with an even larger flurry of supportive messages from states that had ratified. As suffragist women packed Senate galleries to hear the final debate, Republicans shifted to support of the amendment. On 18 February the Senate ratified the amendment seventeen to five. The next day, after a three hour Republican caucus, Dan Padilla withdrew his referendum proposal, Republican leader R. I. Baca shifted to support, and the House ratified thirty-six to ten. New Mexico became the thirty-second state to ratify. Oklahoma, Washington, and West Virginia followed New Mexico, the final battle occurring in Tennessee where, according to Catt, antisuffragists bought votes and instigated opposition of every sort. On 15 August 1920, however, Tennessee ratified.[39] After almost a century of talk about suffrage and more than a decade of campaigning in New Mexico, women had won the vote.

The major problem now for political parties was how to mobilize the new voting public. The Republicans, using lists of women collected in 1916 and tapping leadership developed by the women's movement, acted quickly to organize women. Women moved into three of the eleven slots on the state executive committee, and fifty-seven women became state committeemen, including eighteen Hispanic women and eight former suffragists. The Democrats also drew four women on to their executive committee and appointed fifty-six women to the county committees, of whom only two were Hispanic while three were former suffragists. The difference between eighteen and two Hispanic women in the two parties reflected the relative proportion of Hispanics, although Hispanic women were not equally represented with Anglo women in either party.

Although they believed Republican women would vote, Democrats made little effort until September 1920 to get out the women's vote, when they recruited fifteen women to speak. At this late date it was difficult to form these women into an effective speaker's bureau. One woman had a small baby to care for, another had no experience at speaking, and a third was recovering from nervous exhaustion after stumping the state for prohibition. Meetings scheduled for one woman had to be cancelled because she was a poor speaker. Only Frances J. Nixon, who spoke primarily on the League of Nations, proved to be an effective speaker and organizer. The chairman of the Speaker's Bureau was insistent that wherever possible local women make short addresses at rallies and that several women be on the stage. "Our success depends on getting out the Democratic women voters. Bear this in mind;—*The Republican Women are going to vote,*" he warned. But beyond making women visible, Democrats had no clear-cut policy to attract the new voters. One local organizer suggested "emotional appeals especially to the women"; another recommended picnics to help get women to the polls.[40] Mainly, the initiative remained with local party loyalists who had gained their position in the party by being able to turn out male voters. Late in the campaign a fusion blossomed with Democratic and Independent Republican women joining to issue a bilingual appeal (*"A Las Senoras de Santa Fe"* and "To the Women of Santa Fe") that urged women to choose reform candidates who

A Las Señoras de Santa Fe

Mañana es el día de la elección. Es un día de mucha importancia para las señoras de Santa Fé. Esta es nuestra primera participación en una que no sea solamente elección para escuelas, y las señoras se sienten algo tímidas acerca de ejercer sus privilegios; miedosas de dar un golpe recio con una nueva arma. Pero no debemos tener miedo de pegar con todas nuestras fuerzas en defensa de nuestros hogares.

El gobierno de una ciudad, o de un estado, o de una nación queda solo en las manos de sus ciudadanos. Si el ciudadano no ejercita sus derechos y franquicias no tiene derecho para culpar a los que gobiernan, o mal gobiernan, para sus propios intereses. La cuestión en el condado de Santa Fé es una cuestión para un gobierno mejor. Es para hacer nuestra ciudad un lugar mejor donde vivir, un lugar mejor para nuestros hogares, para nuestros hijos. Se nos ha dicho que los hombres de los partidos van iguales, y que si Santa Fé se ha de 'limpiar' nosotras las señoras debemos hacerlo.

Con este prospecto ante nosotras, ¿vámos a votar por nuestro partido en el condado de Santa Fé, sin importar el registro de los hombres que están corriendo en el boleto de nuestro partido? ¿Es un hombre un hombre bueno para los pobres porque regala unos cuantos pesos de abarrotes o una carga de leña con una mano, mientras que con la orta permite al jugador que se robe el poquito dinero que tienen los pobres, y a la mujer mala que pone en peligro nuestros hogares? ¿Después de la elección se vá a decir que las señoras de Santa Fé han votado para mantener en las oficinas hombres que han probado por sus registros pasados que no sostienen las leyes que ellos han jurado defender? La elección este año en el condado de Santa Fé no es una elección de partido. Es una elección del HOGAR. Por medio de nuestros votos hablaremos en favor de una ciudad más limpia, o bien hablaremos por una continuación de las condiciones presentes. Mientras tales lugares como el "Canary Cottage" y los garitos de juego sean permitidos en Santa Fé, ningún hogar en la ciudad está segura. Esta es la cuestión más importante en Santa Fé hoy día.

¿Vámos a votar por una continuación de las condiciones presentes, o vámos todas a votar para cerrar el "Canary Cottage" y los garitos de los jugadores que infestan nuestra ciudad? ¿Podemos esperar a los que están lucrando con lugares de esta clase que los cierren?

Los miembros de la Comisión Ejecutiva de la Comisión Fusionista del Condado no creen que las señoras de Santa Fé, una vez que comprendan la situación, traicionen la confianza que se ha depositado en ellas. Creemos confiadamente que las señoras de Santa Fé y del condado de Santa Fé estarán firmes en favor de un gobierno sano y limpio.

También creemos firmemente que los hombres nominados para oficiales de la ciudad y del condado, por los Demócratas y los Republicanos Independientes en el movimiento de Fusión del Condado, cuyos nombres se encontrarán en la columna Demócrata en el boleto mañana, nos darán un gobierno fuerte y limpio para la ciudad y el condado, y por esta razón, y nada más por esta razón, pedimos el soporte de las señoras de Santa Fé, de la ciudad y del condado.

Para asegurar el depositar sus votos, todas las señoras deben visitar los lugares de votación al abrise las casillas electorales a las nueve de la mañana, y deben votar antes que los hombres salgan de sus trabajos, cuando la mucha gente hará que sea difícil que se pueda votar, especialmente en los Precintos 3 y 4. Debería saber bien como vá a votar para que cuando llegue a las casillas electorales no se pierda el tiempo ni haya demoras al votar, a fin de que cada uno de los votantes pueda tener tiempo de votar.

Con toda confianza dejamos la cuestión en manos de las señoras votantes de Santa Fé.

Respetuosamente,

LA COMISIÓN EJECUTIVA DE SEÑORAS
de la Comisión Fusionista del Condado de Santa Fé.

Por Ina Sizer Cassidy, Presidenta
Sra. Nicanor Baca, Secretaria
Sra. C. S. Kennedy, Sec. Asistenta
Sra. A. S. Alvord
Sra. A. M. Thebault
Sra. Mariano Durán
Sra. Abel Benavidez

Spanish version of a bilingual appeal to women voters. Miscellaneous Records, Political Issues. Courtesy of the State Records and Archives, Santa Fe, New Mexico.

would eliminate prostitution and gambling—and to vote early before the polls became crowded.[41] This appeal indicated that reform might be a continuing interest of women.

Overall the parties were successful in getting out the vote. The number of adults participating in the election jumped from 40 percent in 1916 to 62 percent in 1920. (See tables 2 and 3.) Only an estimated 11 percent more men than women voted. Mobilization, voter participation, and the newly franchised women can be considered major achievements for New Mexico parties. Although it would take a state referendum to prove that women also had the right to hold office, women campaigned for school superintendent in twenty-one of twenty-nine counties and were elected in nineteen. The governor appointed both Hispanic and Anglo women to every state board, a woman became assistant secretary of state (a position previously reserved to males), and women moved into control of the public welfare board.

Political scientists sometimes list two reasons for the lower nationwide political participation of women than men in the early 1920s: the lack of role models to help women internalize voting and office holding practice and local resistance to women's voting and holding office. Yet in the years from 1920 to 1940, Hispanic women with few role models and no tradition of participation in formal political structures, expanded dramatically their political activities. Like Black women after they gained the vote in the 1960s, these Hispanic women became rapidly politicized.[42]

This dramatic politicization becomes evident by comparing the total mobilization before suffrage with the percentage of adults voting in six predominantly Anglo counties (Little Texas) and a block of five predominantly Hispanic counties. Because women were disfranchised before 1920, the total mobilization of voters was low, with only 27 to 40 percent of the adults voting. (See table 2.) During the years from 1900 to 1916, male voter participation ranged from 51 to 72 percent in New Mexico with Hispanic counties having a much higher voter turnout than Little Texas counties in 1912 and 1916.[43] Regardless of how this turnout was achieved—most historians attribute it to a well-oiled political machine reminiscent of nineteenth century machines that unfailingly delivered the vote among white males—it was impressive. Hispanic women voters moved rapidly into this voting structure. The percent of eligible voters voting in Hispanic counties dipped to 59 percent in 1920,

Table 2. Voter Turnout and Mobilization 1900–1916

	1900	1904	1908	1911	1912	1916
Voter Turnout (T)	72%	63%	69%	51%	55%	73%
Mobilization (M)	40%	34%	37%	27%	30%	40%

$$T = \frac{\text{total vote}}{\text{total population eligible to vote}}$$

(includes a small number of Native Americans, many
of whom were disfranchised)

$$M = \frac{\text{total vote}}{\text{total population over 21}}$$

Table 3. Voter Turnout 1912–1940

	1912	1916	1920	1924	1928	1932	1936	1940
State★	55%	73%	62%	62%	60%	70%	69%	66%
Hispanic Counties[A]	67%	84%	59%★★	68%	70%	82%	83%	80%
Little Texas[B]	46%	70%	59%	46%	43%	56%	57%	53%

★Includes a small number of Native Americans, many of whom were disfranchised.
★★No returns for San Miguel Conty; averaged on basis of four-county vote.
[A]Includes Guadalupe, Mora, Rio Arriba, San Miguel, Taos.
[B]Includes Chaves, Curry, DeBaca, Eddy, Lea, and Roosevelt.

but by 1924, 68 percent were voting, and the count reached a peak of 84 percent in 1936. (See table 3.) Little Texas counties also had 59 percent voting in 1925, but the percentage decreased in subsequent elections before climbing to a high of only 57 percent in 1936. Anglo women in these Little Texas counties tended to follow the voting pattern of the southern region of the country where women had a low overall voter participation, but Hispanic women immediately became active voters, exceeding the average level of women in northern states.[44]

Hispanic support also extended to Hispanic women who ran for political office during these twenty years. Perhaps the change was most dramatically symbolized when Otero-Warren ran for the United States House of Representatives in 1922. During a special election held in the fall of 1921 to confirm the right of women to hold office in New Mexico (*"para tener oficina las mujeres,"* as the ballot read in Spanish) numerous Hispanic males continued to remain opposed to granting this political right as one can see by comparing the county blocks of Hispanic and Litte Texas regions. Of the five core Hispanic counties, four defeated the amendment. Of the six Little Texas counties, four passed the amendment by a majority. Republicans expected organized womanhood to support Otero-Warren in 1922 as the first woman in New Mexico to run for high federal office. Campaigners even took out a full page advertisement in the NMFWC *Bulletin* to remind club women of her past activities on behalf of women. Otero-Warren did not win enough votes to defeat her male Democratic opponent, but this was not too surprising since the Democrats elected a governor and most of the state officials that year. That she carried four of five Hispanic counties and none of the Little Texas counties was a surprise. This willingness of Hispanics to have a woman represent them in Congress one year after voting against women holding office was a tribute to the ability of political structures to triumph over ideology. The first woman representative from New Mexico to the United States Congress would not be elected until twenty-four years later when in 1946 Georgia L. Lusk carried all of the Little Texas counties and none of the Hispanic counties. By then, Little Texas had become so populous that Lusk did not need the Hispanic counties.[45]

While New Mexico women had to wait twenty-six years after suffrage for their first female United States representative and

Figure 1.   Women Holding Office
New Mexico 1900–1940

Number

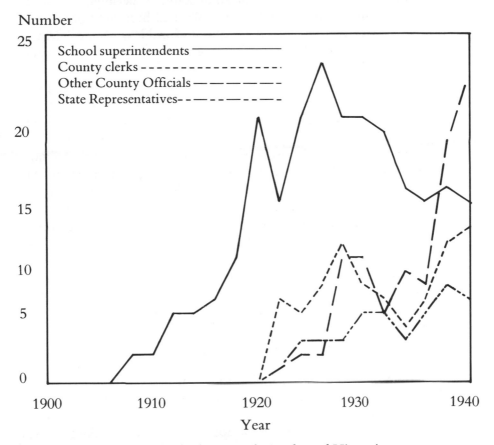

to this writing have never had a second, Anglo and Hispanic women did move into state office holding. (See figure 1.) In the election that Otero-Warren lost, New Mexicans elected a Hispanic Democratic woman as secretary of state and an Anglo Democratic woman as state superintendent of public instruction. Women never gave up the position of secretary of state in New Mexico, and women held the office of superintendent of public instruction for most of the years before 1940. Women reached a peak in county office holding in 1926 when they held twenty-three offices of county superintendent of education and in 1928 when they occupied ten county clerkships and nine other county positions. By 1938, seven women also sat in the New Mexico legislature, although only one of the

women was Hispanic. While these numbers seem meager in relationship to the percentage of women in the population, each of these
political offices, with the exception of county superintendent of education which women held from 1908, had been held previously
only by men and was much sought after in New Mexico. Moreover, women would have difficulty extending these modest gains
after World War II. [46]

The political situation in New Mexico, rather than the presence or absence of role models, seems to have contributed most to
this dramatic change in female political participation and male support for such activity. Because Republicans dominated New Mexico from 1850–1911, Hispanic males were able to protect their ethnic
interests through active participation in the Republican Party. After 1911, the growth of the Democratic Party, traditionally an Anglo party, made the political position of Hispanics more vulnerable.
Hispanic males did not uniformly oppose women's political participation, nor did Anglo males uniformly support it. Indeed, the
issue of women's suffrage became entangled in the complex web
of party loyalties and ethnic fears. Before 1920, few Republican
males—Anglos or Hispanics—looked upon women's political participation as crucial to the party, and neither party had any method
of organizing women or giving them political training. Hispanics
and Anglos reached a political compromise in the state: Anglos controlled most political matters in the legislature in exchange for as-
surance of jobs for Hispanics. Some Hispanics may have feared
women's suffrage would upset this balance, especially if they assumed only Anglo women would be voting or considered Hispanic
women as not being capable of political activity. But Ango males
also feared women's political activities. Suffragist organizers probably allayed the fears of Hispanic males by grooming a woman like
Otero-Warren for political activism. [47]

Republican leaders undoubtedly learned from suffragists a number of tactics for mobilizing women politically. And Republicans
surely learned from suffragists to take women seriously as a political variable so that when they needed votes in the 1920s it was possible to expand the party machinery to mobilize Hispanic women.
When progressive Bronson Cutting began to appeal to the Hispanic vote in the 1920s, many followed him. Cutting, who moved
in and out of the Republican Party during the 1920s, created a vol-
atile situation for the Republican Old Guard. Because of this polit-

ical wavering, Hispanic women found themselves wooed as voters by both Old Guard Republicans who needed votes to shore up the crumbling walls of Republicanism and by progressives who wanted to show the Old Guard they were a real threat. Eventually, of course, Democrats also learned how to mobilize Hispanic women. Unemployment and low farm commodity prices during the Depression of the 1930s swung New Mexico women into the Democratic party, and federal assistance programs helped keep them there.[48]

The enfranchisement of New Mexico women was significant both to women who attempted to translate their needs into political action and to the male politicians who tried to predict and control women's votes.[49] When women voted, their choices affected traditional politics in important ways; where they did not vote, their abstention also affected politics, if only by allowing politicians greater power in determining policies. Although New Mexico women entered politics at a time of declining male participation nationally, Hispanic women, like Hispanic men, retained high voter participation in New Mexico. The implication of this pattern is important to present voting, for Hispanic populations in other southwestern states are now increasing participation previously restricted by gerrymandering and other forms of disfranchisement. The potential strength of Hispanic voting and the strong bargaining position Hispanic women have within their ethnic political groups will be crucial factors as the Hispanic population comes to political power in the Southwest.

Notes

The author would like to thank Darlis Miller of the New Mexico State University History Department and Janet Clark and José Garcia of the Government Department for criticism of an earlier version of this paper.

1. Ada Morley to Anne Martin, 15 March 1916, National Woman's Party Paper, tray 12, box 1, Library of Congress (NWP Papers, LC).
2. Morley to Martin, 2 March 1916, tray 12, box 1, NWP Papers, LC.
3. The debate over the place of political history in women's his-

tory is treated in Carroll Smith-Rosenberg, "The New Woman and the New History," *Feminist Studies* 3 (Fall 1975):186; and Ellen C. DuBois, *Feminism and Suffrage: The Emergence of an Independent Women's Movement in America, 1848–1869* (Ithaca, N.Y.: Cornell University Press, 1978). A review of literature on suffrage in the West is in Joan M. Jensen and Darlis A. Miller, "The Gentle Tamers Revisited: New Approaches to the History of Women in the American West," *Pacific Historical Review* 49 (May 1980):173–213; on recent political activities, see Berenice A. Carroll, "Political Science, Part 1: American Politics and Political Behavior," *Signs* 5 (Winter 1979):289–306.

4. Agnes Morley Cleaveland, *No Life for a Lady* (Boston: Houghton Mifflin Co., 1941), 251, 96, 220. Norman Cleaveland, *The Morleys— Young Upstarts on the Southwest Frontier* (Albuquerque: Calvin Horn Publishers, 1971), 243, gives a more positive view of his grandmother and mentions that Ada campaigned for suffrage for thirty-five years. Also, consult Alan P. Grimes, *The Puritan Ethnic and Women Suffrage* (New York: Oxford University Press, 1967), T. A. Larson, "Woman Suffrage in Western America," *Utah Historical Quarterly* 38 (Winter 1970):7–19, and Carrie Chapman Catt and Nettie Rogers Shuler, *Women Suffrage and Politics: The Inner Story of the Suffrage Movement* (New York: Charles Scribner's Sons, 1923), 389–90. Necah Stewart Furman, "Women's Campaign for Equality: A National and State Perspective," *New Mexico Historical Review* (NMHR) 53 (October 1978):365–74, does not discuss the political activities of the early suffragists.

5. Robert W. Larson, *New Mexico Populism: A Study of Radical Protest in a Western Territory* (Boulder: Colorado Associated University Press, 1974), 92; Robert W. Larson, *New Mexico's Quest for Statehood 1896–1912* (Albuquerque: University of New Mexico Press, 1968), 275, 278, 279; and Holmes, *Politics in New Mexico* (Albuquerque: UNM Press, 1967). Billie Barnes Jensen, "Colorado Woman Suffrage Campaigns of the 1870s," *Journal of the West* 12 (April 1973):264–69.

6. National American Woman's Suffrage Association Papers, Library of Congress (NAWSA Papers, LC). Container 78 has *Woman's Journal* subscription lists for 1892 by which time a large number of women in Utah subscribed. *Woman's Journal,* 25 March 1893. Mimeographed letter dated 28 May 1900, and enclosed memorial are in the Secundino Romero Papers, box 1, folders 8 and 9, Special Collections Dept., University of New Mexico Library, Albuquerque (UNM–SC). NAWSA Papers, LC, container 79, has 1909–10 subscription list.

7. On early clubs see Ruby Mears, "Portales Woman's Club," in *Roosevelt County History and Heritage,* ed. Jean M. Burroughs (Portales: Bishop Printing Company, 1975), 203–5; Olga Atwood, "Roswell Woman's Club," in *Roundup on the Pecos,* eds. Elvis E. Fleming and Minor S.

Huffman (Roswell, N.M.: Chaves County Historical Society, 1978), 370–73; and *The Curry County History Book* (Clovis, N.M.: High Plains Historical Foundation, 1978), 537. Almost all women mentioned in the early club movement had Anglo surnames. For the petition see Albuquerque *Morning Journal*, 15 November 1910.

8. Resolutions are in Santa Fe *New Mexican*, 18 October, 20 October, 9 November 1910.

9. Thomas J. Mabry, "New Mexico's Constitution in the Making—Reminiscences of 1910," NMHR 20 (April 1944):168–84; Rueben W. Hefflin, "New Mexico Constitutional Convention," NMHR 21 (January 1946): 67; and Edward D. Tittmann, "New Mexico Constitutional Convention: Recollections," NMHR 27 (July 1952):177. Larson, *New Mexico's Quest*, n. 53, p. 364, offers Tittmann as evidence of the exchange of limited women's suffrage for Hispanic rights, but Tittmann did not say this. Deane Lindsey, in a later report to NAWSA, claimed the constitution was made difficult to amend to prevent woman's suffrage, but she did not link this plan to Hispanic opposition. Ida Husted Harper, ed., *History of Woman Suffrage*, 6 vols. (1922: reprint ed., New York: National American Woman Suffrage Association, 1969), 6:439. Albuquerque *Morning Journal* and Santa Fe *New Mexican*, 9 November 1910, reported debate. Those reported as favoring complete suffrage were C. M. Compton and R. W. Hefflin; as supporting school suffrage, H. Bursum, H. H. Dougherty, J. W. Childers, John Canning, Albert Fall, E. F. Field, J. J. Lawson, W. E. Lindsey, Solomon Luna, C. A. Spiess, and E. S. Stover; opposing school suffrage, Fred S. Brown, E. A. Miere, E. F. Saxon, and Jose D. Sena.

10. Myra Ellen Jenkins, former chief, Historical Services Division, State Records Center and Archives (SRCA), Santa Fe, to author, 7 November 1979.

11. Lindsey was state chairman from 1913 to 1919. Catt sent Lola Walker and Gertrude Watkins as organizers to New Mexico. Harper, *History of Woman Suffrage*, 6:434–39. Lindsey also signed a 1916 petition to the Republican National Convention as the New Mexico representative, NAWSA Headquarters, *Newsletter* 11 (June 22, 1916):15. No New Mexico correspondence exists in the NAWSA files in the Library of Congress. One letter from Lindsey to Frank Hubbell, 9 September 1916, asking his position on suffrage was written on her husband's stationery and is in the Thomas Benton Catron Papers, Sect. 408, box 1, folder 19, UNM–SC.

12. New Mexico Federation of Women's Clubs, *Yearbook 1* (1914): 10, 16. State legislation desired was equitable community property laws, placing women on boards of state institutions, and a state board of charities and corrections.

13. CU strategy discussed is in undated letter from Ella St. Clair Thompson to Mrs. Jas. M. Young, San Antonio, Texas, and attitudes

towards state referendum in "Notes on Conference of the Congressional Union for Women Suffrage," 28 February 1916, NWP Papers, LC. See also Sidney Roderick Bland, "Techniques of Persuasion: The National Woman's Party and Women Suffrage, 1913–1919" (Ph.D. diss., George Washington University, 1972), 96–100. For the Congressional Union's campaign in neighboring Arizona see Meredith Ann Snapp, "Defeat the Democrats: The Arizona Campaigns of the Congressional Union for Woman Suffrage" (Master's thesis, Arizona State University, 1976).

14. Ethel Church to Thompson, 27 November 1915, Adelina Otero-Warren to Martin, 4 December 1917, tray 8, box 3, NWP Papers, LC.

15. Otero-Warren to Mabel Vernon, 1 March 1920, tray 8, box 3, NWP Papers, LC.

16. Jessi M. Stroup to Alice Paul, 24 April 1914, Paul to Harriet L. Henderson, 19 July 1915, and Henderson to Paul, 5 July 1915. Henderson was president of the New Mexico WCTU at the time; Deane Lindsey vice president. Paul to Thompson, 15 and 26 October 1915. Thompson to Paul, 16 October 1915 described mass meeting. Paul to Doris Stevens, 24 February 1916 on bombardment. Thompson to Mrs. Joshua Raynolds, 24 February 1916 on recruiting tactics. All in NWP Papers, tray 8, box 3, LC.

17. "Notes on Conference of the Congressional Union for Woman Suffrage," 28 February 1916, tray 8, box 3, NWP Papers, LC. Santa Fe *New Mexican,* 26, 27, 29 February 1916.

18. Biographical information on 107 women, prominently mentioned in NAWSA and NWP papers, was collected from: *Women in New Mexico* (Albuquerque: n.p., 1976); *Albuquerque Tribune,* 30 March 1976; Max Binheim, ed., *Women of the West* (Los Angeles: Publishers Press, 1928), 146–50; Ralph Emerson Twitchell, *Leading Facts of New Mexico History,* 5 vols. (Cedar Rapids, Iowa: Torch Press, 1911); Frank D. Reeve, *History of New Mexico,* 3 vols. (New York: Lewis Historical Publishing Co., 1961), 3: *Family and Personal History;* Jose Chavez Papers, Marguerite Medler Scrapbook, Raynolds Family Papers, all in UNM–SC; Nancy C. Benson, *Notable New Mexico Women: A Selected Index* (Albuquerque: n.p., 1976). For methodology see Burton W. Folsom II, "The Collective Biography as a Research Tool," *Mid-America: An Historical Review* 54 (April 1972): 108–22; Richard Jensen, "Family, Career, and Reform: Women Leaders of the Progressive Era," in *The American Family in Social-Historical Perspective,* ed. Michael Gordon (New York: St. Martin's Press, 1973), 267–80; and Barbara Campbell, *The "Liberated" Women of 1914: Prominent Women of the Progressive Era,* Studies in American History and Culture, No. 6 (Ann Arbor, Mich.: University Microfilms, 1979).

19. Thompson to Paul, 16 October 1915, NWP Papers, LC.

20. Morley note on Lindsey to Morley, 16 February 1916, Paul to Otero-Warren, 21 September 1917, NWP Papers, LC.

21. Otero-Warren to Paul, 4 December 1917, NWP Papers, LC.

22. Otero-Warren to Martin, 7 February 1918, NWP Papers, LC.

23. Santa Fe *New Mexican,* 27 October 1915, 29 February 1916.

24. Victor Westphall, *Thomas Benton Catron and His Era* (Tucson: University of Arizona Press, 1973), 348–50, 352–84. Quote from John Paul Wooden, "Thomas Benton Catron and New Mexico Politics, 1866–1921" (Master's thesis, New Mexico State University, 1959), 118.

25. Morley to Martin, n.d., NWP Papers, LC.

26. Morley to Martin, 2 March 1916, Lindsey to Morley, 16 February 1916, NWP Papers, LC. A search of Catron's papers reveals little correspondence from suffragists, but his files for 1915 are obviously incomplete, and no correspondence for 1916 is in the collection, Thomas Catron Papers, sect. 501, box 2, folder 25, UNM–SC.

27. U.S. Congress, *Congressional Record,* 64th Cong., 2nd sess., 1917, 54, pt. 4:3579.

28. For information on Hernandez see Morley to Martin, n.d., NWP Papers, LC, and Donald R. Moorman, "A Political Biography of Holm O. Bursum, 1899–1924" (Ph.D. diss., UNM, 1962), 172.

29. Westphall, *Thomas Benton Catron,* 380–83.

30. Russell correspondence is in Republican Central Committee, Catron Papers, sect. 408, box 1, folder 19, UNM–SC.

31. Russell correspondence, Republican Central Committee, Catron Papers, UNM–SC. See especially Russell to Mrs. A. B. Stroup, 21 October 1916, and Russell to Mrs. George Frenger, 9 October 1916.

32. Willard H. Rollings, "The Congressional Career of Andrieus Aristiens Jones, 1917–1927" (Master's thesis, New Mexico State University, 1975), p. 36. Doris Stevens, *Jailed for Freedom* (New York: Boni and Liveright, 1920), and Inez Haynes Irwin, *The Story of the Woman's Party* (1921; reprint ed., New York: Kraus Reprint, 1971) discuss the work of Jones on the amendment. Strong egalitarian statements by Jones are in U.S. Congress, *Congressional Record,* 65th Cong., 2nd sess., 1918, 56, pt. 7: 6306 pt. 11:10921.

33. Martin to Otero-Warren, 21, 29 December 1917; Lillian Kerr to Paul, 15 February 1920; Paul to Kerr, 15 February 1920; and Hernandez to R. L. Baca, 16 February 1920, NWP Papers, LC. Hernandez was reelected in 1918 and helped in the final state push for ratification.

34. Cora A. Kellman to Paul, 31 January, 18 March 1919, NWP Papers, LC.

35. Carrie Chapman Catt to Aloysius Larch-Miller, 22 October 1919, and "Reporter's Transcript of Jubilee Convention of NAWSA," St. Louis, 24–29 March 1919, NAWSA Papers, LC. Catt to Rosika Schwimmer,

22 October 1921, Catt Papers, container 8, LC. Early NAWSA-CU friction is discussed in Otero-Warren to Martin, 4 December 1917, Jane Pincus to Martin, 20 November 1917, and Stevens to Paul, 28 February 1916, NWP Papers, LC.

36. Catt to Grace Raymond Hebard, 30 December 1918, NAWSA papers, container 84, LC. Harper, *History of Woman Suffrage*, 6:437, for Larrazolo; Vernon to Otero-Warren, 21 January 1920, NWP, LC.

37. Otero-Warren to Paul, 21 January 1920, NWP Papers, LC.

38. Paul to Otero-Warren, 14 February 1920, Paul to Kerr, 14 February 1920, Paul to Clara S. Waller, 15 February 1920, Otero-Warren to Paul, 24 February 1920, NWP, LC. Republicans denied the plot and said the Democrats wanted to divide the Republicans.

39. Otero-Warren to Paul, 17 February 1920, NWP Papers, LC. Albuquerque *Morning Journal*, 18, 19 February 1920. Senate Republicans opposing were Roman Gallegos, Mirabel, M. Lucero, Salazar, and Sanchez. Catt to Mary Gray Peck, 15 August 1920, Catt Papers, box 8, LC.

40. New Mexico State Central Democratic Committee, box 3, UNM–SC. Republican records for 1920 have not yet been deposited in the archives. Women's offices are listed in the *New Mexico Blue Book, 1920–21*.

41. The bilingual appeal is in Miscellaneous Records, Political Issues, SRCA. Three of seven women signing had Hispanic surnames.

42. I have used the listing of Hispanic and Little Texas counties from Holmes, *Politics in New Mexico*. Statistics on 1921 vote from Ernestine D. Evans, *New Mexico Election Returns, 1911–1969* (Santa Fe, 1970).

43. For the participation of women voters, see William H. Flanigan and Nancy H. Zingale, *Political Behavior of the American Electorate*, 3rd ed. (Boston: Allyn and Bacon, 1975), 10–27, and Jerrold G. Rusk, "Comment: The American Electoral Universe: Speculation and Evidence," *American Political Science Review* 68 (September 1974): 1044. For Black women, see Marjorie Lansing, "The Voting Patterns of American Black Women," in *A Portrait of Marginality: The Political Behavior of the American Woman*, eds. Marianne Githens and Jewel L. Prestage (New York: D. McKay Co., 1977), 379–94.

44. John J. Stucker, "The Impact of Woman Suffrage on Patterns of Voter Participation in the United States; Quasi-Experimental and Real-Time Analysis, 1890–1920" (Ph.D. diss., University of Michigan, 1973), and Stucker, "Women as Voters: Their Maturation as Political Persons in American Society," in *A Portrait of Marginality*, eds. Githens and Prestage, 264–83.

45. Moorman, "A Political Biography," 340–43, claims Otero-Warren's candidacy "spelled disaster" because of Hispanic opposition to women in high legislative office, but fusion between Independent Repub-

licans and Democrats, including the popular leaders Cutting and Larrazolo, was probably more important for the worst Republican defeat since
statehood. Everyone was defeated. Statistics from Evans, *New Mexico Election Returns*.

46. Post-1940 political participation remains to be studied, but a preliminary survey seems to indicate that, with the exception of Lusk's election during World War II, it was a period of retreat by women from public
life. Two of the most powerful state legislators, Senator Louise Coe and
Representative Concha Ortiz y Pino, retired from the legislature in 1941
and 1942 respectively (Furman, "Woman's Campaign," p. 370). Information on office holding is taken from *New Mexico Blue Books, 1911–1941*.
Lusk's campaign is discussed in Roger D. Hardaway, "Georgia Lusk of
New Mexico: A Political Biography" (Master's thesis, New Mexico State
University, 1979). For a recent analysis of the political progress of women
and Hispanics, see Cal Clark, Janet Clark and Jose Z. Garcia, "Policy Im-
pacts on Hispanics and Women: A State Case Study," in Marian Lief Pal-
ley and Michael B. Preston, eds., *Race, Sex, and Policy Problems* (Lexington,
Mass.: Lexington Books, 1979).

47. Holmes, *Politics in New Mexico*, 175–97; Thomas C. Donnelly,
ed., *Rocky Mountain Politics* (Albuquerque: UNM Press, 1940), 101–3,
231–32; E. B. Fincher, *Spanish-Americans as a Political Factor in New Mexico, 1912–1950* (New York: Arno Press, 1974), 108.

48. William Hickman Pickens, "The New Deal in New Mexico:
Changes in State Government and Politics, 1926–1938" (Master's thesis,
UNM, 1971), 92–143.

49. Walter Dean Burnham, "The Changing Shape of the American
Political Universe," *American Political Science Review* 59 (March 1965):7–28,
noted declining male participation before enfranchisement of women as
parties lost their hold on masses of voters. Much of the decline in the
South was due to disfranchisement of poor white and Black male voters.
In the North, progressive measures such as voter registration and civil
service reform also caused a decline. The trend bottomed out in 1924 and
peaked again in 1940. Thus women's participation was a part of this overall trend (Flanigan and Zingale, *Political Behavior*, 15).

≈12≈

The Campaign For Women's Community Property Rights in New Mexico

1940–1960

Joan M. Jensen

In 1972, the people of New Mexico voted overwhelmingly for a state Equal Rights Amendment. The state ERA went into effect the following year and under it 60 state laws were revised by the end of 1975. Among those laws was one that had prohibited a wife from disposing of her share of the community property by will. New Mexico women had battled for nearly half a century to change that law. And now it came, certainly not effortlessly but seemingly without the hard political battles that earlier women had mounted. "I was overjoyed," recalled Gina Allen who had been one of those early women, "but I could also hardly believe it."[1]

The following chapter is based primarily on the correspondence and memoirs of three women, Carmen Freudenthal, Gina Allen, and K. Rose Wood who campaigned hard to effect this change in the law. They were but three of hundreds of New Mexico women who worked for legal reforms for women over almost half a century. They worked to change two laws that affected women: the right of a woman to inherit her husband's property when he died intestate (without a will) and the right of a woman to will her property to whomever she wished. Reformers were successful in obtaining the first change in 1959; the second

333

did not come until after the state Equal Rights Amendment had been approved thirteen years later.

This campaign of New Mexico women for community property rights is significant in several respects. These political activities spanned a period of American history during which historians portray women as "politically inactive." According to most general histories of the period between 1940 and 1960 women did not see themselves as a bloc or group with separate political interests. Nor were they organized as political pressure groups to demand change in the American legal structure. Such political activity did not emerge until the 1960s as the new women's movement arose and swept through the country on the crest of feminist discontent. But here is an example of hundreds of women organizing state wide for over twenty years, during a period of supposed political quiescence. That they were not successful in gaining all they wanted is testament to the intrasigence of the male legislators and the inability of women to make the political system responsive to their legal needs. Their story also tells us much about the difficulty women had at the state level in securing reform in the absence of a national movement for women's rights. Moreover, it provides an excellent case study to examine the tactics and strategy of a state women's rights movement that eventually merged with the broader reform of the 1960s.

Community property reform is an important part of the history of family law. New Mexico was one of the few states which had community property laws during the nineteenth and early twentieth centuries, laws which are now becoming the dominant form of family and property law in the United States, and which generally expand the rights of women. Women in New Mexico did not, however, have greater rights under community property until the state ERA was passed in the 1970s. This chapter points up the constraints that could exist even under a community property law.

As pointed out in a previous chapter, laws regulating family relations had changed under a century of American jurisprudence. Although Americans adopted community property laws in the 1840s, American judges trained in United States common law applied common law procedures to New Mexico laws. These procedures expanded some of the rights of women and restricted others. In 1906, however, the legislature adopted a new and vastly more restrictive family law based on a California model. Among the most important rights denied to a woman under the new law was the right to inherit her husband's property when he died intestate and to will her community property to whomever she wished.

On the death of the wife, the husband automatically inherited her estate. He paid no tax and had no probate fees. The husband, on the other hand, could will his estate to whomever he wished. When a husband died intestate, the woman had to have the estate probated, to pay an estate tax, and frequently had to go to court to be appointed guardian for her own underage children. Those children over legal age had an immediate right to their portion of the estate even though that might mean the widow had to sell her home or the family business. Women also had special legislation that gave them certain advantages over men in a few cases. Most commonly, however, women had the greater disadvantage. They had some control over their own privately owned and personal property but none over joint or community property obtained in marriage. They had no control over their community property during their lives and no control over its dispersal at their death. In 1940, only women in Nevada and New Mexico had no testamentary rights. Nevada women obtained these rights in 1959. In 1972, of the eight community property states, only New Mexico still denied women these rights.[2] New Mexico women saw these conditions as unjust, and that belief led them to organize in an attempt to obtain these two essential rights.

Some club women had tried to change the laws in the 1930s but the real battle began in 1944 before World War II had ended. The war had given women new political leverage in New Mexico. This occurred in both the private and public spheres. Privately, thousands of wives received part of their overseas husbands' military salary directly thus giving them for the first time *de facto* management and control over part of the community property. Publicly, women increased their hold on important state offices in New Mexico, especially as Secretary of State and State Superindendent of Public Education. By 1944, two women from southern New Mexico, Cecilia Tafoya Cleveland of Hot Springs (later renamed Truth or Consequences) and Georgia Lusk of Carlsbad, held these high elected offices. Women had also mobilized on the homefront during the war. By the end of the war, there seemed to be a growing consciousness of the unfinished business of legal rights for women in New Mexico. Newspapers were discussing the fact that women still had no jury rights and that there were serious inequalities in community property laws.[3]

The campaign for revision of these laws resurfaced in southern New Mexico. There women's clubs taxed members twenty-five cents each to finance the campaign and pressured politicians to support legislative change. The largest women's clubs in the state sponsored changes in the community property laws: the New Mexico Federation of Women's Clubs (NMFWC), the New Mexico Federation of Business and Professional Women, the Associated Women of the State Farm Bureau, and the American Association of University Women (AAUW). A women's club based at the New Mexico College of Agriculture and Mechanic Arts (later New Mexico State University) in Las Cruces sent summaries of the laws to every club woman in the state and every women's club in Las Cruces had a special program to discuss the proposed legislation. Clubs contributed over $200 to help finance lobbying efforts. Democratic governor John Dempsey pledged his support and Democratic delegates in Congress agreed to help. The Republican Party even carried a plank in its platform supporting the revisions. The Republican Women's Club was active in this campaign as well as non-partisan women's clubs. The Republican women of Doña Ana County made a contribution and worked hard to collect additional funds.[4]

As the bill made its way through the legislature in Santa Fe in early 1945, however, it became clear that the men would again kill the bill as they had in the past. Governor Dempsey gave the women no assistance. The Democratic floor leader fought the bill. The Democratic Senator who introduced the bill did not work for it. The Republicans opposed efforts to record votes on the bill. Only one senator from Silver City carried through for the women. Nor could the southern women hold the northern women to the cause. The Santa Fe Women's Club withdrew its support because it did not like the final provisions of the bill. Other northern clubs did not send women to Santa Fe to work for passage. In addition, even the money collected was not spent effectively by southern women to get important attorneys to Santa Fe to testify in their behalf. This was the analysis of their inadequate strategy by Carmen Freudenthal, the woman who organized the southern campaign. Ten years later Freudenthal would also spark the second campaign for legal rights.[5]

Carmen Freudenthal was a woman already skilled in community affairs when she turned her attention to community property reform in 1944. She was born Carmen Kahn in the small northern town of Sedalia, Missouri into a comfortable Jewish family. Her parents were able to send her to a preparatory school in St. Louis after she attended public schools in Sedalia. From there she went on to Washington University and to Smith College in Massachusetts where she graduated *cum laude* in Sociology and Economics. Following graduation in 1920 Carmen worked in a settlement house in Chicago but welfare work in those days seemed to her to involve separating families so she returned to St. Louis. There she worked in sales, then moved to San Francisco, and then to New York City in the early 1930s. At a time when men were selling apples on street corners, she was able to make an excellent income selling encyclopedias in the Bronx. The families of her assigned area, mostly lower middle-class Eastern Jews, were concerned about their children's future and would make any sacrifice in those Depression days to increase their chances of success in school. Encyclopedia sales were so good that Carmen was living on Park Avenue when she met Louis Freudenthal. He had gone East from Las Cruces to discuss the needs of Mesilla Valley farmers with the Secretary of the Interior and then traveled on to New York to visit his mother who was living with her family there. Carmen and Louis met on New Year's Day and, and after a short courtship by mail, married in March, 1934. They returned to Las Cruces where she began her New Mexico career.[6]

Carmen Kahn Freudenthal joined a family well known and well established in the community. Louis was a native of the Mesilla Valley and from an old New Mexico family. He had gone to an eastern preparatory school and studied agriculture at Cornell University, but he planned to return to New Mexico to help run the family farms, to engage in business, and to continue his community work in groups like the Farm Bureau and the State Historical Society. Although Carmen made the local newspaper once for wearing white satin pajamas at a party, she fit easily into the small southwestern community. During her first decade in Las Cruces she was busy helping to design a new home, giving birth to and raising a son and a daughter, and managing the household of a husband who successfully combined business with an active community life. Louis was Board Director of the American Farm Bureau and Carmen soon became interested in agricultural problems and in her own project to have the Farm Bureau support a federal child labor amendment that would outlaw child labor in agriculture. The Farm Bureau never yielded to her efforts but years after she still remembered the ugly sores that she had seen between the fingers of children who had worked in the Mesilla Valley cotton fields.

Carmen's mother-in-law, Amalia Freudenthal, had already established a tradition of community services for the women of the family as well. Mrs. Phoebus Freudenthal had been well known among the club women of Las Cruces, mostly married middle-class women, who had organized formally and publicly as the Women's Improvement Association (WIA) in 1894. Members of WIA had launched important municipal projects—providing a hearse to replace the ice wagon used for funerals in the city, getting drinking fountains, having the dusty streets watered in summer so that women had less work with the clouds of dust that regularly filtered into their homes, establishing a park, starting a library. Amalia Freudenthal held the presidency of the WIA in 1896 and 1903. By 1940, Carmen held that position. From the presidency, she moved to the chairmanship of the WIA legislative committee. From there she organized her first attack on the community property laws.[7]

After that brief and disheartening first campaign Freudenthal busied herself with other community affairs. In the early 1930s, she joined the Las Cruces branch of the AAUW. One of the primary concerns of this women's group, new at the time, was that graduates of the Las Cruces based land-grant college could not join the new group because the college was not recognized by the Association. To be recognized, the college had to be certified as having equal conditions for women faculty and students. Among the inequities was the lack of a women's gymnasium. Carmen and other AAUW women went to college officials to insist they build equal facilities. By 1954 the gymnasium was built and the Association recognized the college.[8]

Meanwihile, as the AAUW worked to improve conditions on the campus, it also began to organize in the community. Members of AAUW focused on low income families, set up a hot lunch program at the segregated black school, studied the needs of low income families, and after Carmen became president in 1947, worked to end racial discrimination in Las Cruces schools and restaurants. In 1949, at the end of her presidency, she formulated a statewide survey on the health and safety of school pupils that called the attention of public officials to the inadequate facilities for most rural students in New Mexico. By 1956, then, Freudenthal had over two decades of experience in public service as a community organizer and developer. That year she became legislative chairman of the WIA again, an office she held for the next five years, until 1961. From that strategic position she launched her second battle for women's equal rights.[9]

By 1956, however, some things had changed in Doña Ana County. One of the most important changes was the beginning of the Democratic Women's Club. In 1950 a dramatic event occurred in state politics: the Democrats, safely in control of the governor's mansion since the days of the New Deal, lost the gubernatorial election to Las Cruces Republican Edwin L. Mechem. As Gina Allen later wrote: "In our traditionally one-party state, this was a major upset. It was the women, commentators said, who had elected our Republican governor." The Democrats began a search for a county chairwoman—in those days the County Chairman was always a man, the County Vice Chairman a woman—who could organize a Democratic Women's Club. The woman they found was Gina Allen.[10]

Allen, like Freudenthal, was a dedicated and confirmed community worker. Raised in the Black Hills of South Dakota, Allen had married before her graduation with a Bachelor's degree in journalism from Northwestern University in 1940. She and her husband Ted moved to New York, then to Oklahoma in 1943 where Ted was to teach chemistry to new Army recruits. When they could not find a place to live in the crowded university town of Stillwater, they rented a farm. While her husband taught and learned farming, Gina stayed on the farm and learned farming too. That experience, she later described in a warm and humorous account called *Rustics for Keeps*, a book published after the family moved to Las Cruces in 1945 with a new baby daughter, Ginita. In Las Cruces, the Allens established the Allen Acres Dairy Farm, and settled comfortably into community life. In addition to driving a tractor, milking cows, and delivering milk, Gina cared for animals, raised a garden, and canned fruits and vegetables. She did work then considered by some rural women to be "men's work." At Allen Acres, Gina explained later, "the idea was that anybody should be able to take over wherever needed." Her husband Ted was active in the Farm Bureau, she recalled, but she could not be because "they were

very much into sex roles and woman's place was in the kitchen."
But both Ted and Gina were active in the Guernsey Cattle Breeders Association and other dairy and cattle organizations. For some years, Gina wrote a column called "The Dairyman's Wife" for *The Western Dairy Journal*.

The young couple plunged into other community work. Ted became involved in community theatre. He organized the "Cinema Club" to show foreign films for newcomers working at the expanding White Sands Missile Range but living in Las Cruces and hungry for films other than westerns—the typical fare of the time. Both helped found the first Unitarian Fellowship. Gina joined the university women's club, the AAUW, the League of Women Voters, the PTA. Her energy seemed inexhaustible.

Soon after coming to Las Cruces, Gina met Carmen. "Of course," wrote Gina later, "Carmen couldn't keep quiet about her community activities and these interested me tremendously—particularly testamentary rights. The result was that Carmen took me to the women's club working on testamentary rights and I began working too. I got into politics because I felt an active participation in this area might help pass our testamentary rights bill and also improve our school system. Both concerned me. But lack of testamentary rights infuriated me." Allen had taken little interest in partisan politics previously. When the Democratic county politicians announced to her that they wanted her to be Doña Ana county chairwoman, it seemed like politics might open up new possibilities for the stalled community rights campaign. "They told me I had been chosen. I was honored, and at the same time frightened," she wrote. The county machine pushed her nomination through at the county convention and she began her new political career.[11]

Immediately after the convention Allen organized a Democratic Women's Club to rival the Republican Women's Club. These clubs were outside the regular party structure and gave women no voice in party affairs. What they did do, as Allen recalled, "was get women working in politics so that they learned about the party, attended conventions, and sometimes took over precincts so that they would have a voice in the party and how it was run. Prior to the Democratic Women's Clubs the Party looked like (and often behaved like) an all male stag party."

As another early organizer of the Doña Ana County Democratic Women's Club, Mary Ellen Triviz, recalled, one of the women's first jobs was to feed poll workers, something very traditional for women. Before long, however, the women were figuring out ways to make the Democrats more effective in the 1954 campaign. The men seemed stumped on how to beat the incumbent Governor Edwin L Mechem, the popular Las Cruces attorney who was then challenging Clinton P. Anderson for his seat in the United States Senate. Las Cruces had undergone a building boom in the early 1950s as White Sand Missile Range employees and their families settled in town. Part of the strategy suggested by the women was to concentrate on the new housing tracts—to register the new-comers and ignore the oldtimers who knew Mechem. Painstakingly, they worked in teams of three, knocking at each door to register the new families. They had already determined that most of these families would register as Democrats. Then the women went on to organize "Meet the Candidate" programs at the county courthouse. They arranged to bring Lyndon B. Johnson, then Senate floor leader, to Las Cruces to campaign for Anderson. They filled the courthouse to overflowing. While the Democratic men had said there was no hope, the women managed a winning campaign. Not only did they get voters to give Anderson a whopping majority in Mechem's home territory, they also helped elect a young Democrat and former speaker of the House, John F. Simms, Jr. as governor.[12]

While the Doña Ana Democratic Women's Club did not claim all the credit for electing the two Democrats, its winning strategy got Allen the position of Chairwoman of the New Mexico Democratic Central Committee in 1956, a position she held for three years, through hard-fought presidential and senatorial campaigns. Then she turned her attention to the community property campaign, intending to collect some political debts that Democratic politicians owed her.

When members of the New Mexico Federation of Women's Clubs again passed resolutions at their annual meeting of 1958 to get the property laws passed, Freudenthal and Allen took the project seriously. The two southern women linked up with a Santa Fe club woman, K. Rose Wood, who was the Public Affairs Chairman for the NMFWC and Legislative Program Chairman for the New Mexico Division of the AAUW. Wood shared the other two women's love of the political process and willingness to take on the male politicians. She headed a Santa Fe command center, writing almost daily to Freudenthal in the heat of the campaign during the early months of 1958, and swinging into the political battle with great enthusiasm.[13].

Carmen Freudenthal and K. Rose Wood were already old friends. As K. Collet-Peterson, she had come to Las Cruces in 1935 as a state field representative for the New Mexico Department of Welfare. Between 1936 and 1941 she helped organize nineteen of thirty-two welfare offices. Born in Chicago, a graduate in education and a certified social worker from the University of Minnesota, K. Peterson first met Louis Freudenthal and his family through a mutual friend in public welfare, and through Louis she met Carmen. They can no longer remember exactly when or where they met, only that they instantly became friends. They respected each other for their intelligence, wit, and competence. In 1941, K. married E. A. Rose, an engineer in the Works Progress Administration and was out of the state during the 1945 property rights campaign.

When the Roses returned to New Mexico in 1946, it was to Santa Fe. There K. Rose began to work for the legislative programs of the AAUW and a joint state committee of women's clubs. When her husband died intestate in 1948, K. Rose had to spend a year and a half in probate court settling the affairs of their modest community property estate. In 1949, she went to work for the Department of Public Health but she remarried again in 1953, to Charles Wood, a school superintendent and then a field representative for the New Mexico Education Association (NEA). Between 1953 and 1959 she was free to devote most of her time and attention to lobbying for women's issues. High on her list of priorities was a change in the community property laws. By 1959, K. had made valuable friends in the legislature, knew the political "ropes," and was ready for an all out campaign as a registered lobbyist for legislation of benefit to women.

The strategy of the 1959 community property campaign was not new. Women had been lobbying for their legal rights for over a century. During the campaign for suffrage, New Mexico women had organized through clubs to bring political pressure on male legislators to vote for bills that would expand the political rights of women. In this sense, the women of New Mexico were continuing an old lobbying tradition. The political and organizational experience that the women brought to their task and their realization of just how hard it would be to expand the legal rights of women was new, however. Particularly Gina Allen, after her experience of campaigning throughout the state, had little illusion about the disabilities of their own political allies and the potency of the tactics that would be used against them.[14]

The women felt that the politicians had easily outmaneuvered the reformers in their previous campaigns. Particularly galling was their experience with the Twenty-First Legislature in 1953. The Senate had established an Interim Committee on Community Property, ordered a study, and then let the matter rest. The committee's report, *The Community Property Law of New Mexico*, written by Joe Wood in 1954 while he was an attorney for the Legislative Council Service (a state research agency), clearly set forth the inequities of the law and discussed solutions. But women called the action of the Committee "whitewash" because that seemed to be all they intended to do about the matter—issue a report. The senators soon let it be known that women should stay out of the matter, that they wanted, as the women said, "no swish of feminine skirts."[15]

During previous campaigns, from the late 1930s to 1955, bills always failed in the Senate. The House had always seemed more supportive of women's reform bills. Therefore, the women decided to concentrate on the Senate—to get a senator to introduce the bill and work for its passage, to get it reported out of the Senate Judiciary Committee favorably, then to get it on to the floor of the Senate, and line up support. They planned to organize club women in each district to write and call on their senators urging passage. Once the Senate had passed the bill, the women expected little trouble in the House. They also expected no difficulty in getting the Democratic governor, John Burroughs, to sign the bill.[16]

What the women had to face was no ordinary political opposition; it was also well-intrenched discrimination. It was not that men were unwilling to recognize the political abilities of women who knew how to play the game like men. Indeed, Ernestine Duran Griegos, Cala Wolf, and Concha Ortiz y Pino had all held important political places in the state legislature during the 1930s and 1940s. Georgia Lusk had been the first woman elected to the United States Congress in 1946 on the basis of her superb ability to use traditional male political networks. But these women had not used their political offices to work for women's issues. Women were mistrusted if they used female rather than male networks, worked for reforms in the structure of politics, or worked for women's interests. As Gina Allen described it a few years later in an article for the *Ladies Home Journal*, party politicians had already developed ways to deal with women political activists. They attacked their morals—being active in politics was good evidence of loose morals according to male politicos. They ridiculed women. And they loudly protested that "real" women did not want change.[17]

Allen recalled one example of ridicule. She wrote a puppet show for club women to present before the Senate Judiciary Committee. Women came from all over the state for the hearings. Allen wrote:

> After we had presented the puppet show—a heart rendering dramatization of women's plight in New Mexico, we thought—I was walking back to my seat in the auditorium when one of the members of the committee said, "What do these women want anyway? They already have the right to fall off of bar stools."[18]

Such comments by legislators were not at all uncommon, whether in hearings or on the floor of the Legislature. K. Wood, keeping her legislative vigil in Santa Fe, reported to Freudenthal in February, 1959 that Senator William Osborn of Roswell, who opposed the bill in the Senate, said that, "Only business women and those in professions are urging that women *be made equal* with men in the eyes of the law. Majority of feminine women are housewives and they are not for this as they lose protections now granted." At this wrote Wood, "the Balcony booed and groaned!"[19]

Of course, the balcony was full of women who were housewives. Like the women who led the campaign, these women did not consider themselves radical but concerned citizens fighting for necessary reforms for women. Freudenthal, Allen, and Wood were all successful housewives, happy with their married state, and attentive to the needs of their families. Although it was true, as one daughter remembered later, their children did not see much of their mothers during the campaign, the women certainly saw the campaign as absolutely consistent with their concerns as married women. There was no evident conflict with husbands; they supported the women in their political campaigns. In fact, the women used their secure places at home from which to launch their political activities. Still, it hurt when in the heat of the campaign politicians used such tactics to discredit their efforts. After listening to Osborn, Wood wrote from Santa Fe about support for the bill, "if the old girls—*especially Haus fraus* will only *come out* in *bunches next week & corner representatives* in *person* at their *seats*—it might squeeze into the Governor's hands."[20]

Although these women had comfortable secure middle-class homes, they had few independent financial resources upon which to draw. Clubs tended to turn yearly from one project to another and those interested in legislative reform had to ask the clubs for financing. During the campaign of 1945, clubs in the southern part of the state had contributed over $240 to the campaign. When Freudenthal did not use the entire amount, however, she returned over $80 to the clubs instead of setting up a permanent legislative fund. Thus in 1958, the women once again had to go begging. The WIA donated $100 to the campaign and the AAUW spent about $75; other clubs were less supportive. Freudenthal collected only $245 from the clubs but spent over $400 on trips to Santa Fe, telegrams, phone calls, and supplies. Wood estimated that she had come out only $1.94 in the red. "What the hell, what other group tries to do a serious job on that kind of peanuts," she wrote to Freudenthal at the end of the campaign. However, the Freudenthals were out several hundred dollars, a sizeable sum even in the 1950s.[21]

Financing was only one of the problems that the political activists encountered. The difficulties in financing reflected a more serious problem with political strategy, as Allen later pointed out. Most women's organizations refused to be involved in partisan politics even though their causes called for action. The women's organizations also did not support women candidates because they believed that "nice women" would not be able to do as well as men. "That the men are committed to do the work of the groups that put them in office doesn't occur to the nonpolitical women," wrote Allen. "When the election is over they take their proposals to the men who can make deals in the smoke-filled rooms. Naively, they announce that they represent 4000 (or 40,000) women voters who are members of the organization. The men are courteous. They introduce the women to their colleges. But they don't take their proposals into the smoke-filled rooms. They have more important things on their minds—namely, re-election."[22]

Beyond strategy was the issue of the nonpolitical attitudes of women. Women's advocates like Allen, Freudenthal, and Wood knew the political disabilities that women faced in organizing themselves. It was true that the networks club women had created throughout the state were stronger than ever. The NMFWC claimed 5,000 members. The Business and Professional Women's Club (BPW) and the AAUW claimed hundreds more. The BPW would have seemed to be one place from which to draw political expertise. However, many of these women were so busy with their careers that they had little time left for politics.

The clubs also did not reach deeply into the Hispanic communities, into most rural parts of the state, or into the poorer Anglo female population. In addition, there was a strong interest within the women's clubs in social rather than political activities. Many women were concerned more with developing social contacts and creating activities than with using their organizations to lobby for changes that could benefit the women and children of New Mexico. This lack of support for political activities could cause deep fissures within the clubs, seriously weakening any political activity mounted by the more political women. The internal weaknesses combined with external opposition made campaigns such as that for community property rights difficult to organize successfully.

Lack of political leadership within the clubs plagued the campaign from the start. In November 1958, as the three key women began to formulate their strategy, Wood wrote to Freudenthal about Pearl Crossett, head of the NMFWC, "Pearl doesn't seem able to spell out essentials and get consensus & she's left me to lug a great big amorphous ball and bounce it to suit myself." When Crossett arrived in Santa Fe in early 1959, Wood fairly groaned to Freudenthal about "a lot of swishing around in silks and satins at the Santa Fe Women's Club annual tea at which distaff members of the Legislature are special guests." She went on: "I don't give a damn about getting the federation program, because I don't feel there is one . . . it seems to me that unless the females of Doña Ana and Otero Counties where the experts and leaders are can get together and stay together, everything is doomed this Session." Then she added thoughtfully, "I think the men love to see women fighting among ourselves and not agreeing."[23]

The women kept the quarrels to themselves but support did not increase during the struggle in the Legislature. The state federation had passed the resolution supporting the legislation, had not criticized the activities of the women who organized the campaign, and had the precedent of collecting funds in 1944. Still when Freudenthal tried to solicit financial support, Crossett told district clubs that it was contrary to the constitution to collect funds for "political purposes." Freudenthal wrote indignantly to several women's clubs after the campaign about this lack of support. Crossett, said Freudenthal, "knew perfectly well that we were promoting legislation for the good of the women and children of New Mexico and that such work is far from being 'political activity.' " The Legislative Committee, said Freudenthal, once geared for "aggressive, energetic action," had become merely a "research" committee.[24]

Aside from this one impatient letter, Freudenthal dropped the issue rather than increase dissension among the women. "I wanted to write a scorching attack on Crossett's do-nothing attitude and her complete failure to implement the Convention Resolutions," she wrote to Wood, "but I'm not sure how I can do this without causing even more dissension than Crossett has caused. The reason women don't get anything done is exactly because of this kind of jealously bickering . . . . I want to make just exactly that point of the importance of women pulling together. Otherwise all the impetus of this year's work will be lost and we'll have to start with another Club generation entirely."[25]

Meanwhile, the men seemed to be working together smoothly to defeat the women's bill. Although the women had extracted a promise from Senator Earl Hartley of Clovis to introduce the bill and support it, when the time came, he introduced the bill "by request." It was, wrote Freudenthal, "the kiss of death." What happened? Freudenthal, on a trip to Santa Fe, spent an hour talking with Senator Hartley at La Fonda, the hotel usually used for political lobbying. He had said how pleased he was to introduce the bill, that several senators had asked to co-sign it. That was on Thursday. After the weekend, however, when the Legislature reconvened, Senator Hartley backed off. Hartley later claimed the lawyers in the state legislature opposed the bill. The word had gone out to the political leaders and then to Senator Hartley that he was not to support the bill.[26]

The women refer frequently in their correspondence to the "lawyers," meaning the legislature. The "lawyers," for example, were responsible for their not having one of the women representatives introduce the legislation in the House. Freudenthal wrote to Wood in January, "you know that your work must be with the lawyers in the Senate. Get past them and we are all set." In early February, when Freudenthal realized that the "lawyers" were against the bill, her confusion was genuine, for she did not know why they opposed the bill and the lawyers would not say. She suspected some had personal reasons but not one ever gave her a reason. Were they reacting as men who would lose control of their wives' property? Did they fear women would attack the "management and control" of community property next? Or was it simply fear of their male constituents? Freudenthal wrote to the acting dean of the University of New Mexico Law School, Robert Clark, "Why are the lawyers so afraid we'll upset the Community Property applecart?"[27]

Wood later explained the opposition this way. "Male politicians, as I remember were husbands and fathers. They *PROTEC-TED wimmin* and were frustrated over all the 'furor' women were causing 'busy legislators' with more important *issues* on their minds, like oil and gas and cattle—& money—deals." For most, she concluded, their opposition had no legal basis but was "personal, familial, and sexual."

Certainly the reason for the opposition was not because legal experts opposed it. Dean Clark's 1956 study, *Community Property and the Family in New Mexico*, pointed out how American common status concepts had deprived women of testamentary rights held under Spanish law and why change in the intestate law was necessary. When Freudenthal first wrote to Clark in 1955 to ask him about his writings in community property law, he had replied cordially. Later, she invited him to be her guest while he was at a state bar convention held in Las Cruces. After Freudenthal had the community property bill drafted and introduced, Dean Clark wrote a long supporting letter to Senator Hartley who was chairman of the Judiciary Committee. Clark testified before the Judiciary Committee in support of its passage and urged former students, now practicing legislators, to support it. He did not appear on the Senate floor to help answer technical questions from the lawyers, however, something that the women thought may have weakened their position. Probably, however, Clark did everything that could have been done at the time. The law school, still relatively new in the state with few graduates, was simply not influential enough. In 1972, another expert on the law, Professor Leo Kanowitz, who supported passage of the state ERA, had a much larger group of students in the law school, as well as University of New Mexico Law School graduates in the legislature and in communities across the state.[28]

In the absence of a strong law school influence, the women had to depend upon their own understanding of the law and their political expertise to convince the lawyers in the Legislature to change the law. And they had to depend upon the lawyers themselves. The women took the advice of these lawyers only to find that advice being undercut by their subsequent actions. After the "lawyers" had advised them to avoid the women representatives in the House and instead have a male lawyer introduce their bill in the Senate, another lawyer in the House immediately went to representatives Helen Wells and Jane Cosper to co-sign a bill that cut out the testamentary rights provision and provided only for intestate succession. This maneuver, calculated to kill the bill, confused other club women and caused a great deal of trouble for the organizers who had to explain that their bill was the one that women's clubs had been backing for so many years. The tactics also increased tension. Two letters written by Freudenthal on February 20, as the bill was making its way through the Senate, reflected the tension. One was to an Albuquerque lawyer, a friend from Las Cruces who was supporting the bill. "We should pass the Senate to-day—but I'll confess I'm nervous and Gina is about to go crazy. Fact is we're all wound up as tight as a Spring!" At the same time, Freudenthal wrote to Wood that their concern was now shifting to the House and to Representative James Martin who had introduced the substitute bill. "And we're worried about the House, worried that Martin will give us trouble . . . . At this point we're seeing boogie men everywhere," she wrote.[29]

And well they might. During all this time Carmen and Gina talked several times a day, and into the night, about developments. Gina also called legislators in Santa Fe, and frequently drove up to see them. They treated her handsomely, she recalled, giving her seats beside them and introducing her. But when she was gone, they voted against her, or did nothing.

The hopes of the women sank as they tried to analyze what had happened. Hartley was not their enemy but he was no longer their friend, that they knew. In addition, they realized now that they did not have the support of the House. Freudenthal wrote to Allen from Santa Fe after talking with Senator Hartley, "when he got thru his weak protestations I knew our bill was doomed." One of the politicos confided to her, she wrote, that "every lawyer in the House was against our bill but that the key person was Gene Lusk—that he had given orders and he was *the boss*." A political confidant had told her, Freudenthal wrote later to Wood, "They were laying for us and intended to lick us, and that there wasn't enough pressure from back home." Ironically, Gene Lusk was the son of Georgia Lusk, first New Mexico woman representative to Congress who had later been reelected to the post of State Superintendent of Education and recently retired. Her son was now majority leader in the Senate, chief spokesman for the Democratic Party, and interested in running for Congress in the next election.[30]

Despite the retreat of the women's supporters, the battle in the Senate went on successfully. On February 16, 1959 the women spoke effectively before the Senate Judiciary Committee and created a sympathetic response with their puppet show. Mostly, as Allen recalled, "they were astonished by the hundreds of women who had come to the hearing, which had to be moved to an auditorium to accommodate them. It suddenly occurred to them that these women were concerned, could talk and influence other women, and *vote*."

The Committee voted the bill out by seven to two. The women lobbied hard and the bill passed the Senate by four votes. The women, elated, went home to celebrate. Allen explained what happened then: "We drove back to Las Cruces from Santa Fe happy as children at Christmas. I had just got into bed and was dozing off when the phone rang. It was a newspaper reporter. 'What are you going to do now?' he asked. 'Live happily ever after,' I said, 'if people will stop waking me in the middle of the night.' 'Then you don't know,' he said. 'After you left the legislators voted again. This time against.' " This was the maneuver that Freudenthal had worried might enable the bill to be killed. The Senators recalled the bill for revision and defeated it by a voice vote. "By clever maneuvering the bill was killed by just two votes," Freudenthal wrote to Lenore Snell, president of the BPW, "We were not to feel that we had been clobbered, it was all to look as if it were on the up and up."[31]

Over twenty years later, the Senators' maneuver still rankled. Why, Allen asked, "did they wait until the 'ladies,' as they called us, had gone home to do their recalling. And why did they revise it so that they could subsequently defeat it? That bill had been before them for a quarter of a century at least. They had plenty of time 'for revision' during that time."

Next morning, however, the women immediately began work to salvage the House bill that gave them half of what they wanted. They urged support of the Martin bill, introduced to kill the larger bill, but identical to their provision on intestate succession. This bill gave women control over community property of husbands who died without a will and enabled them to avoid costly taxes and estate fees. It was an important change that benefited widows, especially those with small estates. The women lobbied hard in support of this bill, and thus were able to salvage a part of their campaign. The bill passed the House unanimously and the Senate by only a few votes. Governor Burroughs signed the bill into law in March 1959.[32]

"*You* are the Heroine of this Novel," wrote Wood to Freudenthal in jubilation. Freudenthal too was elated. "I *do* think I put up a good scrap," she replied. But the ease with which the men had defeated their hard work increased the women's determination to punish politicians for their actions. "Now we must speak at the polls and will the women do that?" she asked Wood. To Lenore Snell, she wrote, "We *must* make ourselves heard even before nominations and certainly before elections if we ever expect to get our rights."[33]

But the voices of women were drowned in 1960 as Republican Edwin Mechem swept back into the governor's office. In the political volatility of state politics, the women could not mount a successful non-partisan campaign. Republican women seemed quiescent, satisfied to play a supportive role for their husbands. First Lady Dorothy Heller Mechem even made it a rule never to voice her opinions or to campaign for her husband. Democratic women engaged in more campaign activity for their husbands and other male politicians during this period. First Lady Jean Burroughs, a club woman from Portales, campaigned for her husband in the 1958 gubernatorial campaign. But Governor Burroughs offered no leadership to state women who wanted changes in the law. Why did women not run for office themselves? Allen asked herself that later and answered: "I am amazed that it never occurred to me to run for County Chairman and and run the party. I just worked for a chairman whom I hoped would let the women do their thing. Women's consciousness had not been raised very high then."[34]

In the years that followed the community property rights campaign, the three women who had led the campaign turned to other activities. Allen finished a fictionalized account of racial integration in the schools, *The Forbidden Man*, for which she received an Anisfield-Wolf Award, presented by the *Saturday Review* in 1962. That same year she also published a fictional account of her political experiences in New Mexico politics in the *Ladies Home Journal*; her literary success led her to accept a contract to write another book. The Allens then sold their farm. Ted took a job on an agricultural project in Africa, and later accepted the presidency of an agricultural college in Iran. Gina Allen moved to California. She joined the National Organization for Women in 1968, founded the Women's Caucus of the American Humanist Association, and continued to be politically active in the new women's movement. Wood went back to work in July, 1959 in the Department of Public Welfare and organized and directed the State Program on Aging. What time she had for legislative reform was given to this growing and predominantly female group of older New Mexicans. Freudenthal also supported women's issues. She helped set up Planned Parenthood in Las Cruces, served as its president in 1962, and continued active in civil rights and civil liberties campaigns. There were always new causes for which she lobbied, organized, and lent her voice.[35]

The battle over community property rights was, it seems clear, an important example of one stage in the development of women's political perceptions. It revealed a new group of women emerging into active state politics. Those women had enough political experience and clout to launch effective battles and to get some of what they wanted. Perhaps most important, they kept alive at the state level a tradition of women working for women's rights in a period when there was little visible activity at the national level. Until the national women's groups like the AAUW and LWV supported a national ERA, there was little organized support for its passage. Like other women reformers, the New Mexico women worked on local issues that could benefit women by fostering social change. That local tradition, kept alive through the difficult times of the 1950s and early 1960s, merged with the new political wave of young women who came of age in the late 1960s. It helped make early passage of the state and the federal ERA possible in New Mexico. As such, the campaign for women's community property rights in New Mexico, and the women who led and supported that campaign, deserve a place in the history of the women's movement.

Notes

The author would like to especially thank Gina Allen, Carmen Freudenthal, and K. Rose Wood for their cooperation and support in gathering material for this article.

1. Gina Allen to the author, October 22, 1983.

2. Robert Emmet Clark, *Community of Property and the Family in New Mexico* (Albuquerque: University of New Mexico, Department of Government, 1956), 13–14; Anne K. Bingaman, "The effects of an Equal Rights Amendment on the New Mexico System of Community Property: Problems of Characterization, Management, and Control," *New Mexico Law Review*, 3(Jan. 1973): 15.

3. Roger Dale Hardaway, "Georgia Lusk of New Mexico: A Political Biography," (Unpublished master's thesis, New Mexico State University, 1979), 54, 62; Roger Hardaway, "New Mexico Elects a Congresswoman," *Red River Valley Historical Review*, 4(Fall 1979): 75–89. John J. Bodine, "A Tri-Ethnic Trap: The Spanish Americans in Taos," in June Helm, ed., *Spanish-Speaking People in the United States* (Seattle and London: University of Washington Press, 1968), 148.

4. Carmen Freudenthal to Canutillo Aladdin Woman's Club, Doña Ana County, April 1, 1959, mentions tax in southern New Mexico, the 4th District of the New Mexico State Federation of Women's Clubs. See also Carmen Freudenthal to Mrs. Scofield, May 4, 1945; Freudenthal form letter, Dec. 15, 1944; and Financial Report, 1944-1945. Freudenthal Papers, Rio Grande Historical Collection. Hereafter cited as RGHC. As the papers relating to the community property campaign are not processed, no box numbers and record groups can be assigned.

5. Updated mimeographed sheet by Carmen Freudenthal, "Final Appraisal of Legislative Campaign," Freudenthal Papers, RGHC.

6. Information on Carmen Kahn Freudenthal is in Box 30, Folder 14, Freudenthal Papers, RGHC, and Doña Ana County Historical Society, *Sixteenth Annual Banquet Program, May 20, 1982*, 8–9 or drawn from an interview with her by the author, November 14, 1983.

7. Mrs. Pheobus Freudenthal, *Las Cruces Sun-News*, June 11, 1961, clipping, Box 30, Folder 15, Freudenthal Papers, and Woman's Improvement Association Collection, RGHC.

8. Nehema G. Maynard, "A History of the Las Cruces Branch, AAUW, 1923–1978," typescript, RG81-27, Freudenthal Papers, RGHC.

9. *Ibid.* and various reports in RG81-27, Freudenthal Papers, RGHC.

10. Gina Allen, "Party Girl," *Ladies Home Journal*, 79(Nov. 1962): 68.

11. *Ibid.* and Gina Allen, *Rustics for Keeps* (New York: Odyssey, 1948). Other biographical information and comments by Gina Allen are in two letters to the author, Oct. 22, 1983 and Dec. 4, 1983.

12. Interview with Mary Ellen Triviz, Dec. 1, 1983.

13. Correspondence from K. Rose Wood is in the Freudenthal Papers, RGHC. Additional biographical information and recollections are from a phone call on Dec. 2, 1983 and letters to the author, Dec. 6 and 16, 1983.

14. See chapter " 'Disfranchisement is a Disgrace:' Women and Politics in New Mexico, 1900–1940."

15. Joe W. Wood, *The Community Property Law of New Mexico: A Report to the Senate Interim Committee on Community Property Pursuant to Senate Resolution No. 3* (Twenty-First Legislature, State of New Mexico, Legislative Council Service, 1954), 137–151 contains a resume of inequalities.

16. Strategy discussed in various letters. See especially Carmen Freudenthal to Robert Clark, January 5, 1959, Introduction to puppet show, Freudenthal Papers, RGHC.

17. Allen, "Party Girl," 129.

18. Gina Allen to the author, Oct. 22, 1983.

19. K. Wood to Carmen Freudenthal, Feb. 20, 1959.

20. *Ibid.*

21. Carmen Freudenthal to Canutillo Aladdin Woman's Club, April 1, 1959, K. Wood to Carmen Freudenthal, March 9, 1959, Financial Report, 1944–1945, List of 1959 Contributions, Freudenthal Papers, RGHC.

22. Allen, "Party Girl," 138.

23. K. Wood to Carmen Freudenthal, Nov. 3, 1958, Jan. 29, 1919, Freudenthal Papers, RGHC.

24. Carmen Freudenthal to Canutillo Aladdin Woman's Club, April 1, 1959, Freudenthal Papers, RGHC.

25. Carmen Freudenthal to K. Wood, March 14, 1959, Freudenthal Papers, RGHC.

26. Carmen Freudenthal to K. Wood, Feb. 6, 1959, Freudenthal Papers, RGHC.

27. Carmen Freudenthal to Bob Clark, Feb. 4, 1959, Freudenthal Papers, RGHC.

28. Robert Emmet Clark to Senator Earl Hartley, Jan. 15, 1959, Carmen Freudenthal telegram to Emmet Clark, Feb. 29, 1959, Freudenthal Papers, RGHC. Leo Kanowitz, "The New Mexico Equal Rights Amendment: Introduction and Overview," *New Mexico Law Review*, 3(Jan. 1973): 1–10.

29. Carmen Freudenthal to K. Wood, Jan 13, 1959, Carmen Freudenthal to Bob Clark, Feb. 4, 1919, Carmen Freudenthal to Fran Levin, Feb. 1, 1959, Freudenthal Papers, RGHC.

30. Carmen Freudenthal to Peter Gallagher, Feb. 20, 1959, Carmen Freudenthal to K. Wood, Feb. 20, 1959, and Mrs. Robert Lytle & Carmen Freudenthal to Mrs. A.K. Jayroe, President, Mountainair Woman's Club, Feb. 20, 1959, explaining their bill as one they had worked so long for and asking her to write to women legislators urging passage of their bill. Numerous other letters of February 18–20 to other club women do similar explaining. See also Freudenthal to Zoe, Feb. 19, 1959, re Martin bill, Freudenthal Papers, RGHC.

31. Freudenthal to Wood, Feb. 6, 1959, Freudenthal to Lenore Snell, March 4, 1959, Freudenthal to Gina Allen, undated letter for the record, Freudenthal to Wood, March 14, 1958, Freudenthal Papers, RGHC. Hardaway, "Georgia Lusk of New Mexico," 144. Gene Lusk later committed suicide.

32. Freudenthal to Lenore Snell, March 4, 1959, Freudenthal Papers, RGHC.

33. K. Wood to Freudenthal, Mar. 18, 1959, Freudenthal Papers, RGHC.

34. Freudenthal to Lenore Snell, Mar. 4, 1959, Freudenthal to K. Wood, March 14, 1959, Freudenthal Papers, RGHC.

35. Eunice Kalloch and Ruth K. Hall, *The First Ladies of New Mexico* (Santa Fe, New Mexico: The Lightening Tree Press, 1982), 114; Gina Allen to the author, Oct. 22, 1983.

36. Gina Allen, *The Forbidden Man* (Philadelphia: Chilton, 1961).

37. See various correspondence in Freudenthal Papers, RG82-80, RGHC.

⇜13⇝

"Thank You for My Bones"

Connections Between Contemporary Women Artists and the Traditional Arts of Their Foremothers*

Vera L. Norwood

From Sappho onward, the evaluation of women's achievement in the arts has been problematic and subject to intense debate. For some, women's art is important only to the extent that it fits Anglo-European aesthetic standards of "high" art.[1] For others, folk and domestic art is of crucial importance to any evaluation of women's creativity.[2] This chapter is a study of the ways in which a group of contemporary women artists and writers working in the American West have incorporated the less valued forms of verbal artistry such as lullabyes and gossip, and of needlework such as embroidery and quilting, in the more traditionally valued art forms of written literature, painting, and photography.

Folk and domestic art forms are often viewed by these modern women as inheritances from the past that provide a means of connecting with their forebears. Texas poet Jan Seale provides a clear beginning point from which to study this connecting pro-

*Reprinted by permission of the regents of the University of New Mexico and the editor of the *New Mexico Historical Review*.

cess. Seale has written eloquently of her grandmother's life in "Pearl Bell Pittman: 1888–1976."[3] The poet offers a picture of a woman's life on the frontier by recounting bits of stories Pearl Pittman told her and by describing artifacts from Pittman's life:

> I want to pick through the homestead
> in the Indian territory
> for corset stays, sachet bags,
> her churn lid, next year's dehlia bulbs.

The poem is not particularly sentimental or nostalgic. Seale is very careful to point out the connections between the hard life her grandmother has lived and her death: "Now my Amazon grandmother / lies a great broken continent, / a land over-grazed."

It is important that the life presented is not romanticized, for the author is giving a credibility to that life on its own terms, and she is acknowledging her debts. The concluding stanzas to the poem express the connection the artist feels between herself and her grandmother:

> A part of me lies in her eighty-year-old
> death-ridden body.
> A part of her walks in my thirty-six-year-old
> death-ridden body.
> Goodnight, my Amazon lady.
> Thank you for my bones.

The "bones" are both literal and figurative. Not only do the poet and her relative share a genealogy; the grandmother's life has provided structure for the work of art. What her death means is a loss of "the next part / to the story she is telling." Through this poem, Jan Seale recaptures the verbal artistry of her grandmother and places it in the framework of her more educated voice.

Historians are increasingly concerned with understanding the place of such domestic and folk arts in women's lives. Several fine studies have been done on those home-based art forms that until very recently constituted the bulk of women's creative activity.[4] For a complex set of reasons, domestic arts were particularly important to women as they first crossed, then settled the western frontier. As Lillian Schlissel discovered in her study of women's overland trail diaries, women depended on female bonding to preserve the equalibrium of their former lives.[5] John Faragher and

Christine Stansell note that crucial bonding activities included song fests, gossip, sewing, and sharing favorite recipes in groups that met separately from men. That women greatly valued these creative activities is borne out by Faragher's further comment that women's loss of their "homely treasures" to the exigencies of a wagon trip over difficult terrain destroyed "a psychological lifeline to their abandoned homes and communities, as well as to elements of their identities . . . ."[6]

Women's attachment to their art forms was not due simply to a need for female connectedness, as Schlissel and Faragher realize. The extent to which a woman valued those "homely treasures" depended on her stage in life and the degree to which she had been affected by the "cult of true womanhood."[7] Many historians have documented the changed nature of women's role in the home that postindustrial society and Victorian morals wrought in America.[8] Basic to this role was life in a "woman's sphere": separate roles for men and women and a valuation of woman's place in the home based on her spiritual and cultural contributions. As Faragher points out, many women carried these roles with them to the frontier, where the restrictions such roles imposed limited women's abilities to support and participate fully in the westward movement. Julie Roy Jeffrey's study of women in the trans-Mississippi West supports Faragher in noting the divergence between popular visions of domesticity that women held and the actual life lived on the frontier:

> 'Home,' crude and impermanent though it might be, received the kind of attentions which would have pleased the proponents of domesticity. Though the cabin or sod house might not be the cozy nook pictured in stories of Western life, women hoped to make it one as they papered their walls with old newpapers or tacked up cloth to make the house snug and cheery. Old rags became rugs, old dresses curtains.[9]

In the introduction to her study, Jeffrey notes that she began her work hoping to prove that the West had freed women from suffocating roles, but discovered that this "feminist" hope was not proved by the data; she goes on, however, to explain that the resulting text documents the "strength and courage" of women surviving in difficult times. Elaine Hedges completes a study of women's quilts with a similar ambivalence:

> Our response to quilts as an art form rooted both in meaningful work
> and in cultural oppression will therefore inevitably be complex: a
> combination of admiration and awe at limitations overcome and of
> sorrow and anger at limitations imposed.[10]

As these statements indicate, scholars' grasp of how to place value
on the creative sources out of which domestic art is woven, without also seeming to value the limitations that seem to be inextrica-
bly part of the weave, has been difficult to achieve. In reading the
above descriptions, one has the feeling that domestic arts are inex-
tricably connected to a historical past that "modern" women have
left behind. No matter how carefully phrased the analysis, the creativity of these earlier women is diminished in the process.

The artists studied here offer a different method of regarding
the domestic arts of their forebears. Their work is useful to those
historians attempting to reevaluate women's traditional domestic
arts in that they find methods for giving the creative act primacy
over the attendant suffocating roles their artistic forebears suffered.
The crucial point these artists make is the absolute necessity of valuing the female creative traditions. Nationally recognized artists
such as Judy Chicago and Miriam Shapiro and writers such a Adrienne Rich have taken fairly radical steps to force their audiences to
look at the full range of women's creative contributions.[11] While
such women never deny the difficulties women have faced in achieving an artistic voice, their emphasis is on the importance of female
traditions to the making of that voice.

Two recent appraisals of women artists have made significant
contributions to new understanding of the problems women artists face and the solutions they have found. In *Silences*, Tillie Olsen
graphically portrays the "unnatural silences" that have affected
women writers; in the process she provides clues to strategies for
overcoming these blocks. Discussing the contrasts between lives
of very successful male writers and lives of women, she describes
the fragmentation and diversity in women's lives, the repetitive
processes that suffocate creativity. But, as Olsen goes on to note,
she first found artistic voice in one of the most mundane of women's activities: "It is no accident that the first work I considered
publishable began: 'I stand here ironing, and what you asked me
moves tormented back and forth with the iron.' "[12] While the life
itself blocks creativity, it is only through that life that a voice is
defined.

Eleanor Munro's *Originals: American Women Artists* begins with a vision of the "suppressed artist's cry" of several of her own female ancestors such as "my maternal grandmother, Berthe Clerc Nadler, who wrote sonnets and sewed many a fine seam as she followed her husband Westward and raised . . . three artist daughters . . . ."[13] For Munro, a crucial component in the success of women artists and an aspect that makes women's art unique is the artist's sense of connection to her past. Rather than rejecting the past, rather than following the classic modern injunction to artists—perhaps best expressed by Ezra Pound—to "Make it new," Munro sees contemporary female artists as "daughters [who] now looked on their gifted but voiceless mothers' sufferings with new understanding, pity, and a will to 'make it better' in their own time span."[14]

The artists studied in this paper have found creative sources in the domestic arts of earlier times and have made those arts "better" (in the sense of being more closely akin to traditional Anglo-European forms of "high" art) by integrating their materials into the arts of painting, photography, and literature. Each artist lived in the West in the 1970s. The West as place is important to some, particularly those with family ties to established populations (such as Native Americans Paula Gunn Allen and Leslie Marmon Silko) or to pioneer families of the nineteenth century (such as Jan Seale). For others the region is less important; for example, Betty Hahn's work shows little regional impact. What is important to their work as a group is the participation of each in the feminist artistic ferment of the 1970s that engendered new scholarly methods for assessing the aesthetic values of domestic art forms.

Each artist takes that which was "voiceless," in the sense of having no acceptable aesthetic form, and places it in a context that meets accepted artistic standards. Recent critiques of the structures underlying "folk art" forms provide a basis for understanding how the connecting process works. An example is Shiela de Bretteville's analysis of the structures of such "women's work" as quilts and blankets, "which are an assemblage of fragments pieced together whenever there is time . . . . The assemblage of fragments, the organization of forms in a complex matrix, suggests depth and intensity as an alternative to progress."[15] Bretteville's analysis of how such "women's work" is organized provides the final touchstone by which we may understand the work of the following artists: they are involved in assembling from their past those creative voices that give their work "intensity." Thus they use materials from the past with a sophisticated and self-conscious sense of the underlying structure to the domestic art forms.

Bretteville uses quilting merely as an example of the structures underlying traditional women's arts. Women's domestic arts encompass a wide variety of creative activities. Sewing included such diverse activities as quilting, embroidery, and lace making. Weaving has also been a traditional art of women. Other visual art forms include jewelry, metal work, and pottery. In addition, women were heavily involved in illustration and hand printing; even fine penmanship was considered at one time a requisite quality in a potential wife.[16] Recent scholarly work indicates that women's verbal artistry is no less diverse nor less understood. Women have long established bonds by handing down stories and songs to their childern. Even gossip is beginning to be included as an object for aesthetic revaluation.[17]

Within such diversity there are, however, common attributes that inform the arts of the past and that are manipulated by contemporary artists. It does not matter whether the artist is working with visual products or words, whether she is a poet or a photographer; even ethnicity does not change the approach significantly. All of the artists considered create their work by assembling fragments of experience not only from their own time but from earlier periods in women's history. Each speaks as a collaborator in a story or product that began in a preceding generation. Each thus maintains a tradition in the face of contemporary pressures for change. This emphasis on tradition connects the artists' works to the sense of "depth and intensity" rather than "progress" that Bretteville finds in the works of quilters. Finally, each is concerned with universal experience rather than with the unique or time-specific event.

Women's folk and domestic arts, with their emphasis on the ordinary, repetitive, often conservative, family-based life provide a perfect base for such contemporary statements. What the contemporary artist then adds (for this work is indeed a collaboration) is the self-conscious decision, in the face of historical concerns for the limited lives out of which domestic art sprang, to find a way of retrieving those forms from the past and utilizing them in her contemporary world.

One of the best contemporary examples of the connections

women artists make between the "folk" arts of their foremothers and the "fine" arts of today is provided by photographer Betty Hahn who works and teaches at the University of New Mexico. While Hahn has won wide recognition for the innovative, experimental nature of much of her work, she acknowledges a debt to traditional folk arts, particularly those most often practiced by women. Hahn's work, both in subject matter and technique, contains echoes of stitched portraits, embroidery, quilting, and botanical drawing. Some of Hahn's earlier work done in this vein harks back to stitchery traditions of the nineteenth century, in particular the creation of hand-done "personality portraits." Fairly standard portrait photographs are done in fabric with embroidery added to highlight and outline.

Other work extends the content past the individual, almost hermetically sealed portrait, to studies of family. It is in this work that one finds connections to quiltmaking, particularly pictorial quilts. Early quilting materials came from left-over scraps of family clothing; many quilts provided visions of routine family lives; quilts were often perceived to contain a woman's life.[18] Hahn plays with all these emotional connections between women's lives and the needle arts in her family portraits. The photography deals with mundane, middle-class subjects; "Dover Park Family" depicts a nuclear family grouped in front of their house; "Double Portrait: Roger and Joni" shows a young couple formally seated in their plant room. The color, the simple stitches emphasizing a bed of flowers, the line of a house, provide an organizing principle to the lives in much the same ways as the the grid systems and borders in pictorial quilts organized an otherwise diverse jumble of images. One photograph of a family walking along a road with a simple half-rainbow embroidered above is an outstanding example of the technique through which routine family activities become stylized and take on a more symbolic weight than the photograph alone would ordinarily provide. Yet the simple stitchery technique is absolutely compatible with the familiar scene presented (Photograph page 137).

Since doing the stitchery in the early seventies, Hahn has moved in several directions. In 1979 she completed a series of Polaroid prints using flowers; such prints remind one that botany and flower-drawing were accepted "occupations for ladies" during the eighteenth and nineteenth centuries in Europe and America.[19]

Hahn follows the tradition with a series of photographs of flowers laid over botanical sketches and flowers laid on patterned wallpaper.

Hahn also completed two Polaroid assemblages of artifacts retrieved from the lives of her aunt and grandmother (Photograph page 138). The assemblages contain things the women cherished—pieces of lace, letters—and things to give a sense of the past—newspapers, photographs. The whole vision is of a humble, structured life. (The work is framed and cross-hatched with a tape measure in one case and a white ribbon in another.) The photographs are memorials not only to individual women, but also to the creative lives of those women—the arts that they practiced but that have gone largely unrecognized.

These last photographs become artifacts—they are the shape and form of the past, particularly women's past. Hahn has completed one other series of such artifacts in what she calls "soft daguerreotypes." These are xeroxed photographs on plastic-coated fabric presented in old-fashioned velvet and satin casings. In an interview Hahn stated that she sees photography as a "folk art."[20] The daguerreotype replaced portrait painting, which was, in many cases, done by folk artists. Although clearly working in a "fine arts" tradition of individual statement, experimental style, and sophisticated techniques, Hahn has used content, attitudes, and styles of the folk arts to give her work meaning and form. Most often the folk arts she has tapped have been those of women.

The introduction of photography in America provided many young women with an opportunity to enter an art field and even support themselves once they learned the techniques. But the technological innovation also ended the opportunities for self-taught portrait painters, many of whom were women, to support themselves by their creative endeavors.[21] While Hahn feels no loss in the move to more sophisticated art forms such as photography (possibly *because* she sees it as another folk art, not different from earlier forms), other artists feel the disjunction and inherent conflict the change from traditional forms of domestic expression to more contemporary art forms caused, and struggle to reconcile this conflict in their creations.

Several writers have commented upon problems inherent in the move from the spoken to the written word, from gossip to novelist, or from singer of lullabyes to poet. Tillie Olsen asks: "How many of us who are writers have mothers, grandmothers, of limited education; awkward, not at home, with the written word, however eloquent they may be with the spoken one?"[22] Bobbie Louise Hawkins's novel *Back to Texas*, graphically illustrates the freedom and the pain felt by the generation of daughters who are more literate than their forebears. For while the ability to read and write opens new vistas for creative activity, it can also at first mean a loss of connectedness.[23]

Back to Texas is ostensibly about a car trip that a grown daughter and her mother make to visit relatives in the Texas panhandle. The primary narrator, the daughter Jessie, begins the novel with a discussion of the most important event of her life: "Nothing in my life ever happened that was as important to me as learning to read."[24] This event initially separates her from her more uneducated family, particularly her mother. By the end of the novel, however, the daughter has come to an acceptance of her connections with her mother and grandmother, while still acknowledging their differences.

This final reconciliation is achieved through the structure of the novel. Hawkins provides an initial clue to her intentions in an early chapter in which Jessie, the novelist's voice, describes the format of the book: "In a book like this, the 'plot' is whether it can come together at all. It might help to think of it as having *gathered* more than having been written. It's got about as much plan to it as tumbleweeds blown against a fence and stuck there."[25] Again we are dealing with lives lived in pieces, put together much as a crazy-quilt might be, with more interest in pattern than in progress. Each chapter is essentially a piece of family history spoken or written by Jessie, her mother, or grandmother. The book then becomes an "assemblage" of memories of the lives of three generations.[26] Its success depends upon typical stories and gossip that go on every day in southern and western families, particularly among women. *Back to Texas* constitutes a retrieval and reevaluation of women's verbal arts. By writing down such mundane conversations and shaping them to create a coherent work of art, Hawkins stresses the worth of the verbal act itself.

Back to Texas pays tribute to the creativity hidden and repressed in lives of mothers and grandmothers by telling their stories when they could not, ironically using the one gift (reading/writing) that sets the artist apart from her forebears. Such acknowledgements, such attempts to reevaluate the creative contributions of previous generations, do not, however, necessarily imply valuing and acceptance of all the conditions of that life. The point is that the surrounding conditions of that earlier life, not the quality of these unrecognized creative arts, cause the anonymity.

The work of Barbara Nugent while she was a student in New Mexico in the 1970s provides a visual example of such concerns for the limitations in women's lives. Nugent's best early work utilizes a common working woman's activity—shorthand—to comment on the stereotypes that define us. Her work of this period combined advertising images of women, which confine them to domestic spheres, with shorthand comments on the advertisements. At this point in her career, she was speaking very consciously to a specific audience—those women who knew shorthand.

The works slowly became memorials to skills that, while limiting and stereotyping, have also gone undervalued in previous generations. At one point Nugent moved from direct re-creation of shorthand pages in spiral notebooks to more stylized creations combining decorative wallpaper with shorthand. This work is in the tradition of samplers with the combination of skilled writing with decorative visual imagery and in the tradition of the "arts of writing" with the emphasis on the decorative aspects of shorthand.

A last work in this vein takes the technique even further by combining reversed images of shorthand on black background, over which is superimposed a black and white photograph of a rose. At this point, Nugent was beyond the "message" emphasis of the earlier works. Shorthand became even more of a "secret" language, appreciated primarily for its beauty, suggesting ancient hieroglyphics, gaining a timeless quality.

The gradual change in Nugent's work from that specifically meant to be a woman's message for a special group of other women to that which, while continuing the earlier forms, speaks to a wider audience, provides another aspect from which to study women's use of domestic art forms. Nugent found creative methods for escaping what Tillie Olsen has described as "restrictions" and "constrictions": those forces that deny women the right to express themselves outside a traditional woman's sphere of "bed and childbed."[27] Women taking shorthand, women in the working world, represent some of those arenas of life that Olsen thinks have not been seriously enough considered in our art. In finding her voice in that slightly larger context, Nugent was able to escape from some of the restrictions and constrictions. By pulling shorthand beyond its immediate, utilitarian image and into a more timeless context, Nugent gave the traditional craft validity as art.

Nugent exemplifies one approach whereby the artist can escape the restrictions that almost inevitably follow from emphasis in the "women's sphere": take the restricting situation and convert it into another form.[28] Other artists have chosen to separate the idea of domestic arts from the negative historical framework in which the "cult of domesticity" has been described and to return to earlier traditional sources for their creative statements. As most critics of the "cult of true womanhood" have stated, the problem began when women's role was no longer equal to men's in the maintenance of economic stability and culture, when as one historian has noted, women were "forced to play hostess to male inventions."[29] One solution for the artist inheriting this situation is to return, through her work, to those traditions that provide women with equal power in the world and reject those that do not. The concluding section of this study concerns women artists engaged in this renovation of almost preindustrial lifestyles in their work.

It is especially in this framework that the work of some American Indian and Hispanic women writers provides an excellent beginning. As Elaine Hedges has noted, needlework is an art form that crosses cultures as well as generations—and it becomes a significant touchstone for Hispanic as well as Anglo writers in finding their way to powerful images of their and their foremothers' lives.[30] A particularly fine example of such work is California poet Lorna Dee Cervantes's "Beneath the Shadow of the Freeway."[31] Meaningful life in an urban setting, with an omnipresent freeway across the street, is the concern of the speaker. As in many families in transition (in urban times or on the wilderness frontier) there is disjunction among the generations:

> We were a woman family:
> Grandma, our innocent Queen;
> Mama, the Swift Knight, Fearless Warrior.
> Mama wanted to be Princess instead.
> Myself—I could never decide.
> So I turned to books, those staunch, upright men.
> I became Scribe, Translator of Foreign Mail . . . .

The mother and grandmother are radically different sorts of

women, living different roles. The mother fits the image of women caught in the "women's sphere" yet living in a contemporary world that no longer supports such roles. She "dreams of taffeta" while counseling her daughter to "count on nobody." She has a man who drinks and threatens to molest the daughter; her life slowly grinds out in bitterness as "she spends her hours / washing down the bile." The grandmother is full of "woman's wisdom," but it is pre-technological, prescientific, making her seem a relic of the past. She passes on "old wives' tales" about predicting rain, hand sews her own quilts, and "trusts only what she has built / with her own hands." The daughter chooses to live her life as her grandmother has done before her, even in the face of the freeway.

What is the difference between the mother and grandmother? Their advice is identical—make your way in life yourself. Yet one never truly does so, waiting for the rescuing Prince, consuming her life rather than producing it, while the other creates her life from materials at hand. One waits to be given her role; the other takes an active part in making it. Importantly, the images that provide solutions for the daughter are of domestic arts practiced as they were before the great technological changes that made women's work in the home less valuable. Through fantasizing a return to a way of life that existed before her urban situation, the speaker is able to find a way to overcome the continuing effects of the "cult of true womanhood" that still afflict her mother.

Celebration and remembrance of women's importance in ritual and religious custom provides yet another source for moving beyond the restricted visions of women's sphere that limit their creativity. Antonia Quintana Pigno's poem, "The Miracle of Santuario" provides an initial example.[32] The poem concerns the yearly trek to a religious shrine at Chimayo, New Mexico. Told from the perspective of children, the central focus is on the new shoes and cape the mother makes for the santo figure in the church. The "miracle" is that at the shrine the children find "Indeed upon Your tiny feet / Last September's white shoes / Now scuffed and worn." The key person in the miracle is the mother, who remembers the time while the children are forgetful and who knows that the saint will require new clothes. The simple act of sewing for the family is thus extended to a broader, more "powerful" sphere of action, indeed is crucial to the religious tradition presented.

The technique of using traditional women's creative arts as a vehicle for defining women's place in a larger, more powerful sphere is prevalent also in the work of American Indian writers. Leslie Marmon Silko's novel, *Ceremony*, addresses the nature of women's power in our daily lives by combining the simple act of story-telling with the religious act of myth-making. *Ceremony* tells the story of a young Navajo's return to his home following the Korean War and his difficulty in reestablishing meaning in his life. Although a woman is not the central character to the novel, through her the young man's (Tayo's) final reintegration with his life is achieved. Women are presented not only in "bed and childbed" but bearing all the consequences of both places. Alongside this very real vision of women's lives another image is developed, one that acknowledges power behind the mundane, a power that ultimately provides the resolution to the novel.

The clearest expression of woman's centrality to the novel is Tayo's Grandmother. She is very *real* in her crotchety old age: "They were the same—the mule and old Grandma, she sitting in the corner of the room in the wintertime by the potbelly stove, or the summertime on an apple crate under the elm tree; she was as blind as the gray mule and just as persistent."[33] But she is also the primary source of the stories that finally give Tayo a way back to himself. Through her status as story-teller she gains power—she is able to create a world that exists in spite of other "realities."

What Tayo learns is that his Grandmother's stories are still true today; the trick is to be able to find them in the contemporary, routine life he lives. Grandmother also knows this truth, and she is the only character in the novel who may directly express it. Her voice essentially concludes the novel. As the family engages in some final "gossip" that ties the novel together, Grandmother's only comment is: " 'I guess I must be getting old . . . because these goings-on around Laguna don't get me excited any more . . . .It seems like I already heard these stories before . . . only thing is, the names sound different.' "[34]

While *Ceremony* offers a fairly traditional narrative structure, an overlay of Silko's poems adapted from Navajo myths is added. In many cases the myths are updated, are redefined in the context of the novel. A central figure in the myths is "Spider Woman," one of the few women given the power of a creation myth.[35] The novel begins with a poem playing on this myth:

> Thought-woman, the spider
> named things and
> as she named them
> they appeared.
> She is sitting in her room
> thinking of a story now.
> I'm telling you the story
> she is thinking.[36]

From the beginning, the novel is defined as a story told by a woman created by another woman. It is only consistent that the character in the novel who best knows the story is the old story-teller herself.

While Silko's novel never avoids pointing out the constrictions/restrictions that women live under, the implication is that strength/connection comes from those aspects of our lives that are beyond those limitations, even though the connection may on its face be as simple an act as a grandmother telling a story to a child. This is a great leap for women artists to make: from valuing their forebears' voices *because* they have gone unnoticed to valuing those "mundane" arts for their connection to much larger spheres of life. When the second acknowledgement is made, the humbler modes can be expanded, stretched, and included in contemporary voices. A poem by Laguna poet Paula Gunn Allen, "Grandmother," directly embodies this sense of making a connection with a tradition ripe with power. The first stages of the poem again allude to "Spider Woman": "Out of her body she extruded / shining wire, life, and wove the light / on the void."[37] Having created the world, the old woman leaves and "After her, / the women and the men weave baskets into tales of life." The artist follows the tradition, even in the humble duty of maintaining the rug, the life, Spider Woman has created: "After her I sit on my laddered rain-bearing rug / and mend the tear with string." Rather than breaking with the past, the move is to build upon it, to preserve and retrieve that which was important.

Eleanor Munro, speaking of the visual arts, defines the process in which such artists are engaged as "retrieving what otherwise would be irrevocably lost and fixing it in a form."[38] She sees many young artists as essentially "conservationists" in the sense that their art is a type of preservation. Regardless of ethnic background or art form, for the women discussed here, such preservation is accomplished through a quilt devised of materials inherited from their forebears. They preserve that part of the past that is at the core of the need to continue traditional materials, and they begin to create, visually and verbally, a multifaceted image of the contemporary woman.

The work of New Mexican Deborah Cole is illustrative of the visual imagery of preservation. Cole began in 1978 to work on a piece built around a photograph of her mother. The xeroxed series went through various modifications, but throughout the organic, gaudy flower pattern in the mother's dress carried the visual interest in the work. In one of the final works, the photograph was subsumed by the pattern, and that natural, colorful pattern became the final definition of her mother. The dress came to be the strength, the freedom not initially perceived in the first, almost historically trapped images. Cole moved in the series from a concern with the specific, historic, personal details of her mother's life to a sense of what in her life was beyond the personal and part of a larger universe. She made the transition, however, by remaining in touch with the ordinary, by pulling from it the extraordinary.

The technique is similar to that used in a poem by Texan Naomi Clark. The poem utilizes a found object just as Cole's xerox uses an initial, casual photograph. "Found Poem: First Letter from Aunt Cat"[39] alternates between the text of the note, obviously written by an almost illiterate relative and the unheard, graceful voice behind that limited by circumstance and education. Aunt Cat's letter tells the tale of her increasing sickness. Alternate lines tell the stories Aunt Cat really has hidden within her:

> If I cd tell you
> But to get to that—is this something colors you never did see
> have started loosing 10 lbs. a week
> bluegill sunfish
> for no rime or reason
> swim round thru in
> I have some kind spell
> blossums
> I just leave this world . . . .

Like artist Cole's mother, Aunt Cat becomes directly connected to nature, becomes a part of, one with, natural forces. And she gains mythic power in this connection: "scoop a drink / . . . moon in my hands / . . . drink moon." Cole and Clark have "retrieved" an image, a way of living, from the past and given it significant "form" though their techniques. That past becomes a valued artifact, a link, without which the work could not exist.

Clearly, this study of the use of traditional women's arts in contemporary art is really only part of the larger issue of how women's experiences and lives affect and inform their art. The discussions of Cole and Clark may have more to do with the broader issue than with concerns specific to traditional women's art forms. Such a fact, however, comments only on the need to study further what Munro calls "psycho-[a]esthetics"—the connections between one's art and one's life. One recognizes, finally, the strength that each of these artists gains through acknowledging her connections with the past. It seems that the willingness to make those connections is an expression of the type of creative female artist we may expect in the future. She is the artist who is not afraid to present any aspect of her, or any woman's life, with the realism and the sense of seriousness and purpose that has in the past been missing in much of our art.

This paper has been itself a crazy-quilt; an assemblage of many women's works collaboratively leading to one voice. The vision is one of strength and beauty in lives that have for so long gone unnoticed. There is hope and reaffirmation in their voices— reaffirmation of the importance of women's past to our present condition and hope that a stronger future may be built out of the valuable lessons of earlier times. A short poem by Bobbie Louis Hawkins provides a fitting close to this discussion:

> Own your body,
> as good a property
> as any other.
> Say, from this point
> far as the eye can see,
> It's me.[40]

The sentiment expressed, particularly the feeling of the land being one's to mold, is reminiscent of the pioneer urge; the need to discover all there is to see. These women artists are embarked on an adventure that opens up new frontiers, including frontiers of the past. In the same sense that the frontier was an ancient land, new only to the eyes of the pioneer beholders, so the artistic traditions in which many women are working contain age-old voices made new by the contemporary insights and more sophisticated techniques of the present generation.

Notes

1. See particularly Linda Nochlin's classic essay "Why Have There Been No Great Women Artists?" in *Art and Sexual Politics,* ed. Thomas B. Hess and Elizabeth C. Baker (London: Collier-Macmillan, 1973), 1–44.

2. One of the most important recent reevaluations of women's domestic art is C. Kurt Dewhurst, Betty MacDowell, and Marsha MacDowell, *Artists in Aprons: Folk Art by American Women* (New York: E. P. Dutton in association with the Museum of American Folk Art, 1979). Elaine Hedges has a fine article on the aesthetic aspects of quilting entitled "Quilts and Women's Culture" in *In Her Own Image: Women Working in the Arts,* ed. Elaine Hedges and Ingrid Wendt (Old Westbury, N.Y.: Feminist Press, 1980), 13–19.

3. Jan Seale, "Pearl Bell Pittman: 1888–1976," *Southwest: A Contemporary Anthology,* ed. Karl and Jane Kopp (Albuquerque: Red Earth Press, 1977), 97–9.

4. A particularly fine historical study of women's participation in such art forms in England is Anthea Callen's *Women Artists of the Arts and Crafts Movement: 1870–1914* (New York: Pantheon Books, 1979). Dewhurst, MacDowell, and MacDowell, *Artists in Aprons,* provides the most comprehensive study of women's folk and domestic arts in America.

5. Lillian Schlissel, "Mothers and Daughters on the Western Frontier," *Frontiers* 3(1978): 30.

6. Johnny Faragher and Christine Stansell, "Women and Their Families on the Overland Trail to California and Oregon, 1842–1867," *Feminist Studies* 2(1975): 158.

7. Schlissel, "Mothers and Daughters," 31, and Faragher, "Women," 153.

8. There is an extensive bibliography pertinent to this area. Exemplary sources include Anne Douglas, *The Feminization of American Culture* (New York: Knopf, 1977); Ann Oakley, *Women's Work: The Housewife, Past and Present* (New York: Pantheon, 1974); Gail Parker, *The Oven Birds: American Women on Womanhood, 1820–1920* (Garden City, N.Y.: Anchor Books, 1972); Katherine Kish Sklar, *Catherine Beecher: A Study in American*

Domesticity (New Haven: Yale University Press, 1973); Carroll Smith-Rosenberg, "The Female World of Love and Ritual: Relations Between Women in Nineteenth-Century America," *Signs* 1(Autumn 1975): 1–29; and Barbara Welter, "The Cult of True Womanhood: 1820–1860," *America Quarterly* 18 (Summer 1966): 151–74.

9. Julie Roy Jeffrey, *Frontier Women: The Trans-Mississippi West, 1840–1880* (New York: Hill and Wang, 1979), 73.

10. Jeffrey, *Frontier Women,* p. xvi, and Hedges, *Image,* 19.

11. Judy Chicago and Miriam Schapiro directed "Project Womenhouse" (1974), the renovation by art students of a house in Los Angeles as the first "all-female art environment." Many of the resulting images depended upon domesticity for their statement. Schapiro's comments on "Womenhouse" in Eleanor Munro's *Originals: American Woman Artists* (New York: Simon and Schuster, 1979), 272–81, stress the "new release of energy" she experienced as a result of the project.

12. Tillie Olsen, *Silences* (New York: Delacorte Press, 1978): 19.

13. Munro, *Originals,* 5.

14. Munro, *Originals,* 53.

15. Sheila de Bretteville, "A Reexamination of Some Aspects of the Design Arts from the Perspective of a Woman Designer," *Arts in Society* 11 [special issue on "Women and the Arts"] (Spring-Summer 1974): 117–18.

16. For comprehensive surveys of women's creative activities outside the "fine arts" tradition, see Callen, *Women Artists,* and Dewhurst, MacDowell, and MacDowell, *Artists in Aprons.*

17. The idea that lullabyes and even gossip are forms of women's art of equal power to male myth-making traditions is explored in Marta Weigle, "Women as Verbal Artists: Reclaiming the Sisters of Enheduanna," *Frontiers* 3 (1978): 1.

18. Dewhurst, MacDowell, and MacDowell, *Artists in Aprons,* 46–54.

19. Alice Coats, *The Treasury of Flowers* (London: Phaiden Press, 1975), 28.

20. Interview with Betty Hahn, 12 December 1979.

21. Dewhurst, MacDowell, and MacDowell, *Artists in Aprons,* 91.

22. Olsen, *Silences,* 184–5.

23. Lillian Schlissel notes the sacrifices mothers made to enable their daughters to have an education, commenting that such sacrifices were often made in the hope of reaffirming traditional bonds rather than breaking them apart (Schlissel, "Mothers and Daughters," 32).

24. Bobbie Louise Hawkins, *Back to Texas* (Berkeley: Bear Hug Books, 1977), 1.

25. Hawkins, *Texas,* 4.

26. Marta Weigle's work on gossip and other forms of women's ver-

bal arts describes the connections between narratives and ordinary conversation, noting particularly the "collaborative" styles of many women's narratives (Weigle, "Women as Verbal Artists," 1).

27. Olsen, *Silences,* 41–2.

28. A fascinating study of the way one group of artists have used images of domestic madness and fantasy to explore the "women's sphere" is provided in Carolyn J. Seifert, "Images of Domestic Madness in the Art and Poetry of American Women," *Women's Art Journal* 1(Fall 1980-Winter 1981): 1–6.

29. Douglas, *Feminization of American Culture,* 166.

30. Hedges, *Image,* 13.

31. Lorna Dee Cervantes, "Beneath the Shadow of the Freeway," in *The Third Woman: Minority Writers of the United States,* ed. Dexter Fisher (Boston: Houghton Mifflin Co., 1980), 378–81.

32. Antonio Quintana Pigno, "The Miracle of Santuario," in *Southwest,* ed. Kopp and Kopp, 166.

33. Leslie Marmon Silko, *Ceremony* (New York: New American Library, 1977), 28.

34. Silko, *Ceremony,* 273.

35. Marta Weigle's work on women and/in myth provided background for this aspect of the paper (Weigle, *Spiders and Spinsters: Women and/in Mythology* [Albuquerque: University of New Mexico Press, 1982]). Paula Gunn Allen, in a comprehensive essay on *Ceremony,* argues that Tayo's success depends on his not only understanding but becoming female (Allen, "The Psychological Landscape of *Ceremony,*" in a special symposium issue on Leslie Silko's *Ceremony,* ed. Kathleen M. Sands, *American Indian Quarterly* 5 [February 1979]): 7–12).

36. Silko, *Ceremony,* 1.

37. Paula Gunn Allen, "Grandmother," in *Southwest,* ed. Kopp and Kopp, 184.

38. Munro, *Originals,* 331.

39. Naomi Clark, "Found Poem: First Letter from Aunt Cat," in *Southwest,* ed. Kopp and Kopp, 125.

40. Bobbie Louise Hawkins, "Own Your Body," *Sparrow* 15 (December 1973): unpaginated.

Appendix A

Early Woman
in New Mexico

The first record of women's work is in the stone artifacts found by archaeologists in North Central New Mexico. Sometime about 12,000 years ago, our paleo-foremothers with their children and their men moved into northern New Mexico in small bands to take advantage of the abundant supply of large game. The climate was colder then and large animals like mammoth and bison provided two important sources of heat, protein from meat and warmth from hides. Artifacts left by these early people indicate that the bands carefully chose base camps after which, scholars speculate, women and men may have divided. The men established hunting camps where they prepared arrow heads and organized expeditions. Women established processing camps. To these camps, women brought gathered roots, berries and herbs, an important source of food among these early nomadic bands. Men also brought their kill to these processing camps where women took charge of skinning the animals and scraping the hides, as well as drying and roasting the meat. Together, then, each sex using skills developed over centuries of experimentation, these people survived on the cold plateaus of New Mexico.[1]

Women in these paleocultures, if later ethnology gives some hint as to what the cultures were like, probably worked no more than a 20-hour work week to provide their share of adult subsistence. In addition, they provided through their own bodies, milk for the younger children whom they may have breast fed for as long as four years. There is no evidence of high fertility among later women from gathering and hunting cultures and as with later groups women may have had an average of only two children. Women may have used herbs as abortifacients or contraceptives as did later Native American women but the long period of lactation, perhaps combined with sexual abstinence, probably kept mother and child in close proximity for several years. Lactation may also have decreased fertility. During these first years of life, women trained young children in basic survival skills, how to find edible roots, seeds, and berries, how to trap small animals to feed themselves, and how to shelter themselves from the cold.[2]

At around five or six years, women's work training young boys was probably done and the men took over their education, teaching them to hunt. The young girls now began specialized training that would enable them to process foods and hides with their mothers. The status of women was probably high in these early cultures, for they provided subsistence essential for the survival of the group, probably controlled their sexuality and perhaps their fertility, and performed a reasonable amount of work.

About 5,000 years ago, this combination of women's work and culture disappeared from New Mexico as it did from other areas of the world. The work of these paleopeople was so efficient that, combined with the changing climate, larger animals disappeared. The early people disappeared along with the large animals from North Central New Mexico.[3]

The next documented evidence of early women comes from small groups of people who lived on the fringes of these rich food areas and who had evolved a way to survive without large animals. In the southwestern corner of New Mexico, women of what anthropologists call Desert cultures had learned to process less palatable crops by grinding them. Between about 5,000 and 2,000 years ago corn was domesticated in the highlands of Mexico. As more drought resistant strains of corn developed, the cultivation of corn spread north into the drier lowlands of New Mexico. The evolution of the small wild corn to its larger domestic variety involved a major genetic change, similar to the changes in grains in the Old World that allowed a settled population to develop. Wild grains and corn were probably collected very early in prehistory. An earlier variety of cultivated corn retrieved by anthropologists from Bat Cave in central New Mexico was between 4,000 and 5,000 years old.[4]

The collecting of wild corn seems to have been the primary mechanism of domestication. Wild grains scatter easily. Gatherers tend to collect the grains that are the last to scatter. Thus, through repeated collections of the type of grain most shatterproof and through experimental planting, selection for tougher connective tissue holding the seed pods to the stem (called rachis) developed. For corn, this meant the development of extremely tough outer leaves covering the kernals completely. The husks kept the grains so tightly together that a form of external pollination developed using the corn silk. Such tight husks also meant, however, that this new form of grain could no longer survive without domestication. Corn was now as dependent upon people as people were upon it. Scholars think that because women had a large role in the systematic gathering of wild food, that they may also have played a large role in the domestication of grain. There is no way to document this at present but there are hints in the gathering activities of primates and of gathering peoples today that this was the case.[5]

More than 2,000 years ago, domesticated corn spread into the southwest together with domesticated beans and squash. These three plants spread north along with the information on how to plant and harvest them. Women were soon at work in small plots of land that they had cleared with the men, using digging sticks to plant and storing surplus so that their families would not have to depend entirely on wild plants and animals.[6]

Metates and manos became much more elaborate and numerous now that women had to grind corn. Archaeologists believe that the metates and manos were used by prehistoric peoples long before corn was domesticated, perhaps even before paleolithic times. These grain grinding tools are the first tangible evidence of a shift of interest toward hard seeded grains as an important food supply. In southern New Mexico mesquite beans may have been an early food gathered and ground by women. Asian and African metates have been found that were in use more than 49,000 years ago but in America firm evidence of their use dates from 10,000 years ago. In fact, knowledge of grinding probably facilitated the introduction of corn.[7]

Collection of wild food had already necessitated the development of weaving to create containers to transport food. Women may have created these carrying containers because most prehistoric women probably had already created slings to carry their young children on gathering expeditions. These, again according to anthropologists' still preliminary work, probably evolved into the first burden baskets used to transport and store surplus food for the winter months when food was scarce.[8]

A few remains of weaving have been recovered from sites in New Mexico but the introduction of corn necessitated the creation of an artifact that provided a much more durable object—pottery. Because corn not only had to be ground, something that prehistoric women had done even before the paleolithic period, but also cooked, a more durable water and fire proof container was needed. Again, women seem to have created this new food container.[9]

Scholars are not yet agreed as to why large mammals became extinct in most of the world about the same time that producing food began to supplement the process of gathering and hunting it. Two rather contradictory schools have emerged, one that argues that population pressure on resources caused changes in food gathering strategies and one that argues that once population settled down to agriculture, a population explosion followed. Among the most persuasive arguments in favor of the population pressure are those of Mark Cohen whose *The Food Crisis in Prehistory* marshals an impressive amount of material supporting his view. But others, like Kent V. Flannery, have argued that the population densities of Mesoamerica seem quite low at the time corn was being domesticated. Flannery thinks that since cultivation of corn required twice as much labor as collecting mesquite beans, corn had to produce more than twice the amount of food per area before it was worth while to cultivate. He speculates that populations may have settled down in some areas before agriculture began, then population densities increased, and agriculture followed. Because food production seems to take so much more effort than hunting and gathering, Flannery argues that people must have needed to produce, not just wanted to produce. At any rate, settled groups did seem to grow at a greater rate than hunting and gathering cultures. The fact that early agricultural populations could control production to a greater extent than gathering populations may have caused a greater investment of time and effort for intensification.[10]

For whatever reason, the intensification of agriculture probably intensified women's work. Increased population meant that women had to spent more time in child care, they had children at more frequent intervals and more of them, they spend an increased amount of time weaving and potting, and more time processing crops and preparing food. Men did an increasing amount of agricultural work but they still did some hunting. Since women still worked in the fields, their work relative to men probably increased. Anthropologist Carol Ember argues that the status of these agricultural women may have decreased because they lost opportunities for obtaining information and friends while males continued to be in greater public view.[11]

Around 3,000 years ago, women in southwestern New Mexico probably began to manufacture pottery for storage and cooking of the new tougher vegetable foods. Together with smaller animals, like deer and fish, the new vegetable diet allowed bands not only to survive but to create more elaborate life styles. Eventually women of this culture, usually called Mogollon by archaeologists, created the Mimbres pottery, leaving behind the first visual picture of women's work in New Mexico.[12]

In this southwest corner of New Mexico, Native American women created thousands of pottery bowls on which are left pictures of their work. On this pottery, called Mimbres from the valley in which archaeologists found this record of past culture, there are pictures of women potters, women gatherers carrying burden baskets, women birthing children. It is an amazing picture of the working lives of New Mexico women and an example of the rich heritage of women's history in New Mexico.[13]

By the time Mimbres pottery reached its most creative point, about 1000 years ago, the Mimbrenos were cultivating large corn fields. They also grew sunflowers, agave, amaranth (a plant similar to sorgum), chili pepper, bottle gourds, tomatoes, and other plants. This extensive irrigated cultivation, combined with hunting small game animals and fishing, allowed an estimated population of 10,000 people to live in the Mimbres Valley. They lived in cobble and adobe walled pueblos. The walls were of round stones chinked and held together with adobe and faced with a smooth adobe plaster. Floors sometimes had adobe and stone slabbing. Because later native women specialized in pottery making and decorating, as well as wall building and plastering, anthropologists believe most of these artifacts to be the work of women.[14]

Around the twelfth century, the Mimbres culture also disappeared. Probably it disappeared because the ecosystem could no longer support such a large population. Perhaps the people were absorbed by invaders from the south who established themselves in what is now the Salt River Valley and who created large irrigation works and the first stratified culture in southern New Mexico. This culture, the Hohokam, which existed side by side with the Mogollon for some centuries, dispersed as the Anasazi or Pueblo culture spread throughout the Southwest.[15]

In the Pueblo cultures, women probably also farmed and ground corn, but they made increasing amounts of pottery and a large number of adobe houses. Women did not leave the visual record of Mogollon women but they produced such a vast amount of pottery that archaeologists have identified the history of this group almost entirely by broken pottery shards. As the climate became warmer and game even more difficult to procure, men began to assume more of the burden of agriculture, working in the fields by the side of women. Some men also began to weave cloth of cotton so that they continued to contribute to subsistence but in new ways. As the groups came to depend almost entirely on food crops, women concentrated more on pottery that could be traded as well as used to store food and to prepare increasing amounts of plant food needed for nourishment, once more easily provided by gathering and hunting. And women developed new tools and new techniques of grinding corn.[16]

In southwestern New Mexico, by the fifteenth century, a new culture had developed. Here people built not with stone and adobe but completely with adobe walls that had stone footings and plaster. These women had slab-lined hearths, some had mealing bowls embedded in the ground at the end of metates to accumulate corn meal, they had large numbers of metates, manos, and some corn griddles, along with large quantities of various sized pots. They had ladders and covered hatchways and their homes resembled those the Spanish would find among the Pueblos when they arrived in the sixteenth century.[17]

In most areas of the Southwest, the fifteenth century was a period of movement and change as the climate became dryer. In northern New Mexico, many villages established along outlying streams were abandoned as people moved back toward the Rio Grande and major streams. By examining the skeletal remains in Rio Hondo, an abandoned village just south of Santa Fe, archaeologists have determined that the diet of corn and beans when not supplemented by meat and fish was unable to sustain a healthy population. They estimate the infant mortality rate at Arroyo Hondo was 50 percent and that almost 60 percent of the population died before reaching adulthood. Anemia caused by the predominance of corn in the diet may have been the cause. Women breast feeding for long periods of time during periods of drought probably developed iron deficiencies, thus their feeding children in turn became anemic, susceptible to diarrhea, and early death. Although women who survived to 15 could expect to live to over 40, they often developed osteoarthritis.[18]

At this point, the archaeological record merges with the historical record. The Spaniards arrived in New Mexico and the records become much fuller. The story is taken up in chapter one.

Notes

1. W. James Judge, *Paleoindian Occupation of the Central Rio Grande Valley in New Mexico* (Albuquerque: University of New Mexico Press, 1973), 187–207 and James E. Fitting and Theron D. Price, "Two Late Paleo-Indian Sites in Southwestern New Mexico," *The Kiva,* 34(Oct. 1968): 1–7.

2. Frances D. Dahlberg, *Woman the Gatherer* (New Haven: Yale University Press, 1981). The work of Eleanor Burke Leacock is also relevant here. See her *Myths of Male Dominance: Collected Articles on Women Cross-Culturally* (New York and London: Monthly Review Press, 1981), 33–81 and Eleanor Leacock and Nancy Lurie, eds., *North American Indians in Historical Perspective* (NY: Random House, 1971).

3. Vernon L. Smith, "The Primitive Hunter Culture, Pleistocene Extinction, and the Rise of Agriculture," *Journal of Political Economy,* 83(1975): 727–56, and Douglass C. North and Robert Paul Thomas, "The First Economic Revolution," *The Economic History Review* 30(1977): 229–41.

4. Paul C. Mangelsdorf, "The Mystery of Corn," *Scientific American,* 183(July 1950): 20–24 and "Ancestor of Corn," *Science* 128(Nov. 28, 1958): 1313–20.

5. Philip J. Wilke, Robert Bettinger, Thomas F. King, and James F. O'Connell, "Harvest Selection and Domestication of Seed Plants," *Antiquity*, 46(1972): 203–8.

6. Walton C. Galinat, "The Evolution of Corn and Culture in North America," *Economic Botany*, 19(1965): 350–57.

7. Nancy Kraybill, "Pre-Agricultural Tools for the Preparation of Foods in the Old World," and George F. Carter, "The Metate: An Early Grain-Grinding Implement in the New World," in Charles A. Reed, *Origins of Agriculture* (Hague: Mouton, 1977), 485–521, 693–709. See also Katharine Bartlett, *Pueblo Milling Stones of the Flagstaff Region and Their Relation to Others in the Southwest: A Study in Progressive Efficiency* (Flagstaff, Arizona: Northern Arizona Society of Science and Art, 1933).

8. Dahlberg, *Woman the Gatherer*, 8.

9. For the importance of pottery and its origins see H. M. Wormington, *Prehistoric Indians of the Southwest* (Denver: Denver Museum of Natural History, 1947), 12, 44, 52.

10. Mark Nathan Cohen, *The Food Crisis in Prehistory: Overpopulation and the Origins of Agriculture* (New Haven and London: Yale University Press, 1977) and his "Archaeological Evidence of Population Pressure in Pre-agricultural Societies," *Antiquity*, 40(1975): 471–4. The best general overview is "The Emergence of Food Production," in Clifford Jolly and Fred Plog, *Physical Anthropology and Archaeology* (3rd edition, NY: Knopf, 1982), 305–37.

11. Carol R. Ember, "The Relative Decline in Women's Contribution to Agriculture with Intensification," *American Anthropologist*, 85(1983): 285–304.

12. "The Pre-Historic Mogollon Culture and its Regional Aspects in the El Paso Area," *The Artifact*, 10(1972): 1–57.

13. The best visual account is J. J. Brody, *Mimbres Painted Pottery* (Albuquerque: University of New Mexico Press, 1977). See also O. T. Snodgrass, *Realistic Art and Times of the Mimbres Indians* (El Paso, Texas: privately printed, 1975).

14. Steven Leblanc and Ben Nelson, "The Salado in Southwesten New Mexico," *The Kiva* 42(1976): 71–9.

15. A helpful overview of these changes is Irving Rouse, "Southwestern Archaeology Today," in Alfred Vincent Kidder, *An Introduction to the Study of Southwestern Archaeology* (New Haven and London: *Yale University Press*, 1962), 27–42. See also Charles C. DiPeso, *Casas Grandes: A Fallen Trading Center of the Gran Chichimeca* (3 vols.: Flagstaff, Arizona: Northland Press, 1974).

16. Marjorie Lambert, *Pueblo Indian Pottery: Materials, Tools and Techniques* (Santa Fe: Museum of New Mexico Press, 1966) and Alfred E. Dit-

tert, Jr. and Fred Plog, *Generations in Clay: Pueblo Pottery of the American Southwest* (Flagstaff, Arizona: Northland Press, 1980).

17. Jack P. and Vera M. Mills, "The Dinwiddie Site: A Prehistoric Salado Ruin on Duck Creek, Western New Mexico," *The Artifact,* 10(1972): 1–50.

18. Ann M. Palkovich, *The Hondo Skeletal and Mortuary Remains* (Santa Fe: School of American Research Press, Arroyo Hondo Archaeological Series, Vol. 3, 1980), 30, 44, 75.

Appendix B

Sources

Researchers who wish to write about women's experiences in their own neighborhoods and counties will find that sources are both rich and readily available. Local newspapers provide information about prominent women, especially in the twentieth century, but they also document events and phenomena that were important to all nineteenth and twentieth century women, including economic trends and natural disasters, political issues such as suffrage and equal opportunities, and community improvement projects. Many New Mexico newspapers have been microfilmed and are available for use at most libraries or through interlibrary loan services. A handy guide for locating newspapers on microfilm is *Newspapers in Microform*. Also available on microfilm at most university libraries are manuscript census reports for 1850, 1860, 1870, 1880, 1900, and 1910, which provide information about family size, residence patterns, literacy, and occupations.

Of major importance for any local history project are records housed in county courthouses. These records will vary in subject matter from one county to another, but among the most valuable for recovering women's history are probate records for both men and women. The amount of information included in probate files is astonishing. Community and personal property of the deceased usually is listed, as are the legal heirs of the deceased, all of which helps the researcher reconstruct family composition and illuminates what happens to families over time. In documenting the extent and condition of the estate, probate records may reveal important economic information, such as the current price of wool or the number of men and women employed on a ranch or in a household. Sometimes probate files reveal something about the education of daughters of the deceased—where they went to school and the type of courses taken. Other files may list the cause of death and the care provided elderly widows in their final years.

County deed records provide important information about land ownership among married and single women. Women like Susan Barber of Lincoln County, who purchased land in their own names and speculated in land, can easily be located in the direct and indirect indexes of county deed records, as can women who took out homestead and desert land entries. Some courthouses in the nineteenth century kept separate contract books and brand books, wherein researchers may find evidence of women entering partido (leasing) arrangements for sheep and cattle or women registering their own brands. Since mortgage records are also housed in courthouses, something can be learned about women's borrowing habits. Other helpful county records include records of county commissioners, which provide insight into community problems, and civil marriage records, important to researchers wanting to document cross-cultural marriages or trends in marriage-age among women and men.

Many local churches, particularly Catholic churches, have extensive marriage, baptismal, and death records, which help document family histories, common-law marriage practices, and compadre-comadre relationships. Some New Mexico church records have been microfilmed by the Church of Jesus Christ of Latter Day Saints (Mormons), and researchers have access to these records through local Mormon genealogical or history libraries. Then, too, the Archives of the Archdiocese of Santa Fe is available on microfilm at the State Records Center and Archives in Santa Fe.

University and community libraries generally have many resources pertaining to New Mexico women. Because of current interest in women's history, some libraries have started special files on women of local interest. Many libraries have collections of private papers that include information about individual women and their families. The Amador Collection at New Mexico State University, for example, proved invaluable for documenting the daily concerns of a remarkable group of sisters. Furthermore, records of some women's clubs are deposited in various state repositories. Business records and private papers of prominent male politicians and community leaders, such as those located in special collections at the University of New Mexico library, frequently contain important information about women and their activities. And many libraries, as well as county historical societies, have important collections of oral interviews with women, some documenting conditions in New Mexico in the late nineteenth and early twentieth centuries. For the later twentieth century, researchers can make valuable contributions by conducting their own oral interviews with New Mexico women and depositing transcripts of the interviews in nearby libraries and archives.

Some university libraries have extensive microfilm collections pertaining to New Mexico's history, and these contain information on New Mexico women, even though it takes time and effort to locate relevant material. Most universities own copies of three important series of documents microfilmed by the State Records Center and Archives: The Spanish Archives of New Mexico, 1621–1821, The Mexican Archives of New Mexico, 1821–1846, and The Territorial Archives of New Mexico, 1846–1912. There are calendars available for all three series describing the documents on each roll of microfilm. Several microfilm publications pertaining to New Mexico's history have been produced by the National Archives in Washington, D.C. and contain some information on women. These publications include Territorial Papers of the Interior Department, Territorial Papers of the State Department, Records of the New Mexico Superintendency of Indian Affairs, and Records of the War Department (including correspondence of the Military Department and District of New Mexico and Compiled Military Service Records for the Civil War). Service records may seem an unlikely place to locate women's history, but some list servicemen's debts to company laundresses and others document soldiers' misconduct involving women.

Also available on microfilm are Agricultural Extension Service Records, which are extremely valuable for documenting rural women's history in the twentieth century. And some libraries have on microfilm a complete record of laws passed by the territorial legislature, important for researchers investigating family and inheritance laws. Useful background material on women, their families, and communities can be found in published histories of towns and counties, which are available at most public libraries.

Once researchers have exhausted local resources, a trip to the State Museum and to the State Records Center and Archives in Santa Fe will prove profitable. The State Museum has a fine photo archive which may contain photographs appropriate to the researcher's topic. Many other repositories, such as the Rio Grande Historical Collections at New Mexico State University and the Silver City Museum, have important photographic collections that can help document women's experiences working the land, participating in community activities, and managing families and homes. Oral interviews compiled by WPA workers during the Depression are deposited both in the State Museum and in the State Records Center. Some of these interviews help document family histories of New Mexico women reaching into the 1850s.

A wide variety of documents—too numerous to adequately summarize—are housed in the State Records Center. Among them are Spanish and Mexican land grant records, useful in compiling histories of certain New Mexico women, and some county records, including territorial court records that are so important in writing social and cultural history. Court cases document an endless variety of problems and events that affected the lives of ordinary women: cases involving cheating and swindling, divorce, disorderly conduct, and improperly documented land and mining claims. In many cases, women appeared as claimants, defendants, or witnesses.

Of major importance in understanding the finances and economic activities of women and their families are territorial assessment records and agricultural schedules for the 1860, 1870, and 1880 censuses. Assessment records provide information by counties on individual land ownership, improvements on the land, and the value of livestock owned; agricultural schedules list by individual farmers and ranchers the amount of land cultivated, amounts and value of crops raised, and the number of animals on the property. Both sets of records have been microfilmed by the State Records Center. Also helpful for understanding local demographic and economic conditions are published census materials on population and agriculture.

In seeking to document women's experiences in New Mexico, researchers can also use material culture. Most museums, whether state, university, city, or privately owned, house artifacts that directly relate to women's lives. Clothing, household furniture, kitchen equipment, and even toys help reveal the reality of our female ancestors. Researchers may want to visit locations where women lived and worked, describing the land and the buildings as they appear today and documenting changes through time that affected these women.

Appendix C

Methods for
the Study of
New Mexico Women

During the past fifteen years, the study of women's history has developed as an exciting and rigorous discipline. Although much remains to be discovered about the history of New Mexico women, studies in other areas have tested methods that seem particularly helpful in recreating women's past. Below are some of the works that are good models for methods to use in the study of New Mexico women.

The family, household, and life cycles of women provide important access to women's private lives. By analyzing the lives of groups of women, scholars can do much to recreate the environment in which most women worked and cared for themselves and others. These studies range from analyses of the household composition (who lived with whom), to age of marriage and fertility, divorce, and the kinds of tools used by women. One of the best sources for these studies is the collection edited by Nancy F. Cott and Elizabeth H. Pleck, *A Heritage of her Own: Toward a New Social History of American Women* (New York: Simon and Schuster, 1979). Included here also are articles on cross-gender relations and homosocial bonding among women, both important subjects for which a careful examination of unpublished letters and diaries should give clues. Mary P. Ryan's *Cradle of the Middle Class: The Family in*

Oneida County, New York, 1790–1865 (Cambridge: Cambridge University Press, 1981), is a classic local study that can serve as a model for other areas. Robert L. Griswold, *Family and Divorce in California, 1850–1890* (Albany: State University of New York Press, 1982) and *Family and Community in Colonial America: Two Perspectives, Women & History,* No. 4(Winter 1982) provide models for the study of divorce and property holding by women. For examples of early New Mexico wills by women see Carmen Espinosa, *Shawls, Crinolines, Filigree: The Dress and Adornment of the Women of New Mexico, 1739 to 1900* (El Paso: Texas Western Press, 1970).

For the twentieth century, oral history is an important supplement to more traditional documents. Here the best guides to methodology are the two special issues put out by *Frontiers,* Vol. 2(Fall 1978) and Vol. 7(Fall 1983). Together these issues discuss a great variety of approaches to gathering and using oral histories of women in diverse cultural backgrounds.

The use of statistical information to ground oral history is particularly important. A model of how that can be done is in Joan M. Jensen, "Farm Women in New Mexico, 1900–1940," in Robert Kern, ed., *Labor in New Mexico: Strikes, Unions, and Social History Since 1881* (Albuquerque: University of New Mexico Press, 1983).

Very little has been done on land ownership and homesteading among women of the West. Some of the important questions are asked and answered in a Colorado study by Sheryll Patterson-Black, "Women Homesteaders on the Great Plains Frontier," *Frontiers* I(Spring 1976), 67–88.

Political history, in many ways the most traditional area of women's history, remains poorly studied. Newspapers give an important view of women's political campaigns. So too do election returns. Important legal rights can be traced through court decisions and probate records. Oral histories and the papers of women in public office can yield important views of women's public activity. Studying the kinds of questions women's studies scholars are asking about women and contemporary politics often help formulate questions about the political lives of women in the past. Especially helpful here are Ellen Bonepath, *Women, Power, and Policy* (New York: Pergamon, 1982), Joan Rothschild, ed., *Machina Ex Dea: Feminist Perspectives on Technology* (New York: Pergamon, 1983), and Rosalind Rosenberg, *Beyond Separate Spheres: Intellectual*

Roots of Modern Feminism (New Haven and London: Yale University Press, 1982).

The history of religion is a field revitalized by historians of women in recent years. Women have played significant roles in American religions. Several volumes offer a variety of approaches to analyzing the role of women as spiritual leaders, educators, missionaries, and members of churches. See especially Janet Wilson James, ed., *Women in American Religion* (Philadelphia: University of Pennsylvania Press, 1980), which contains several articles on Catholic and Jewish as well as Protestant women. Judith L. Weidman, *Women Ministers: How Women Are Redefining Traditional Roles* (San Francisco: Harper & Row, 1981) offers many insights into women's role in organized religion. Amanda Porterfield, *Feminine Spirituality in America: From Sarah Edwards to Martha Graham* (Philadelphia: Temple University Press, 1980) traces the Protestant tradition. For early New Mexico Virgin cults see Fray Angelico Chavez, *Our Lady of the Conquest* (Santa Fe: Historical Society of New Mexico, 1948).

The material available on individual American Indian tribes is voluminous. An essential guide to the literature on women is the new bibliography by Rayna Green, *Native American Women: A Contextual Bibliography* (Bloomington: Indiana University Press, 1983), the best starting place for methodology.

Hispanic women have also been the subject of important new studies, a number of them still unpublished. The best reference to sources is in the *Teaching Guide to Accompany Las Mujeres,* Oliva Evey Chapa (Old Westbury: Feminist Press, 1981).

Black women have been less well studied in the West than in the East. For an overall analysis of the methodology of the history of black women see Sharon Harley and Rosalyn Terborg-Penn, *The Afro-American Women: Struggles and Images* (Port Washington, NY: Kennikat, 1978).

For western women, the best introduction remains Joan M. Jensen and Darlis A. Miller, "The Gentle Tamers Revisited: New Approaches to the History of Women in the American West," *Pacific Historical Review* 49(1980), 173–213. A supplementary bibliography is available from the Sun Valley Institute of the Arts and the Humanities.

Contributors

Joan M. Jensen, professor of history, teaches women's history at New Mexico State University. She has published *With These Hands: Women Working on the Land* (1981) and *Decades of Discontent: The Women's Movement, 1920–1940,* coedited with Lois Scharf (1983).

Darlis A. Miller, associate professor of history, teaches western history at New Mexico State University. She coauthored with Joan M. Jensen, "The Gentle Tamers Revisited: New Approaches to the History of Women in the West," which won the Billington and Koontz awards in western history in 1980. She has published *The California Column in New Mexico* (1982).

Cheryl J. Foote is a doctoral candidate at the University of New Mexico. She has published "The History of Women in New Mexico: A Selective Guide to the Published Sources," *New Mexico Historical Review* (1982) and "Changing Images of Women in the Popular Western Film," *Journal of the West* (October 1983).

Salomé Hernández is currently Assistant Cultural Affairs officer at the United States Embassy in Mexico. She is completing her doctoral dissertation on the role of women in the settlement expeditions into the Provincias Internas of New Spain.

Janet Lecompte is an editorial consultant of the *New Mexico Historical Review*. She has published *Pueblo, Hardscrabble, Greenhorn: The Upper Arkansas 1832–1865* (1978), *Rebellion in Rio Arriba, 1837* (1985) and numerous articles on western history.

Vera L. Norwood is assistant professor in American Studies at the University of New Mexico. She has published "The Photographer and the Naturalist: Laura Gilpin and Mary Austin in the Southwest," in the *Journal of American Culture* (1982) and edited a special issue of *New America* in 1982, *Changing Women: Women Writers and Artists of the Southwest.*

Terry R. Reynolds is a contract anthropologist. Her dissertation at the University of British Columbia was on "Residential Ideology and Practice Among the Sheep Springs Navajo."

Sandra Kay Schackel, a doctoral candidate at the University of New Mexico, is assistant editor of the *New Mexico Historical Review*. She has published in New Mexico history in *El Palacio* and *Journal of the West.*

Sandra L. Stephens is a contract historian who recently completed her Master's Project on the women of the Amador family.

Index